Eco-Joyce
The Environmental Imagination of James Joyce

Eco-Joyce

The Environmental Imagination of James Joyce

Edited by

Robert Brazeau and Derek Gladwin

First published in 2014 by
Cork University Press
Youngline Industrial Estate
Pouladuff Road, Togher
Cork, Ireland

British Library Cataloguing in Publication Data
A CIP catalogue record for this book is available from the British Library.

ISBN 978-1-78205-072-8

Typeset by Tower Books, Ballincollig, County Cork
Printed in Malta by Gutenberg Press

www.corkuniversitypress.com

To my daughter, Ailsa.
R.B.

To Patricia Barkaskas for her support and for believing in the project from the beginning.
D.G.

Contents

II JOYCE AND THE URBAN ENVIRONMENT

III JOYCE, SOMATIC ECOLOGY AND THE BODY

Acknowledgements

Both editors would like to acknowledge the writers who have entrusted their work to us and without whom this volume would not have come into being. We would also like to thank the Department of English and Film Studies and the Faculty of Arts at the University of Alberta for the financial support they have extended, in various forms, to both editors. Robert Brazeau would also like to acknowledge the generosity of his institution's sabbatical structure, which offered timely assistance as this manuscript was nearing completion. He has also received generous support from the Social Sciences and Humanities Research Council of Canada, and would like to acknowledge the importance of that granting body for research in the humanities.

This project has received generous support from Joyceans and Irish studies scholars too numerous to name, many of whom offered helpful criticisms and suggestions as some of these papers were presented at the annual conferences of the International and North American James Joyce Foundations. Tony Thwaites, Sheldon Brivic, Anne Fogarty and Kim Devlin were especially supportive figures at these events. There is little doubt that this volume was strengthened in concrete ways by the efforts of the many strong scholars who attend this valuable conference. As well, a number of the essays in this volume were first presented at the *Ireland and Ecocriticism* conference (2010) organised by Maureen O'Connor.

Finally, we owe an inestimable debt of gratitude to the staff and editorial board at Cork University Press, especially Maria O'Donovan for her meticulous handling of this project as it progressed through the press. Both Maria and Mike Collins have been a pleasure to work with.

ACKNOWLEDGMENTS

Contributors

FIONA BECKET, University of Leeds. Co-editor of *Culture, Creativity and Environment: New Environmentalist Criticism* (2007) and *Ireland in Proximity: History, Gender, Space* (1999). Becket's current research investigates the eco-critical consciousness at work in the canonical texts of modernism.

ROB BRAZEAU, University of Alberta. He has published scholarly essays on Seamus Heaney, Thomas Kinsella, Medbh McGuckian, Brian Friel, nineteenth-century Irish nationalism as well as recent papers on Synge and O'Casey. He is presently writing a monograph on Joyce and modernity and has an article based on that project in a forthcoming issue of the *James Joyce Quarterly*. He has also guest edited a number of scholarly journals.

CHRISTINE CUSICK, Seton Hill University. Editor of *Out of the Earth: Ecocritical Readings of Irish Texts* (2010) and author of numerous articles in Irish studies and ecocriticism including, 'Moments of Story: Rachel Giese's *The Donegal Pictures*' and '"Our language was tidal": Poetics of Place in the Poetry of Moya Cannon'.

JAMES FAIRHALL, DePaul University. Author of *James Joyce and the Question of History* (1996). Fairhall has also presented a number of papers on Joyce, embodiment and nature, and has published articles on Joyce in leading journals in the field.

Anne Fogarty, University College Dublin. She is Professor of James Joyce Studies at UCD and founder of the *Dublin James Joyce Journal*. She has been Academic Director of the Dublin James Joyce Summer School since 1997 and was President of the International James Joyce Foundation, 2008–2012. She is co-editor of *Joyce on the Threshold* (2005), *Bloomsday 100: Essays on 'Ulysses'* (2009), *Imagination in the*

Classroom: Teaching and Learning Creative Writing in Ireland (2013) and *James Joyce: Multidisciplinary Perspectives* (forthcoming, 2014). She has published widely on aspects of modern Irish writing. She is currently completing a study of the historical and political dimensions of *Ulysses*, entitled *James Joyce and Cultural Memory: Reading History in 'Ulysses'*.

DEREK GLADWIN, University of Alberta. He has recently published an essay on Irish ecocritical drama in *Irish Studies Review* entitled, 'Staging the Trauma of the Bog in Marina Carr's *By the Bog of Cats*'. He has articles on Ireland and ecocritism in *Culture and Photography* and *Gothic Studies*.

CHERYL HERR, University of Iowa. Author of *Joyce's Anatomy of Culture* (1986), *For the Land They Loved: Irish Political Melodramas* (1991), *Critical Regionalism and Cultural Studies* (1996), and *Ireland into Film: The Field* (2002). In completion is a book tentatively entitled *Rock Britannia: World War II and British Popular Music*. Herr has published numerous articles on Joyce and other topics in Irish studies.

BRANDON KERSHNER, University of Florida. Author of *The Culture of Joyce's Ulysses* (2010), *Joyce, Bakhtin, and Popular Literature* (1989), as well as editor of *Cultural Studies of Joyce* (2003), *Joyce and Popular Culture* (1996), and *Joyce's Portrait of the Artist* (1992).

YI-PENG LAI, Queen's University, Belfast. She has presented on *Ulysses* as an ecological text at many conferences and is author of 'Through the Arc of the Tropical Forest: Imagining an Environmental Dystopia', in Karen Tei Yamashita's *Through the Arc of the Rain Forest*.

GARRY LEONARD, University of Toronto. Author of *Reading Dubliners Again: A Lacanian Perspective* (1993) and *Advertising and Commodity Culture in Joyce* (1998) as well as some twenty or so articles and book chapters on various aspects of Joyce's fiction.

MARGOT NORRIS, University of California, Irvine. Author of six books, four on the work of James Joyce and two on other topics. Her Joyce studies include *The Decentered Universe of 'Finnegans Wake'* (1976), *Joyce's Web: The Social Unraveling of Modernism* (1992), *Suspicious Readings of Joyce's 'Dubliners'* (2003), and a monograph on the 1967 Joseph Strick film of *Ulysses* published in 2004. Norris has also published many articles on Joyce in leading journals in the field.

EUGENE O'BRIEN, Mary Immaculate College, University of Limerick. Author of *Examining Irish Nationalism in the Context of Literature, Culture and Religion: A Study of the Epistemological Structure of Nationalism* (2002) and *The Question of Irish Identity in the Writings of W.B. Yeats and James Joyce* (1998), as well as editor of the *Irish University Review: A Journal of Irish Studies* (1998–2005). O'Brien has also published two books on Seamus Heaney.

BONNIE KIME SCOTT, San Diego State University. Author of *Gender in Modernism: New Contexts, Complex Intersections* (2007), *James Joyce* (1987), and *Joyce and Feminism* (1984).

ERIN WALSH, University of California, Irvine. She has recently completed her PhD dissertation entitled, *Analogy's Territories: Ethics and Aesthetics in Modernism, Darwinism, and Cybernetics* (2011). She has also presented on *Finnegans Wake*, *Ulysses* and Darwin at numerous conferences.

GREG WINSTON, Husson College. He is the author of 'Dublin Dreadfuls: Race, Imperialism and Boys' Story-Papers in "An Encounter"' and 'Barracks and Brothels: Militarism and Prostitution in *Ulysses*'. Winston's book, *Joyce and Militarism* appeared in 2012.

Foreword

ANNE FOGARTY

James Joyce is first and foremost an urban writer. All of his revolutionary creations, *Dubliners*, *A Portrait of the Artist as a Young Man*, *Exiles*, *Ulysses* and *Finnegans Wake*, centre on Dublin, his native city. It is not simply the case that Joyce uses Dublin as a setting or imaginative backdrop; rather he conceives of it as a symbolic locale with universal import. The city is at once Joyce's raw material, an experimental terrain, the site of the modern, and the fundament for a radical vision of the future. In his work, moreover, Dublin is a historical locus whose irreducible particularities demand painstaking artistic recreation and act as an inexhaustible wellspring of linguistic invention. Only a few of his texts, amongst them the 'Penelope' episode of *Ulysses*, his playful children's story *The Cat and the Devil*, the prose fragment, *Giacomo Joyce*, and some of the lyrics in *Pomes Penyeach*, venture outside of this foundational setting.

Moreover, the decision to focus on the urban as opposed to the rural had a pointedly political dimension for Joyce. In 'The Day of the Rabblement', his diatribe against the Irish Literary Theatre, he stridently voiced his dissension from the aims of writers such as W.B. Yeats whom he felt had sold out to populism and reneged on their duty to produce an outward-looking, cosmopolitan literature.[1] The turn to the peasant play, the embrace of an Irish primitivism and the glorification of west of Ireland locations such as the Aran Islands were seen by Joyce in this polemical essay and elsewhere as retrograde and contrary to the objectives of his own aesthetic and to his commitment to bring about the spiritual and cultural renewal of his country.

To view Joyce solely in this manner is, on the face of it, to hold him far removed from the environmental turn in current criticism. His programmatic urbanism and underscoring of the anti-pastoral aspects of 'dear dirty Dublin' are at odds, it would appear, with an ethical movement concerned with the rescue and preservation of the natural environment. However, as Raymond Williams has pointed out, the city and the country have historically always been interdependent even in Britain in which cities grew at the expense of the countryside.[2] In Ireland, moreover, a greater contiguity between the rural and the urban existed in the late nineteenth and early twentieth centuries because an industrial revolution had not altered the landscape or created divisions between agricultural and urban populations in the way that it had in other countries.

Indeed, it is the very resistance of Joyce's works to pastoralism and conventional nature writing that makes them so amenable to contemporary ecocritical scrutiny, many of whose principal debates they anticipate. As several critics have noted, second-wave ecocriticism has questioned the very notion of nature as a thing apart, endowed with a primal purity.[3] They point to the fact that the natural is very often a human concoction or projection, and that it frequently merges with or is overlaid by the built and man-made environment. Further, many have made the case that it is more pressing to take account of urban, degraded and polluted landscapes and the sullied slums and back-streets occupied by the poor and the outcast in the modern metropolis than to continue to hanker after comforting notions of pristine natural spaces or of untouched wilderness. Timothy Morton has gone so far as to claim that theories of ecology need to jettison notions of nature altogether and to question the validity of what he terms 'ambient poetics' in which the writing self and the environment fuse, and retire the conceit of immersive outdoor scenes where subject and object coalesce organically.[4]

Natural images in Joyce tend to be jagged and discontinuous, and to suggest political and social faultlines, discountenancing Romantic views of the alliances intermeshing the human and the environment. The image of the subvervient herdsman driving his cattle 'above Cabra' in 'Tilly', the opening poem of *Pomes Penyeach*, cedes to the inexplicable suffering of an anonymous persona bleeding 'by the black stream/For my torn bough!'[5] The conjoint rural and semi-urban landscape traced in this poem seems to provide succour for the cattle, but to be inhospitable to the humans who inhabit it and witness its destruction or violation. In fact, animal tropes are frequently used by Joyce to disturb hierarchies of the human and the non-human rather than to suggest continuities between them.[6] The ominous 'moocow' in the fragmented fairy tale that opens *A Portrait of the Artist as a Young Man* acts as a metonymy for Stephen Dedalus and a refracted image of his struggle to find a place for himself in the over-determined narratives that he inherits.[7] Leopold Bloom's conversation with his cat in the 'Calypso' episode of *Ulysses* at once establishes his otherness, his lack as a human agent and his atypicality as a fictional character.[8] The cat, whose language is approximated through onomatopoeia but never fully captured, in turn points to another gap and source of disquiet. It functions as an inexact proxy for Molly Bloom who likewise is rendered partially and obliquely on her first appearance in the text and is associated throughout with disruption and loss. Her night-time ruminations close *Ulysses*, mimicking notions of a subjectivity that can still be ordered by narrative but also raising the spectre of a selfhood that has become post-human.

The concern of *Ulysses* with the abject and with urban detritus conveys not just a sense of the squalor and poverty of Dublin, reflexes of its colonial status, but also of the anti-pastoral aspects of the modern city. Maritime settings or littoral (that is shoreline) scenes are further deployed by Joyce as a means of disrupting a Romantic aesthetics of place that hinges on notions of harmony and wholeness. Stephen Dedalus' contemplation of the bird-girl wading in the water at Dollymount strand in *A Portrait of the Artist of the Artist as a Young Man* rewrites John Millington Synge's appreciative anthropological account of the girls washing clothes with tucked-up petticoats in the sea on Inis Meáin, 'beautiful as tropical sea-birds'.[9] It recasts it as an urban fantasy that unevenly links the sublime and the erotic, and counterpoints an ecstatic artistic vision with the teasing corporeality of this anonymous and cryptic woman whose answering gaze breaks with decorum.[10] In transposing a west of Ireland scene to a Dublin shoreline it advertises the capacity of an urban space to cast a pastoral spell of its own and to be the purveyor of modern affects. Leopold Bloom's voyeuristic dalliance with Gerty McDowell in the 'Nausicaa' episode of *Ulysses* in turn replays the scene in *Portrait* and overlays it with multiple ironies.[11] The seascape at Sandymount becomes the site of fantasy, subterfuge and of linguistic pyrotechnics rather than of epiphany. The shoreline is used not as a source of revelation or of abstract contemplation but as an impetus for a phantasmal and abortive encounter, and for the fertile intermingling of sexual and religious discourses and of popular and literary fictional plots and devices.

The chthonic images of HCE as the sleeping figure linking the Hill of Howth with the Phoenix Park and Anna Livia Plurabelle (ALP) as the River Liffey flowing through Dublin in *Finnegans Wake* act as further instances of Joyce's disembedding of the human and political traces in an urban topography that refuse to be accommodated in traditional overarching stories or conjured according to Romantic myths of place. The merging of Anna Livia with the sea at the end of the text, although allowing for a possibility of fusion, is also rendered bleakly as an inevitable and protracted cycle of ageing and decay, a self-immolation, a surrender of the mother to the all-powerful father-son and a chilling cessation of Being.[12]

The 'greening' of modernist literature, as Bonnie Kime Scott has dubbed it, opens up numerous interpretative possibilities.[13] It allows us to historicise early twentieth-century writing and to reflect on the ways in which capitalist expansion, the spread of cities and the rise of new technologies have impacted on the environment and blinded us as readers to consequent imbalances, moments of destruction and acts of social injustice and to the role of ideologies of nature even in fictions centring on the city. Joyce's works, in their resistance to myths of a harmonising, recuperative nature, their emphasis on biopolitics, their blurring of the human and the non-human, their depiction of landscapes and urban settings in particular as sites of conflict and loss and their quest to voice the post-human, invent global idiolects, and reach beyond the limiting confines of the subject, invite ecocritical inquiry even as they also urge us to rethink many of the contentious precepts governing this critical field. Above all, they alert us to problematic mystifications of nature and organic life still dominant in Western culture and attendant concepts of the aesthetic, and to the need to expand notions of environmentalism to include the urban and the abject.

Introduction: James Joyce and Ecocriticism

ROBERT BRAZEAU and DEREK GLADWIN

This collection brings together fourteen previously unpublished essays that introduce and examine the overarching ecological consciousness evinced in the writings of James Joyce. Although Joyce is one of the most critically examined writers in the English language, and easily the most in all of Irish literature, there has never been a volume that focuses on the environmental themes found in his writings. These essays approach Joyce's ecocritical consciousness from a variety of overlapping and mutually informing perspectives and address two broadly conceived but fundamental questions: why should Joyce be considered a writer of interest to ecocritics and how does investigating the ecological dimension of Joyce's work contribute to both existing Joyce scholarship and ecocritical theory?

Ecocriticism clearly represents a new and important direction in literary studies, and scholars who are compelled by this critical outlook will, we hope, find this collection of interest in the context of their work. The essays presented here will help to suggest new and profitable pathways for future work in ecocriticism. In addition, scholars working within Irish studies draw on a wide variety of critical outlooks, including cultural studies, post-colonial studies, transnational studies and, of course, modernist studies; this book will help that community become better acquainted with how ecocriticism elucidates the work of Irish writers, and will encourage further research in this direction. As we show here, even writers like Joyce, who are usually regarded as primarily urban, exhibit a strong ecological dimension in their work, and there are many other Irish writers who have produced work that directly engages issues in ecology and environmental studies.[1] *Eco-Joyce* covers a multitude of disciplines in an attempt to serve as a point of entry into Joyce and ecocriticism of course, but it will also suggest ways in which Irish studies and modernist studies could gain energy from this relatively new and vital approach. Before moving into critical analysis of Joyce's individual works, however, this introduction briefly outlines the ecocritical field for readers of Joyce who are unfamiliar with this critical outlook; it then discusses recent advances in ecocriticism and Irish studies, as well as contemporary work in Joyce scholarship; and, finally, it offers a brief overview of the essays in this collection and how they engage with issues of space, place and environment in Joyce's fiction and non-fiction.

A Brief Look at Ecocriticism

Once regarded as peripheral to cultural studies, ecocriticism is now central within contemporary scholarship. Ecocritical works have come to be featured more prominently on course reading lists, conferences are devoted to the critical outlook and an increasing number of publications appear each year that offer ecocritical readings of literary works or cultural and aesthetic objects. The definition of ecocriticism, nevertheless, can be more difficult to sort out than its history, especially since ecocritical investigations can range from reading texts with an eye towards environmental degradation to more expansive approaches taken up in ecofeminism, postcolonial ecocriticism, animal studies, genetic engineering, geography and travel writing. More recently, biopolitics has emerged as a new, compelling and heavily theorised area that shares much in common with ecocriticism. Due to the recent proliferation of ecocritical themes in scholarly work, we will briefly contextualise ecocritical theory by cataloguing some of the historical and contemporary currents in the field.

William Rueckert was the first to introduce the term 'ecocriticism' in his 1978 article, 'Literature and Ecology: An Experiment in Ecocriticism'. Rueckert's goal was to expand the critical discourse of literary studies in order to 'join literature to ecology'.[2] By Rueckert's coinage, the term 'eco' connotes environments that are natural, but the prefix has been reappropriated from the science of ecology and is used synonymously with 'environmentalism' or 'green'.[3] Ecocriticism, however, did not fully emerge as a recognised sub-theory of cultural studies until the publication of *The Ecocriticism Reader: Landmarks in Literary Ecology* (1996). This collection brought together historical and contemporary work that sought to stress the importance of an environmental engagement within literary and critical practice. As the co-editor of the volume, Cheryll Glotfelty, points out in the introduction, 'Ecocriticism takes as its subject the interconnections between nature and culture, specifically the cultural artifacts of language and literature.'[4] Subsequently, ecocriticism has come to focus on literary texts that address both general and specific issues dealing with the environment, language and culture.

Once a sufficiently elaborate critical lens for engaging with literature, culture and ecology had been established, ecocriticism burgeoned throughout North America relatively quickly. At about the same time *The Ecocriticism Reader* was being assembled for publication, the Association of Literature and the Environment (ASLE) was formed along with the allied journal *Interdisciplinary Studies in Literature and the Environment* (*ISLE*); *ISLE* is still considered the definitive journal in the field. This 'first-wave' movement of ecocriticism grew rapidly until only recently, when it came under fire for not challenging the definition of terms like 'nature', 'ecology' and 'culture' within a more rigorous theoretical framework. Thus, the introduction of a 'second wave' of ecocriticism began when Greg Garrard published the first pragmatic overview of the movement, *Ecocriticism* (2004). In many ways, Garrard bridged the first and second wave by looking at the ten or so years prior to the publication of his book even while offering a kind of programme for the future of ecocritical studies. Furthermore, it should be noted that Garrard has sustained a critical rigour in his numerous publications in this field.

The 'second wave' of ecocriticism has offered new ideas about how this theory can speak to issues beyond the aesthetic and literary. Ecocritical works frequently engage with ethical, practical and political concerns. This wave of ecocritical thinking, as it reimagined the entire approach, also called into question the assumptions laden into the familiar terms of the movement and, because of the evolving nature of green cultural studies, the term 'ecocriticism' no longer serves as a sufficient catch-all for the various forms that ecologically oriented criticism can take; such work is often now referred to as environmental criticism, cultural ecology, ecofiction, literary ecology, ecotheory, or literary environmental studies, depending on the objective and direction of the critic.[5] For example, Lawrence Buell is considered a prominent figure of both the first and second wave of ecocriticism because his trilogy bridged both eras: *The Environmental Imagination* (1995), *Writing for an Endangered World* (2001), and *The Future of Environmental Criticism* (2005). After reflecting upon the greening of literary studies, he now prefers the term 'environmental criticism' in order to escape the association that 'ecocriticism' often has with the first wave. He contends,

> Although I believed then and continue to believe that the literatures of nature *do* bear important witness against 'the arrogance of humanism' (Ehrenfeld 1978), I found myself agreeing with those who thought the concentration on 'environment' as 'nature' and on nature writing as the most representative environmental genre were too restrictive, and that a mature environmental aesthetics – or ethic, or politics – must take into account the interpenetration of metropolis and outback, of anthropocentric as well as biocentric concerns.[6]

As Buell suggests, the tension in ecocriticism has arisen around how we view and define ideas of 'nature' and 'environment', moving from predominantly North American nature writing – which is often compelled by an epiphanic experience of nature, which was initially hailed as the quintessential environmental literature – to more recent advancements in literatures examining issues dealing with urbanism, gender, resource management, contested landscapes in colonial zones, Darwinism, environmental justice and issues of space and place in various geographies. While we are mindful of the value of Buell's careful application of the term, we have preferred the use of the older term 'ecocriticism' in the current volume because we feel it may be more familiar to readers who are coming to this material from an interest in Joyce studies.

As with many critical schools, these internal debates can forge new terrain for critics in exploring the boundaries and possibilities of the approach. Fortuitously, debates in ecocriticism have sent many critics back to Raymond Williams' *The Country and the City* (1973) as the text where culture and nature (in the form of pastoralism) are explicated in pragmatic and historical terms. Williams' work has remained important for ecocritics both because he sketches a history of the development of a literature of urban and rural consciousness, and also explicates how both the urban and rural have come to denote an entire structure of affect. Engaging with Williams' discussion of the historical and materialist nature of representations of urban and rural environments and extending the argument in explicitly ecocritical directions, Kate Soper's *What is Nature? Culture, Politics, and the Non-Human* (1995) suggests that the philosophical concept of 'nature' does not adequately stand in for the myriad and conflicted representations of the external environment. Other critics, such as Timothy Morton, whose *Nature Without Ecology: Rethinking Environmental Aesthetics* (2007) challenges the aestheticisation of nature, suggest that ecocriticism should employ a more robust theoretical aptitude and methodology in order to gain a wider audience and professional legitimisation.

The first and second wave divide in ecocriticism notwithstanding, ecocritics collectively agree that they are generally concerned with humanity's mutual deep and abiding connection to the environment and with developing a critical discourse that speaks of the text's ability to articulate a sense of our shared belonging to the natural world. As the subtitle of this collection suggests, we want to be inclusive of theories of space, place, culture and embodiment in Joyce's writings. We believe, along with a rising number of scholars of Irish writing and ecocritics, that issues surrounding place and subjectivity, urban and rural landscapes, ecological degradation and climate change, as well as gender, sexuality and embodiment all represent pertinent issues in Joyce's writings. Perhaps above all, then, *Eco-Joyce* looks at the writings of James Joyce in broad ecocritical terms in order to include many voices and approaches in this promising direction in Joyce studies.

The Emergence of an Irish Ecocriticism

As with the rest of the Western world, Ireland faces increasingly difficult questions about the environment, and an explicitly Irish ecocriticism has emerged as a response to this significant concern. During the era of the Celtic Tiger, urban development, pollution from industrialisation, lax regulations for business and unsustainable economic growth had a deleterious effect on the environment. These contemporary shortcomings (or worse) mark our era as especially challenged where the environment is concerned and much has been written about Ireland's short-term and long-term challenges in relation to the environment.[7] As we will see, Joyce's Dublin also confronted many important environmental issues (such as air pollution, clean water distribution and waste removal, to name a few) and Joyce was a keen reader of the importance of these issues in his own time and place. Our view, then, is that engaging with literary and cultural works that confront environmental issues is not only pressing, but also long overdue. And while the exilic writer Joyce is simultaneously bound to late nineteenth- and early twentieth-century Dublin, he nevertheless demonstrates an abiding interest in environmental issues that reflect this period of history as well as contemporary Ireland. As this collection reveals, Irish geography, especially when it is figured as cultural geography, occupies a central place in Joyce's work.

Gerry Smyth was the first scholar to discuss the relevance of ecocriticism to Irish writing. In '"Shite and Sheep": An Ecocritical Perspective on Two Recent Irish Novels' (2000), Smyth stressed the relationship between Irish space, geography and environment. A year later in *Space and the Irish Cultural Imagination*, he contended that 'the study of the relationship between culture and environment overlaps significantly with the study of Irish cultural history, and more specifically with analysis that addresses the issue of Irish space'.[8] Since Symth's publications, a few ecocritical treatments of Irish subjects have followed, leading up to three prominent publications: Tim Wenzell's *Emerald Green: An Ecocritical Study of Irish Literatu*re (2009), Christine Cusick's edited collection, *Out of the Earth: Ecocritical Readings of Irish Texts* (2010) and Eamonn Wall's *Writing the Irish West: Ecologies and Traditions* (2011). And while these texts substantiate the immediate critical need for ecocriticism in Irish studies, they do not include Joyce as a figure under consideration. Michael Rubenstein's roundly (and deservedly) praised *Public Works* (2010) looks at the centrality of the sewer system in *Ulysses* and in so doing helps to demonstrate the importance of an ecological reading of Joyce's work, although Rubenstein's own approach is more historicist and materialist than ecological in orientation.

In addition to these significant publications, the conference 'Ireland and Ecocriticism: An Interdisciplinary Conference' was held at Mary Immaculate College, University of Limerick, in June, 2010, and constituted the first conference devoted exclusively to Irish ecocriticism. The success of this conference and the works referenced above adequately demonstrate Smyth's point, 'Irish studies and ecocriticism will have a lot to say to each other. . . . Geographical peculiarity and historical discontinuity have produced a situation in Ireland in which questions concerning space, landscape, locality, gender, urban and rural experience and nature have become central to both the cultural and the critical imagination.'[9] Following the emergence of a strong ecocritical dimension in Irish studies, the

Association for Literature and the Environment-UK added Ireland to the association, which is now called ASLE-UKI.

Even though the development of Irish ecocriticism is relatively recent, it should not go without mentioning that its trajectory follows the work of many Irish geographers and some literary critics who have helped to locate culture, nature, rural history and the city as central to the Irish imagination. That is, there have been many texts that ecocritics can turn to in order to add to the emerging and robust ecocritical discussion in Ireland. One particularly relevant example is John Wilson Foster's comprehensive volume, *Nature in Ireland: A Scientific and Cultural History* (1997). As ecocriticism was taking shape in North America, Foster was anthologising the work of writers who were exploring the historical and contemporary meaning of 'nature' in the context of Irish intellectual and cultural production. This massive undertaking clearly demonstrates an abiding interest in the subject of sustained reflection on the natural world among Irish writers, and even while Foster does not offer his volume under the rubric of ecotheory, it is clearly animated by the same kinds of interests, concerns and ethical thinking that suffuses contemporary ecocriticism. Foster, it should be noted, was preoccupied with the century-old gap between science and culture in Ireland, and argues in the preface for a return of Irish natural history that is inclusive of culture. According to Foster, debate regarding three important cultural issues should surface as a result of bridging this gap: environmentalism, animal rights, and genetic engineering.[10] In short, Foster, though predominantly a literary critic and without articulating a self-consciously ecocritical stance, nevertheless succeeded in formulating at least one potentially prosperous approach to a decidedly Irish ecocriticism.[11]

Many geographers have focused their work on environmental concerns within the Irish landscape. Patrick J. Duffy's *Exploring the History and Heritage of Irish Landscapes* (2007) identifies the cultural, historical, ecological, literary and social relationships that have formed in any discipline discussing both the built and natural environments in Ireland. Brian Graham's collection, *In Search of Ireland: A Cultural Geography* (1997), investigates issues of gender, postcolonialism and land management within Irish cultural geography. The historical geographer, Kevin Whelan, has, throughout his prolific career, focused on the relationship between space and cultural and communal memory, and has therefore contributed inestimably to a body of work that is decidedly ecocritical in orientation if not in name. Moreover, Irish geographers have identified environmental, cultural and historical problems within the culture of tourism, an industry that has become central to the Irish economy. In the co-edited volume, *Tourism in Ireland: A Critical Analysis* (1993), Barbara O'Connor and Michael Cronin address spatial, geographical, cultural and environmental issues within Irish tourism that also speak broadly to ecotheory. For instance, travel writing and photography, rural imagery and heritage centres in Ireland are surprisingly ripe for ecocritical investigation. In fact, many of the representations of Ireland that inhere in contemporary tourist documents derive from the Literary Revival and its aesthetic inflation of rural Ireland. Contemporary Irish geography has become infused with an ecocritical dimension even though the practitioners in the field do not typically define themselves with this term.

The Future of Eco-Joyce

There has yet to be any sustained attention given to James Joyce's relationship to ecocriticism. There have been some appeals, however, toward a greening of Joyce criticism among Joyceans. Alongside a handful of presenters at various Joyce conferences in the last several years, Michelle McSwiggan Kelly's essay, 'Oceanic Longing: An Ecocritical Approach to Joyce', came out in *Joyce in Progress: Proceedings of the 2008 James Joyce Graduate Conference in Rome* (2008). In addition to Kelly, Margarita Estévez Saá and Marisol Morales Ladrón both have chapters on ecocritical approaches to Joyce in the edited volume, *New Perspective on James Joyce* (2010).[12] Furthermore, Seán Latham recently emphasised that the 'lack of attention Joyce scholars in general have paid to the vibrant field of ecocriticism' needs to increase with 'an awareness of ecology and a critical attentiveness to Joyce's own theory of nature' as the growing trend in ecocriticism takes shape in modernism and Irish studies.[13] As this volume demonstrates, there are many ecocritical points of entry to Joyce's work, and ecocriticism is amenable to some of the more popular rubrics, including modernism, studies in empire/colonialism, feminism, nationalism and urbanism, through which Joyce's work is more typically examined.

Two distinct schools of thought have come to dominate Joyce studies: the view that Joyce is a high modernist, or an historically and politically engaged Irish writer. These two labels are not exclusive of each other and in many ways are complementary. Nonetheless, they can be determinative of how one critically engages with Joyce's *oeuvre*. Questions of landscape, nature, colonialism and geographical identity arise in discussions of Irish nationalism and Catholicism, on the one hand and, on the other hand, questions of narrative, language, aesthetics and the city arise in connection to Joyce's engagement with literary and cultural modernity. These two perspectives – Joyce the universal writer of the modern era or Joyce the nationalist – permeate the scholarship. This collection does not prescribe to one reading over another; however, the essays in *Eco-Joyce* concentrate on Joyce's interest with a variety of compelling linguistic and literal environments, and as such collectively work to bridge the false dichotomy that is still evident in Joyce scholarship.

Recently, ecocritics have begun to investigate issues like empire, modernism and gender as part of the greater pantheon of ecological inquiry. Alfred Crosby began the discussion of the ecology of empire in his seminal *Ecological Imperialism: The Biological Expansion of Europe, 900–1900* (1986), arguing that imperialism, both biological and political, alters the local ecology of place through biological emigration and invasion. Edward Said also reminds us, 'If there is anything that radically distinguishes the imagination of anti-imperialism, it is the primacy of the geographical element.'[14] Crosby's book predates much of the ecocritical expansion in the 1990s, but more recent works have analysed imperial expansion as an important, even decisive, environmental event. Both Graham Huggan's and Helen Tiffin's *Postcolonial Ecocriticism: Literature, Animals, Environment* (2010) and Laura Wright's *'Wilderness into Civilized Shapes': Reading the Postcolonial Environment* (2010) are prime examples. Although the evidence for Joyce's own interest in colonial and anti-imperial Ireland is vast and has been explicated in contemporary scholarship, the connection between Joyce and postcolonial ecocriticism has not.

For all of its focus on urban cityscapes, alienation and psychological and philosophical contingency, modernity itself has to be seen as ushering in a new conception of the natural world and our relationship to it. Usually regarded as antipathetic to nature and as precipitating contemporary environmental degradation, modernity and the assumptions that underwrite its megamyths (scientific progress, social order and personal liberation), all require that nature become subordinate to some other perceived ethical, social or commercial imperative. Accordingly, many critics have begun to explore the ways in which modernist writers documented and critiqued the emergence of modern urban and suburban development. Important modernists like Joseph Conrad, Virginia Wolfe and D.H. Lawrence have become significant figures within an ecologically engaged 'greening' of modernism, owing to the attention to forests, rivers and rural landscapes that suffuse their work. This reconsideration of literary modernism as engaged with the dichotomous relationship between built environments and the natural world is obviously significant and compelling, and as this collection shows, Joyce was a keen reader of modernity as an ecological event.

However, Joyce was also clearly interested in Irish modernism as containing a distinctive historical trajectory, one that emphasises nationalist symbols of agrarian landscapes and Yeatsian metaphors for an anti-modern, anti-imperial, and mythologically-oriented Ireland. Admittedly, Joyce took issue with the Literary Revival's atavistic representations of Ireland, but it is also undeniable that he too recognised and, at times, championed Irish modernism as an alternate form of literary modernism and philosophical modernity. Indeed, collectively these essays point up the salutary manner in which Irish modernism is underwritten by a consciousness of region and centre (or rural and urban) and that Joyce located this distinction as primary in his explication of the consciousness of modern Ireland.

While reading Joyce's ecocritical imagination alongside his interest in modernity and the history of imperialism helps to focus critical attention on previously under-considered aspects of his writing, the somewhat more established view that Joyce's work speaks to the modern relationship between the genders is also amply evidenced in the present volume. Ecofeminism – considered by some critics to be part of the third wave of feminism[15] – treats two significant historical events as almost synonymous; in this work, a history of environmental manipulation and exploitation is regarded as congruent with the essentialisation, subjugation and oppression of women. However, some feminists suggest that the tension between 'eco' and 'feminism' contributes to re-essentialising women as synonymous with 'nature', thereby nullifying female agency and autonomy and reinscribing prescriptive gender norms. One such ecofeminist reading could be made of Joyce's Molly Bloom as an oversimplified embodiment of the earth mother with concomitant goddess associations related to Celtic mythology.[16] Ecofeminism underscores that issues of discursive readings of nature and gender can be explored and articulated in increasingly expansive readings of texts. A number of essays in this volume take up the ways in which Joyce's reading of gender is central to a consideration of his engagement with ecological realities.

It seems, then, that for the many reasons outlined here and for others that will only be explicated by others, Joyce studies and ecocriticism are mutually informing and of relevance to contemporary scholarship. We cannot enumerate all of the possible theoretical matrices among ecocritical readings of Joyce in this introduction, but just as Derek Attridge points out that 'The number of entrances to the Joycean mansion . . . is potentially infinite,'[17] our edited collection serves to punctuate this already compelling and growing body of collective and imaginative work by bringing together fourteen previously unpublished essays by pre-eminent Joyceans, scholars of Irish literature and ecocritics, in its examination of the overarching ecological consciousness evinced in James Joyce's fiction and non-fiction. *Eco-Joyce* is thematically arranged into three sections: I. Nature and Environmental Consciousness in Joyce's Fiction; II. Joyce and the Urban Environment; and III. Joyce, Somatic Ecology and the Body. To enable a varied readership, each section allows both the broad/concise and supportive/sceptical critic to engage with Joyce and ecocriticism. The essays in this volume address many of the challenges, contexts and dimensions that emerge when we read Joyce's writings with an ecological sensibility.

The essays presented in the first section, 'Nature and Environmental Consciousness in Joyce's Fiction', investigate Joyce's general approach to the subjects 'nature' and 'environmental'. These essays collectively work to describe the ample purview for an ecological reading of Joyce's fiction. Fiona Becket's essay examines the relationship between high literary modernism in the writing of Joyce and a contemporary understanding of eco-poetics. It is a discussion that focuses on aspects of *Ulysses* and *Finnegans Wake* but draws on examples of mid-century writing including J.G. Ballard's *The Drowned World* and *The Drought*. In Ballard, as represented by these novels of the 1960s in which the 'real' returns in a Žižekian sense, there is in fact little that can be theorised and understood beyond the self, beyond subjectivities. Becket's essay considers the legacy of Joycean self-representation in relation to this mode of writing, which invokes the environment in order to disavow it and to invite a critical concentration on Joycean 'place'. The point is not only to subject the Joycean texts to a 'reading', but more significantly to invite these texts, which are brought to bear on Ballard's work, to contribute to the development of an eco-poesis, and in doing so to contribute to debates about the future of ecocriticism.

Cheryl Herr's essay similarly points to ways in which contemporary ecocritics may formulate their responses not only to Joyce's work, but to literary texts more broadly. Indeed, Herr's essay compels a new space for ecocritical attention on the level of syntax rather than strictly reading the verisimilitude of literary works for markers of positive or negative ecocritical attention. Herr argues that scatological themes in Joyce have often been addressed from a psychoanalytic perspective, especially when Joyce's 1904 letters to Nora are taken into account. Rather than concentrate on the writer's putative anal fixation or simply chronicle the scattered references to excrement that punctuate his works, this paper looks at the problems of human waste disposal in Ireland during the lifetime of James Joyce and his parents. Building on the argument in Michael Rubenstein's brilliant book *Public Works* (2010), which concludes that *Ulysses* is Joyce's mature reflection on modernisation and sanitation in Dublin, particularly in reference to the waterworks, electrification and sewage disposal, Herr's paper argues that *Finnegans Wake* in fact marks a new stage in Joyce's address to the long-standing and persistent problem of waste disposal. Joyce specifically addresses the task of sanitisation at the sentence level; in the *Wake* sentences periodically feed on culture, fatten and assume what we might call peristaltic faecal shapes.

Bonnie Kime Scott's chapter, 'Joyce, Ecofeminism and the River as Woman', embarks from the view that despite all the due attention that has gone to modernity, technology, consumerism and 'making it new' in modernist studies, the category of 'nature' has a persistent, if little recognised, presence in the works of many modernists, including James Joyce and other Irish writers. The Irish male literary establishment has also tended to equate their nation with woman, which as Eavan Boland has noted, is problematic for a woman writer. Taking an ecofeminist approach, Scott considers Joyce's gendering of nature, and particularly the River Liffey, as feminine. Finally, she compares Boland's poem, 'Anna Liffey', to Joyce's ALP coda in *Finnegans Wake*, finding a comparable grappling with history and dissolution in both authors, but a more personally grounded gender identification with the river in Boland's work.

Erin Walsh's 'Word and World: The Ecology of the Pun in *Finnegans Wake*' also examines Joyce's engagement with Irish history in the *Wake*, but Walsh moves from city to nation in her exploration of how the *Wake*'s variable puns suggest a model for an ecological discourse of nation – nation not only in process, but as process – that supplants the fiction of nation as unitary organic whole with the self-adulterating word-world of the *Wake*. Walsh contends that by destabilising the conceptual and linguistic boundaries of the word 'nation', the *Wake* articulates nation not as romantic metaphor but as ecological pun. In the *Wake*'s final pages, ALP, appearing as both tree and river, sheds her leaves as the reader's hand turns the final material leaves of the book, further entailing the reader in a material-symbolic discourse that models an ecological negotiation of national boundaries. Walsh suggests that the reader's return to the beginning of the *Wake*'s 'riverrun' emerges as a suturing that restores rather than effaces the *in medias res* of the text's opening, producing not a totalising self-contained whole, but a readerly bridge that still honours the rift.

Yi-Peng Lai concludes this section by outlining Joyce's connection to Ireland's history of deforestation in 'The Tree Wedding and the (Eco)Politics of Irish Forestry in "Cyclops": History, Language, and the Viconian Politics of the Forest'. Focusing on the Tree Wedding scene in the 'Cyclops' episode of *Ulysses*, Lai's essay delves into the problematics of deforestation and Irish politics, and ponders the question of history in relation to environmental consciousness and cultural nationalist propaganda in Ireland at the turn of the twentieth century. She examines the wedding procession of 'the chevalier John Wyse de Neaulan, grand high chief ranger of the Irish National Forests, with Miss Fir Conifer of Pine Valley',[18] and proposes a critical discussion of the intertextual technique of the chapter and the politics surrounding environmental issues during Joyce's time, as revealed by this specific tree wedding passage. In particular, Lai examines the catalogue's specific location within the text apropos Giambattista Vico, referencing Viconian historiography regarding the myth of Vulcan and Cyclops. Also, Lai's essay reconsiders Joyce's Cyclopean catalogue as a sustained reflection on commerce, colonial/capitalist exploitation, the Celtic Revival (especially its language politics) and the deforestation of Ireland.

The second section of the volume focuses on 'Joyce and the Urban Environment'. Margot Norris begins by arguing that the urban setting of the 'Wandering Rocks' episode of *Ulysses* poses severe challenges to ecocriticism precisely because the city already constitutes a 'paved civilisation', as Irish ecocritic Tim Wenzell calls it. Indeed, a number of images cited or alluded to in the text point to ecological disaster: the 1904 General Slocum riverboat catastrophe, for example, and the malnutrition of the Dedalus girls with its gesture toward Ireland's 'Great Hunger'. But in general, Norris maintains, the ruination of nature is less directly represented in the episode than obliquely expressed through a series of anti-ecocritical world views produced by narrative and character in the text. The extrusion of nature from the perspectives of the narrative voices and the Dubliners in 'Wandering Rocks' threatens its perceptual extinction in ways that constitute an ecological casualty of a discursive kind.

In 'Joyce Beyond the Pale', Brandon Kershner asserts that Joyce's work has seldom been addressed from an ecological perspective because he is an overwhelmingly urban writer. But on closer examination, his portrayals of the city are closely bounded by a vaguely conceived and rather brutal vision of nature, a vision clearest in 'A Painful Case' and 'The Dead'. According to Kershner, in *Portrait* Joyce struggles with the Yeatsian, ideologically charged idea of a nature associated closely with Irish racial purity and with spirituality, an idea Joyce rejects. *Ulysses*, whose action does not leave the city, invokes as its most powerful vision of nature Molly and Bloom's memory of Howth Head, Molly's memories of Gibraltar, and the scenes on Sandymount Strand, like scenes of the park, all liminal spaces mediating between the city and what lies beyond.

Greg Winston's essay on the '"Aquacities of Thought and Language": The Political Ecology of Water in *Ulysses*' investigates how ecocriticism has tended to neglect the topic of water resources and to look past urban, modernist texts it deemed unconducive or irrelevant to environmental readings. Winston proposes to fill both of these critical gaps by reconsidering Joyce's allusion in 'Ithaca' to the Dublin water system (also known as the Vartry Scheme), particularly for how it demonstrates the social inequalities that underlay the technological marvel of that massive public-works project. Bloom's thoughtful digression on his household water supply flows directly from an account of civil engineering to a revealing reference to a 1904 legal dispute over water use by the Dublin poor. Doing so, it raises questions about political control of water, including whether the resource should be treated as a market commodity or universal right. In this regard, Joyce's novel can be read as articulating a discourse of political ecology that is concerned with how the power relationships in a human community can be both cause and consequence of that community's relation to its environment and exploitation of its resources. A century later, as water moves increasingly to the centre of regional and global political conflicts, *Ulysses* offers us a valuable framework and localised example by which to contemplate issues of water regulation and accessibility.

In '"Clacking Along the Concrete Pavement": Economic Isolation and the Bricolage of Place in James Joyce's *Dubliners*', Christine Cusick invokes the theoretical compass of social ecology to study humans' economic relationship with the built environment as a channel for processes of self-actualisation. Offering a close reading of Joyce's characters of Eveline and Little Chandler, she asserts that the desire to escape the built environment of Dublin life is ultimately thwarted by actual and perceived want of economic agency. Attention to this materiality of place presents a new lens through which to interpret Joyce's implication of modernity, a lens that diffuses emphasis on the alienated individual and gives voice to the reciprocal relationship between the situated human life and its material and social environments. Through this reading, Cusick examines what Joyce might teach critics about the praxis of urban ecocriticism, arguing that the epistemology of Joyce's Dublin offers critics a model of how to study human nature's psychological and physical embodiment of urban space.

Derek Gladwin takes us out of Joyce's Dublin and into the urban/rural divide of the Irish West by examining two of Joyce's nonfiction essays, 'The City of the Tribes: Italian Echoes in an Irish Port' and 'The Mirage of the Fisherman of Aran: England's Safety Valve in Case of War', published in the Italian-language newspaper, *Il Piccolo della Sera*. Although many would consider these articles Joyce's pragmatic foray into journalism, Gladwin suggests that Joyce goes beyond this, functioning as a travel writer in order to probe the deeper historical and cultural geographies within his Irish itinerary by using a spatial practice called place-attachment, accessing place through personal and cultural experience in the landscape. Joyce explores the region's underlying cultural and environmental currents, at times controversial and conflicted, revealing his deeper emerging interest in the land's geography. To this end, Gladwin argues that Joyce's environmental impulse lies within the fabric of the cultural representation of place.

In the final section of *Eco-Joyce*, 'Joyce, Somatic Ecology and the Body', writers look at the centrality of embodiment, sexuality and corporeality in Joyce's textual ecology. Eugene O'Brien argues that art, and specifically that of *A Portrait of the Artist as a Young Man*, offers a corrective to the Cartesian dualism of mind and body that has been a pervasive influence on not only aesthetics and philosophy, but also on the subject and object, and pits humans against the environment. Joyce's aesthetic theory, which is worked out through *Portrait*, is a holistic one that values all aspects of experience as part of the aesthetic. O'Brien also underscores the homologies between Joyce's thinking on art and that of a number of philosophers and thinkers, such as Martin Heidegger, Giorgio Agamben and Jacques Derrida. The politics of such a view has strong implications for a criticism that sees the world not as an object to be used and mastered, as in many discourses, disregarding the importance of environmental legitimacy, but rather as a partner in aesthetic apprehension and experience.

Robert Brazeau takes up issues of embodiment and wayfinding in his essay, 'Environment and Embodiment in Joyce's "The Dead"'. This chapter examines Joyce's engagement with all of the behaviours (including eating, drinking, wayfinding and reproduction) that come to reveal the animality and connection with nonhuman nature of his human subjects, especially Gabriel Conroy, in 'The Dead'. Brazeau argues that, in this story and others in *Dubliners*, Joyce reveals a strong ecological consciousness through his sustained attention to how humans draw on instinctual and somatic clues to orient themselves – physically and psychologically; alone and with others – in their world.

In '"Sunflawered" Humanity in *Finnegans Wake*: Nature, Existential Shame and Transcendence', James Fairhall takes a phenomenological and ecocritical approach to *Finnegans Wake*. Fairhall indicates that the *Wake* reflects Joyce's long-standing interest in nature and the body, particularly in the duality of human beings as uniquely self-conscious products of evolution whose spirit-like minds, seeking transcendence, are tragicomically tethered to animal-like bodies. As they morph into each other and into nonhuman entities, the *Wake*'s characters remain embedded in a web of natural relationships.

Garry Leonard's essay concludes this section and the collection as a whole with an expansive and theoretically compelling approach to the relationship between the body and nature. Leonard argues that nature seems to manifest itself in Joyce the way a 'correction' alters the stock market. It comes from an unimagined 'nowhere' that clearly becomes a 'somewhere' as its presence takes irrevocable effect on what now is, in a way that can no longer be ignored, a false construction that has always kept the person 'elsewhere'. In this essay, he compares Stephen Dedalus as he experiences two 'corrections' from the natural environment. The first, from his so-called 'bird girl' epiphany in *Portrait*, is a corrective that ecstatically banishes all nagging thoughts of perhaps entering the priesthood, stirring him instead to announce his vocation as an artist, 'a priest of the eternal imagination'. The second correction, also on a beach (Sandymount Strand), occurs in the 'Proteus' episode of *Ulysses*, after Stephen has crash-landed, yet again, in true Icarian fashion, from his over-hyped flight 'to forge in the smithy of [his own] soul the uncreated conscience of his race'. Ultimately, Leonard suggests that Joyce is 'green' in a profoundly radical way: nature is what your body smashes up against if you persist long enough in self-serving, self-delusion.

To conclude, *Eco-Joyce* offers work from a number of established Joyceans, as well as incisive critics of ecocriticism, Irish studies, modernism, and contemporary theory. This expansive and interdisciplinary collection prompts readers of Joyce to address pressing issues around the environment as we move on in the twenty-first century while also contextualising Joyce's writings as relevant in this discussion. It is our sincere wish that this collection will prompt readers to re-examine Joyce as a writer engaged in a wider ambit of themes than has been previously imagined, and that this work will contribute to the ongoing and fruitful dialogue between Joyceans and environmental critics.

I

Nature and Environmental Consciousness in Joyce's Fiction

James Joyce, Climate Change and the Threat to our 'Natural Substance'

FIONA BECKET

A cloud began to cover the sun wholly slowly wholly. Grey. Far.
(*Ulysses*)

This essay considers whether the conditions of anthropogenic climate change – transhistorical, indifferent to the survival of species and, in relation to human life, indifferent to the claims of deterministic categories such as gender, class and race – can produce a meaningful critical practice. It assumes the prevalence of environmental reference in Joyce's work, but asks whether the protean, 'Circean', poetics of disembodiment and re-embodiment in James Joyce, in particular, can usefully modify, supplement or challenge the presuppositions of environmental poetics and literary ecology. As we acquire an increasingly detailed awareness of the environmental consequences of global capitalism, we also take on board the fact that capitalism's priorities overwhelmingly obstruct the implementation of effective solutions (however remedial these 'solutions', there are too many short-term interests to be protected). The imperative within literary ecology (for this reader) is to connect with the rich field of the symbolic and approach that which exceeds the symbolic, that which is most threatened by ecological catastrophe, which Slavoj Žižek has called our 'natural Substance'.[1] In this context, in this essay, examples from *A Portrait of the Artist as a Young Man*, *Ulysses* and *Finnegans Wake* identify the principal aspects of a Joycean poetics, set alongside examples from John Cowper Powys (with his vision of a 'vivisected' earth) and, mid-twentieth century, J.G. Ballard's fictions of climate change. Ultimately, aspects of an ecology inflected by Deleuzean/Guattarian 'geophilosophy' are signalled in the hope of exposing the barest traces of an ethics of reading.

Kate Soper articulates a commonly held position when she describes Joyce's resistance to ruralism (in which she included Celticism) as decidedly political, 'motivated by a desire to expose the bigotries masked by Irish nationalism and its mythical status as a pure, indigenous cultural legacy', and highlights the fact that, despite his understanding of the 'mythologising functions and regressive effects of nationalism', he nevertheless developed in *Ulysses* 'an essentialist and mythologising conception of the feminine (as earth-bound, cosmic, cyclical, the representative of humanity in its reproductive immanence)'.[2] Nevertheless, it is easy to accept at face value, as the title of this volume suggests, that there is an eco-Joyce, and that *eco-* might be a prefix that one could usefully attach to any, or a range of, writers so named, perhaps to insert them unproblematically into a familiar and recognisable framework of understanding that would add to the ways in which their works can be seen to 'read' the relations between the habitually dichotomised categories of nature and culture. To assume so is to presuppose that the politics and cultural theories of 'environmentalism' and 'ecology', or 'literary ecology', are already written, and that they have achieved a coherence which renders available newly wrought or adapted versions of the self, the body and world (totalising categories, all), re-appropriated and re-presented for straightforward critical consumption. That is far from the actual situation (and how thankful we might be for that).

If Joyce's concentration on the urban is an aspect of his critique of the enlightenment project (about man, nature, and perception) that is not the last word that can be uttered about Joyce's environments. Joyce's odyssey, let us call it his *geodesy*, comprehends the ethical force of environments, those which surround us, comparable to the ethical force of language in positing degrees of difference that challenge repressively certain categories of thought and value: at the beginning of *A Portrait of the Artist as a Young Man* Stephen thinks, 'But you could not have a green rose. But perhaps somewhere in the world you could.'[3] Throughout his works Joyce refers to environments, not as background but, as often as not, poetry and song, mediated forms of language that challenge Stephen's egocentricity in terms of an often ironic ecocentricity: Shelley's 'Art thou pale for weariness/Of climbing heaven and gazing on the earth' (*PAYM* 88); the 'fragrant' verses of Horace, 'as though they had lain all those years in myrtle and lavender and verbain' (163); Nashe's 'Brightness falls from air' (211) which Stephen has misremembered, transformed to the image of lice ('His mind bred vermin' [211]). Throughout *A Portrait of the Artist as a Young Man* Stephen's moral, ethical, reflections are mediated by reference to non-human nature, most effective, arguably, in the vision of hell when the purgation of the *world*, an entirely cultural concept, is limned in terms of the *earth*: 'The very air of this world, that pure element, becomes foul and unbreathable when it has been long enclosed. Consider then what must be the foulness of the air of hell' (111).

As we know, in *Ulysses* aspects of *A Portrait of the Artist as a Young Man* are re-introduced, developed and transformed. In 'Calypso', the retreating sun intervenes to change the train of Bloom's thought from 'On earth as it is in heaven' to its contradiction, 'No, not like that', and then to an account of a waste, a 'dead sea in a dead land, grey and old'. The broader context is Bloom's reverie on settler colonies in Palestine, stimulated by his perception of 'Agendath Netaim', land acquisition and the cultivation of produce for trade. Bloom's recollection of Molly spitting out olives, and his pleasure in the 'wild perfume' of oranges freighted in from Jaffa, of Moisel's description of the trade routes, all these combine to produce a narrative of the inextricability of commerce, economics, politics and religion. The change in his environment as he walks home from the butcher, in the light and the temperature ('A cloud began to cover the sun wholly slowly wholly. Grey. Far'), works subtly on Bloom, whose thoughts are transferred from *Sukkoth*, in which flawless citron and palm branches become a symbolic language of unity and redemption, to an apocalyptic description of the 'then' of Biblical judgement ('Sodom, Gomorrah, Edom. All dead names'). The Biblical accounts of divine wrath produce in Bloom (whose name, as it punctuates the novel, offers a quietly insistent challenge to the certainty of devastation) an image of the degree zero of the natural world, against which all other accounts of growth, birth and fecundity in the novel must be measured: 'No, not like that. A barren land, bare waste. Vulcanic lake, the dead sea: no fish, weedless, sunk deep in the earth. No wind would lift those waves, grey metal, poisonous foggy waters' (*U* 73). That image – of poisonous foggy waters – connects the raining brimstone with contemporary Dublin; the 'bent hag' who 'crossed from Cassidy's', with the poor old woman (the Shan Van Vocht), nation, the earth. The 'dead land' which 'bore the oldest, the first race' in the time of myth, ante-diluvian, is exhausted, epitomising the end of time, finitude represented as feminised decrepitude against which the mythic figure of Molly Bloom will compete: 'It lay there now. Now it could bear no more. Dead: an old woman's: the grey sunken cunt of the world. / Desolation' (73).

If myth offers a digestible pre-history of climate change, in our own moment it returns in fictional accounts (notably film) in inevitably epic proportions – no other scale will do. I hope my reasons for choosing to focus on anthropogenic climate change become clearer as this essay progresses. It is not an obvious way of framing a reading of *Ulysses*, or even parts of *Ulysses*, and that is not the objective here, but it is to acknowledge the totalising narrative about 'finitude' that cannot seriously be excluded from one's usual practice of reading or engaging with a text from a different but not unrelated cultural moment. Marx, across a range of his writings, described the complex interrelations between nature and human nature and refused any polarising distinction between them. Much current environmentalist writing, without characterising its stance as owing anything much to Marx's thought, begins and ends with alienation. To Marx, the concerns of the human, the natural and the social operate dialectically. When capitalism produces the conditions for radical distortions of these relationships, the result is a familiar social and economic environment of the kind we now inhabit:

> Capitalist production [. . .] disturbs the circulation of matter between man and soil, i.e. prevents the return to the soil of its elements consumed by man in the form of food and clothing; it therefore violates the conditions necessary to lasting fertility of the soil.[4]

Giving an account of the alienating results of agricultural hyper-productivity, Marx concludes:

> Moreover, all progress in capitalistic agriculture is a progress in the art, not only of robbing the labourer, but of robbing the soil; all progress in increasing the fertility of the soil for a given time, is a progress towards ruining the lasting sources of that fertility. [. . .] Capitalist production, therefore, develops technology, and the combining together of various processes into a social whole, only by sapping the original sources of all wealth – the soil and the labourer. (*C* 298)

This is not an argument for the cessation of agriculture, of course, but for a better-regulated, socially responsible – we might say, environmentally aware – economics. The human contribution to anthropogenic climate change – global warming as a result of the unchecked polluting processes of human activity – is the natural extension of the alienation described in these passages from *Capital* and I would argue that ecocriticism should acknowledge the importance of a Marxist ecology as part of its theoretical framework. Is it too facetious to suggest that, in its manifestation and effects, climate change shares some of the characteristics of the commodity?[5]

Ecocriticism has its origins in writing about non-urban, regional, local environments – wilderness, mountains, national parks – and ecocritics have commonly represented themselves as populating the spectrum from those benign consumers of the great outdoors, those with an investment in conservation, nature writers (photographers, documentary-makers etc.) and activists, and all places between. It is ironic, therefore, that anyone wishing to develop debates within the environmental humanities, and write about the totalising narrative of climate change that dominates a high proportion of debates on ecology and environmental politics – ecocriticism and its environments, we could say – will discover it only by its absence in most ecocritical literary criticism. Timothy Clark has recently made this point in an important article which calls ecocritics to account,[6] and in his comprehensive introduction to the field, *Literature and the Environment* (2010), in which he comments on the contrast between the prevalence of environmental plots (plots that allude to, or highlight, global warming and eco-catastrophe) in contemporary fiction, including science-fiction, and the inattention paid to climate change in works of literary analysis.[7] The observation itself begs the question of what kind of response to climate change (as the context superseding all others according to which our subjectivity can be determined) might our discipline produce? What ethics of reading, if any, is proposed by the fact of climate change and, no less relevant, to what extent is it desirable that ecocriticism remains a critical practice confined to a number, even a significant number, of university departments with almost no political significance beyond them?

To date, ecocriticism has not matured a theory of discursive and symbolic practices as found in literature, although in positing the formulations of 'deep ecology', as some ecocritical interventions have, it has already attracted opposition to what are perceived to be its unexamined assumptions about the ideological formations of nature, and human subjectivity, as well as the relations between human and non-human beings. The most developed arguments put pressure on deep ecology's romantic organicism.[8] For some, 'deep ecology' asks the wrong questions because it seems to be embedded in dualistic notions, the logic of which it labours, unsuccessfully, to reject; ultimately it repeats or seems to reconfigure, some might say distort, the dominant conceptual configurations of romantic arguments, romantic thought. Critics have shown how deeply indebted modern environmentalism is to the most pervasive myths of the romantic imagination in its constructions not least of place and space, but also indigeneity.

To return to Clark's lucid and surgical critique of the objectives and impasses of ecocriticism: he argues that it constitutes nothing more effective than a 'simulative' or pseudo-politics because it fails to engage critically with climate change, and it manifestly fails in the way that political solutions manifestly fail because climate change offers to the human subject 'no simple or unitary object *directly* to confront or delimit'.[9] Clark is highly critical of ecocriticism's concentration on the local and the individual at the cost of a more global perspective. He writes critically of a perceived fidelity to liberal consensus so that 'simulative' ecopolitics appear to be merely another version of the 'symbolic' politics of liberal democracy, whereby attempts to fashion social attitudes and behaviour according to 'green' imperatives (he invokes the example of getting cars off the road) conflict with personal freedoms (the freedom, or the perceived right, to own a car). Clark does not deny the achievements of green readings, green critical practice. (This description bestows it with a coherence that the situation belies somewhat, although 'seminal' texts have rapidly emerged particularly in North American environmental writing, invoked as part of a 'green' canon of foundational works.) However, in his view it is a question of relatively small advances in the face of extraordinarily difficult conditions:

> To describe ecocriticism as engaged in a simulative politics [. . .] is not to deny that individual readings – of representations of the nonhuman, environmental racism or of bioregional ideals etc – are often valuable and desirable, like efforts to preserve ecosystems or reform energy infrastructures, but only to acknowledge the inadequacy of their scope in relation to national and global contexts whose practices so overwhelmingly negate them.[10]

In its multifaceted, dynamic response to the totality of polluting human activity, climate change – that is to say, the effects of anthropogenic global warming – undermines and confounds (for Clark it *deconstructs*) the pieties and parochialism of ecocriticism born out of the values of liberal-democratic capitalism ('consumer democracy'), that it also seeks to expose and critique. Hence, Clark proposes that ecocriticism, contrary to its initial promise, is an expression of what environmental politics, 'embedded in the modernist, liberal tradition',[11] also manifest: 'the politics of closure in self-denial'.[12]

It is in the context of this critique that the current essay hopes to proceed. To presume an eco-Joyce might be to presume a convenient fiction under the circumstances; a rather artificial attempt to expand or further the 'greening' of modernism (up to now in relation to Joyce the description, 'green', has operated metonymically for nation). *Contra* Soper, Seamus Deane asserts that, 'Joyce was, and knew himself to be, part of the Irish Revival. [. . .] The country and culture he repudiated was also the country and culture he re-imagined', so establishing Joyce firmly in relation to debates on literature, identity and cultural nationalism.[13] The current essay does not seek to claim Joyce for environmentalism and it proceeds in the full glare of Clark's challenge to ecocriticism. It also pays heed to a supplementary observation in the course of his argument, introduced via reference to the conclusions of Ursula K. Heise, that the extra-human scale of climate change demands modes of representation in which techniques 'previously associated with the urban novel of literary modernism (James Joyce, John Dos Passos)', or with a 'secularised magic realism', are foregrounded.[14] For Heise, the extra-human scale of climate change demands narrative forms that problematise the human subject as a discrete consciousness; subjectivity set off or apart from the world of objects. Hence, she invokes Joyce – of *Ulysses* and *Finnegans Wake* – to account for the narrative styles of John Brunner's novel about the consequences of over-population, *Stand on Zanzibar* (1968) and, more recently, David Brin's fable of a self-consuming planet in *Earth* (1990). According to Heise, John Brunner develops the horizon of the urban modernist novel in order to accommodate the planetary scale:

> In narrative terms, he configures this sense of the global in terms of a far-flung mosaic of discourses that extends the matrix of the modernist urban novel to the planet as a whole, in an effort to capture both its heterogeneity and its complex connectivity.[15]

The question, for Heise, is in great part one of representation. She insists on the influence of Brunner on Brin, and also invokes John Cage's 'Overpopulation and Art'. Both Brin and Cage are seen to 'deploy experimental narrative and lyrical forms to reflect on the question of how global ecological and technological systems might be represented, what kinds of human collectivity they enable, and what modes of inhabitation planet-wide communities entail'.[16] It appears that, like the terrain of the unconscious and its systems of translation and repression for the so-called 'high' modernists, so the phenomenal scale and complexity of 'the global' defined by the 'connectivity' of ecologies at a time of crisis also produces a renewed concentration on modes of representation. Both Clark and Heise identify 'representation' and 'form' as absolutely central to the debate. It is interesting that Slavoj Žižek, in 'looking awry' at ecological crisis, insists on the irreconcilability of 'the real' (environmental disaster; ecological catastrophe) and 'its modes of symbolisation', and urges that we acknowledge and *preserve* the awkward disjunction between the 'real' (as the 'nonsymbolised kernal') and the symbolic.[17] As Richard Kerridge, who examines Žižek's argument in his introduction to *Writing the Environment*, puts it, for Žižek '[t]he real is that which disrupts representation'.[18] Addressing more recently (post Hurricane Katrina) the contexts of ecological catastrophe, Žižek has warned that in prioritising hyperproductivity and developing the conditions for continued, unchecked, economic wealth, we risk 'the loss of our natural Substance',[19] beyond the commodified and the symbolic.

When Terry Eagleton asks 'What is James Joyce's style?' he invokes Franco Moretti's argument on the commodification of discourse in *Ulysses*, and asserts that '*Ulysses* marks the historic point at which capital begins to penetrate into the very structures of the symbolic order itself, reorganising this sacrosanct terrain in accordance with its own degraded, emancipatory logic'.[20] Following the logic of the 'eternal return' (of the commodity in monopoly capitalism, of 'myth' in the historical time of capitalism), the Homeric subtext in *Ulysses* permeates and regulates social, quotidian experience but, Eagleton argues, a studied and strategic distance is retained between these levels, producing surfaces that are 'fragmentary and chaotic'. At the same time, the totalising function of myth – producing unity from chaos – replaces the function of historical explanation particularly discredited after the Great War.[21] When contemporary environmental criticism looks to high or classic modernism for guidance in appropriate aesthetic responses to anthropogenic climate change, it matters that it situates particular texts and styles in their historical moment, rather than regarding a particular mode as providing a palette of possibilities on the basis of superficial resemblance.

It may be that Heise, in her analysis of genre writing, is nostalgic for an aestheticised politics of which Joyce's writings, notably *Ulysses* and *Finnegans Wake*, are taken to be exemplars. If this is the case, she is perhaps understating the operations of a fundamental optimism in these works, and perhaps risks decoupling Joycean politics from its immediate preoccupations with, for example, nationalist myth-making, in the rush to align observations that are generated out of an analysis of Joycean modernism in the context of a highly specific, twenty-first-century understanding of the relation between the local and the global. Heise admires in Brin's *Earth* a 'reactivated collage structure that turns into a template for later literary attempts to consider attachments to the local in the context of an increasingly crowded global society'.[22] It is also to overlook the fact that, in the early part of the twentieth century, debates about artistic and literary form were developed in relation to debates about the social role of an avant-garde which identified its aesthetic origins in relation to the *symbolistes*, constructivism and expressionism, theorised by, not least, Benjamin and Adorno. Heise's nostalgia, therefore, presupposes a high degree of comparability between the contemporary moment of anthropogenic climate change and the context of bankrupt bourgeois values, the cataclysmic effects of the Great War and the growth of fascism as the historical conditions that informed symbolism, expressionism and modernism.

However, if Marx's view of the fundamental integrity of human and non-human nature teaches us to regard changes in the natural environment and revolutionary social change as analogous,[23] or, indeed, as occupying different positions on the spectrum of change, this perhaps provides a context for reading the position articulated by Clark (and Heise), that:

> A geographical and geological contingency, the finitude of the earth, now compels us to trace the anthropocentric enclosure of inherited modes of thinking and practice. The enlightenment project to render all the elements of nature part of a calculable technics is made to face its own dysfunction in the agency of what had previously been excluded from reckoning, or, more precisely, in that which had always been included-as-excluded.[24]

To some extent this is an instruction to revisit one of the aspects of the romantic sublime which in its 'chastening, humiliating power [. . .] decentres the subject into an awesome awareness of its finitude, its own petty position in the universe, just as the experience of beauty shores it up'.[25] But the reference to the agency of features (bodies, processes, systems and cycles presumably) historically 'excluded from reckoning' extends the field of vision. We are, in part, in the sphere of influence of 'the Kantian imaginary' and the paradigmatic resemblance of the aesthetic and the ideological, as Eagleton expresses it.[26] One of the intellectual effects of climate change then may be to explode the distance required for the operations of aesthetic comprehension. 'Environmentalism', Timothy Morton asserts, 'worries that we are disconnected from the world. But what if one of the problems were *this idea itself?*'[27]

These are some of the intellectual contexts that might productively inform a study of influence that seeks to align the polymorphous *poesia* of James Joyce with literary production in the epoch of climate change. I want to turn to a work which is not, I think it is fair to say, as culturally situated in general consciousness as Joyce's novel in order to draw attention to the ways in which a text roughly contemporaneous with *Ulysses* can be freshly encountered in relation to debates about literature and environmental degradation in our own time. A modern writer, whose work has yet to feature in literary ecology despite his 'green' credentials, is John Cowper Powys. In Powys' novel *Wolf Solent* (1929) the narrator establishes the eponymous hero as, variously, embedded in and at a remove from his world in ways which, strategically located at the start of this novel, force us to concentrate on the functions of aesthetic distance, and does so in the context of a narrative which enacts the redemptive power of myth and nature.[28] The novel begins with Solent sitting in 'an orgy of concentrated thought' (*WS* 13), a state which is only possible because of his isolation, apart from a fly, in a train compartment whose open window nevertheless does not disturb the atmosphere of dusty sunlight which surrounds him and allows into this space 'the sweet airs of an unusually relaxed March morning'(13). Through the windowpane of the moving train Solent perceives the continuous passage of static objects which themselves make possible Solent's self-projection. (Stephen Dedalus, on the night mail to Cork, fits the four-second intervals of telegraph poles to the 'furious music' which allays his dread of the unseen sleepers in the cottages beyond the train, and closes his eyes to the external world [*PAYM* 81].) Solent's self-projection, in contrast, privileges mythic 'green' forms in opposition to the hard and unyielding objects of the modern world, and these forms proliferate and mutate to sustain a highly personal metaphysic:

> As he stared through the open window and watched each span of telegraph-wires sink slowly down till the next telegraph-post pulled them upward with a jerk, he indulged himself in a sensation which always gave him a peculiar pleasure, the sensation of imagining himself to be a prehistoric giant who, with an effortless ease, ran along by the side of the train, leaping over hedges, ditches, lanes, and ponds, and easily rivalled, in natural-born silent speed, the noisy mechanism of all those pistons and cog-wheels!
>
> He felt himself watching this other self, this leaping giant, with the positive satisfaction of a hooded snake, thrusting out a flickering forked tongue from coils that shimmered in the sun. And yet as the train rushed forward, it seemed to him as if his real self were neither giant nor snake; but rather that black-budded ash tree, still in the rear-ward of its leafy companions, whose hushed grey branches threw so contorted a shadow upon the railway bank. (*WS* 17)

At the heart of Solent's self-projection is the dynamic recurrence of natural forms, and throughout the novel his experiences will be understood in terms of this symbolic language. Solent's imaginary production of an alter ego corresponds to a fantasy of a pristine, pre-industrial, pre-historical world in which specific forms (giant, snake, tree) give shape to what Powys calls in the 1960 preface to the novel, 'the self within us' (*WS* 9). In ways redolent of D.H. Lawrence, Powys manifests an attraction to dualism, 'the necessity of opposites' (*WS* 9).[29] The long passage quoted above gives an instance of personal self-making and cannot be extrapolated into a universal. On one level it is entirely expected and an aspect of the resurgence of myth that characterises the work of Powys' modernist contemporaries as they re-forge human subjectivity in the context of modern social experience and modernist space. It is not fanciful to perceive Pound's 'faces on a wet, black, bough' in Powys' black-budded ash tree. Indeed, the central image of *Wolf Solent* is that of the figure of the (every)man Solent had previously spied on the steps of Waterloo Station and that he now recalls:

> The inert despair upon the face that this figure had turned towards him came between him now and a hillside covered with budding beeches. The face was repeated many times among those great curving masses of emerald-clear foliage. It was an English face; and it was also a Chinese face, a Russian face, an Indian face. [. . .] And the woe upon the face was of such a character that Wolf knew at once that no conceivable social

> readjustments or ameliorative revolutions could ever atone for it – could ever make up for the simple irremediable fact that it *had* been as it had been! (*WS* 15)

The faces of, respectively, imperialist, revolutionary and subjugated human subjects share the bad destiny of a world exhausted of resistant, revolutionary possibility.

Solent has lost his post as a school-teacher and is on his way, at the novel's opening, to a new post, that of 'literary assistant' to John Urquhart, Squire of King's Barton. The reason for his dismissal: in the act of discoursing on Swift he experiences the involuntary annihilation of the forces that have regulated his social self – 'all of a sudden some mental screen or lid or dam in his own mind completely collapsed and he found himself pouring forth a torrent of wild, indecent invectives upon every aspect of civilisation' (*WS* 14). This expression of internalised negativity shows Solent preconditioned for his vision, on the train out of London's developing suburbs, of a 'vivisected' earth, a vision which operates as a motif to connect the novel's subsequent exploration of the relation of surface appearance to underlying truths. Stimulated by the sight of dust raised by a 'motor-lorry' on a rural lane, Solent's vision establishes Powys' investment in the imagined power of a transcendent nature diametrically opposed to technological modernity:

> There arose before him, complicated and inhuman, like a moving tower of instruments and appliances, the monstrous Apparition of Modern Invention.
>
> He felt as though, with aeroplanes spying down every retreat like ubiquitous vultures, with the lanes invaded by iron-clad motors like colossal beetles, with no sea, no lake, no river free from throbbing, thudding engines, the one thing most precious of all in the world was being steadily assassinated.
>
> In the dusty, sunlit space of that small tobacco-stained carriage he seemed to see, floating and helpless, an image of the whole round earth! And he saw it bleeding and victimized, like a smooth-bellied, vivisected frog. He saw it scooped and gouged and scraped and harrowed. He saw it hawked at out of the humming air. He saw it netted in a quivering entanglement of vibrations, heaving and shuddering under the weight of iron and stone. (*WS* 15–16)

Powys, like Lawrence, develops the 'metaphysical' novel out of an imperative to critique the deepest mores and prejudices of his historical moment. Here, via the 'Apparition of Modern Invention', Powys re-presents nature in such a way as to gain what we might now call 'anti-ecology'. The planes, iron-clad motors and vivisected earth, the creatures, are an expression of the fundamental continuity and connectedness of humanity and nature gone wrong. The 'Apparition' is a device to show Powys' despair at an earth denatured by the unregulated domination of its resources (Powys' version of 'knowledge, which is power'). The 'moving tower' recalls Tatlin's tower, something of an icon of constructivism at its most ambitious and, paradoxically, most reductive point.

* * *

Powys' novels deserve more attention than can be given here, but the details alluded to above, from *Wolf Solent*, offer a sense of 'natural Substance', to borrow Žižek's formulation, being eroded. The solipsistic Solent is yet able, by the power of imagination, to objectify the earth as eviscerated corpse, and to hold it at a distance so that the multiplicity of earthly life is reduced to the messy status of laboratory specimen.

Powys 'objectifies', and thereby creates a fictive space that will 'contain' the Apparition of Modern Invention. Joyce, in contrast, develops the space of the text in *Finnegans Wake* (1939) in an arcane recycling of his previous texts, managing thematic reversals and rhetorical complexity in the service of scale. The final book is founded on a paradox: regressive progression, a return to the womb and first things, a gargantuan play on the double-meanings contained in 'wake'. It was the scale and ambition of Joyce's poetic prose that appealed to a later generation of writers concerned with pushing the human to its limits of which J.G. Ballard, whose sense of Joyce is not irrelevant here, is the exemplar. Ballard argued in 'Which Way to Inner Space' (1962) for a re-visioning of science-fiction:

> I'd like to see more psycho-literary ideas, more meta-biological and meta-chemical concepts, private time-systems, synthetic psychologies and space-times, more of the sombre half-worlds one glimpses in the paintings of schizophrenics, all in all a complete speculative poetry and fantasy of science.[30]

Heise's view is a version of this, in its invocation of modernist poetics inflected with Freudian psychoanalysis and surrealist disassociation. Ballard's wish-list broadly describes the modes of *The Drowned World*

(1962) and *The Drought* (1966), novels in which the effects of climate change (in one, rising sea levels, in the other, desertification) are written on the body and on the mind heightened by 'psychic' powers, Ballard's 'inner space'. In *The Drowned World*,[31] the shock of the emergence of the city's forms, when anarchic, insane, Strangman drains the tropical lagoon to reveal the formerly submerged Leicester Square, has the scientist Kerans fighting 'to free his mind' (*DW* 121), and the equally marooned Beatrice declares, 'I *need* the lagoon' (123). The greater part of the novel accompanies Kerans on his 'neuronic odyssey' (174) which culminates in Kerans heading south, alone, 'a second Adam searching for the forgotten paradises of the reborn sun' (175).

If the still, uncanny, lagoons are a figuration of the human mind withdrawn from the public world of action and reaction, and in a world in which human beings are out-sized and out-competed by the giant fauna of Ballard's novel, more recent science-fiction has sought to develop tropes that express diversity and connectivity as well as the decentredness of human beings. Heise praises Brin's *Earth* for establishing 'digital connectedness', the 'digital network', as the 'counterpart and in some senses the master trope for [. . .] ecological connectivity' and, by implication, an affirmation in our time of the radical potential of polyvocal, heteroglossic, associative modernism.[32] The perceived translatability of styles, though, threatens to disengage cultural modernism from its moment.

By way of re-asserting eco-Joyce out of this proposition, Joyce's nature would seem to confirm Joseph Meeker's view that the original genre of literary ecology is comedy, because comedy's foundational idea is adaptation and survival; it is venal, sexual, propagatory. The 'satyric' *nighttown* episode of *Ulysses* might seem to confirm the unorthodoxy of Meeker's thought in this regard. Robert Pogue Harrison, writing with T.S. Eliot as his model high modernist, sees in Joyce's *oeuvre* a literature that 'exploited the almost limitless resources of the sayable' but failed to heed the '"nature" of the times', being, instead, 'luxuriant' and eschewing the waste land, the 'dessicated ground of the modern habitat'. Joyce's work 'thrives', argues Pogue Harrison, who seems to have overlooked Bloom's contemplation of desolation in 'Calypso', 'on the illusion of plenitude – the plenitude of nature, of the vigorous body, of meaningfulness in every dimension of being'.[33] Such plenitude (if we overlook the exceptions to this rather inclusive judgement) is not unthinkable in relation to

Meeker's thesis of comedy, except that 'Circe' is intensely, literally, anthropomorphic, even while the extra-Bloom dreamscapes are vivid with subjects and objects that exceed their habitual limitations: the sun's disc with the face of Sweny, the druggist, that displaces Christ at its centre; the objects endowed with speech and song (the cycle bells, the gong, the soap, the gulls, the whore's fan, the waterfall, the yews, the cap and so on). Bloom's potato, a sick joke redolent of the famine and Ireland's subjugated and self-punishing past; an object which is talismanic, a *memento mori*, a 'relic', of his mother(land). A mode of reading that establishes (or only establishes) the connections – and the differences – which produces the play of signification in *Ulysses* is not, or not usefully, 'ecocritical'. As Dana Phillips says, poems are not ecosystems.[34] The problem might be the emphasis on representation, as was intimated earlier. As Deleuze and Guattari assert, 'Writing has nothing to do with signifying. It has to do with surveying, mapping, even realms that are yet to come.[35]

* * *

The *planetary* body is conceivable in the thought of Deleuze and Guattari as a body without organs, containing others *ad infinitum*. An inconceivably vast connectivity of assemblages, in which the bounded human body is not a distinct unity but networks integrated with other networks (in this, Morton's work builds on the perceptions of Deleuze and Guattari). In their 'geophilosophy' Deleuze and Guattari outline the basis of their materialism – 'All we talk about are multiplicities, lines, strata and segmentarities, lines of flight and intensities, machinic assemblages and their various types, bodies without organs and their construction and selection, the planes of consistency, and in each case the units of measure' (*TP* 4). In *Anti-Oedipus* they assert that:

> we make no distinction between man and nature: the human essence of nature and the natural essence of man become one within nature in the form of production or industry, just as they do within the life of man as a species. [. . .] man and nature are not like two opposite terms confronting each other [. . .] rather, they are one and the same essential reality, the producer-product.[36]

Attracted by the materialism of Spinoza, they propose the 'real' of 'Nature' in terms of an 'Abstract Machine'; not a poem, or an idea with its beginning and end in the realm of the symbolic:

> Thus each individual is an infinite multiplicity, and the whole of Nature is a multiplicity of perfectly individuated multiplicities. The plane of consistency of Nature is like an immense Abstract Machine, abstract yet real and individual; its pieces are the various assemblages and individuals, each of which groups together an infinity of particles entering into an infinity of more or less interconnected relations (*TP* 254).

As impersonal as this may (of necessity) sound, it is underpinned by an ethical imperative, the ethical imperative to 'connect'. Deleuze and Guattari are as far away from Powys' 'Apparition of Modern Invention' as they could possibly be, but much less despairing of a critical response to a 'vivisected' earth.

In *A Thousand Plateaus* a suspicion is articulated about a totalising operation in Joyce: 'Joyce's words, accurately described as having "multiple roots", shatter the linear unity of the word, even of language, only to posit a cyclic unity of the sentence, text, or knowledge' (*TP* 6). The criticism is not dissimilar to Eagleton's view, and, anyway, cyclic unity is part and parcel of the conception, the idea, of Joyce's architectonics as we know from his interest in Vico. What 'Circe' insists upon, meanwhile, is that the body is present, and porous; that the Cartesian containments of the body are and can be suspended. In particular, Bloom is permitted to maximise the number and nature of transformations available, within the logic of the over-riding preoccupations of *Ulysses*. Bloom's body enters a field of unprecedented (terrifying, stimulating and joyous) possibilities, for which he is, of course, unprepared by anything that has gone before. 'Circe', not least, underlines the operations in Joyce's poetics of assemblage, uncanny juxtaposition, the breakdown and inversion of hierarchies, parodies of governance, a relentless play with the categories of subject and object, a democratisation of voices and the re-formation of the body. In 'Circe', 'natural' laws are suspended to initiate a new kind of reckoning of, and with, the world, in ways that implicate the earth. The 'more or less interconnected relations' carry an ethical charge; the 'infinity of particles' carry a Joycean one since quantum physicist Murray Gell-Mann named the quark, the sub-atomic particle which is a fundamental unit of matter, from *Finnegans Wake* ('Three quarks for Muster Marks' [*FW* 383]). In the humanities, across the disciplines, anthropocentric climate change is increasingly named for its material effects and its conceptual power, as 'ecology' forces the examination of the Gordian knot that ties together nature and culture with a heightened awareness of the relationship between 'oikos', economy, alienation and extinction.

Joyce and the Everynight

CHERYL TEMPLE HERR

The turd swiftsure
Flew down the sewer
& the sleuce-hounds
Flushfleshed after
(*Buffalo VI. B.3*, 67–69)

Readers first meet Stephen Dedalus as a child who has wet the bed. His mother puts oilcloth, with its distinctive aroma, under the sheet, and it's fair to surmise that the boy thinks no more of it. Soon, however, he becomes keenly aware of the anthropological danger zones threatening his physical purity. At Clongowes, Stephen's fall into the square ditch makes him ill. When his family moves to Blackrock and he visits Carrickmines with the milkman, he reacts strongly against 'the filthy cowyard at Stradbrook with its foul green puddles and clots of liquid dung'; his 'heart' is 'sickened' (*P* 66) by seeing these things. Soon his 'boyish conception of the world' as eternally the same is shattered, and the stage is set for Stephen's long-term anger and disillusion. He resents his family's 'change of fortune' and the 'squalor' – a previously unseen portion of a larger and much less predictable world (*P* 69) – that he is forced to acknowledge.

When the family's disastrous move from Blackrock to the city occurs, Stephen finds his way to the Liffey, where he encounters a 'multitude of corks that lay bobbing on the surface of the water in a thick yellow scum' (*P* 69). Why doesn't the text register the stench that was at that time associated with the river? Stephen's fresh sensory experience ('new and complex' [*P* 69]) surely provides an opportunity for the narrative to notice the Liffey's famous stench and to make something of it. That is, unless Stephen has already become aware that bodies of water around Dublin tended to smell of sewage, that waterways and sewers were sometimes synonymous. Joyce was writing about the Liffey at the same time that a series of parliamentary discussions were ongoing about sanitation and acceptable levels of pollution in Ireland. To some extent Joyce screens out of *Portrait* and *Ulysses* the more dire evidence of water pollution and of Ireland's struggle with waste disposal. In the context of his entire *oeuvre*, Joyce relocates these topics from everyday life to what we might call the 'everynight' of *Finnegans Wake*. In the everynight, riverine waste disposal becomes an issue that infiltrates every aspect of the narrative, and Joyce's many connections between the Liffey and all the other rivers of the world speak to the impossibility of disentangling purity from pollution, humanity from excrement, post-colony from empire, and past from present.

The Odour of Ashpits

The view that in Joyce's era waterways and sewers could not be disentangled finds ample confirmation in the twenty-seven volumes of testimony and reports obtained in 1902 by the 'Royal Commission on Sewage Disposal', a body then newly convened to discuss conditions in Great Britain's major cities from Birmingham to Belfast, from London to Dublin. The Engineer to the Dublin Corporation provided a description of the main drainage project (over forty years in the making), designed so that a northern and a southern main would intercept both existing and new connections. The discourse lays out contemporary arrangements in cold detail. Some of the oldest piping leading out of homes had cracking cement and thus leaked effluent.[1] Incoming tides drove sewage back up the channels down which it had flowed: 'All the old sewers, which at present discharge into the Liffey . . . are connected by short lengths of pipe sewer large enough to take the sewage proper and rainfall equal to one-quarter of an inch in twenty-four hours. If the flow in the sewers exceeds this rate the storm water will pass over a weir into the river . . .'[2] Diameters and lengths, gallons and cubic feet, cast-iron and blue brick, pumping and dredging, 'filth hoists' and inner flaps form the vocabulary of sewage design and punctuate the rhetoric of this lengthy report. At one point, the Royal Commission's interrogator states, 'I see that you are making arrangements to remove the sludge out to sea?' Yes, says the Engineer, 'at present we are proposing to take the sludge six miles out to sea'. What about the ocean currents near the outfall, asks the Commission, to which the Engineer responds, 'Yes, there is no question at all but that some of the effluent will absolutely go out to sea and at other times some may not.'[3] The delights of reading official records are, of course, endless, and moments of absolute ambiguity are chief among these pleasures. However, nothing can mask the fact that in the early twentieth century, as in days earlier and later, the Liffey often stank, and the estuary and nearby seaside likewise were characterised by intermittent periods of foul smell. Even when he first reaches the quays in *Portrait*, Stephen has apparently learned to think of bodies of water with sufficient consistency that the narrative does not mention this prominent sensory fact. Either that, or simply living in Dublin produced a certain amount of olfactory fatigue.

Whatever the state of Stephen's nose, during the Commission's examination of an informant named Dr Adeney, we do find mention of those corks that astonished the boy, and they form part of an emergent argument about estuarial tides and waste management. These copious corks formed part of the materials that Adeney calls 'domestic sewage . . . light, flocculent stuff',[4] which moved in the sea currents differently from the way that heavy organic matter shifted. Adeney explains:

> I paid special attention at neap tides to the condition of the estuary water, and . . . I have given data to show that at neap tides the water is nowhere anything like seriously polluted. There is undoubtedly a good deal of sewage lying in the estuary, but . . . it is not sufficient to go anywhere near fouling the surface water; it affects very slightly the water at a depth below 7 feet, and it is all cleared out at the ensuing flood and ebb tides.[5]

Apparently seeking to be meticulously fair in giving evidence, Adeney does note that 'the floating matters that go to Clontarf shore after two or three days of south-easterly wind give the whole shore an extremely bad appearance'. To the Chair's pointed question about whether the array of corks 'merely make the shore look ugly', another examinee reminds the Commission that 'you must approach the question of the disposal of sewage at a seaside resort with very different ideas from those with which you might regard a place with a sea border like the South Wall, the Dublin estuary'. Earlier in this discussion, evidence included the distinction between 'a sentimental point' (the desire to sustain a waterway free of floating corks, matches and paper) and the 'reality' of actual danger from such matter. Judging by this exchange and many similar cross-examinations by the Commission, it is clear that Joyce was writing at a moment when official distinctions were being made among a merely visual degradation of a landscape, an all-things-considered acceptable olfactory assault and the threat of disease from water pollution.

Sandymount Strand lies directly south of Clontarf, the two sites separated by the Liffey, yet Stephen, with his apparently unerring instinct for waste, later observes seaside refuse on Sandymount Strand, too:

> Unwholesome sandflats waited to suck his treading soles, breathing upward sewage breath, a pocket of seaweed smouldered in seafire under a midden of man's ashes. He coasted them, walking warily. A porterbottle stood up, stogged to its waist, in the cakey sand dough. A sentinel: isle of dreadful thirst. Broken hoops on the shore . . . (*U* 3.150–154)

In contrast to the strand scene in *Portrait*, *Ulysses* allows Stephen to de-romanticise seaweed and to accept tacitly that at least on Bloomsday its smell of decomposition reinforces the tang of seaborne sewage. Historically a midden town, Dublin – or at least its outskirts – is metonymically described as an ashpit, a garbage dump into which many bottles and many more corks have found their way. By 1905, the author himself pointed out to his potential publishers that his short stories smelled bad, expressing his belief that 'people might be willing to pay for the special odour of corruption which, I hope, floats over my stories'.[6] In June of 1906, he took an even stronger stance, writing to Grant Richards, 'It is not my fault that the odour of ashpits and old weeds and offal hangs round my stories.'[7] Aware of the writer's need and even artistic duty to present scents along with sensibilities, Joyce attends to the flavour of the Irish everyday as his characters move through Dublin.

Stephen's not noticing the river's stench is not merely a sign that his era preceded our own widespread concern over ecology and environmental justice. Rather, his double gestures of both denial and unstated awareness of the river's degradation speak to the colonial cringe, a collective inferiority complex forced upon occupied nations by way of their underdevelopment. Further, in all of his work Joyce understates, partly in the service of the taken-for-grantedness of everyday life, that the Liffey – then the city's main artery for commerce – was in very poor condition. Before the 1906 completion of the Main Drainage, the river was at times quite literally a cesspool.[8]

There can be no doubt that Dublin's unsavoury reputation was behind the famous review of *Portrait* written by H.G. Wells and published in the *New Republic* in 1917. Wells overstates the case when he claims that Stephen Dedalus pays no attention at all to bad odours, as he does the view that Joyce himself must have lacked 'a normal sensory basis' for his writing. Wells framed his review in a way that allowed him to claim that Joyce introduced offensive materials by-the-by and thus gave his fiction an 'incidental insanitary condition'. Wells writes:

> It is no good trying to minimise a characteristic that seems to be deliberately obtruded. Like Swift and another living Irish writer, Mr Joyce has a cloacal obsession. He would bring back into the general picture of life aspects which modern drainage and modern decorum have taken out of ordinary intercourse and conversation. Coarse, unfamiliar words are scattered about the book unpleasantly, and, it may seem to many, needlessly. If the reader is squeamish upon these matters, then there is nothing for it but to shun this book, but if he will pick his way, as one has to do at times on the outskirts of some picturesque Italian village with a view and a church and all sorts of things of that sort to tempt one, then it is quite worth while.[9]

In England, Wells says, 'modern drainage' makes life much better than it is in Ireland. Were he growing up in England, Stephen would never have suffered as much as he does in his backward country. Wells then moves directly from Ireland's lack of modernity to what he views as the pure hatred of England expressed in *Portrait*: 'a cant cultivated to the pitch of monomania'. Recall that Wells was writing during World War I, a fact that makes him worry over an atmosphere in which Irish nationalists seem to him 'narrower and intenser than any English Tory'. When the war ends, he opines, the Irish nationalist will be 'the natural ally of the Tory'. This warning is addressed to 'the American observer', whom he wants to inform that 'these bright-green young people across the Channel are something quite different from the liberal English in training and tradition, and absolutely set against helping them'. Ireland is revealed in Joyce's writing – no, in Joyce's imagined insensitivity to bad odours – to be dangerous, dirty, atavistic, overwrought and not British.

Bilgewater

Some time before Joyce came on the writing scene, Gerard Manley Hopkins gave a lot of attention to the condition of Dublin. In 1884, Hopkins was sent by the Jesuit order to teach at University College (then the Royal University). Never robust, Hopkins suffered from almost constant ill health and fatigue, so the physical environment was important to his sense of wellbeing. Wherever he lived, he was especially attentive to water quality. For example, in 1876, while the Jesuits were on holiday in Wales, Hopkins wrote to his mother that 'the town empties its sewage, like other well-watered shores, into Neptune's salt wash, and bathers have sometimes "gone nigh to suspecting it"'.[10] Not long after, Hopkins accused his good friend Robert Bridges of having written 'bilgewater' in response to his long poem *The Wreck of the Deutschland*, and Hopkins' explanation of that term of abuse shows his interest in water purification. Hopkins explained that 'vessels sailing from the port of London . . . used to take Thames water for the voyage: it was foul and stunk at first as the ship worked but by degrees casting its filth was in a few days very pure and sweet and wholesomer and better than any water in the world'. Similarly, Hopkins says, his poem had 'worked very much and unsettled you, thickening and clouding your mind with vulgar mudbottom and common sewage . . . and just then unhappily you drew off your criticisms all stinking'. Had he waited longer to let the whole thing settle, the poem would have been more palatable.[11]

In a later sermon, Hopkins described hell as a pit full of foul water, and many 'bilgewater' moments made their way into his poetry. But nothing assaulted his sensibilities more than Dublin in the 1880s. As he described the city to his friends, Dublin was 'surrounded by slums', and most of the houses around Stephen's Green were owned by irresponsible absentee landlords: 'Many of the buildings look crestfallen and bedraggled, some having been turned into apartments in which whole families occupy a single room each.'[12] The area around St Patrick's Cathedral featured pubs, brothels and redolent slaughterhouses. Paul Mariani writes:

> though there has been some progress in making potable water available, efforts to modernise the public drainage system have foundered for lack of money, so that the River Liffey, which empties directly into the sea, continues to serve as the major sewer line, those living in the old stately buildings along its

> banks so defeated by the stench that they have abandoned the city for the countryside if and when they can.
>
> Worse still are the private drainage systems and subsoils of the houses themselves, including the ones at 85–86 St Stephen's Green. Scarlet fever, bronchitis, and tuberculosis are only some of the diseases that continue to claim the lives of the middle and professional classes as well as the poor, and typhoid, carried by infected milk and diseased drainage, is far more prevalent here than in London, Edinburgh, or even Liverpool.[13]

So it is that in 1889, when Joyce was seven years old, Gerard Manley Hopkins succumbed to typhoid fever. Hopkins' biographers believe that the cause of death was linked to the drains in 85 Stephen's Green (now Newman House), which he unhappily inhabited. Indeed, Norman White discovered that after the poet's death, the drains at the attached No 86 were inspected and found to be full of rats and filth, and a Mr McGarvey was engaged to carry out extensive plumbing operations costing £250.[14]

Hopkins' terrible experiences in Dublin are carefully and precisely described in his letters. They form part of his image of hell. Joyce could not have been aware of Hopkins' poetry before Bridges published the work in 1918, and in any event we have no evidence that Joyce read Hopkins. On the other hand, the intertwined human and natural history of Dublin – in all of its smelly particularity – was an essential aspect of Joyce's lifelong theme. The river and the city did not release their histories spontaneously into characters' recorded perceptions but rather exerted pressure on Joyce to bring their several pasts into his total narrative vision.

'Plumbing Consciousness'

Regarding the role of sewage in *Ulysses*, the go-to person as of 2011 is Michael Rubenstein, whose book *Public Works* includes a chapter on Joyce. When Rubenstein addresses drainage in *Public Works*, he does so as part of his exploration of 'plumbing consciousness' in *Ulysses*, of a 'communion between an imagined community and its built environment'.[15] The encompassing structure of *Public Works* places this ambitious claim in context. Rubenstein puts forward a new category, the 'postcolonial comedy of development', which he sees in Ireland as an encounter between the history of public works in the Irish Free State and Irish literary modernism. Rubenstein avoids the usual inquiry into the relative good or ill of technology itself, choosing the far more useful strategy of exploring how public utilities both create entitlements and constrain the nature of citizenship. Thus James Joyce is joined by Flann O'Brien in testifying to plumbing challenges and initiatives in Irish literature at the municipal and national levels, while Denis Johnston requires us to study up on the Free State's Shannon Scheme, which liquidly propelled Ireland into the era of total electrification. Implicit in these works is an ideal nation in which the state provides public utilities as a matter of course and through those public works alters the citizen's ways of thinking, being and writing.

To some extent, this description belies the internal complexities and even unresolved challenges that Rubenstein has tackled in *Public Works*. Hence, it is instructive to track precisely where the seams show in the enterprise. Although the book falls into two parts labelled 'Water' and 'Power', in the introduction the author also includes gas power and lights under his inquiry into public utilities. At the same time, water issues (reservoirs, sewage disposal, domestic plumbing and more) never fully recede; the Shannon Scheme involved *hydro*electricity, after all, and while this overlap from water to power undoubtedly helps the book's argument to flow, it also points to the difficulty of talking about modernity in its parts while development was, however unevenly, chugging ahead as a whole. Rubenstein defines the titular term 'public works' as itself 'a kind of synthetic summation' of his argument, which is 'that works of art and public works – here limited to water, gas, and electricity – are imaginatively linked in Irish literature of the period for reasons having to do with the birth of the postcolonial Irish state'.[16] Wanting to shore up its sovereignty, the new Free State strategically used public utilities and the powerful metaphors connected with them to bring the social into domestic space and into the collective psyche. The waterworks at Vartry and the Shannon Hydroelectric Dam made the state's engineering a part of public and literary consciousness while allowing some distance between aesthetic representations and the inevitability of personal invasion by capitalist machineries. So it is that Joyce might be seen as offering literary routes both through and around the prison house of modernisation. Rubenstein submits that we cannot understand modernist literature without understanding how modern states produced power and how that power was homologous with imagined communities.

In this unstable context, then, Rubenstein proposes that in 'Ithaca' the reader encounters the virtual voice of the waterworks. In fact, he sees the waterworks as the 'narrating consciousness' of the chapter and extends his point to include a reference in 'Wandering Rocks':[17] 'From its sluice in Wood quay wall under Tom Devan's office Poddle river hung out in fealty a tongue of liquid sewage' (*U* 10.1196–97). Rubenstein writes that 'the Poddle River appears where it merges with the Liffey and offers its salute' to accompany those of Simon Dedalus and other Dubliners.[18] Rubenstein's argument coordinates the sardonic respect shown by the tongue in question with Joyce's counterfactual liberty in relocating the Poddle from Wellington to Wood Quay (credit is duly rendered here to Clive Hart, who first observed the transfer) because, Hart believes, the Dublin Corporation Cleansing Department Offices were located at Wood Quay.[19]

Indeed, Rubenstein points out that the relocation 'evokes the Poddle's civic role through a long history, a tragicomic image of urban ecological degradation through time'.[20] Reaching back to the first Viking settlement in Dublin (AD 841), Rubenstein observes that both in time and in space Joyce chooses his spot with care, the original Dubh Linn having become black with human waste. Meanwhile, 'The Poddle's tongue asks us to make a big conceptual-metaphorical leap by way of simple word association from river to tongue to stream to "stream of consciousness" to "sewer of consciousness"'.[21] As the argument develops, the river-sewer becomes for Rubenstein Joyce's own omniscient point-of-view, a nonhuman narrator, and very much what Victor Hugo claimed in 1862 in *Les Misérables* as 'the conscience of the city'.[22] Here, Joyce's technique seems to keep pace with the engineering technology that accounts for the public sewers and for the utopian state that the Main Drainage was meant to produce.

Of course, Wood Quay is only a few blocks east of the Four Courts, across the Liffey from which we find the Church of the Immaculate Conception (aka Adam and Eve's). The site of pollution in *Ulysses* arguably offers some form of spiritual and/or historical renewal in *Finnegans Wake*. If we choose to accept the circularity of *Finnegans Wake* as a given, ALP's fearsome plunge into the sea always returns us to what appears, at least at first, to be a more pellucidly running river. Does this Viconian cyclic cleansing seek to undo the historical facts of the Liffey's condition? Is Joyce gesturing toward a utopian 'Drainophilias' (*FW* 110.11) that Dubliners have engineered? Is Dublin sometimes 'better' in the *Wake* than it could ever be in *Ulysses* and *Portrait*? Is the *Wake* an ecologically progressive text?

Nightsoil

The route to the first location shot in *Finnegans Wake* is a 'commodius vicus' (*FW* 3.2), a time and space already caught up in civilising processes. Lawrence Wright cites the tradition, out of Sir Arthur Evans, by which King Minos at Knossos hired Daedalus to build his palace and his labyrinth. Among the wonders that the archaeologist Evans documented was the palace's plumbing: 'Minoan skill in hydraulic and sanitary engineering far surpasses that of the Chaldeans, the Egyptians or the Greeks.'[23] Interlocked and cemented terracotta pipes dating from 2000 BC carried waste into stone sewers that were flushed by rainwater.[24] The ancient latrines are thought to have had wooden seats and water reservoirs akin to those of eighteenth-century England.[25] Bathtubs, sinks and cisterns stand behind the famous Minoan dolphin mosaic dear to today's travelling photographers. In contrast, Joyce's Dedalus will have seen Irish people squatting to defecate in back alleys. He will also be aware that working-class Irish women were averse to being seen entering the squalid waterclosets in their tenement courtyard and thus improvised their disposal of faeces, often using scavenging bins or ashpits.[26] He will know the smell and perhaps the taste of the Liffey in its premodern state. These conditions frame Joyce's single and salient use of an evocative word: nightsoil.

In *Finnegans Wake*, the word 'nightsoil' appears on page 544 in a five-page paragraph that reaches from 540 to 545. This often glossed paragraph begins, 'Things are not as they were. Let me briefly survey.' The speaker then puts himself forward at length in the manner of a politician stumping for votes and pointing to his previous public initiatives, which quickly decline into a register of public failures. The 'beginning of all this order' (*FW* 540.23), he claims, will bring 'New highs for all!' (*FW* 540.20–21). In fact, the town already experiences fewer 'Thuggeries' (*FW* 540.31) than in the old days. Both 'mains' and 'drains' (*FW* 541.9,10) briefly and somewhat incoherently enter the speechmaking, as do the 'slobodens' at 'faireviews' (sloblands/Fairview: *FW* 541.25,26) passed by

Stephen Dedalus in *Portrait* and the ultimate destination of much solid waste at the time.

This glib lip-service to the debates of the era points us toward the plumbing terms in which poverty was framed in Joyce's day. We spot a 'bathtub' (*FW* 542.5) and some 'longertubes' (*FW* 542.6–7) but also a house 'blocked with refuse' (*FW* 543.33). We read of a 'reformed philanthropist [who] whenever feasible takes advantage of unfortunates against dilapidating ashpits' (*FW* 544.12–13) and a circumstance in which the 'nearest watertap [is] two hundred yards' run away' (*FW* 544.16–17). There is the perennial woman who 'cleans stools' (*FW* 544.21) and an 'outlook marred by ne'er-do-wells using the laneway' (*FW* 544.29–30). Several shared waterclosets occupy this scene, which despite all of the speaker's best intentions to glorify himself cannot screen out the dire settings in which many Dubliners lived.

Many years ago James Atherton traced the descriptive content of this long paragraph to B. Seebohm Rowntree's 1902 book *Poverty*.[27] Rowntree had catalogued the conditions of life for wage-earners in his native town of York at the turn of the century. Rowntree's views of individual homes include vivid details that would have caught any reader's eye: tenements damp from the soaked and polluted soil directly beneath their broken brick floors, cottages steeped in unbearable stench from clogged privies, courtyards littered with human excrement. One description in Rowntree will have to stand in for the whole. When he describes the third house that he encounters, he includes measurements that intensify a reader's embodied awareness of the claustrophobia suffered by the poor inhabitants:

> House No. 3. Eight single-roomed tenements, situated on the ground floor, and the first, second, and third storeys of a building, and approached by a staircase rising from a dark passage 3 feet wide. . . . Interior of rooms very dilapidated, having uneven wooden floors, the woodwork round the doors broken away, and deep cracks in the walls. There is no water-supply in the house, the eight families having to share one water-tap, situated in a passage at the back of the buildings, with eight other families who are living in other houses. The grating under this water-tap is used for the disposal of human excreta, and was partially blocked with it when inspected. The above sixteen families also share six water-closets, which are situated in the same passage. The length of the passage is roughly 25 yards, the width 52 inches. The whole is cobbled, and pools

> of water are standing in some places. A heap of rubbish measuring 3 yards long, 2 feet wide, and 1 foot deep lies in one part, but a considerable portion of the passage, perhaps a fourth of the whole, is strewn with tin lids, dead flowers, broken bottles, old rags and bones, etc. At the extreme end is an unused privy even more filthy than the passage generally.[28]

In comparison with York's conditions, the housing of the Irish poor often backed onto a courtyard in which many families shared a single water-tap along with blocked-up waterclosets and replete privies. Add in congested street drains, ashpits whose deodorising work was overwhelmed by quantities of ordure and a local slaughterhouse or two, and the setting is complete for the horrors that Joyce, in the *Wake*, would inflect toward satire.

Making extensive use of Rowntree, Joyce at times simply copied phrases from this source. Atherton says, 'The effect of parody is produced through one statement being piled on top of another, often with the words unaltered, as lilies that need no gilding, but more usually intensified and enlivened.'[29] In short, 'Joyce took a scrap or two from almost every chapter of *Poverty* and rearranged them in an order of his own.'[30] Little extrapolation is required to note that Joyce experienced many of his primary texts as used-up goods, as the stuff of scraps, to be jotted down on his own bits of paper and transferred into his book of the night, which is also notoriously a midden or book of waste.

'Ireland in the early twentieth Century', an online exhibition based in the National Archives of Ireland, confirms that both church and state failed tenement dwellers in the early twentieth century:

> In 1911 Dublin had the worst housing conditions of any city in the United Kingdom. Its extensive slums were not limited to the back-streets or to impoverished ghettos. By 1911 the city slums also incorporated great Georgian houses on previously fashionable streets and squares. As the wealthy moved to the suburbs over the course of the nineteenth century, their huge, red-brick buildings were abandoned to the rent-paying poor. Tenements in inner-city Dublin were filthy, overcrowded, disease-ridden, teeming with malnourished children and very much at odds with the elite world of colonial and middle-class Dublin.[31]

With this underwriting noted, we can turn to Atherton's comment that in Joyce's text 'the shared closet . . . is a detail repeated *ad nauseam*' (Atherton 77). In *Finnegans Wake*, the sharing of closets comically escalates from eight dwellings to 'fourteen similar cottages and an illfamed lodginghouse' (*FW* 545.2–3). Joyce adds that 'nightsoil has to be removed through snoring household' (*FW* 544.7). Indeed, those living in the midst of these wildly unsanitary conditions objected most of all (and not only in Rowntree's study) to the removal of privy waste directly through their living areas. Rowntree says, 'There are great complaints about this state of things.'[32]

In an online local history archive of Wolverhampton, George Peck (b. 1910) gives us further insight into the process of nightsoil removal:

> We used to have 2 or 3 toilets to 5 or 6 houses. One board with a hole cut in and a big galvanised tank with 2 handles, underneath. They used to come every so often to empty it. They would come in rough sort of clothes, rough sort of blokes, they'd come with their horse and cart. It was just an open cart, you see, with roll-up waterproof covers. It would carry about 10 of these things. They would put a big hook on and drag them across the yard. It was a big yard, the things used to come over bricks and there was nothing made on the level, just up and down. They had got to drag them down the entry. They used to overspill and it would be all over the floor. Two men would lift them onto the cart and when it had got the 10 or 12 vessels in, they used to drive it through the main street and down to Crown Street, where they were emptied.[33]

Nightsoil, then, is a euphemistic but in the Joycean context highly accurate and evocative term for human waste that had already made it from the human intestines into the social system but was not carried through sewage pipes. In England, as in many other countries around the world from time immemorial, the nightsoil men arrive at homes only under cover of darkness.[34]

Another term for nightsoil men is 'gong men', whom the *Wake* also refers to in the II.1 paragraph that begins 'It darkles, (tinct, tint) all this our funnaminal world' (*FW* 244.13) and proceeds 'We are circumveiloped by obscuritads' . . . 'What era's o'ering? . . . Lang gong late' (*FW* 244.15, 25). The possibility of the next day's work is suggested by 'Send leabarrow loads amorrow' (*FW* 244.34). The loads in question are filled by those who move through 'troublebedded rooms' (*FW* 245.30–31). Nightsoil, then, sits comfortably in a book of the night. Here, amid 'droppings of biddies' (*FW* 79.30) and 'festering rubbages' (*FW* 79.31) and 'scavenging' (*FW* 79.34), a 'dungcart' (*FW* 79.25) and a 'dungcairn' (*FW* 479.34), night soil is right at home. The mode of labour described reaches back to a time 'Ere were sewers' (*FW* 4.14), coincident with the earliest and original middenheap. This everynight is the prehistory of Dublin's Main Drainage.

Having gathered the waste, what did the nightsoil men do with it? Some of this material was used for landfill; some of it found its way to the sea. In his classic work *Dear, Dirty Dublin*, Joseph O'Brien describes the circumstances of waste removal in these terms:

> Day after day and year after year, the 500 men and 160 horses of the scavenging department emptied over 20,000 dustbins (supplied to householders by the Corporation at cost) and conveyed the refuse from these and from the streets and ashpits to the Destructor at Stanley Street, to the sloblands at Clontarf, and to the reclamation area that was later to become Fairview Park. Until 1906 a portion of the unsalable house refuse (300 tons daily) was taken to one of Dublin's less pleasing attractions – the Eblana hopper barge moored in the river facing the Custom House at the Tara Street railway station. There the noxious heaps would gather daily pending removal out to sea. Considering that the dustbins (one for each tenement house) were also used as receptacles for all kinds of slops and filth and that loads of manure were frequently disposed of via the barge, the crosswinds must have put many an admirer of Gandon's Custom House to flight.[35]

The 1903 report of the Royal Commission is useful in pointing to difficulties in the existing system. One of the experts states ominously, 'I have seen the contents of the Eblana barge on the shore . . . [in Kingstown, seven miles from the outflow near Howth] after two or three days of an easterly wind.'[36] Here the concern turns out to be those same corks and other flocculent matter rather than solid human waste. On the other hand, another examinee, who strongly favoured processing all waste into liquid form before ejecting it into waterways (and using the heavy sludge to reclaim foreshores), commented, 'Anyone who had made a voyage on the Corporation barge "Eblana" would tell them how unpleasant it was.'[37] Is this notoriety the reason that Joyce uses the term 'Eblannah' only once in the *Wake*? That reference, which plays on Ptolemy's use of 'Eblana' to name the city of Dublin (McHugh), is in the form of a maxim: 'it is easier to found a see in Eblannah than for I or you to find a dubbeltye in Dampsterdamp' (*FW* 138.22–24). While much else is at stake in this citation, the alignment of the sea ('see') and poverty (lack of a 'dubbeltye' even in Amsterdam) establishes the Eblana barge as a smelly cipher for Dublin itself.

After 1906, the Eblana was put out of use, and the tramway system carried refuse 'to the foreshore (in the dead of night, naturally) where years later the Fairview recreation grounds would emerge',[38] while the Main Drainage carried off much of Dublin's waste in somewhat (but only somewhat) less pungent circumstances. Did Joyce want to rewrite historical conditions, to depict a river that has an infinite capacity to carry off waste, and to purify Ireland's riverine environment as part of the narrative work? Or did he want to assert that despite technological advances, the social forces that produce nightsoil as such – the irreducible connection between human beings and excrement – remain not only part of the historical record but also impediments to environmental reform over time? However we imagine the answer, in *Finnegans Wake*, the whole history of waste disposal is mobilised; everything is dumped into the Liffey, and all of it is carried off into the textual sea. Even in dream-states, modernisation cannot efface the long memory of Ireland's humiliating colonial situation, its mediated traces everywhere in language and form.

Rivers

In the first two waves of *Wake* criticism – say, from the thirties to the seventies – opinion about Book I, Chapter 8 was binary. Either Joyce's extensive use of river names in I.8 was ideally full of meaning, or the steady introduction over time of almost a thousand river names was a sign of Joyce's obsessive mentality and consequent self-deception about the impact of this accumulation on the reader's understanding. In 1939, Edmund Wilson famously paved the way for future naysayers when he declared most of the river names to be gratuitous. In 1960, Fred Higginson compared six stages of revision for I.8 and offered scholars an opportunity to debate the issue with many more facts at their disposal. In 1961, A. Walton Litz expressed his decision that a probably unfortunate *idée fixe* controlled the composition of the Anna Livia Plurabelle chapter.[39]

In 1978, Louis Mink presented *A Finnegans Wake Gazetteer* and a special format for the geographical references in I.8 that privileged river names: 'Rivers named only in this chapter appear only in the indented columns and are not listed in the alphabetical gazetteer; rivers named elsewhere in *FW* as well are listed in both the indented and unindented columns and are cited in the alphabetical gazetteer.'[40] This note implies that Joyce's perhaps mechanical addition of river names at a certain point rendered those watery domains less present than rivers also cited in other chapters. Mink's introduction isolates I.8 as one of the three principal set pieces in *FW*, and he clearly has mixed feelings about these more routine compositional strategies:

> In the river chapter, however, the river-names cluster so thickly and are so artfully disposed that they virtually cease to bear any meaning as individual names. In this new language, they are more like phonemes than like morphemes. In his drafts of this chapter, Joyce returned again and again to the task of adding river-names to the expanding text, which in its final version flows without any sign of effort, like the river it celebrates. About the middle of October 1927 he wrote to Valery Larbaud, 'I have just finished revision of Anna Livia for transition no 8 . . . Her fluvial maids of honour from all ends of the earth now number about 350 I think' (*Letters* III, 164). A few weeks later, on 9 November 1927, he wrote to Harriet Weaver, 'Since [*transition 8*] came out I have woven into the printed text another 152 rivernames and it is now final as it will appear in the book' (*Letters* I, 261). But in fact he was not finished, and in late 1930 he wrote to Eugene Jolas asking him for the names of Austrian rivers . . . .[41]

Mink dutifully notes that his list drew on Fred Higginson's work, 'which not only lists about 800 river-names but analyses . . . the entry of names at four stages of revision of the text between 1925 and 1939. In Professor Higginson's view, the endless revisions and additions to this chapter very much complicate the text, but at the same time they sharpen its focus. In this respect the river-names were structurally effective in the process of composition, not merely ornamental as they have often been taken to be.'[42]

The most recent published foray into Joyce's revisions of I.8 is Patrick McCarthy's contribution to *How Joyce Wrote Finnegans Wake* (2007). Arguably, the genetic approach to Joyce that this volume summarises and furthers came about because readers have long been frustrated in their efforts to evaluate Joyce's accomplishment – the many different elements in his elaborate designs. For his part,

McCarthy notes Litz's belief that Joyce had 'overrevised' I.8 but advises that 'it is probably more useful to try to understand the text we are faced with than to wish for a simplified version that would call for less work on the part of readers'.[43] This judgement might be taken either as laying the matter to rest or as avoiding the issue posed by Joyce's diligence.

However, fully to understand Joyce's apparently obsessive narrative strategy in I.8 we must turn to Pare Lorentz's *The River* (1937), a film that Joyce deeply admired. W.L. White's discussion of Pare Lorentz in *Scribner's* (1939) cites Joyce's accolades for Lorentz's lyrical prose.[44] Although the fact that has so far gone unnoticed in the literature, *The River* undoubtedly reinforced Joyce's copious use of river names in I.8 and throughout the *Wake*. This thirty-minute documentary film, written and directed by Lorentz, tells the story of the Mississippi watershed. Thomas Chalmers resonantly narrates the historical conditions that created flooding in the Mississippi valley in the late 1930s. A close reading of the film suggests that Joyce responded not only to the written text but also to the concatenation of voice (Chalmers was a noted opera singer), orchestration, and other sound effects – the soundtrack as a whole.

The River purports to show that the Mississippi watershed had been devastated by erosion, that mishandling of agricultural lands had removed the natural impediments to flooding. The river is swollen as a result of human stupidity, human waste and human failure to notice the consequences of building levees to contain the Mississippi. And the watershed draws water, mud and more:

> Down the Yellowstone, the Milk, the White and Cheyenne;
> The Cannonball, the Musselshell, the James and the Sioux;
> Down the Judith, the Grand, the Osage, and the Platte,
> The Skunk, the Salt, the Black and Minnesota;
> Down the Rock, the Illinois, and the Kankakee
> The Allegheny, the Monongahela, Kanawha, and Muskingum;
> Down the Miami, the Wabash, the Licking and the Green
> The Cumberland, the Kentucky, and the Tennessee;
> Down the Ouachita, the Wichita, the Red, and Yazoo.[45]

Virgil Thomson's music eloquently punctuates Lorentz's images, fluty rivulets in the Alleghanies becoming streams that built the rivers named above and many more. Here the power of naming and water power dovetail in relentlessly downstream ecological teleology. All of America's agricultural and industrial history is here: from King

Cotton in the steamboat days to the Civil War and the closing of the frontier. We see not only the cotton in the south but also the lumber in the north. Everything topples into or is carried along the waters as they head downstream.

Then clouds gather over the stripped mountains and hills devastated by human activity. Drums beat as rain begins to fall. Faster and faster, more and more drops, spring and fall rains, mud falling and slipping, men working in sandbags and mud; white water; makeshift dams; men battling the 2,000 miles of danger to the built environment: two-thirds of the continent was involved in this annual destruction of the natural environment. 'At what a cost?', the narrator repeatedly intones. In Lorentz's day, four million tons of topsoil careened down the Mississippi every year, leaving the land eroded. Writing during economic depression, Lorentz had no trouble making the claim that 'Poor land makes poor people', and the pathos-tinged cinematic depiction of sharecropping in the US is as close to showing the Irish famine as makes no difference, all of this happening 'in the greatest river valley in the world'.[46] The final section of *The River* is a paean to the Tennessee Valley Authority, the Farm Security Administration and similar government programmes engaged in rebuilding land, conserving soil, controlling flooding, constructing dams, electrifying rural areas and creating model farming communities.

The River is now a classic in documentary filmmaking. For anyone thinking seriously about agricultural and natural history, this film provides powerful images expertly calibrated with a lyrically persuasive soundtrack. The rhetorical power is such that one can step easily from the filmscript to an imaginary scene in which Joyce sits at a table weaving river names into I.8. Given this cinematic context and Joyce's avid interest in emergent film culture, that additive process was surely an effort to make the *Wake* continuous with Lorentz's movie and with the issues that it lays bare. Like the levee-laden Mississippi, the Liffey is a river enclosed by quays. In Joyce's day, the Liffey was a working river; barges carried Guinness and other goods to and from the North Wall. Like the Mississippi, the Liffey opens onto the sea. Like the Mississippi, the Liffey carries materials that seriously compromise the environment.

One might well wonder how Joyce came to hear Lorentz's prose, that is, to see this documentary film. The answer is that *The River* achieved a worldwide cultural presence owing to exceptionally canny promotion and considerable good fortune. During pre-production, Lorentz had written a detailed factual narrative about the Mississippi watershed; recognising that the story was too detailed, he condensed his material into the rhythmic, lyrical version that forms the filmscript. The May 1937 issue of *McCall's* magazine – then a popular periodical – published both of these pieces as its opening editorial statement, and from there the item was widely reprinted in serials and newspapers.[47] Not only this, but after an unprecedented meeting with Roosevelt in which he screened *The River* for the president, Lorentz received direct help from the US government in staging the film's opening. Rather than take the obvious route to New York City, Lorentz chose New Orleans as the opening site, a location that guaranteed not only positive reviews but also the endorsement of numerous local celebrities.

Lorentz tells the story of how his good luck became a public relations coup:

> There were many cities where Walt Disney was locked out because he would not agree to the terms of the big chain theatre companies. For that reason he would let me have a print of a new Walt Disney cartoon wherever I previewed *The River*. This time he sent me a print of a short that introduced Pluto, the dog, to the world. Along with that I told my theatre owner that I knew of a fine feature film that was having a problem getting released in England . . . *The Thirty-nine Steps*, directed by Alfred Hitchcock.[48]

So it is that in October of 1937 *The River* opened in New Orleans before being released to copycat critical acclaim in New York, securing distribution by Paramount, and receiving the award for best documentary film at the Venice Film Festival (August 1938). In short, Lorentz played his cards admirably, and *The River* gained a purchase on the widest possible audience.

Aware of the film, admiring its musicality and its message, Joyce could only have taken Lorentz's style as a cosmic confirmation of his approach to I.8. Given the context offered by Lorentz in Joyce's historical moment, an *au courant* reader need only discover the Nuvoletta neologism 'Missisliffi' (*FW* 159.12–13) to trigger a connection not only between Joyce and Mark Twain but also between Joyce's fiction and Lorentz's documentary.[49] Following the filmmaker's suit, the writer conjoined the Liffey with the rivers – often environmentally damaged – of the world: hence we find 'the dneepers [Dnieper] of wet and the gangres [Ganges] of sin' (*FW* 196.19), the 'slobs della Tolka' (*FW* 201.18) (Dublin's Tolka River running down toward the so-called 'sloblands'), the 'ems of embarras (Embarrass River, Wisconsin) (*FW* 207.35), Germany's Moselle River (*FW* 207.23), and hundreds more. That said, if Joyce's textual interweaving of river names is obsessive in anything like a clinical sense, this phenomenon speaks to his increasing attunement to the interconnectedness of waterways around the globe. Issues of colonial neglect and postcolonial carelessness converge where the Liffey meets the sea.

'Here Comes Everything'

In both *Portrait* and *Ulysses*, Stephen Dedalus thinks about philosophical realism. He tries to work out whether the world exists independently of his concepts of it. But which world? The reader's or the text's? Timothy Morton, in a 2010 essay on 'Ecology as Text, Text as Ecology', asserts, 'Life forms cannot be said to differ in a rigorous way from texts', and he ponders how deconstruction has fetishised, in the process of making meaning, the immediate linguistic environment of any sign. Following this post-structuralist logic through several semiotic and structural layers of experience, Morton makes his key move, which is to argue that 'the matter-sign distinction breaks down at a certain point, because one of these environments is *the* environment'.[50]

For Morton, the way beyond philosophical realism has to do with understanding that everything, even so-called subjects, are objects, each of which is never fully available to any other object. Morton's own ecology-centred writings have posited a 'strangeness' of objects that cannot be thought away: 'Ecological philosophy that does not attend to this strangeness is not thinking coexistence deeply enough.'[51] Hence '*human* being is just one way of being in a mesh of strange strangeness – uncanny, open-ended, vast'.[52] If this definition sounds like the aesthetic of *Finnegans Wake*, it's no surprise, as Morton calls this essay 'Here Comes Everything'. Morton also looks to Gerard Manley Hopkins' poetry for depictions of strangeness, for what he calls the irreducible withdrawal of each object in relation to all other objects, the simultaneous speaking and silence of each object. Throughout this article, Morton freewheels his efforts to convince the reader that the world works as he imagines. Although he never mentions Joyce, Morton depicts an interpretive situation deeply familiar to readers of the *Wake* in which nothing ever goes away, nor is anything ever fully plumbed. In this essay, I have surveyed waste disposal in Joyce's Dublin from Morton's vertiginous perspective. As Joyce was aware, much of the heavy lifting was done not only in the everyday but also in the everynight.

Joyce, Ecofeminism and the River as Woman

BONNIE KIME SCOTT

Despite all the due attention that has gone to modernity, technology, consumerism and 'making it new' in modernist studies, the category of 'nature' has a persistent, if little recognised, presence in the works of many modernists. As unlikely as this might seem, this includes James Joyce. From a discursive standpoint, 'nature', like 'gender', is a cultural construction, and various eras, cultures and individuals bring different qualities to natural entities, and make more or less strict divisions between nature and culture. Recently the anti-modern strands of modernism have accrued increasing attention, and many of the same questions raised by post-colonial theory, racial studies, feminist studies, queer theory, trauma studies and even aesthetics can be applied to the re-insertion of the natural world into modernist studies.[1] Though known for its arcades and cityscapes, modernism also has its beachfronts, and it churns down rivers through much of the world: in Conrad's *Heart of Darkness*, the riparian landscape of the Thames in Eliot's 'The Waste Land', the Amazonian waterway of Woolf's *The Voyage Out*, Langston Hughes' 'The Negro Speaks of Rivers', and all Joyce's major works, culminating in the catalogue of the world's rivers and the pervasive presence of Anna Liffey in *Finnegans Wake*. Modernists noted the capacity of rivers to connect through time and global distance and they detected the growing threat of human pollution to their beauty and viability.

Ecofeminist analysis draws attention to ways that gender and sexuality have been related to concepts of the 'natural world', including power dynamics that seek to control both woman and nature and impose heterosexual norms in conceptualising it. Ecofeminism has begun to make its presence known in modernist studies. It is probably most evident in studies of the ways various modernist writers have represented nonhuman animals.[2] Virginia Woolf and D.H. Lawrence are far more immediate subjects for this angle of inquiry than Joyce. Ecofeminist approaches have been in existence since the 1970s and their variety allows for considerable selection of methodology. Approaches closely allied to cultural feminism include mythic models of the earth mother, inspiring the Gaia principle that sees the whole earth as a living being. Psychological theories of female cultural development, such as the work of Carol Gilligan, emphasise relational values and this contributes to 'ethic of care' ecofeminism. Greta Gaard was in the vanguard of ecofeminists who queered heterosexual models for nature. Environmental justice movements have been recognised as an important alliance for ecofeminism, as seen in Rachel Stein's 2004 collection, *New Perspectives in Environmental Justice*, though they are distinct in origin. Led at the grassroots by women of colour, this work emphasises local analysis and action, recognising that the poor – consequently women and children – bear an inordinate share of environmental degradation. Though creative work related to the injustices of class and race was classified more in the realist than the modernist tradition, left-leaning writers of the 1930s, such as Meridel LeSueur and Muriel Rukeyser, brought this vision to early twentieth-century literature.[3] Their projects had something in common with Joyce's representations of the urban poor in *Dubliners*. Still other ecofeminisms orient toward posthumanities and the post-human, seeking to break down the species barrier and hierarchy inspired by androcentrism, read as, not just human, but male-centred.[4] Such work explores ways of becoming animal and strives toward new concepts of democracy that are environmentally sustainable and broadly egalitarian.[5] A proponent of the post-human, starting with her work defining the cyborg, Donna Haraway offers a blended concept of 'natureculture' in defiance of the western binaries and the tendency to position the human more in cultural than natural terms. This move encourages us to see various rural and urban environments, and even the suburbs, in a new light. It is also sensitive to the mixture of natural and cultural elements that comes in when nature serves national iconic purposes, as it long has done in Ireland.[6]

Admittedly, Joyce has numerous counts against him as a writer of nature. First of all, he is so obviously an urban writer that it seems unpromising to go to him for a sense of nature, of which he had only limited experience. His large family was too fragile economically to afford the extended childhood vacations in the countryside enjoyed by other modernists such as T.S. Eliot, W.B. Yeats and Virginia Woolf. Nor have critics encouraged us to see him in a natural frame. Much of his early publicity came via modernist promotions that identified with classicism and conscious crafting of language. This includes the 'men of 1914' whose gender-biased version long enjoyed academic prowess. In manifestos and reviews, Wyndham Lewis, T.E. Hulme and Ezra Pound conjure up formless, dark, decayed manifestations of nature to condemn what they consider inferior forms of writing, further associated with decadence and the feminine. Hugh Kenner carried on the torch. Science and mechanics, including the futurist engines of war, furnish preferred masculine metaphors. Indeed, they fit beautifully with binary, hierarchical thinking and models of rational, technical dominance over woman as nature challenged by ecofeminist theory. Here one might turn to the catalogue of gendered binaries offered by Val Plumwood and the revolution in thinking that turned from organic to mechanistic models of nature identified by Caroline Merchant. The recent collection, *Out of Earth: Ecocritical Readings of Irish Texts*, does not contain an essay on Joyce.

* * *

Joyce fell right in with the female gendering of nature, at least as he represents the growing artistry of Stephen Dedalus. Dumas and the Romantic poets provide models for the feminine gendering of nature. When Stephen conjures up a garden in *A Portrait*, it is to place his own Mercedes within it. His representations of the nature of the beach are carefully cultivated, mannered and aesthetic, his clouds drawn from a 'treasure' of saved images. He famously combines bird with wading girl, crafting her appearance, 'Her bosom was as a bird's, soft and slight; slight and soft as the breast of some dark-plumaged dove',[7] his words caressing human-becoming-avian parts of her body. He soon leaves behind this approximation to nature, however, re-tooling the young woman as his guide toward the 'fair courts of life' in order to further his artistic ambitions. Describing his own crafting of Molly Bloom to Frank Budgen, Joyce suggests that the 'Penelope' episode 'turns like a huge earth ball slowly, surely and evenly round a round spinning, its four cardinal points being the female breasts, arse, womb and cunt'.[8] ALP, Anna Livia Plurabelle, is the river as woman, infiltrating much of his final work, representation we will return to extensively. As hen on her midden heap, ALP has another feminised interpretation of nature in the form of a domestic animal, something very much in tune with the Victorian ordering of the species as detailed by Harriet Ritvo.

All is not despair for those seeking to make a connection between Joyce and ecofeminism, however. Modernism as expressed in Ireland has its own characteristics that set it apart from the technological bent of modernists elsewhere. Ireland has long been feminised in its own mythic representations and by those who sought to dominate it. Irish modernism reflects a setting permeated by agrarian traditions and economy, its nationalism embracing this identity, as set against a more aggressively capitalist and industrial English culture. Of course, Joyce was no easy fit to the Irish traditions of his day, an attitude borne out by his satirical writings and some of his statements of exile. Eavan Boland also has resisted the national poetic she entered with difficulty; Boland offers resonances with, as well as challenges to, Joyce's coping with Irish nationalism and his representation of woman as river.

Though he lacked privileged exposure to nature in its more pristine places, as an inhabitant of Dublin at the turn to the twentieth century, Joyce lived in close association with animals. Horses and moocows still frequented Dublin streets. His beasts have enjoyed some critical interpretation, though little of this has taken an ecological turn.[9] Joyce also had pets, especially cats, and it might be argued that Bloom makes an effort to cross the species barrier during his interview with his cat in the 'Calypso' episode of *Ulysses*. Bloom is in good company in addressing his cat; he has been joined by Jacques Derrida, who had an increasingly famous bathroom encounter with his own cat, a drama enhanced by the philosopher's own nudity. Derrida's own discourse in *The Animal That Therefore I Am* has been subjected to ecofeminist criticism. While she is impressed with Derrida for viewing his own cat as a responding being, Donna Haraway finds that he falls short of making a companion species of her. This would require greater curiosity about what the cat was 'doing, feeling thinking' and offering to him.[10]

Bloom's brief exchange with his unnamed cat displays a variety of attitudes on the part of both individuals, as well as the narrator. Cheryl Herr argued over twenty years ago that 'natural behavior is subsumed by cultural vision' in this interaction.[11] To his credit, Joyce attributes language to the cat, and she has the first word in 'Calypso', inventively spelled 'Mkgnao!' Bloom's reply, 'O, there you are', need not be to a creature of another species.[12] Joyce's free indirect discourse, as it merges the narrator's descriptions with Bloom's thought, also blurs boundaries. Bloom attributes intentions to the cat, the desire to be scratched on the head and '– Milk for the pussens, he said,' which is replied to with another 'Mrkgnao!' Its intonation apparently calls for one additional letter, 'r'.[13] Bloom disagrees with anyone who would consider cats 'stupid': 'They understand what we say better than we understand them. She understands all she wants to.'[14] But Bloom's attitude is not consistent. A few lines later he is taunting the cat and her intelligence via baby talk: '– Afraid of the chickens she is, he said mockingly. Afraid of the chookchooks. I never saw such a stupid pussens as the pussens.'[15] Indeed he may be underestimating the offensive potential of a hen at the top of the pecking order. Before his cat is offered a saucer of milk, Bloom describes her as having 'shameclosing eyes' and 'eyeslits narrowing with greed'.[16] Earlier, thinking about her companion species' household function of mousing, Bloom pronounced her 'vindictive' and 'cruel', this being part of 'her nature'.[17] An ironic reading reveals this as an imposition of his own limited conception of predation. Though he does well interpreting the cat's request for milk, Bloom does not always know what the cat wants. He bids her wait and he will open the door for her to go out. But it turns out that she has another destination in mind, becoming the first that day to be called to Molly's bed. Joyce's cat has a will and makes plans of her own with companion species collaborators besides himself.

Through most of his youth in Ireland, Joyce lived a short walk from the beach. In *A Portrait*, there are visionary moments when Stephen is seen as yielding and even merging with earthly forces:

> His eyelids trembled as if they felt the vast cyclic movement of the earth and her watchers, trembled as if they felt the strange light of some new world. His soul was swooning into some new world, fantastic, dim, uncertain as under sea, traversed by cloudy shapes and beings. A world, a glimmer, or a flower? Glimmering and trembling, trembling and unfolding, a breaking light, an opening flower, it spread in endless succession to itself.[18]

While there are many possible esoteric sources for this passage, and abundant room for satire, this moment resembles others in Proust and Woolf that suggest porousness of the self, and oceanic feelings of ecstasy that Marianne DeKoven has charted for modernism.

In *Ulysses*, Joyce's capacity for ironic handling of natural references is clear in the 'Cyclops' episode, where we are entertained with a shifty forest scene. The political issue of the deforestation of rural Ireland comes through in the nationalist discourse of the 'Citizen', who blusters that one must 'save the trees of Ireland for the future men of Ireland on the fair hills of Eire'.[19] With its feminine fair hills and its trees serving as a masculine preserve, this gendered discourse serves Joycean irony. The speech is undermined further when it morphs into the description of the wedding pageant of the 'grand high chief ranger of the Irish National Foresters with Miss Fir Conifer of Pine Valley',[20] delivered in the rhetoric of a newspaper's society column, a discourse designed to have feminine, but hardly naturalist, appeal.

In writing as early as *Dubliners*, Joyce shows a great affinity for images of excretion, compost, decay and recirculation, separating him from the metaphors of masculinity favoured by favoured makers of modernism, and distinguishable from the Viconian cultural structure – thunderclap and all – favoured by early interpreters of the *Wake*. Describing 'Penelope' to his patron, Harriet Shaw Weaver, in a different version from that offered to Frank Budgen, Joyce says, 'I tried to depict the earth which is prehuman and presumably posthuman,' the latter a designation that has recent currency among ecofeminists such as Donna Haraway in seeking to decentre humanisitic, and thus androcentric, understandings of the earth. Joyce explores a connection between nature and language itself: 'These heavy sands are language tide and wind have silted here.'[21] Like Bloom's cat, rivers also are in possession of language. This should remind us of the discursive quality of the culturally constructed term 'nature' itself, which we inescapably use in discussing the environment.

* * *

Throughout his life, both in Dublin and in continental Europe, Joyce frequented cities traversed by great rivers, many with estuaries to the sea. His vast catalogues feature rivers among other features of landscape, including flowers and trees at bankside. Its presence in *Dubliners* is relatively modest amid the urban social geography of streets and squares. In 'The Dead', Julia and Kate's house faces the Liffey River. Lights reflecting on its surface contribute to the mood as their party disperses. The river promises adventure to the boys in 'An Encounter', though their planned expedition stops well short of their goal, the Pigeon House, situated well out the estuary. The narrator and Mahoney cross from quay to quay on the ferry, see the commercial port in full operation and dream of setting forth on tall foreign ships. As the mood darkens, they explore mean streets inhabited by fishermen. The main protagonist offers a gentle contrast to his more masculine mate, who has brought along his catapult to 'have some gas with the birds'.[22] Before setting forth, the young narrator appreciates 'tall trees . . . gay with little green leaves' and notes how 'the sun slanted through them on to the water' beneath Canal Bridge; taking in the warmth of the sun in its granite structure, he briefly experiences happiness.[23] The estuary represents an escape not taken in 'Eveline', whose own imagination offers images of drowning. Characters in *Ulysses* repeatedly take notice of the Liffey, which serves as a conduit for the 'throwaway' and a significant social boundary. However polluted, it attracts birds to the metropolis, if only in quest of garbage or snacks the likes of Leopold Bloom might provide. Serving as a much-treasured coda to *Finnegans Wake*, Joyce's Anna Livia Plurabelle traverses both country and city on her way to her dissolution in the sea. As discussed by Margot Norris and Kim Devlin, among many others, the river is presented via numerous possible narrative removes, including its composition by a male author, attribution to a male dreamer and association with a female character who has appeared at different ages and guises, including that of a hen, a typical assignment of woman to the category of domestic animals and those useful for dairy products. Finally, we cannot overlook the linguistic proliferations available in Joyce's highly allusive, inventive and suggestive language and spelling.

All of this representation of rivers constitutes a great many narrative removes from nature, already discussed as a discursive human construct, even if we do assume there is an earth-given river out there in the cosmos. Joyce continues his *Finnegans Wake* litany of rivers of the world to the end, with Amazia and Nulina (the Amazon and the Nile) joining the list in the final pages. The ALP coda performs as flowing water, rushing and bubbling energetically, or meandering through memories, slowing with loss of altitude, suggesting age, as it approaches the estuary, then whipped up by the wind. It is lisping, sibilant and alliterative, occasionally escaping from multifarious language and into sound that defies human meaning. Even thus, it suggests emotion and instils a mood. Joyce's play with language layers nature with culture in the forms of legend, history and literary allusion. Indeed, one of Donna Haraway's ecofeminist tenets is that we do best to consider the environment in a blended way defying the binary, as the merged concept of naturecultures, and this surely the text creates. Through Joyce's play with language and though resonant with cultural symbolism, a large bestiary comes to the river (dogs, stags, a possum, foxes, the ram, trout, salmon, a porpoise, a seal, an ox, a mare, the lobster and a great variety of birds, the last merging into the holy ghost), as do hunters, invading warriors, buccaneers and the washerwoman. Ferns, mushrooms, moss, grass, flowers and trees border the river, offering their own sounds and motions. Anna Livia carries at first many leaves, which disperse in number, dwindling down to one.

To the extent that the river is a woman, she is much occupied with family: mother, daughter, sons, husband, father. If the river cycles back to its origins, so she cycles back to the blue bedroom suggestive of her source in a sky mother. Just as she came down sweet 'out of me mother', now comes a new 'daughterwife from the hills . . . Swimming in [her] hindmost'.[24] This has frequently been glossed as female competition, rather than life cycle, reflecting the critical current as much as the text. Anna can see herself leaving behind her bumpkin, HCE, to frolic among the sea hags. As a female-centred cycle, hers may occasionally seem to offer an escape from patriarchy. But she is also much occupied with, and threatened or even traumatised by, both father and husband. She must rouse up HCE, her man of the hooths, clothe him, dress for him; she thinks about breakfast or their golden wedding.[25] Like the land of Ireland, it seems that she has been subjected to bodily invasion, the evidence dropped in her tale of one who 'aims to hazel me from the hummock',[26] or the recollection, 'You'd rush upon me darkly roaring'.[27] Nor, despite the memory of being carried by Taddy as a girl to the toy fair, there is still the threat of the 'therrble prongs' of 'my cold father, my cold mad father, my cold mad feary father, or even one come from the Arkangels "bearing down on me now under whitespread wings"'.[28] Still she recycles: she may abjectly 'die down over his feet but [this is] "only to washup" hushed by grass, aware of gulls, giving a final lisp to riverrun again'.

* * *

In an article entitled 'James Joyce: The Mystery of Influence', Eavan Boland discusses her gradual approach to Joyce as an influence, arriving at something they had in common. It was her sense that she had 'gone into exile in my own literature'.[29] Boland spent much of her childhood away from her native Ireland, having a father in the diplomatic service; now she spends a part of each year with an academic appointment in California. She identifies not just with Joyce as a migrant but also with the monarch butterflies that pass this way. Her intellectual exile, as pertains to Joyce, had to do with Irish literary and national traditions that equated woman with nation, such that the Irish woman as she understood her existence did not exist in Ireland's poetry, and certainly not in the models offered out of the Celtic Twilight. John Eglinton, who had his own walk-on role in *Ulysses*, offers a vintage example:

> Fortunately there is in Ireland something older than the Catholic Church, older than the Irish language, older than archeology, older even than the gods – Mother Nature herself, in whose presence the poet can forget the squalid animosities of race and creed, and the various contentious sobriquets – 'West Briton', 'Irish Irelander', and the like – which at times make him sick of the name of his country. The future of Irish literature is mainly an affair between the poet and this kindly mother, as she manifests herself to the solitary thinker on the hills and plains of Ireland.[30]

Boland's own 'Mother Ireland' – described in a poem that bears that title – evolves from being 'land', when she 'lay on my back to be fields' or turned on her side to make hills and at this stage let words fall on her. Having obtained a name, she transforms into the teller of her own story, gaining mobility, she explores the fields and finds among the detritus a 'rusted wheel and . . . pram chassis'. She gains the perspective to look back at 'gorse-bright distances', demand of her sceptics their trust.[31]

Boland had long appreciated the capacity the exiled Joyce had to represent Dublin and Dubliners in his work, places and character types that she could still encounter in her youth. What she appreciated was that Joyce 'removed the local from the manipulation of the historic'. 'He became an Irish writer by denouncing the previous definitions of the term.'[32] Boland has described what she takes to be the 'false pastoral' of the Celtic Twilight, seeing this as a 'heavy and corrupt investment' of a nationalist nature, a construction she addresses in much of her poetry.[33] Boland argues in this and other essays that women's poetry opens up the flaws in the relation between Irish poetry and national ethos.[34] She led the feminist response to the inequities of the original *Field Day* anthology, as one of only three women included in it, who could speak from the inside for those left on the margins, and she was a memorable speaker to the all-female women's caucus audience of the James Joyce Symposium in 1992.

Boland has her own version of Joyce's Anna Livia in the poem 'Anna Liffey', used both to name the third section of her 1994 volume, *In a Time of Violence*, and the first of the five poems in that segment. The title poem starts with the story of a legendary woman named Life, who 'loved the flat-lands and the ditches' of Kildare as well as its 'unreachable horizon'. Being the 'daughter of Canaan', she could ask to have the place named for her: 'The river took its name from the land./The land took its name from a woman'.[35] Legendary woman and land are one, so far as naming goes. Like Joyce, Boland follows the river's course first above and later in its course through Dublin: 'Around a bend at Island bridge/and under thirteen bridges to the sea'.[36] Plants and later birds lend context to the river. The Liffey rises in the hills 'in rush and ling heather and Black peat and bracken' and 'strengthens/To claim the city it narrated'.[37]

But this is a much more personal work of art than Joyce's *Finnegans Wake*, and in it the poet risks communicating much more directly her own being. The poet's persona, at first younger, still with red hair, is 'a woman in the doorway of a house', watching the landscape and the weather she shares with 'a river in the city of her birth'. With this recurrent element, Boland places the Irish woman, as she knows her, in the poem. Part of her struggle, having returned as an exile in childhood, is to relate to Ireland as a nation, the nation so long having claimed woman as its sign, both mythologising and victimising her. The Liffey's taling is a telling in her case as well as Joyce's. Asked by the poet to serve as a narrator, Anna Liffey reflects, 'Fractions of a life/It has taken me a lifetime/To claim',[38] entering her into a woman/river analogy. To her, the river, like 'Mother Ireland', is an active player. It engages in 'shiftless and glittering/Retelling of a city'. It is a 'Maker of/places, remembrances'.[39] It also shows 'patience at twilight' when there are 'Swans nesting by it'.[40] She insists that 'A river is not a woman . . . Any more than/A woman is a river'. But there are 'signs' shared, a history of suffering from Vikings and Redcoats, the glare of 'the flames of the Four Courts',[41] serving as did Joyce's invaders in *Finnegans Wake*. In many of her most memorable poems, Boland imagines Irish women who have suffered and striven in a distinct place – holding a dying baby on an emigrant ship, striving to survive in a workhouse, or serving the garrison as a sex worker – such that a decaying building, a ship, a river, or the domestic objects left behind in what once was a home, build a case for environmental justice.

In 'Anna Liffey', the poet includes her own activities in the narrative, representing a mother's role of calling her daughters home in the summer dusk. A trope repeated in many of her poems, it is perhaps her equivalence to the protective mother swan on the Liffey. She is unapologetic in expecting to find the suburban mother in Irish poetry. Boland points out that in the tradition of Irish poetry set by Yeats 'you could have a political murder . . . but not a baby. You could have the Dublin hills, but not the suburbs' and presumably the suburban mothers 'under them'.[42] The rain represented in this poem falls off of car-ports and clipped hedges in Dundrum. She turns out a 'harsh yellow/Porch light'.[43] In the course of the poem, the young woman in the doorway puts on the body of the 'ageing woman', who has a different relation to language: 'Single words she once loved/Such as "summer" and "yellow"/And "sexual" and "ready"'are someone else's dwelling. She sees her body as 'a source. Nothing more' and that 'it seeks its own dissolution'.[44] The names that were part of Liffey's narrative are claimed by the sea. The rain, coming off the sea, brings in the shore birds and cycles back to the hills where the river rises. Aspects of the poet's identity as river/body/language are 'Particular and unafraid of their completion' in the sea. Like Anna Livia Plurabelle, she yields. Still she does state conclusively, as the Irish woman poet, 'I was a voice'. It is a poetic ecosystem that rises, acts, represents suffering, cycles and may even evolve from environmental failures of history, nation and poetry of the past.

Word and World:
The Ecology of the Pun in *Finnegans Wake*

ERIN WALSH

'In the beginning was the pun'.
Samuel Beckett, *Murphy*[1]

Word and World in the *Wake*

Much critical attention has been given to the Wakean portmanteau word as a structuring principle and a source of the *Wake*'s proliferative meanings.[2] While Ruben Borg argues that the arbitrariness of the portmanteau exceeds that of the pun, I would argue that the particular linguistic instability of the pun – and specifically the word-world pun – in the *Wake* impels an evolutionary-cybernetic process which in turn reveals the correspondence of textual and material phenomena.[3] Louis Gillet recalls Joyce himself characterising the pun as central to the *Wake*, 'such a book, all in puns'.[4] As we trace appearances of the word-world pun in the text, we find it to be not merely iterative, but *variable*, exploiting the instability inherent to puns more generally. In these puns the homophonic and orthographical similarities of 'word' and 'world' also produce metonymic relations between material and linguistic phenomena, revealing the word-world as dynamic process rather than stable essence, a foundational notion of evolutionary and cybernetic theory with far-reaching ethical implications. Ultimately I argue that the *Wake*'s variable puns suggest a model for an ecological discourse of nation – nation not only in process, but *as* process – that supplants the fiction of nation as unitary organic whole with the self-adulterating word-world of the *Wake*. By destabilising the conceptual and linguistic boundaries of the word 'nation', the *Wake* articulates nation as fundamentally heterogeneous and contingent, nation not as romantic metaphor but as transgressive pun. In the *Wake*'s final pages, ALP appears as tree, but also as river, and it is her accordingly hybrid discourse that actualises the famous recirculation of the text's 'riverrun', offering a model for an ecological negotiation of national boundaries. The reader's return to the beginning of the *Wake*'s riverrun emerges as a suturing that restores rather than effaces the *in medias res* of the text's opening, producing not a totalising self-contained whole, but a readerly bridge that honours the rift.

In order to examine the word-world pun in the *Wake* and its implications for the *Wake*'s status as an ecological text, I would like to first examine the pun's more famous debut, as malapropism in *Ulysses*. In *Ulysses*, Martha Clifford chastises Bloom-as-Henry Flower: 'I called you naughty boy because I do not like that other world. Please tell me what is the real meaning of that word?'[5] Martha's error makes the tantalising possible meanings of an already obfuscated allusion (to a word from a letter the reader cannot access) proliferate through substitutions. Later, in 'Hades', when Bloom recalls the line from Martha's letter, the sense of error has disappeared: 'There is another world after death named hell. I do not like that other world she wrote. No more do I. Plenty to see and hear and feel yet' (6.1001–3). Both the line and Martha's intended meaning here appear transformed, the memory of the error effaced as the line appears in the new context of Bloom's will to live. Joyce's wordplay here can be seen as a making-ecological of the word-world of the text: Martha's error, which is also Joyce's deliberate pun, mixing word and world, makes the conceptual boundaries of the terms permeable, both to each other and to the surrounding textual environment. The context of 'Hades' permeates Bloom's memory of Martha's error, redefining its significance in terms of Paddy Dignam's death and Bloom's memory of his father's suicide. Shaped by textual process – Bloom's thoughts, Dignam's funeral – the meanings of world and word emerge as expansive processes rather than stable essences. That Joyce's word-world substitution first occurs in a letter may suggest a kind of meta-wordplay, as the orthographical difference between world and word is 'a letter', the letter 'l'.[6] Although these letters might be seen to exist in synecdochic relation with the text as a whole, the notions of whole and part that underlie synecdoche become inchoate in the word-world of letters and are replaced by shifting relations of continuity. The letter is a text within a text (a world within worlds and words within words), a text generated by a text (Bloom's letter) and a text *about* that text that generated it. The word-world of the letter is thus insistently in flux, opening itself to the textual ecology that it both generates and is generated by.

The self-reflexivity and recursivity of the word-world pun suggests that it might also be read as a site of cybernetic transformation. My view is that the *Wake*'s variable puns produce not only a cybernetic system but a symbolic-material *ecology*. I use the term 'ecology' here and throughout this essay in the sense of Gregory Bateson's formulation of the term as co-evolving systems whose boundaries are blurred through their interaction. In his emphatically interdisciplinary work *Steps to an Ecology of Mind*, he articulates a philosophy of mind in which individual psychology cedes to an 'ecology of ideas in systems or "minds" whose boundaries no longer coincide with the skins of the participant individuals'.[7] Drawing on a variety of disciplines, including cognitive science, philosophy, psychology and evolutionary biology, Bateson argues that in these ecologies of mind, disciplinary boundaries, epistemological categories, distinctions between mind and body, text and world dissolve. Bateson equates his concept of mind with that of the cybernetic system, which he defines as 'the relevant total information-processing trial-and-error completing unit' (466). I argue that the *Wake*'s conflations of word and world and of world and mind accord with this notion of the cybernetic system. That cybernetics, often defined as the science of 'control and communication in the animal and the machine',[8] harbours in its disciplinary bounds the dream of not only cross-disciplinary communication but of universal language, suggests that it is completely at odds with the polyglot wilderness of the *Wake*. Yet cybernetics, like the *Wake*, speaks in many overlapping languages, invites succinct definition only to exceed it, and resists disciplinary boundaries. Fritz Senn's comment that 'all analogies for *Finnegans Wake* seem useful at times, and all break down sooner or later' also applies to the discipline of cybernetics:[9] within the world of cybernetic thought, jokes abound about the difficulty of articulating a definition for the discipline.[10] Seen in these terms, cybernetic process undoes the very notions of control and universality at which it purports to aim. Thus, the ethics of the *Wake*'s textual ecology, as cybernetic system, might also suggest an alternate perspective on the problem of cybernetic ethics more generally.[11]

The word-world pun first appears in the *Wake* in one of the text's many self-reflexive comments, this one an injunction to the reader: '(Stoop) if you are abcedminded, to this claybook, what curios of signs (please stoop), in this allaphbed! Can you rede (since We and Thou had it out already) its world?'[12] As in *Ulysses*, the confusion of word and world here appears in conjunction with a pun on letter (epistle and semiotic character), this time compounded with an additional pun on litter: the text surrounding the line is littered with references to a dump, at once the midden heap from which the hen unearths the letter incriminating HCE and the 'mnice old mness' of letters that is the text itself (19.7). The injunction to '(Stoop) if you are abcedminded' and the repeated insertion of the parenthetical 'stoop' recapitulates the stooping and pecking of the hen in the midden heap and the onomatopoeic verbal tic, 'Tip', of the janitrix-hen, Kate, our tour guide through the historical dump of the 'museomound' earlier in the chapter (8.5). The line thus analogises the discovery of the letter (epistle), which promises to reveal HCE's sin, to the reader's rummaging through the text's elemental particles, its disordered 'abced' alphabet. In the Mutt and Jute dialogue immediately preceding this line, the site of the Battle of Clontarf appears as a historical dump, 'Dungtarf', (16.22) and Jute comments: 'Simply because as Taciturn pretells, our wrongstory-shortener, he dumptied the wholeborrow of rubbages on to soil here' (17.3–5). The historical scope of this section (the Battle of Clontarf occurred in 1014) suggests that the 'wrongstory' – perhaps a long story of wrong – has been compressed. And while it is difficult to think of the author of the *Wake* as a 'shortener' of anything, this statement presents a meta-commentary on Joyce's authorship as a kind of composting: a figure in which *homo faber*, man the maker, works ecologically with biological process; and as we know, the *Wake* was developed out of the leftover scraps or 'rubbages' of notes from Joyce's composition of *Ulysses*. As William Tindall notes, 'from the litter comes the letter as from the dump (18.16–35) come letters'.[13]

The proximity of the pun on litter, letter (grapheme) and letter (epistle) and the word-world pun in this memorable and patently self-reflexive section of the *Wake* suggests that puns more generally are crucial to our understanding of the litter of letters and world of words that is the *Wake*. John Marvin sees the injunction to the reader as an instance of the Wake teaching us how to read it: 'To read *Finnegans Wake* one must stop and stoop – get down to earth, appreciate the moment at this space in time.'[14] And indeed, 'stoop' suggests a kind of materialisation of close reading that accords with my own sense of the text as blurring word and world. But in the context of the section's concern with historical clashes, specifically here the Battle of Clontarf, the injunction to 'stoop' here is perhaps the utterance of the conqueror, injecting ambivalence into the directive. If the quality of mind the text prescribes for the reader is that of being 'abcedminded', the alphabetical disordering points to another reading of the word that challenges the injunction to focus on the *Wake*'s elemental units: read phonetically, 'abcedminded' is 'absedminded', a pun on 'absentminded'.[15] To read the pun – a skill which seems fundamental to reading the *Wake* – begins with alphabetical-mindedness (required to recognise the disordered sequence of 'abced') but must then suspend this deferential stooping to letters in order to see and then hear the letters as integrated in a phonetically-spelt word. To 'rede its world', then, is perhaps to read the text's puns – its intentional mistakes of its 'wrongstory' – rather than its letters or its words, as its fundamental units.

Indeed, the instability of the pun undermines the very notion of unit; puns are units of meaning in flux, open to and influenced by their textual environment. Here Bateson's notion of ecology is useful: for Bateson, the unit of evolutionary survival is not the breeding organism, but rather the 'flexible organism-in-its-environment' (457) and elsewhere, 'mind' (as ecology) itself (466). In the *Wake*, the reader, through engaging the Wakean pun, participates in an ecological mind that is both 'abced' and ab*sent*-minded: a mind that can suspend the logic of reading (conscious stooping to letters) and open itself to the associative play of unconscious thought processes (the absorptive being-somewhere-else of the absentminded). Importantly, the quality of absentmindedness also produces humorous errors of distraction – confusing salt and sugar, for instance – reminding us that our readings of puns must attend to their levity and to that of the *Wake* as a whole.

Bateson notes that 'the cybernetic nature of self and the world tends to be imperceptible to consciousness' (450). I would argue that it is precisely this cybernetic quality that the 'abcedminded' (absentminded) reader reveals through engaging the word-worldplay of the *Wake*. Like Bateson, for whom minds are ecologies and ecologies minds, the *Wake* sees mind and world as interchangeable concepts; later on in this particularly self-reflexive section of the text, which begins with the injunction to stoop, the speaker notes 'but the world, mind, is, was and will be writing its own wrunes for ever, man on all matters that fall' (19.35–6). Mind, here, is semantically and grammatically equivocal, at once an interjected imperative and an appositive for 'world'. We are instructed here to 'mind', as we were instructed to '(Stoop)' (another parenthetical). The 'abcedminded' reader here must also 'mind' the suggestion that mind and world are doubles, just as the punning 'writing its own wrunes' is also 'righting its own wrongs'. The grammatical ambiguity of mind, at once noun and verb, makes permeable the categories of thing and action and suggests the possibility of mind as process rather than essence and as ecological 'world' rather than discrete subject/individual consciousness. And it is the 'minding' reader here who, in 'righting' the punning 'wrunes' of the text, opens up the notion of textual ecology and participates in the permeable mind-world of the text. Meaning in the *Wake*, then, might productively be seen not as semantic architecture, accessible by key, but rather as an ecology of structures – minds, grammars, words – that in their transgressions of categorical boundaries initiate processes.

That this world-mind is presented as eternally 'writing' and 'righting' suggests an ethical dimension to writing, and perhaps in particular to the *Wake*'s writing of 'wrunes', a word that in the context of the historical 'dump' presents a pun on 'ruins', situating ethical practice as affecting both material and linguistic phenomena. This ethical preoccupation recurs in another word-world pun which concerns HCE's remembrances of his fall, in Book One, Chapter Four: in a self-reflexive and parenthetical comment, the text declares 'this is nat language at any sinse of the world' (83.12). The pun coupling 'sins of the world' and 'sense of the word' not only recapitulates the word-world conflation, but also layers on top of it the pun on sense and sin, evoking the Fall as a fall into language, a replacement of the natural sign with 'nat language'. The paradigmatic shift Bateson proposes from an evolutionary model based on hierarchies of discrete entities (individuals, family groups, species)[16] to an evolutionary model whose fundamental unit is mind (ecologies with shifting boundaries) has important ethical as well as theoretical implications (466). *Finnegans Wake*, apotheosis of modernist textual experimentation, does not initially seem to lend itself to ethical commentary. But the text, in its use of Darwinian and cybernetic principles, dissolves the boundary – indeed often opposition – between ethical and aesthetic concerns. That is certainly not to say that the text equates aesthetic merit with ethical principles; rather, ethics and aesthetics become ecologically negotiated categories, matters of process rather than of essence.

'The war is in words and the wood is the world': Bio-Symbolic Trees in Darwin and the *Wake*

Wake criticism is characterised by both hyper-close reading (Umberto Eco's mapping of 'meandertale')[17] and totalisation (Campbell and Robinson's 'skeleton key').[18] While both methods are useful, their extremes might be respectively glossed as not being able to see the wood for the trees (or for that matter the trees for their wood) and seeing the forest as a product of intelligent design. This analogy is not an idle one, as the word-world *Wake* is all of the above – a wood, a tree, the wood of the trees and the shifting play of the many and the one, the singular and the universal: 'The war is in words and the wood is the world. Maply me, willowy we, hickory he, and yew yourselves' (98.34–6). Here, in the chapter in which HCE, dead and remembering his fall, is most overtly connected with Parnell, the word-world correspondence expands to include the notion of the forest-text as a site of war. The self-reflexive metaphor of the text as wilderness – a wood of words – is voiced by Kate, the museyroom tour guide from the first chapter. Here Kate returns to discuss the unearthing of the elusive letter – the never-deciphered key to the mysterious sin of HCE – from the midden heap by 'that original hen' (110.22): 'Tip. You is feeling like you was lost in the bush, boy? It is a puling sample jungle of woods. You most shouts out: Bethicket me for a stump of a beech if I have the poultriest notions what the farest he all means' (112.3–5). Here the pun on words and woods is dependent on the meta-textual implications of Kate's comment (the 'you' easily read as a direct address to the reader) that the reader is lost in the jungle of the *Wake*.

But the word-world-wood correspondence exceeds metaphor, producing not only relations of similarity, but also of contiguity, arising from the *Wake*'s merging word and world. It is important to note that the correspondence I see here is not a Steinian production of the materiality – the thing-ness – of the word, nor a claim that the *Wake* imagines a pre-lapsarian fantasy of natural language. Rather, I see the *Wake* as situating word and world in a common ecology.[19] The quotation linking wood, world, word and war, for instance, both iterates and undoes the metaphorical notion of the text as a wilderness by metaphorically comparing humans to trees: 'Maply me, willowy we, hickory he, and yew yourselves.' The line also implies an adversarial separateness between text-wood and the individual that navigates it; in relation to the *Wake* the reader is at once the tree *of* the woods, and a lost babe in the woods. The collective singular 'wood' becomes, in the course of the sentence a diversity of individuals-as-tree species, and hence a shifting image of the many and the one with which the reader must contend.

Sandra Tropp has shown that Joyce was not only conversant with Darwinian concepts, but deeply engaged with Darwinian texts, specifically Darwin's *Descent of Man*, from which, she argues, Stephen Dedalus' formulation of the 'esthetic instinct' in *A Portrait of the Artist as a Young Man* is derived.[20] Tropp argues that the appeal of Darwin's *Descent of Man* for Joyce lay specifically in its universal (rather than relativist) theory of beauty and its expressed hope that reason will ameliorate the imperfect human faculty of sympathy so that it might be extended in equal measure to all fellow humans, an ideal that Stephen defends argumentatively but does not achieve in practice in *Portrait*.[21] In *Finnegans Wake*, too, Joyce's use of Darwinian ideas and language, specifically the figure of the tree, challenges readers to extend their faculties of sympathy, to see as fellows even those who have betrayed each other, warred against each other and ultimately slain each other. While Stephen Dedalus' engagement with Darwinian concepts in Tropp's reading of *Portrait* is polemical, *Finnegans Wake* engages with Darwin ecologically, merging text and world through the Darwinian figure of the tree.

'Treefellers' in the Woods

The figure of the tree develops the implications of the *Wake*'s word-world ecology and signals the Darwinian origins of that ecology: in both Darwin and the *Wake*, the tree appears as a material-symbolic figure whose taxonomic transgressions create overlap between word and world. The pervasiveness of the material-symbolic tree in both texts has important ramifications for the ethical discourse of *The Origin of Species* and *Finnegans Wake*: if the tree is to be thought of as both symbol and organism, ethics cannot be founded by taxonomic order. In order to investigate the continuity between symbol and matter in the *Origin* and the *Wake* and between Darwinian and Wakean trees, more particularly, I would first like to read two passages in the *Origin*, which show how Darwin constructs the tree as a bio-rhetorical figure, simultaneously material and discursive.

In the pivotal third chapter of the *Origin*, 'The Struggle for Existence', Darwin discusses the companion concepts of Natural

Selection and the Struggle for Existence, introducing each term by justifying its fitness as a figure: Natural Selection is chosen to express the analogical relation of evolutionary process to 'man's power of selection', the artificial selection of animal husbandry; the Struggle for Existence, Darwin emphasises, is to be understood 'in a large and metaphorical sense'.[22] That metaphor and analogy are constitutive of Darwin's theory is well established and here emphasised by the author himself. But I would argue further that Darwin's uses of metaphor and analogy suggest a continuity between the material and symbolic – between text and nature – that exceeds both theoretical discussions of the constitutive role of metaphor in scientific theory and work on the literary reverberations and narratological implications of Darwinian theory.[23]

To illustrate his concept of the Struggle for Survival, Darwin provides anecdotes that demonstrate the various 'checks' placed on the tendency of a species to increase, from climatic events to competition amongst species for scarce resources. In one significant passage, Darwin situates the Struggle for Survival between (or perhaps beyond) the alternatives of chance and determinism, which bookend his discussion, by imagining tree groves that testify to an epic history of species interdependence and warfare. Darwin introduces the twin phenomena of interdependence and warfare with the famous metaphor of the 'entangled bank': 'When we look at the plants and bushes clothing an entangled bank, we are tempted to attribute their proportional numbers and kinds to what we call chance. But how false a view is this!' (125). Yet from this Platonic bank, we quickly move to the American forest:

> Every one has heard that when an American forest is cut down, a very different vegetation springs up; but it has been observed that trees now growing on the ancient Indian mounds, in the Southern United States, display the same beautiful diversity and proportion of kinds as in the surrounding virgin forests. (125–6)

The 'ancient Indian mounds'[24] situate the Struggle for Survival between nature and culture: the felled American forests here resonate analogically with the felled bodies and cultural ruins that mark the landscape in the form of tumescent graves. Paradoxically, though, these mounds are also the marks of past human intervention into the 'virgin forests'. That the culture in question is an indigenous one further blurs the distinction between 'virgin' and cultivated territories.

As Darwin continues, the human presence in the forest and the Struggle for Survival ostensibly disappears, but the epic language in which Darwin couches the imagined struggle within the emerging ecosystem on the mounds extends the analogy between human society and the forest:

> What a struggle between the several kinds of trees must here have gone on during long centuries, each annually scattering its seeds by the thousand; what war between insect and insect– between insects, snails, and other animals with birds and beasts of prey – all striving to increase, and all feeding on each other or on the trees or their seeds and seedlings, or on the other plants which first clothed the ground and thus checked the growth of the trees! (126)

The notable shift from 'struggle' to 'war' in this passage and the figuring of vegetation as having domesticated – 'clothed' – the ground refuses easy distinction between human cultural change and ecological change, and queers the notion of 'virgin' Edenic wilderness: the 'struggle' in this ecology is already fallen – a war. But just as surely as it refuses easy distinction, the passage also refuses simplistic equivalency: the tree does not swap its identity as organism nor the forest its identity as ecology for allegorical identity as human culture because natural selection is not only symbolic but biological. Darwin's references to 'ancient' indigenous culture in this passage evoke the dangerous fallacies of Social Darwinism (a misnomer, as the concepts are Spencerian and Malthusian in origin). I would argue, however, that the resistance of allegory demonstrated by the passage also constitutes a resistance of Social Darwinism's 'progressive' teleology.

The end of the passage sees Darwin closing the dichotomy between chance and determinism with which the passage opened and returning us to the site of human cultural ruins integrated into the landscape:

> Throw up a handful of feathers, and all must fall to the ground according to definite laws; but how simple is this problem compared to the action and reaction of the innumerable plants and animals which have determined, in the course of centuries, the proportional numbers and kinds of trees now growing on the old Indian ruins. (126)

The epic struggle by which the forest returns to the burial mound is here integrated with the epic of human culture, neither random nor determined, but *ecological.* The dichotomy of species and environment – and in particular man and the forest – is in this passage unhinged not only by the analogy between men and trees, but by the becoming-symbolic of the biological tree in the course of the passage. What began as 'virgin forest', in the course of human history and in the course of the passage becomes a symbolic territory, marked by human intervention, transformed by language. By the end of the passage, the forest is at once an ecosystem and a former Eden, a diverse ecology of species and a testament to epic war, a landscape artificially marked by man and an analogue for the 'forests' of human society, a discrete example of the 'Struggle for Survival' and an encompassing symbol of the same. Darwin thus begins to construct the tree and the forest (already shifting territories of the many and the one) as bio-linguistic and bio-historical phenomena.

The *Wake* goes even further than Darwin in signalling a making-ecological of the world and its texts in its use of the tree, particularly in its treatment of the tree as not only an organism and symbol, but also as a word. The forests of the *Wake* show history as the shared territory of word and world. Like the fallen Indian culture represented by the burial mound in Darwin's natural history of the American forest, at once the fellers of trees existing in a relationship of historical contiguity with the landscape, and at the same time resonating as a symbolic parallel of the felled trees, human figures in the *Wake* are described both as trees (fallen or otherwise) and as the fellers of trees. In fact, humans appear as 'treefellers in the shrubrubs' (420.8). This pun, which occurs twice in the *Wake*, is dependent on the notions of tree as species, as symbol, and as word, and here also as spoken word, as *parole*: it is the overlap in pronunciation of 'fellow' and 'feller' and 'tree' and 'three' that produces the pun on 'three fellows in the suburbs'. That 'treefellers' signifies at once those who fell trees and fellows who are trees invests the term with a similar sense of conflicting affiliations as that evoked by Darwin's example of the Indian culture as both felled trees and fellers of trees.

In that trees in the *Wake* often cluster in the location of Phoenix Park – figurative site of HCE's unnamed sin and historical site of the Phoenix Park murders – these 'treefellers' become aligned with the fall of Ireland's 'Uncrowned King', Parnell. Although the discovery that a letter purportedly written by Parnell and expressing sympathy for the Invincibles and the murders was revealed to be a counterfeit written by journalist Robert Piggott, the incident damaged Liberal support for Parnell, delaying the achievement of Home Rule. Although Parnell's ultimate downfall would be caused by moral outrage on the part of the clergy and many Irish citizens, spurred by his being named as co-respondent in the divorce case of Captain William O'Shea against his wife Katharine, the aspersions cast on Parnell's character due to Piggott's libel foreshadow his ultimate betrayal by the public. These events suggest a succession of 'fellings' rather than of falls, culminating with the felling of Parnell as a potent political figure.

That Joyce chooses to present these political events in ecological language suggests that he may have envisioned ecology as an alternative to historical narrative. This ecology of history emerges saliently in references to Phoenix Park in ways that undermine the distinction between organism and environment. As simultaneously a civic space whose monuments materialise Ireland's colonial history, a material ecology that sustains trees and wild deer, and a metonymic signifier within the *Wake* for the murders that took place within its boundaries, Phoenix Park entangles discursive and material phenomena. More specifically, in the *Wake* Phoenix Park presents an ecology of historical and material 'trees'. In the *Wake*'s third chapter, a disordered, dreamlike rendering of the second chapter in which Phoenix Park is identified as a possible site of HCE's sin, the text presents a vanquished Christlike king, torn 'limb from lamb' by his countrymen (58.7):

> But, lo! lo! by the threnning gods, human, erring and condonable, what the statues of our kuo, who is the messchef be our kuang, ashu ashure there, the unforgettable treeshade looms up behind the jostling judgements of those, as all should owe, malrecapturable days. (58.18–22)

The 'unforgettable treeshade' here evokes Joyce's characterisation of Parnell in 'The Shade of Parnell', refiguring the dead 'king' as a shade-tree, a reading reinforced by the Chinese words 'shu' (tree) and 'kuang', which means light, but also suggests both the English 'king' and the Chinese 'wang' (king).[25] In the following chapter in which HCE, also dead, remembers his fall and is subjected to dreamlike judicial proceedings, the pun on 'tree' and 'three' recurs in another evocation of the Phoenix Park Murders and HCE's alleged sin: 'But it oozed out in Deadman's Dark Scenery Court through crossexanimation of the casehardened testis that when and where that knife of knifes the treepartied ambush was laid (roughly spouting around half hours 'twixt dusk in dawn' (87.33–36). Although the ambush of Thomas Burke and Lord Cavendish by the Invincibles involved approximately twenty conspirators and as many as nine assailants wielding surgical knives, the 'treepartied ambush' may refer to the three parties of the Invincibles' ambush: the two cars, one a decoy driven by Skin-the-goat, aligned with Eumaeus in *Ulysses*, and the other the primary conveyance of the assassins, and the posse who entered the Park and carried out the murders, stabbing Burke and Cavendish to death. 'Treepartied' also evokes the three parties that dominated the House of Commons in Parnell's time: Liberal, Conservative, and Parnell's Irish Parliamentary Party. The language of testimony, guerilla tactics and bodily injury overlap in this quotation: the bodily 'casehardened testis' of the 'when and where' of the ambush 'ooze[s] out', as blood from a wound during 'crossexanimation' to illuminate the circumstances surrounding an ex-animated body. Similarly, 'laid (roughly spouting', changes 'speaking' to 'spouting', evoking both the 'laid' plans and the bleeding, laid-out body that those plans produced. The overlapping puns of 'treefellers in the shrubrubs' of the earlier quotation and the 'treepartied ambush', then, can both be seen to evoke bushes and ambushes, the fraternal bonds that create 'fellows', and the severing of bonds by 'fellers'. And here it should be remembered that the guilt of the Phoenix Park conspirators was revealed in part by two members of the group, James Carey and Michael Kavanagh, who turned Queen's evidence and testified against their fellow Invincibles. Material and symbolic trees here converge on the political and judiciary and force a consideration of constitutive role of conflict in society, the mutual constitution of 'fellers' and 'fellows'.

The wordplay integrating historical, biological and symbolic trees in these sections of the *Wake* presents history as an ecological phenomenon constituted by shifting material-symbolic territories. The wordplay also revises the binaries of historical narrative: evoking both fraternal bonds and their betrayal, the 'treefellers' of the *Wake* figure history not as narrative, but as material-symbolic pun. Without erasing the horror of the Phoenix Park murders, the tree-puns in these sections create perspectival shifts, allowing for 'fellers' to be recognisable as 'fellows'. For Stephen Dedalus, history is a nightmare; the dream-text of the *Wake* awakens the reader to the collaborative constitution of that nightmare, presenting a model for history not as narrative, but rather as material-symbolic ecology, open to diverse interpretations and interventions.

ALP and the Healing of the (N)ations

The *Wake*'s blurring of text and meta-text, organism and environment, word and world is enacted most saliently and lyrically in the final monologue of one of the *Wake*'s whirling 'characters', ALP, who appears as both tree and river, as 'leafy speafing'. ALP's identification with both tree and river challenges the imagination in its confusion of natural categories. Cognitively constrained by our conventional separation of organism and environment, we are perhaps inclined to conceive of ALP as a tree growing alongside the river, its leaves carried 'A way a lone a last a loved a long the' text's cyclic 'riverunn' (628.15–6.1.1). But the language of her monologue in this final section encourages the reader to adopt a dynamic perspective that ameliorates those conceptual limitations, opening up the possibility of seeing not merely the tree by the river, but the river-tree. The eternal return of the text can only be actualised by the reader who sutures the last page of the text to the first, ameliorating the limitations of the book's material form; perhaps another sense in which the book is, as Joyce claimed, a square circle.[26] Seen in these terms, the *Wake* produces both multiplicity and reconciliation, the healing of seemingly fundamental rifts materialised in the suturing of the text's first and last pages. This 'healing' does not erase rifts, but rather re-envisions relations of difference and similarity as fundamentally in process, neither essential nor eternal. In resisting closure and unilateral reading, the *Wake* opens its word-world to a diversity of readers and readings and allows for their mutual coexistence, a making-ecological of conflict.

ALP's language in the final monologue reflects her dual status as tree and river and invites the reader to merge those divergent natural phenomena. Her monologue begins: 'Soft morning, city! Lsp! I am leafy speafing. Lpf! Folty and folty all the nights have falled on to long my hair. Not a sound, falling. Lispn! No wind no word. Only a leaf, just a leaf and then leaves' (619.20–23). In this section, ALP-as-tree presents a decentring centre.[27] Here ALP's 'I' is equated with the grammatical consolidation of subjectivity, with the leaf, which bridges the biological and textual, and with the Babelian condition of speaking. More precisely, though, ALP's 'leafy speafing' presents a kind of decentring upon decentring that blurs the categories of speech, text and world. The present progressive 'speafing' emphasises the continual unfolding of the *Wake*'s ecology of material and symbolic phenomena. The text's characteristic self-awareness, too, emerges as ecologically contingent: ALP's 'I', the paradoxical silent speech of leaves, appears as a process of diffusion and dispersal, literally as leaves falling away from their branches.

References to Anna Livia's leaves bookend her final monologue, the ending of the text determined by the falling of her onomatopoeic lisping leaves that is also the reader's turning of the book's final leaves or pages.[28] Lest we forget ALP's fluidity and association with the Liffey, she is named in this section 'Alma Luvia Pollabella', the first two words together suggesting the alluvial nature of *Wake* – that which is washed up by the river – and the last presenting ALP once again as a hen (the Italian *polla*) but also as a spring of water (*pollo*) (McHugh, 619.16). 'Leafy' is also, of course, Liffey, and the sounds 'Lsp!' and 'Lfp!' are ambiguously arborial and alluvial (619.20). As the reader turns the final page of the text, ALP's final leaf falls: 'My leaves have drifted from me. All. But one clings still. I'll bear it on me. To remind me of. Lff!' (628. 6–7). Anna Livia's leaves are simultaneously strewn upon and constitute the final leaves of *Finnegans Wake*; her 'leafy speafing' is textual and meta-textual, a lyrical blending of the material and the textual, the page and the language, organic and symbolic trees, tree and river. Thus in this final section of the *Wake*, ALP invites the reader to participate in an ecology of life and language constituted by the shifting play of difference and identity, an imaginative suturing of material and textual phenomena that remembers the fissure.

Much as ALP's lisping leaves herald the text's ending, the conceptual suturing that constitutes the reader's participation in ALP's ecological 'polylogue' (for her 'speafing' resists univocality) foreshadows the suturing that the reader will perform in connecting the text's last words grammatically to its first. *Finnegans Wake* begins, paradoxically, both *in medias res* and with Genesis: the reader begins in the midst of a sentence, plunged into and yet already borne along by the Liffey's 'riverrun, past Eve and Adam's' (1.1).[29] The realisation that the *Wake*'s beginning emerges from its ending requires both arriving at the end of the text and suturing it to the beginning through cognitive and also physical 'recirculation' back to page one, in essence a revelation that initiates a readerly *revolution*, a turning back to the beginning. Joyce himself thought of the experience of reading the *Wake* in terms of a journey whose key feature is eternal return. As Adolf Hoffmeister recalled, Joyce said of his 'Work in Progress', 'I don't think that the difficulties in reading it are so insurmountable. Certainly any intelligent reader can read and understand it, if he returns to the text again and again. He is setting out on an adventure with words.'[30] While Joyce's insistence on the work's readability and comprehensibility may seem incredible to those who have encountered its obscurity, Joyce's comments on the reader's experience suggest that reading the *Wake* might revise conventional notions of what is meant by 'read and understand'. Joyce continues,

> On the contrary, 'Work in Progress' can satisfy more readers than any other book because it gives them the opportunity to use their own ideas in the reading. Some readers will be interested in the exploration of words, the play of technique, the philological experiment in each poetic unit. Each word has the charm of a living thing and each living thing is plastic. (131)

Here, 'reading' and 'understanding' in the *Wake* is a fundamentally interactive and variable experience, a mutual shaping that occurs between human minds and 'plastic' words whose malleability resembles that of living organisms. Whereas the biological notion of plasticity characterises the organism's malleability in response to environmental change, plasticity in the *Wake* emerges as *mutually* contingent, a shaping of both reader and text. As the *Wake*'s plasticity undermines the split between organism and environment in favour of ecological relations, so too does it perpetuate itself, resisting a determinate form or telos. The shifting multiplicity of meanings created by the changing perspectives of individual readers who return again and again to the *Wake* ultimately makes possible the eternal return of the riverrun from last page to first so saliently associated with the text.

The reader's revelation that the text's final words reinitiate its first words, combined with the text's opening references to Genesis, also invites us to see the text's final lines – Anna Livia's lines – in terms of Revelations, a text which also presents a salient image of reconciliation in the form of a river-tree. While the opening references to Genesis and the overlap between Eden and Dublin are well-established, the potential connections between the final pages of the *Wake* and the final book of the New Testament are less so.[31] And while Anna Livia as tree can and should be seen in terms of any and all of the bio-symbolic trees, Darwinian, Norse, or otherwise, that have entered into the text, Anna Livia's status as simultaneously tree and river in this the final section of the text suggests that we may also want to investigate her as an iteration of the Tree of Life and Water of Life in Revelations. In Genesis, symbolic and biological trees share common territory; the description of God's creation of the garden simultaneously emphasises naturalistic, aesthetic and spiritual concerns: 'And out of the ground the Lord God made to grow every tree that is pleasant to the sight and good for food, the tree of life also in the midst of the garden, and the tree of knowledge of good and evil' (2.9). Like the trees of the *Wake* and of *The Origin of Species*, the trees of Genesis merge the realms of biological and symbolic concerns; those trees that are 'good for food' are given equal precedence in this passage as the symbolic spiritual Tree of Knowledge and Tree of Life, the latter of which is not forbidden to the couple. The Tree of Life, enclosed in Eden and guarded by a flaming sword following Adam and Eve's transgression, is renewed in the New Jerusalem. John reports: 'Then [the angel] showed me the river of the water of life, bright as crystal, flowing from the throne of God and of the Lamb through the middle of the street of the city; also, on either side of the river, the tree of life with its twelve kinds of fruit, yielding its fruit each month; and the leaves of the tree were for the healing of the nations' (Revelations 22.1–3). Although the text identifies the tree and river separately, the image also presents a unity, the single tree cleaved by the river. As in the final pages of the *Wake*, in the final pages of Revelations the reader is invited to imaginatively suture tree and river to produce the surreal image of a tree-and-river.

Reading ALP – whose middle name means 'life' – in terms of the Tree and Water of Life in Revelations invests the reader's recirculation from the last leaf of the text back to the first, and from the Liffey to the sea and back again, with ethical and political significance. The foregrounding of ALP's leaves in this final section suggests that like the leaves of the Tree of Life in Revelations, ALP's leaves and the leaves of the *Wake* may also be 'for the healing of the nations'. One revelation of the *Wake*'s final pages, then, is that the ecological processes of its word-world may ultimately inform a new understanding of nation. To say that nation, nationalism, and Ireland-as-nation, more specifically, are central preoccupations of Joyce's work is both understatement and commonplace. And the *Wake* more specifically has been described in terms of a recapitulation of Irish history[32] and its language as fundamentally 'Hiberno-English', Joyce's reflection of British linguistic imperialism.[33] While the 'healing of the nations' as an heuristic for *Finnegans Wake* might be usefully applied to an ongoing discussion of Joyce and the 'nation' of Ireland, whose self-divided status (political, linguistic, psychic) emerges as the heritage of invasion and empire, such an investigation is beyond the scope of this chapter. I would like to investigate nation in *Finnegans Wake* on the text's own terms, as not only concept but also as word, and also as suffix. The blurred linguistic boundaries of the many 'nations' in the text undermine the concept of nation as homogenous and teleological. The 'nations' that emerge from the *Wake* envision nation as not merely *in* process, but rather *as* process.[34]

In his 1907 lecture 'Ireland, Island of Saints and Sages', Joyce suggests the necessity of revising the 'fiction' of nationality:

> Nationality (if it really is not a convenient fiction like so many others to which the scalpels of present-day scientists have given the coup de grâce) must find its reason for being rooted in something that surpasses and transcends and informs changing things like blood and the human world.[35]

Joyce's argument that the 'convenient fiction' of nationality must reinvent itself in order to evade the scalpel-wielding scientists produces slippage between the 'fiction' of nationality and the dead organism subjected to dissection: the organism is at once the biological entity whose dissection undermines the 'convenient fiction' and the unitary 'organism' of nation itself. Though written years before the *Wake*, Joyce's notion that the 'fiction' of nationality must cease to be fiction and rather become paradoxically 'rooted' in flux – that which informs 'changing things' – permeates the *Wake*'s discourse of nation. In place of the organicist fantasy of nation as characterised by progressive development and completeness, the *Wake* presents a bio-semiotic ecology in which the 'rooted' tree is coupled with the (re)circulating river, in which constitutive binaries of nation – inside and outside, native and foreigner – are dismantled through the self-adulterating language of the *Wake*; the '[in]convenient fiction' of nationality is dissolved in the non-narrative, punning word-world of the *Wake*.

In the *Wake* 'nation' is made conceptually and linguistically unstable in that it is often registered through puns that conflate 'nation' and the 'nations' created by the –ation suffix. The punning technique of *Finnegans Wake* precludes an understanding of nation as discrete, singular, or homogenous; rather, nation appears as semantically independent and dependent, ambiguously whole and part.[36] In the 'Quiz' chapter, for instance, the first question (the answer to which is 'Finn MacCool!') identifies its answer as a fecund entity who 'sas seed enough for a semi*nation* but sues skivvies on the sly' and 'has twenty four or so cousins germinating in the United States of America' (130.17, 27–8, emphasis mine). The language not only merges plant and human sexuality, rooting the concept of nation in the distributed processes of biological reproduction, but also suggests the nation-forming dimension of the entwined processes of human procreation and agricultural cultivation: Finn not only accomplishes 'semination', but ambiguously has seed enough to father and to feed a 'semi-nation', heroic indeed in the context of Ireland's history of famine and population loss. Nation here is both the process of propagation, a 'noun of action', and the entity that results from it, importantly an incomplete entity, a 'semi-nation'. The ambivalence of this pun, combined with the reference to America, recalls Joyce's ambivalence about Irish emigration to America in 'Ireland, Island of Saints and Sages': Joyce celebrates America as a possible site of Irish revival while in the same breath lamenting that 'every year, Ireland, decimated as she already is, loses 60,000 of her sons' (172). Finn MacCool's 'semination', then, presents Irish nation as incomplete and registers the ambivalence produced by this partialness.[37] The propagations of the 'semination' heal, but do not efface the rifts of history. The drawing and redrawing of the semantic and conceptual territories of 'nation' thus presents another suturing of word and world.

In the final chapter ALP enacts a making-ecological of nation that brings together the text's discourse on nation with the bio-semiotic figure of the Liffey, itself suggestive of the river from Revelations. Some pages before ALP's monologue, we encounter her as a body of water teeming with life: 'Polycarp pool, the pool of Innalavia' (600.5). The pool quickly turns to the river Liffey, down which streams Dublin's heterogeneous history: 'the river of lives, the regenerations of the incar*nations* of the ema*nations* of the apparentations of Funn and Nin in Cleethabala, the kongdomain of the Alieni, an accorsaired race, infester of Libnud Ocean, Moylamore, let it be!' (600. 8–12, emphasis mine). In these lines the mythos of national purity is, in Dublin's river, subjected to adulterating process: 'nation' is drowned in a stream of 'ations': 'the regenerations of the incarnations of the emanations of the aparentations'. In the passage, Dublin, or 'Libnud', appears as a kingdom of foreigners, 'the kongdomain of the Alieni', populated by a race of pirates (corsairs), 'an accorsaired race'. 'Cleethabala', resonating with the Gaelic name for Dublin (*Baile Átha Cliath*) shares space with the Danish word for kingdom (*kongdømme*) evoked in 'kongdomain' (McHugh). Importantly, nation-as-adulterating-process appears here as both life-affirming, as registered by 'regenerations', and destructive, as registered by 'accorsaired' and 'infester'. Undermining the mythos of nation by revealing it as a continual process of adulteration does not erase the deep psychic fissures produced by a history of invasion; rather, it refigures them in a way that allows for ambivalence to be registered and processed in language.

The '[n]ations' of the *Wake* subvert the unitary and organic metaphorical underpinnings of nation – of which the notion of shared language is one – by revealing nation as fundamentally heterogeneous and contingent, not a romantic metaphor, but a transgressive pun.[38] In this formulation, linguistic uncertainty undermines the romance of nation, making it a matter of reading. The *Wake* refigures conventional notions of 'reading' and 'understanding' as ecological phenomena. If, as Benedict Anderson argues, the modern concept of nation finds its literary incarnation in the realist novel, it is perhaps in the recursive processes of the *Wake* that the myth of nation is undone.

The variable puns that Joyce propagates throughout *Ulysses* and *Finnegans Wake* merge word and world, ultimately presenting an ecological argument about nation that actively undermines the romance of nation. This ecological transformation is founded on the recognition of the complex metonymic and metaphorical relations between text and world that figure phenomena as collectively constituted: negotiated rather than natural, dynamic rather than essential. Ecological process, produced discursively, refigures the self-limiting unitary mythos of nation as open and dynamic. In the *Wake*, the reader's recirculation to the beginning of the text does not erase the *in medias res* of the text's opening, but rather restores it. The reader's return to incompletion and meaning-in-process in the form of the text's *in medias res* opening produces a physical analogue – the return to page one – for the reader's journey throughout the *Wake*, a process of perspectival shifting and cognitive suturing. In the context of the text's discourse on nation, reading the *Wake* emerges as an ecological antidote to the limiting myth of nation and as a model of ethical behaviour as 'work in progress', the work of reading as continual revolution, rather than self-evident revelation.

The Tree Wedding and the (Eco)Politics of Irish Forestry in 'Cyclops': History, Language and the Viconian Politics of the Forest

YI-PENG LAI

> O Ireland! Our sireland!
> Once fireland! Now mireland!
> No liar land shall buy our land!
> A higher land is Ireland!
>
> James Joyce, V.A.6 Notebook, f. 3v, *Joyce's Notes and Early Drafts for Ulysses: Selections from the Buffalo Collection*, p. 185

James Joyce certainly had the forests in mind when he drafted the above poem in the V.A.6 notebook for 'Cyclops', although it is unclear as to the reason why he later disposed of the passage. The transformation from 'fireland' to 'mireland' in the second line connects the history of ancient land clearings[1] to the contemporary landscape of the Irish bog.[2] As is well known, the Land Purchase Act of 1903 allowed Irish tenants to buy land and precipitate a felling of forests in the following decades.[3] Indeed, the history of Irish forestry up to the early twentieth century can be read as a series of protracted struggles between Crown and rebels, landlord and tenants, environmental preservation and industrial profits, and between Anglo-Irish landowners and, after the practice of Land Purchase Acts, Irish ones. But the question of afforestation is more often than not a more complicated issue than the dichotomies that tend to structure Irish nationalist historiography would permit.[4] It has, like Eoin Neeson comments in his introduction to *A History of Irish Forestry*, 'paralleled the political history of the country'.[5] In fact, it is an Irish political history of its own accord.

This article dwells on the history of trees in Ireland, along with its politics from the time of Tudor Conquest to *fin-de-siècle* Irish economic and nationalist propaganda, to consider dynamics of the Tree Wedding catalogue in 'Cyclops'.[6] Few scholars have paid specific attention to the environmental politics indicated by this catalogue, and those who have drawn passing references to the passage read it either as a parodic journalistic account on Joyce's part or as another example of Cyclopean gigantism. Although both readings provide insightful perspectives on the rhetorics of the catalogue and Joyce's linguistic gigantism, the catalogue and the Tree Wedding itself deserves a closer examination in light of the politics of deforestation and reafforestation in Ireland in Joyce's time, as well as a reconsideration of the forest as a paradigmatic Irish cultural landscape, one which implicates questions of civilisation, matrimony and patriarchal institutionisation.

In *Forests: the Shadow of Civilization*, probably to date the most comprehensive book-length study of cultural politics of the woodlands in Western literatures, Robert Harrison examines the concept of the forest in Western literary history from ancient epics to twentieth-century environmental writings. The forest, in his view, 'appears as a place where the logic of distinction goes astray. Or where our subjective categories are confounded. Or where perceptions become promiscuous with one another, disclosing latent dimensions of time and consciousness'.[7] Forests are imagined as spaces of confusion, of wilderness, but also of escapist relief, of utopian possibility and nightmarish darkness. Above all, they are imagined in relation to the history of Western civilisation; whether that civilisation is seen in its emergence, as in Vico's *New Science* or the epic of Gilgamesh, or civilisation after the Enlightenment and industrialisation, as in works by more modern writers like Joseph Conrad, T.S. Eliot and Ezra Pound. Interestingly, in his passing comment on Joyce, Harrison writes: 'In retrospect it seems clear that a modernist writer like James Joyce, whose literature exploited the almost limitless resources of the sayable, never really heeded the "nature" of the times'.[8] This essay challenges Harrison's argument and attempts to demonstrate that although Joyce may not be a writer as keen for transcendental environmentalism as Henry David Thoreau, especially not in his earlier works of *Dubliners*, *A Portrait of the Artist as a Young Man* and the renowned urban epic *Ulysses*, he is certainly cognisant of contemporary environmental debates around reafforestation, the cultural politics of the forest, Viconian historiography and the question of nature, nation and human civilisation. This awareness is specifically exemplified in his composition of the Tree Wedding catalogue in the 'Cyclops' episode of *Ulysses*.

* * *

I

Natural historians have pointed out the drastic deprivation of trees in Ireland since the time of Tudor conquest. A.C. Forbes, an active advocate of Irish afforestation in the early twentieth century and later the Director of Forestry at the Department of Agriculture and Technical Instruction for Ireland, writes that 'the country during the sixteenth and seventeenth centuries was extremely bare of trees, leaving out of account altogether anything in the nature of woods'.[9] Eileen McCracken also notes how '[i]n 1600 about one-eighth of Ireland was forested', and 'by 1800 the proportion had been reduced to a fiftieth as a result of the commercial exploitation of the Irish woodlands following on the establishment of English control over the whole country'.[10] Such reduction of Irish woodlands was the consequence of extensive clearings during the Elizabethan era, the period in which the word 'woodkerne' was first coined due to the English fear of the woods as strongholds for Irish rebels. Elizabeth I, well aware of the threat woodlands posed to English settlers, 'expressly ordered the destruction of all woods in the country to deprive the Irish of this shelter'.[11] It was a commonly held view at the time that woodlands provided profits (for the English) and shelter (for the Irish), and for both of these reasons the woods had to be felled.

It was perhaps as early as the time of the Ulster Plantation that the problem of deforestation started to interweave with that of land. The Plantation in Ulster and elsewhere in Ireland attracted Protestant settlers from England and Scotland, the farmers who, in due course, would become aligned with the dominant Anglo-Irish landholding class, and who would engage in conflict with their Irish tenants during periods of agrarian agitations. These newcomers shared with the Elizabethans a fearful dislike for the Irish woods for the same reason: they provided shelter for the Irish troops. Similarly, their desire for profits from this resource induced the excessive felling of forests. A number of pieces of legislation were tabled that might have curtailed the amount of felling allowed for the tenants, or to prohibit woodland clearings, but were to little avail. The subsequent centuries saw an explosion in the use of timber; England was 'not to the forefront in European forestry development either in respect of management or legislation'.[12] And while England made efforts to protect its own trees, Irish forestry was, not surprisingly, neglected.

In 1895, Sir Horace Plunkett, founder of the Irish Agricultural Organisation Society (IAOS), coordinated a 'Recess Committee' whose proceedings recommended the establishment of an Irish Agricultural Department. In 1899, the Department of Agriculture and Technical Instruction for Ireland (DATI) was set up, and silviculture was one of its designated functions. In 1902 the Department founded a forestry school on the newly purchased Avondale estate in County Wicklow. In 1907 a Departmental Committee of Enquiry was formed by the DATI to investigate the condition and prospects of Irish forestry. Their report was presented to the UK parliament and simultaneously published in Dublin on 6 April 1908. This is the report 'of lord Castletown's' which, in 'Cyclops', is mentioned by John Wyse Nolan in his interrupted statement on Irish reafforestation.[13] The Right Hon. Lord Castletown of Upper Ossory was among the eight committee members for this enquiry that sought 'the improvement of forestry in Ireland'.[14] It reported upon the present state of Irish forestry, examined the after-effects of the enforcement of Land Purchase Acts, considered financial aid and administrative schemes with regard to forestry, and prompted state forestry and co-operative measures which followed.

The passing of the 1903 Wyndham Land Act enabled the DATI and the county councils to acquire land for afforestation and for the preservation of existing forests; however, a want of funds prevented the scheme from having any significant practical merit. Landowners, old and new alike, saw potential profits to be earned from selling the standing timber on their properties. The Report points out that 'the prevailing spirit of land transfer operations at present is [. . .] hostile to trees', since '[t]he landlord and the Land Commission find them an obstacle to sale, and there is a sort of premium on their removal'.[15] In short, the run on land transactions precipitated by the 1903 Land Purchase Act coupled with no effective corresponding legislation to protect Irish forests meant that an extensive period of wood-felling ensued.

On the Irish problem of deforestation, in 'Cyclops' John Wyse Nolan exclaims:

> As treeless as Portugal we'll be soon, says John Wyse, or Heligoland with its one tree if something is not done to reafforest the land. Larches, firs, all the trees of the conifer family are going fast. I was reading a report of lord Castletown's . . .[16]

His sympathy with the reforestation campaign and the felled coniferous trees a couple of lines later merits the comic metamorphosis of him into 'the chevalier Jean Wyse de Neaulan' who is going to wed 'Miss Fir Conifer of Pine Valley'.[17] The gigantic guest list for the wedding thence begins:

> Lady Sylvester Elmshade, Mrs Barbara Lovebirth, Mrs Poll Ash, Mrs Holly Hazeleyes, Miss Daphne Bays, Miss Dorothy Canebrake, Mrs Clyde Twelvetrees, Mrs Rowan Greene, Mrs Helen Vinegadding, Miss Virginia Creeper, Miss Gladys Beech, Miss Olive Garth, . . .[18]

And the list goes on. It is noteworthy that except for the family of the bride (the M'Conifer of the Glands and the two maids of honour, Miss Larch Conifer and Miss Spruce Conifer), none of the attending guests belongs to the coniferous family. Other attending guests all belong to arboreal species other than the conifer. It is indeed, like John Wyse Nolan's statement, the procession to witness 'the trees of the conifer family [. . .] going'.[19]

This history of the neglect of Irish forests may help to offer a possible explanation for Joyce's writing of the tree wedding catalogue. Afforestation was a popular issue at the turn of the twentieth century, and mass interest was shown in the significant number of articles that appeared in both British and Irish newspapers on this pressing topic. In the *Freeman's Journal* alone, between 1900 and 1920 there were at least 140 entries whose titles touched on Irish afforestation: thirty-nine were issued between the years 1907–08. In the British paper *The Times* the number of related articles from 1900 to 1920 was 198, forty-eight of which were published in 1907 and 1908. But afforestation was more than a popular topic in Ireland; it was a much-debated agenda item regarding colonial politics. It involves the history of plantation and imperialism, and concerns British policies in Ireland. It reflects cultural politics and tenant–landlord conflicts in Ireland over the centuries. Its early twentieth-century supporters include members of the Gaelic League and Sinn Féin, among them Arthur Griffith, who above all 'was persistent in crying out for forestry'[20] at the time when Horace Plunkett was pressing for the establishment of an Irish institution for its own silviculture. Evidently, forestry history is deeply implicated within the historical process of the construction of Irish nationalism and Joyce must have been aware of its essential role.

* * *

II

> This was the order of human institutions: first the forests, after that the huts, then the villages, next the cities, and finally the academies.
>
> Giambattista Vico, *New Science*, §239

Brigitte L. Sandquist's 1996 article may be among the few scholarly works that extensively analyses the Tree Wedding catalogue in 'Cyclops', although numerous critical comments have been made with regard to the gigantic style that is characteristic of the episode. Among others, Fritz Senn singles out its possible sources from Ovid's *Metamorphoses*,[21] and Sandquist incorporates this idea as she develops her analysis of the tree–human transformation and the implicit violence of patriarchal space in the first part of her article. Then she turns toward the structural dynamics of the catalogue within the narrative as a whole and contemplates its thematic eye/I distinction. She parallels the Homeric design of the eye-blinding scene with Joyce's tree wedding catalogue that is situated right between two 'eyes',[22] and interestingly juxtaposes Odysseus' alienness in the context of the Cyclops' land with the tree wedding's alienness in the text 'Cyclops'. Sandquist sees the interpolation of the catalogue as an alien intrusion into the narrative, and signals the performative function of the tree catalogue as it literally 'hits the narrative right between the eyes'.[23]

Situated between 'Europe has its eyes on you'[24] and 'Our eyes are on Europe',[25] the catalogue not only textually becomes the Cyclopean eye in Joyce's contemporary Irish context, but more significantly, it is the one with the 'beam in the eyes'. Joyce's use of the beam-in-the-eye metaphor is, however, far beyond the synchronic structure of the catalogue. In fact, the episode registers a philological historiography which, as critics have observed, Joyce 'absorbs'[26] from the work of the eighteenth-century philosopher, Giambattista Vico. In what follows, I will illustrate how he further internalises Viconian philological historiography and reconsiders the systems of law, patriarchy and the institutionalisation of nation, specifically in an Irish context, within the tree wedding catalogue of 'Cyclops'.

The name Giambattista Vico is not a foreign one to most Joycean readers. Much attention has been directed toward *Finnegans Wake*, which Joyce himself advised Shaw Weaver to read along with Vico's *New Science*, the way he recommends *The Odyssey* to be read as a counterpart to *Ulysses*.[27] Some Viconian traces have been observed in

Ulysses, and it is also noted that '[the novel's] Odyssean parallelism may have been partly influenced by Vico's "discovery of the true Homer"',[28] which bears the same title as the third book in the *New Science*. A few scholars have commented on Vico's influence on Joyce not only in his composition of *Finnegans Wake* but also of *Ulysses*, and it is frequently asserted that Joyce confesses that his 'imagination grows' when he reads Vico as 'it doesn't when [he] read[s] Freud or Jung'.[29] A. Walton Litz lists 'Cyclops', along with 'Nestor', as the two Ulyssean episodes with the most explicit Viconian influence.[30] As early as in the 1930s, Stuart Gilbert indicated *Ulysses'* Cyclopean allusion to Vico's giants. He relates Joyce's technique of 'gigantism' in the twelfth episode to the Viconian mythological historiography, noting that in Joyce's 'Cyclops', 'not only is there an elaborate description of a giant but the technique of the episode itself is, as we have seen, "gigantism"'.[31] Gigantism, Joyce's designated episodic technique for 'Cyclops', can hence be regarded not simply as an Homeric or an Ovidian scheme, but also, if no less significantly, a Viconian one.

Vico's giants appear in Book Two of the *New Science*, where he explains the origin of human civilisation from savagery, the constitution of family, to that of nation. In his view, after the flood, Noah's descendants, who, due to their primitive lifestyle in scattered forests over the earth, grew into giants. They live unaware of divine Providence until the thunder strikes, and, out of corresponding awe and fear for the divine, they stop copulating, hide in the caves and start raising families. This, according to Vico's theory, marks the beginning of religion (fear of God) and matrimony (institution of monogamy under divine surveillance). From then onwards, families develop their genealogical lineage, settle in cities and generate social systems around laws and the power of patriarchy.

Although Joyce's Viconian adoption is most notably demonstrated in the incarnation of circular progression and cyclical history in *Finnegans Wake*, Vico's *New Science* is in truth a piece of politics, since, as Samuel Beckett points out, more than three-fifths of the book is 'concerned with empirical investigations'.[32] Stuart Gilbert, too, specifies that 'the theory of recurrence in the affairs of men and nations' in *Ulysses* is 'not peculiar to mystical thinkers [of the Celtic twilight]; it appears as an empirical deduction from the facts of history, rather than as an a priori dogma, in the works of the Italian philosopher Vico'.[33] The book's full title itself, *Principles of New*

Science of Giambattista Vico concerning the Common Nature of the Nations, signals its political civilisation. It is structurally divided into five sections based on the Viconian plan of a cyclically developmental history of humanity. Apart from Book One, which introduces the establishment of principles, and the last one that marks the historical cycle, the entire piece runs according to Vico's three successive stages of progression: that of gods, of heroes and of men. His discourse of historiography attempts to incorporate diverse myths and legends by narrating a new universal history that dwells on the origin and progression of poetry, language, law, institutions and human civilisation. And it is in this 'theory of the origins of poetry and language, the significance of myth, and the nature of barbaric civilisation', as Beckett claims, 'appears the unqualified originality of [Vico's] mind'.[34] Joseph Mali resolutely asserts that 'It was Vico's analysis of the inner historicity of human institutions – as exemplified, for instance, in the etymological explanation of words or in the psychological conception of theogony as the outcome of traumatic experience – which . . . impressed Joyce so profoundly'.[35]

In a striking passage which demystifies the myth of the one-eyed Cyclops, Vico writes:

> Every clearing was called a *lucus*, in the sense of an eye, as even today we call eyes the openings through which light enters houses. The true heroic phrase that 'every giant had his *lucus*' [clearing or eye] was altered and corrupted when its meaning was lost, and had already been falsified when it reached Homer, for it was then taken to mean that every giant had one eye in the middle of his forehead.[36]

Here Vico associates *lucus*, clearing, with the concept of an eye. His explanation for the Cyclopean myth corresponds to his earlier axiomatic 'universal principle of etymology in all languages' that 'words are carried over from bodies and from the properties of bodies to signify the institutions of the mind and spirit'.[37] Later he asserts that 'in all languages the greater part of the expressions relating to inanimate things are formed by metaphors from the human body and its parts and from the human senses and passions'.[38] Such physical personification of language and geography, Rosa Maria Bosinelli maintains, is the Viconian principle that 'inspires the very first page of *Finnegans Wake*; a page that declares its debt to Vico from the opening word "riverrun"'.[39] It is possible that Vico's account of the triangular *lucus*-clearing-eye analogy also inspired

Joyce's rendering of the 'tree-run' in 'Cyclops'. Sandquist's analysis has already reminded us of the performativity of the catalogue, with the tree list situated between the two 'eyes' within the entire episodic framework. Were we to delete the tree catalogue from the chapter, the narrative would appear as follows:

> – Europe has its eyes on you, says Lenehan.
> [tree wedding catalogue]
> – And our eyes are on Europe, says the citizen.[40]

Sandquist advised that the above structure is rhetorically equivalent to Bloom's previous statement: 'Some people . . . can see the mote in others' eyes but they can't see the beam in their own.'[41] She also notices an 'implicit violence in this catalogue, a violence masked by Joyce's parodic use of the society column', and how this rhetorical violence is used to shatter 'both the vision and the subjectivity of the narrative'.[42] However, it is worth noting that the specific rhetorical structure of Joyce's tree catalogue may actually be visually and subjectively coherent in accordance with Vico's philological interpretation of the Cyclopean myth.

A closer investigation into the context where Vico sets his *lucus*-clearing-eye analogy helps to explain the violent undertone of the Cyclopean myth in both Viconian and Joycean settings. After the development of families and the agricultural instituting of the fathers, Vico introduces the emergence of '*famuli*' who, originally as savages beleaguered by others, came to the fathers to seek asylum. This new social group, a feudal underclass, subsequently grew in number to accommodate martial slaves and refugees, and, many of its social rights denied, was subjected to unequal servitude. They lived with restricted bonitary rights under the 'eternal principles of the fiefs',[43] and were precluded from owning land. In due time, these *famuli* rebelled against the fathers. It is against this feudal background that the confrontation between the Roman plebeians (the *famuli*) and the patricians (the fathers) came to light, the confrontation which, as Thomas Hofheinz observes, is not unlike the history of Irish–British conflicts which Joyce understood.[44] In *Joyce and the Invention of Irish History*, Hofheinz calls for critical attention to Vico's primary avowed purpose in his composition of the *New Science*, which is 'to construct a provincial historiography that would lay the true groundwork for the teleological explanation of political power advanced by various proponents of "natural law" philosophy'.[45] He persuasively argues that 'Joyce recognised in Vico's providential history an anatomy of modern authoritarian forces dominant since the rise of feudalism', and that Joyce's 'parodic treatment of that history in *Finnegans Wake* reflects his sensitivity to ways in which Vico's patriarchal natural law, within the providential scheme, justified England's conquest of Ireland and clarified the complex power politics beleaguering modern Irish experience'.[46] Since Joyce became Vico's 'enthusiastic' reader as early as his Trieste days in 1913–1914,[47] he must have already perceived the analogous relation between Irish historical experience and Viconian historiography before he started composing *Finnegans Wake*. The de-mythologised Cyclopean eye, I propose, is among the Viconian poetic imagining that Joyce 'absorbed' to construct his own re-mythologised historiography of Irish feudalism and nationhood in 'Cyclops'.

After the account on the appearance of the *famuli*, which 'preceded the cities, and without which the cities could not have been',[48] Vico proceeds to illustrate its significance in the development of human civilisation. As the *famuli* gather under the asylum of the heroic families to 'guard and defend each his own prince and to assign to his prince's glory his own deeds of valor',[49] there initiated feudalism, followed by the 'first intimidation of the fiefs'.[50] Vico considers the formation of arms and shields inseparable from the crucial feudal position of the *famuli*, whose alternative name, *clientes*, originally means 'to shine in the light of arms (whose splendor was called *cluer*)', because 'they reflected the light of the arms borne by their respective heroes [in their families]'.[51] He associates shields with the clearing of fields, signalling 'in the science of heraldry the shield is the ground of the arms'.[52] These first shields contain colours denoting fields of arms, the colours which, in black, green, gold, blue and red, are believed to relate to the cultivation of land.[53] And according to him, these first shields were round in shape because 'the cleared and cultivated lands were the first *orbes terrarum* [the circle of the lands]'.[54] It is in this context that Vico elucidates the *lucus*-clearing-eye analogy, and how the heroic phrase 'every giant had his *lucus*', which originally describes the act of land clearing by the giants, is misunderstood when *lucus* is mistaken to mean 'eye' instead of 'clearing'. Hence the myth of the one-eyed Cyclops, made renowned by Homer.

In the 'Cyclops' episode of *Ulysses*, the conversation taking place in Barney Kiernan's pub reaches the debate on afforestation where the gigantic tree wedding catalogue emerges. The catalogue's textual location between the 'eyes' indeed, as Sandquist contends, corresponds to the Homeric 'beam-in-the-eye' myth of the Cyclops. But in Vico's demystified philological account of the Cyclopean myth, it is not the single eye on the forehead, but rather the land clearings, that these giants have. In the tree wedding catalogue we have personified 'beams' between the eyes, but these beams, echoing the call for afforestation in early twentieth-century Ireland, act as witnesses to the country's deforested landscape as well as its afforestation propaganda. While the history of Irish woodlands, like the universal law narrated by Vico, originates with ancient land clearings under feudalism, the 'clearings' between the eyes in 'Cyclops' may correspond to a dichotomy between natural environment and civilisation, between periphery and empirical centre, or between Irish colonial history and British capitalist exploitation. It entails a more dynamic philological examination of history that originates in etymology, the origin of language, to recover the Viconian historiography which 'goes round and round to meet where the terms begin'.[55] While Vico 'looked upon language as fossilised history and sought to recover the past from the radical meanings of words', Joyce 'reversed this process and sought to create new verbal units which would embody the entire history of a theme or motif'.[56] In this way, as Vico recovers the mystification of the one-eyed Cyclopean myth, Joyce certainly makes use of the demystified *lucus* as land clearings by re-mystifying the clearing (*lucus*) with the one-eye myth of Cyclops, locating it between the 'eye's in his episode of 'Cyclops'.

Following his demystification of the myth of the one-eyed Cyclops, Vico continues to illustrate these giants' act of clearing, in association with the antagonist Vulcan. He writes: 'With these one-eyed giants came Vulcan to work in the first forges – that is, the forests to which Vulcan had set fire and where he had fashioned the first arms, which were the spears with burned tips.'[57] In Joyce's 'Cyclops', the lethal spear enters the narrative in the very beginning of the episode, when the sweeper 'near drove his gear' into the anonymous narrator's eye.[58] Later the beam-into-eye allusion reappears when the tree wedding catalogue, as a gigantic list of personified beams, intrudes into the narrative between two 'eye's. These beams, sharpened into spears, become for Vico the earliest weapons and for Homer the instrument with which Odysseus blinds the Cyclops' eye. In the Homeric myth we are familiar with,

Odysseus chars the tip of the olive pike before he and his comrades ram it into the giant's eye socket. In Viconian historiography, the charred spear is Vulcan's weapon equipped with the cleared forests to observe Jove from the cleared ground and to revolt against him. The way Vulcan burns the forest in order to set armies against Jove contrasts the Irish woodkernes, who use woodlands to secure their arms against their enemies from the time of Elizabethan conquest onwards. Yet whereas the Irish National Foresters, the non-militant nationalist society in which the fictional bridegroom of the Tree Wedding is actively involved, is not known to participate in armed nationalist activities, the society demonstrates its pro-nationalist claims in press prints and public street parades.[59] Some of its members were also involved in the 1916 Easter Rising, though due to their double membership in the IRB (Irish Republican Brotherhood), their INF identities were less known to the public. The rebellious nationalist undertone in the tree catalogue's 'woodkerne-run', therefore, is not unlike the rebellious antagonism of Vulcan, but where Vulcan resists the authority of Jove, Irish nationalists marshal their opposition against the colonial government.

* * *

III

Vico lists matrimony, together with religion and burial, as the first three human institutions of civilisation. Throughout *Ulysses* we encounter countless allusions to the Church, not to mention Stephen's much-quoted notion that he has two masters, one of them Italian, by which he means the Roman Catholic Church, and the other being the forces of imperialism in Ireland.[60] The 'Hades' episode of *Ulysses* is devoted entirely to a funeral, whose influence remains in the citizens' thoughts and conversations throughout the rest of the day. On the other hand, there is another dimension to the burial of the dead that is explicitly linked to the Celtic Revival's aspiration for ancient heroism. Such heroic aspiration is exemplified in the mock-bardic catalogue of 'Inisfail the fair' at the beginning of 'Cyclops', where, we learn, there are, in 'the land of holy Michan', 'the mighty dead' who sleep 'as in life they slept, warriors and princes of high renown'.[61] Vico believes that Roman law 'calls for burial of the dead in a proper place', therefore making the ritual of burial a religious act.[62] Furthermore, because 'by the graves of their buried dead the giants showed their dominion over their lands',[63] the burial ground becomes the site from where the genealogical tree germinates. I am not suggesting that every reference to burial or the funereal in *Ulysses* must refer to Vico's theory as elaborated in the *New Science*; however, burials in general, specifically family burials, pave the way for genealogical lineages. Vico points out that the heads of the Latin families 'called themselves *stirpes* and *stipites*, stems or stocks, and their progeny were called *propagines*, slips or shoots',[64] namely youthful branches. Hence comes the ancient heroic saying 'we are sons of this earth, we are born from these oaks'.[65]

Let us return to the tree wedding in 'Cyclops', where the act of burial is absent, but the image of an arboreal family indicative of a genealogical tree is not simply present but 'gigantically' dominant. Considering Vico's three institutions of civilisation, it is curious to notice the scarcity of the marriage ceremony in *Ulysses*, regardless of the book's numerous references to the other two Viconian 'institutions'. In fact, not only are references to nuptials generally absent in the text, the failure of marriage as an institution seems to dominate the book. One of the central storylines of *Ulysses* consists of a strained marriage which leads to the hero's reconciliation with his wife's infidelity. And neither Father Conmee's thoughts on 'the hands of a bride and a bridegroom, noble to noble, . . . impalmed by Don John Conmee',[66] nor Bloom and Stephen's mock-nuptial coupling '*to be married by Father Maher*',[67] seems to offer a satisfactory model of conjugal relationships. Indeed, the marriages mentioned in *Ulysses* are treated either with a sarcastic undertone or with a sense of failure and paralysis. Robert Spoo rightly suggests that Joyce rejects the institutionalisation of marriage in his writings as well as in his personal relationship with Nora Barnacle, whom he did not marry until 1931, after more than two and a half decades of cohabitation. For Joyce, marriage is 'complicit with an oppressive political power system',[68] which he solemnly opposed. In a letter to Stanislaus he commented on the news of Oliver Gogarty's marriage that 'Gogarty would jump into the Liffey to save a man's life but he seems to have little hesitation in condemning generations to servitude'.[69] Joyce sees marriage as a part of the suffocating patriarchal system that he, when fleeing from Ireland, had attempted to free himself from. With regard to Joyce's manifest hostility toward marriage, Spoo concludes: 'No one with opinions like these could have written a novel concluding, as Emma does, with the assurance that "the predictions of the small band of true friends who witnessed the ceremony, were fully answered in the perfect happiness of the union".'[70]

By the same token, the wedding ceremony between Jean Wyse de Neaulan and Miss Fir Conifer of Pine Valley cannot possibly be a manifestation of such an Austenian marriage with 'the perfect happiness'. Joyce does not put his tree wedding ceremony into the journalistic language of a classified board in the newspapers simply to 'reflect' or 'parody' the offerings of popular print culture. Rather, I argue, in this catalogue he intentionally adopts an articulate language alien to the quotidian speech circulated in the bar, and in this way he discloses, through metamorphoses and allusions to contemporary Irish nationalist movements and propaganda, the violence implicated in the institution of marriage, while he puts the Irish questions of law, patriarchy and language 'at the bar'.

Both Fritz Senn and Brigitte Sandquist have signalled the Ovidian metamorphoses that take place within the catalogue, transforming trees into women, the unnamed into names. Senn first observes that 'the twenty-nine wedding guests . . . have common arboreal stock, but different status (some seem to be engaged in social climbing) and linguistic genealogy, all seem to join gleefully in the Cyclopian trickery of naming, a fluctuation between nouns and names'.[71] Elaborating on Senn's earlier observations, Sandquist maintains:

> In Ovid, specific women become generalized into an undifferentiated class of trees; in Joyce's catalogue, this process is inverted – trees become personified as women. In Joyce's catalogue, common nouns for trees become proper names. A 'class' of natural objects (trees) becomes a social class, more particularly a class that designates a highly specific social landscape. The 'fir' becomes 'Miss Fir Conifer of Pine Valley', and a similar thing happens with such trees as the elm, birch, ash and olive. The transformation in Ovid's text is toward the natural and organic; in Joyce's text, the natural and organic enter a system of language and discourse. In fact, Joyce's catalogue goes even further than changing trees into women; more specifically, the trees become names.[72]

What happens in this catalogue, as Sandquist argues, is the humanising transformation of trees.[73] She sees Joyce's human-tree metamorphosis as the inversion of the Ovidian one, retaining the Ovidian violence of transformation with the violence implicit in the very act of naming. She contends that, whereas these tree-women are listed in a highly-structured social space of patriarchy, the naming and titling of the trees designates 'an elaborate root system of kinship', further evidenced by the fact that Miss Fir Conifer, our arboreal bride, is given away by her father, the M'Conifer of the Glands. 'What Joyce seems to be doing in his metamorphosis of Ovid,' Sandquist concludes, is 'highlighting the structures and implications of names, genealogical trees, and kinship systems.'[75]

Whereas I do not intend to refute the Ovidian parallel in the metamorphoses taking place in this catalogue, it might be of help to locate the transformation in another context, the Viconian one. From the myth of Apollo and Daphne,[76] Vico's *New Science* interestingly registers the same tree-genealogy comparison:

> Apollo begins this history by pursuing Daphne, a vagabond maiden wandering through the forests (in the nefarious life); and she, by the aid she besought of the gods (whose auspices were necessary for solemn nuptials), on standing still is changed to a laurel (a plant which is ever green in its certain and acknowledged offspring), in the same sense in which the Latins use stipites for the stocks of families; and the recourse of barbarism brought back the same heroic phraseology, for they call genealogies trees, and the founders they call stocks or stems, and the descendants branches, and the families lineages.[77]

For both Vico and Sandquist, therefore, human lineages, or genealogical trees, trace back to the classical folklores of mythology that transform maiden into trees. While Sandquist asserts that Joyce averts the Ovidian metamorphosis by transforming woman into tree in his tree wedding catalogue, I view the transfiguring process in the catalogue as a cyclical one. Sandquist is correct when she argues that the trees are, in this catalogue, changed into women, and even women with names and titles according to social proprieties. However, as Gibson argues, Joyce is playing with the pun when he composes the 'tree-run' of the catalogue.[78] The tree list, on the one hand, echoes the contemporary afforestation scheme; on the other hand, it implicates the more radical nationalist parades of the Irish National Foresters. Sandquist's argument persuasively supports the first denotation if we read the catalogue's tree-run as a timber-run in light of the environmental crisis in early twentieth-century Ireland. However, if we consider another level of meaning to the tree-run, one that involves the political movement of the Irish nationalists, Sandquist's theory would not work for the woodkerne-run engaged here. In this light, the tree list indeed effectually entails a cyclical process of transformation: from the humans (the woodkernes, the Foresters, or the female republicans in green costumes), to the trees, and then to the humans (the personified arboreal guests) again.

The kinship system of feudalism, which Sandquist identifies as implicated in the social column of this catalogue, reminds us of the ancient Celtic social order of classification: Brehon Law. In Brehon Law, trees were stratified into four classes according to their economic value, with seven species in each class. The highest class is called *Airig Fed*, literally nobles or chieftains of woods or trees, which is composed of oak, hazel, holly, yew, ash, pine and wild apple. The second class from the top, *Aithig Fedo* (commoners or common trees), includes alder, willow, hawthorn, rowan, birch, elm and another one, possibly wild berry. In the third class, namely *Fodla Fedo*, meaning the lower orders, there are blackthorn or sloe-bush, elder or bore-tree, white hazel, spindle tree, aspen, arbutus and crann fir, possibly juniper. Bushes such as bracken, bog-myrtle, furze or whin, brambles, heather, broom, gooseberry (or wild rose) and ivy all belong to the lowest class of *Losa Fedo*, identified as slave-trees.[79] Whereas in principle there are seven trees in each of the four classes, thus totalling twenty-eight different species of tree, the Brehon tree list actually contains twenty-nine trees, with *losa fedo* (ivy) included in the class of slaves. To account for this seemingly idiosyncratic allocation, Eoin Neeson indicates the Celtic mystic preference for certain numbers such as three, five, seven and nine. He informs us that, for instance, the Celtic fighting units 'commonly consisted of eight men plus a leader (nine) banded together into a larger unit of three of these plus another leader, twenty-eight, divisible by seven'.[80] In principle, the Celtic tree list is also divisible by seven, then four times seven, with an extra addition to make the units-digit-nine.

With this number in mind, the twenty-nine arboreal guests at the tree wedding appear like another Celtic tree list. It is worthy of notice that in the *Little Review* instalment where the tree wedding passage was first published in December 1919, there was no indication of a gigantic guest list. Only the wedding couple, along with the two maids of honour, Miss Larch Conifer and Miss Spruce Conifer, were present at the wedding. Even the father of the bride, M'Conifer of the Glands, did not make his appearance in the *Little Review* version of this chapter. In other words, Joyce did not compose the guest list until after the end of 1919. The textual notes to Hans Walter Gabler's 1986 edition of *Ulysses* indicate that the guest list was not added until placard stages three and four.[81] To put it another way, instead of his method of ramification for many of his gigantic lists in 'Cyclops', it is very likely that he added the arboreal guest names altogether into this passage within a fairly short period in October 1921.[82] This hypothesis helps us to identity the entire guest list as a whole, and its wholeness, given its numeric correspondence to the twenty-nine trees in the Celtic tree list and its stratified class structure echoing those outlined in Brehon Law, strongly suggests the guest list's suggestive reference to the ancient Celtic law. Although the tree names in the guest list do not perfectly concur with the stratified arboreal species in the old Irish tree list, many of the trees listed in Brehon Law – such as oak, hazel, holly, ash, hawthorn, rowan, birch, elm, elder, aspen and bog-myrtle – make their way into Joyce's guest names in their original or permuted forms. We have, among others, Mrs Holly Hazeleyes, whose name incorporates both holly and hazel, and the name of Lady Sylvester Elmshade contains both elm and Scots pine, which in Latin is called *Pinus Sylvestris.*

The tree wedding catalogue's resemblance to Brehon Law, however, is by no means confined to its ostensible naming or structural parallel to the old Celtic tree list mentioned above. As the popular legislative system of the society prior to the Ulster Plantations, Brehon Law essentially governed the social order in Gaelic Ireland. In the first part of this article, I remarked on the detrimental effect on Ireland's woodland resources as a result of the replacement of the Brehon Law. The renowned Gaelic chief Hugh Roe O'Donnell, the prototype for M'Conifer of the Glands, was significantly among the last Gaelic clan chieftains in Ireland. After the 1601 siege in Kinsale, which O'Donnell lost, the old Gaelic system collapsed, and Brehon Law was no longer officially in use. In the tree wedding, Joyce makes the fictionalised O'Donnell, one of the last Gaelic patriarchs, give away his daughter to John Wyse Nolan, grand high chief ranger of the Irish National Foresters (therefore representing a contemporary chieftain of Irish nationalism), witnessed by the personified tree list out of the ancient Brehon Law. Interestingly, the INF banners and other nationalist prints, which the Foresters carry during their public parades, are usually dominated by popular feminised figures of Erin. These female icons, usually accompanied by towers, wolfhounds or Celtic harps, are representative of a pure ancient 'Irish' Ireland, to which Irish nationalists and Revivalists aspire. The figure of Miss Fir Conifer on the one hand alludes to the female nationalists exemplified by the members of Cumann na mBan, and on the other she is the representative Erin on the nationalist banners and prints. In this sense, Miss Fir Conifer (in the ideal image of Erin), given away by her father (the Gaelic chieftain whose defeat at the hands of the English represents the loss of the ancient Celtic order of Brehon Law), is married to the INF high chief ranger John Wyse Nolan, whose enthusiasm for the revival of Irish culture is reflected in his mock-Gaelicised name. In fact, Joyce might have made a wordplay with the INF society here not simply in its Forester pun and its nationalist sentiment but also in its benevolent connection. Vico believes that marriage first appeared as the first kind of friendship in the world, claiming that 'the true natural friendship is matrimony'.[83] It is, in Hofheinz's words, 'a principle of connubial "friendship" within a patriarchal framework'.[84] Surely we are not to forget that the Irish National Foresters, though its public performance tends to be outwardly nationalistic, is functionally and fundamentally a friendly society. Sensitive as Joyce is to the institution of marriage as a form of patriarchal oppression, he is very likely to have paid attention to Vico's theory on the marriage–friendship assimilation. Above all, Joyce never loses his sarcastic sense of humour. Henry Flower, Bloom's alternative other, becomes 'Senhor Enrique Flor',[85] who presided at the organ during the tree wedding. Like the mock-Gaelicised name of the bridegroom, his name, too, is ironically transformed into a Portuguese one (echoing John Wyse Nolan's notion: 'As treeless as Portugal we'll be soon'),[86] not to mention that the title Senhor, meaning Lord or Sir, was originally designated a feudal Lord or Sire.

James Connolly regards the two most significant 'institutions' – class divisions and private property – as England's most devastating colonial imposition on the Brehon Law as well as on 'the communal structures of Gaelic civilisation' in Ireland.[87] He singles out the problems of class structure and property ownership as the '"neo-colonial" condition of Irish political culture' under British colonialism.[88] Like Connolly, Irish nationalists and Revivalists looked back on an ancient Gaelic culture that pre-existed the era of Cromwellian confiscations, the period in which the Brehon Law was still in practice. The tree wedding in 'Cyclops' exposes contemporary Irish anxieties regarding the conflict between the old law of feudalism and the new nationalist endeavour to recover the former by 'marrying' the much-desired past. Whereas a wedding as a matrimonial ceremony to unite man and woman is, for Joyce, a form of patriarchal oppression, the tree wedding conveys the same violence, but here removed to the level of patriarchal feudal laws. The personified tree guests from the ancient Celtic tree list in effect not so much witness the wedding ceremony as 'grace' it, thus replacing the colonial obedience to British law with a nationalistic one to the old Celtic order. For Joyce, the Irish nationalist fervour for an ideal Irish Ireland of past glory is as ridiculous as marrying an iconic Erin under the law of the fathers. The metamorphoses from ancient law to human to trees and to human again only testifies to Vico's cyclical historiography and his views on institutions from marriage to burial, and from forest to civilisation. Whether it is the trees, the woodkernes, or the women that are being metamorphosed, the violence of these patriarchal institutions remains.

* * *

IV

> The war is in words and the wood is the world. Maply me, willowy we, hickory he and yew yourselves.
>
> – James Joyce, *Finnegans Wake*, 98.34–6

> Mystery is no longer feared, as the great mystery in whose midst we are islanded was feared by those to whom that unknown sea was only a great void. We are coming closer to nature, as we seem to shrink from it with something of horror, disdaining to catalogue the trees of the forest. And as we brush aside the accidents of daily life, in which men and women imagine that they are alone touching reality, we come closer to humanity, to everything in humanity that may have begun before the world and may outlast it.
>
> – Arthur Symons, *The Symbolist Movement in Literature*, p. 5

Sandquist's argument about the tree wedding seems to run counter to a central Joycean ethic of language when she contends that 'both the Tree Catalogue and the Citizen's words are just words'. Joyce's tree catalogue is by no means 'just words'.[89] As I have elaborated at length throughout this chapter, the historical context of Irish afforestation, its thematic wordplay on the nationalistic Foresters and contemporary Irish politics, the Ovidian or Viconian metamorphosis, its reference to Cyclopean gigantism and Vico's philological historiography, and its implicit patriarchal violence of matrimony, all these issues and techniques interplay within this condensed passage on the tree wedding. If the tree catalogue is just words, then it might indeed be, like the wood to Joyce, just the world in which there are wars and words and war in words. That, in other words, makes the world, and this is the world where Vico's civilisation began: from the Cyclopean myth, the forests of the giants.

Emer Nolan specifically highlights 'the historical context of issues about law, history and government which is at stake' in 'Cyclops'.[90] In the Cyclopean eye of this episode where the forest becomes tree-run becomes woodkerne-run, the law of the fathers is transfigured into the contemporary human forms: figures of personified patriarchal law. The forest, for both Vico and Joyce, is not so much an environmental resource to be preserved, but rather the result of human appropriations that inhere in the history of civilisation and colonialism. 'Cyclops' traces a history of our relationship with the woodlands that is political, cultural and socio-historical rather than ecological, and in this Joyce demonstrates that our attempts to appropriate trees as a resource perpetually distances us from the natural world. The metamorphosis taking place within this catalogue in fact confirms, rather than defies, the distance between the human and the natural. Vico's imaginative metaphysics shows that 'man becomes all things by not understanding them' because 'when he does not understand he makes the things out of himself and becomes them by transforming himself into them'.[91] Becoming is therefore an appropriating act, an act that cannot be negotiated when nature is incomprehensible. And in 'Cyclops' the act of transformation – with the woods becoming tree-run becoming woodkerne-run becoming old Celtic law becoming tree-women guests – becomes, like the linguistic incommunicability of Myles Joyce in 'Ireland at the Bar', the manifestation of an impossible reconciliation between the history of nature and that of civilisation.

Joyce's Viconian road in *Finnegans Wake* goes round and round to where the book begins: 'riverrun'.[92] The running of river, as Rosa Maria Bosinelli indicates, 'contains overtones of the Italian word "riverrun", that is, "they'll come again"'.[93] Like the second coming of the 'riverrun', maybe the 'tree run' in the 'Cyclops' chapter's demystified 'catalogue [of] the trees of the forest'[94] also anticipates the second coming of the forest, which is the beginning of civilisation, and would, though rather ironically, see to 'A Nation Once Again'.

II

Joyce and the Urban Environment

Negative Ecocritical Visions in 'Wandering Rocks'

MARGOT NORRIS

The 'Wandering Rocks' episode of *Ulysses* is named after what we could call an 'unnatural' natural phenomenon described in the *Odyssey*: rocks in the sea that defied their weight and gravity by clashing together to the peril of boats and seamen. These oxymoronic 'wandering rocks' are obliged to serve an ironic function because their scientific impossibility conceptually challenges the assumed stability of the earth's physical foundation. Joyce criticism has inevitably translated this implication as referring to the episode's narrative and stylistic features, its function as 'the endlessly contestable and fundamentally unstable "centerpiece" of *Ulysses*', as Steven Morrison puts it.[1] But the trope's geological referent invites us not to dismiss its grounding (or un-grounding) in nature and this raises the intriguing question of how ecocriticism might help us explore the intertextual, metaphorical and narrative function of 'Wandering Rocks'. The most promising possibility is articulated in Michael J. McDowell's essay 'The Bakhtinian Road to Ecological Insight'. He writes, 'Bakhtin's theories might be seen as the literary equivalent of ecology, the science of relationships. The ideal form to represent reality, according to Bakhtin, is a dialogical form, one in which multiple voices or points of view interact.'[2] Yet this approach could be construed as merely another name for the multi-perspectival analyses that already characterise many of the readings found in the 2002 special issue on 'Wandering Rocks' published as *European Joyce Studies 12*, for example. The challenge of an ecocritical approach to the episode becomes further complicated when we try to reclaim any sort of natural referent in what is finally an urban setting that is by definition inimical to 'the intimate and vital involvement of self with place' as Neil Evernden discusses it.[3] At the same time, the nature/culture binary has itself become challenged in such works as Armbruster and Wallace's 2001 *Beyond Nature Writing: Expanding the Boundaries of Ecocriticism*, which encourages us to find ecological contexts and issues beyond the borders of writing focusing narrowly on 'nature'.[4]

This is the point where an ecocritically oriented discussion of 'Wandering Rocks' might fruitfully begin, by recognising that 'ecology must engage with urbanisation to have critical relevance in the twenty-first century'.[5] Richard Brown's marvellous discussion of the city in the episode was enlivened by the 'postmodernist cultural criticism' found not only in 'the work of de Certeau, but in that of Walter Benjamin, David Harvey, Edward Soja and Henri Lefebvre'.[6] His focus on Dublin as a 'multifarious' space can now be updated with the contemporary concerns voiced by such writers as Tim Wenzell, who begins his discussion in *Emerald Green: An Ecological Discussion of Irish Literature* by lamenting the usurpation of the Irish countryside by the city: '[A] new menace – the underbelly of this Celtic tiger – has moved from the threat of British imperialism to the threat of world capitalism and globalisation, rising across the Irish landscape in the form of urban sprawl.'[7] The landscape of Dublin had by 1904 already been transformed into a 'paved civilisation', as Wenzell would call it.[8] Is the city that is the setting of 'Wandering Rocks' therefore by definition an ecological disaster, and if so, how is its ruination of nature communicated? Certainly not directly, I would argue, but obliquely; not by what the narration shows or represents but in its depiction of sentiments, both by characters and by narrative strategy, that work in opposition to an ecologically sensitive sensibility. An ecocritical reading of 'Wandering Rocks' consequently requires an engagement with a series of anti-ecocritical world-views. Nature, or the natural, is virtually extruded in the visions of life offered by the assorted perspectives in the episode, and it is the threat of its extinction in perception that may be counted as its ecological casualty.

My exploration of this problematic construction of the episode's environment – man-made, urban and social and cultural rather than non-human or natural – will attempt to approximate a critical simulation of 'wandering rocks' by taking one view of nature, the body and place, and letting it collide with other and competing views. This strategy will begin with a disjointed analysis of a number of issues that may appear unrelated, but which can be brought into some relational focus. It is perfectly logical for an episode based on the mythical Sympleglades to evoke a marine disaster even though Jason and his

Argonauts sailed safely through its clashing rocks. Joyce, however, introduced not a fictional maritime catastrophe into the episode, but a historical one. This is the 15 June 1904 destruction of the excursion ship, the *General Slocum*, on the East River in New York. The disaster took the lives of an estimated 1,021 people, at least half of them children. Mention of the *Slocum* disaster can be meaningfully related to the fate of children in the 16 July 1904 Dublin of 'Wandering Rocks', and its echo of such earlier Irish ecological disasters as the Famine. After considering two further contrasting perils to human life – possible death under a street or under water – I will turn to pastoral landscapes that frame the episode in the imagination and the activity of the Reverend John Conmee, SJ. The outcome of these explorations will be to argue that they illuminate competing and conflicting perspectives of disaster and misery that are themselves already decimated and denatured by their inability to register the presence of nature in their conception of the living. This inability to conceptually 'ground' life in nature can be construed as itself a reenactment of perceptual 'wandering rocks'; that is, a peril to both Dubliners and, as Richard Brown has argued, to readers.[9] Ecological disaster is not only material and external, but also imaginary and internal and, arguably, 'rooted' in separations and disjunctions in perceptions of the environment.

The destruction of the steamer *General Slocum* was reported in the *Freeman's Journal* of 16 June 1904, although without the suspicion that its cause was negligence rather than simply a natural collision with river rocks. Gifford's citation of the news item mentions that 'fire broke out in the lunch room', that the crew tried unsuccessfully to put it out and that panic ensued, and that the 'Hell Gate rocks hemmed in the steamer' preventing it from turning, thus having it charge ahead until it beached on North Brother Island.[10] The *New York Times* headline of 16 June 1904 called the ship 'An Unlucky Craft', with numerous prior 'Collisions and Accidents By the Score'. But it was probably not until after a Federal grand jury indicted seven people – including two inspectors and officers of the Knickerbocker Steamship Company – that the extent of the rotted fire hoses and useless life preservers and life jackets, filled with cheap granulated cork that let children sink and drown, became known. Captain Van Schaick appears to have mishandled everything that could have minimised the loss of life, failing to stop after the fire broke out and instead running into headwinds that further fanned the spreading flames. He was eventually convicted of criminal negligence and spent three years of a ten-year sentence in Sing Sing until he was paroled. The *General Slocum* disaster is still reckoned 'the New York area's worst disaster in terms of loss of life until the September 11, 2001 attacks'.[11]

Before looking at the way both narrative and figures in 'Wandering Rocks' conceptualise and comment on the *General Slocum* disaster, it is interesting to look at the way its configuration is posed as an assault or abuse of nature and environment. The image of a ship in a body of water, going back to Greek mythology and the story of the *Odyssey,* intrinsically immerses the human or man-made in, and puts them in potentially disastrous conflict with, the natural. However, the setting of the *Slocum* disaster is a benign landscape, a reportedly calm river in clement weather transporting a ship whose fire is ignited by human or mechanical contrivance and whose sinking was produced not by rocks but by incompetent navigation and unsafe manoeuvres. Burning and drowning could be imputed to the dangerous nature of fire and water only until their cause was more precisely specified as carelessly discarded cigarettes or spilled lamp oil, and soaked cork life preservers and jackets. To an ecologically sympathetic sensibility, nature conceived as malignant in such a disaster is, in fact, maligned. And, indeed, the perceptions of Dubliners seem to put the blame where it belongs. Yet the way the disaster is criticised offers less an ecocritical judgement than its subversion. Father Conmee, learning about the *Slocum* from the newsboard of Grogan's Tobacconist shop, has this to say about the 'dreadful catastrophe in New York': 'In America those things were continually happening. Unfortunate people to die like that, unprepared. Still, an act of perfect contrition.'[12] The victims are not killed living bodies to Father Conmee, not organisms or creatures deprived of life, but souls denied the opportunity to repent before dying and thereby at risk of forfeiting their salvation. We can characterise this as an anti-ecocritical response to the disaster. Although Father Conmee is not the first Dubliner to mention the *Slocum* disaster, Bloom, who learns about it in the paper, offers a response surprisingly similar to Conmee's: 'All those women and children excursion beanfest burned and drowned in New York. Holocaust. Karma they call that transmigration for sins you did in a past life the reincarnation met him pike hoses.'[13] Bloom too de-naturalises the victims and the disaster itself and attributes it to an even more ethereal causality than the Jesuit priest, who blames neither nature, nor human incompetence, nor divine ordination for the event. Conmee instead simply characterises America as a generic producer of misfortune: 'In America those things were continually happening' – a generalisation that smacks of prejudice rather than reasoned criticism.

The *Slocum* disaster is mentioned by name a bit later in a remembered conversation between Tom Kernan and Mr Crimmins, a tea, wine and spirit merchant whom Kernan cultivates as a client for Pulbrook Robertson, his tea distributor: 'Terrible affair that *General Slocum* explosion. Terrible, terrible! A thousand casualties. And heartrending scenes. Men trampling down women and children. Most brutal thing.'[14] Although Kernan recreates for Crimmins a much more dramatic and vivid scene of chaos and suffering than Conmee, his conversational context of wanting to make engaging small-talk with a prospective client robs his account of much of its empathy. Even so, the evocation of a stampede as well as the allusion to 'spontaneous combustion' as a probable cause give his version a more grounded focus. However, in a departure from the historical information available on 16 June 1904, Kernan offers a speculation on the disaster's probable criminal cause: 'Most scandalous revelation. Not a single lifeboat would float and the firehose all burst.'[15] To Crimmins' wonder that inspectors would let a ship sail in that condition, Kernan responds with 'Palm oil',[16] a natural metaphor for the unethical social and economic transaction of bribery. In all three responses to the *General Slocum* disaster, the living and dying bodies of men, women and children are evoked only to be transmogrified into the material of either otherworldly or worldly transactions. The ecological violence of these manoeuvres consists of the rapid transformation of the biological and natural phenomenon of the event into a culturally abstracted form. This reflex stands in marked contrast to Bloom's naturalistic, if repugnant, meditation in 'Hades' on the cemetery underground as harbouring a process in which the soil, 'quite fat with corpsemanure, bones, flesh, nails' is able to renew itself:[17] 'It's the blood sinking into the earth gives new life.'[18]

Joyce makes the point powerfully that life on the planet is ever perilous by making its referent not a fictional but a real-life historical example. Insofar as the historical excursion ship disaster has reference to Ireland, it may point to that country's own worst historical catastrophe: the mid-nineteenth century 'Great Hunger' arising from the famine caused by a potato blight. The failure of the potato crop in

1845 created an ecological disaster, according to Tim Wenzell: 'As a result of this utter failure, the Irish farmer's very relationship with the earth was compromised. Those who had subsisted on this dependency were left in desolation, abandoned by both man and nature.'[19] Given the effects of nutritional deprivation and disease, children were particularly vulnerable to the potato famine's devastating effects. This vulnerability is glossed in 'Lestrygonians' by Bloom, who sees 'Dedalus' daughter there still outside Dillon's auctionrooms. Must be selling off some old furniture'.[20] Bloom deduces quickly that the girl suffers from malnutrition: 'Good Lord, that poor child's dress is in flitters. Underfed she looks too. Potatoes and marge, marge and potatoes. It's after they feel it. Proof of the pudding. Undermines the constitution.'[21] Although it affected children chiefly in western Ireland, Bloom glosses the Great Famine by alluding to a diet of mainly potatoes. But Joyce suggests that urban children in the twentieth century remained as vulnerable to hunger and the effects of nutritional deprivation as those of the nineteenth. 'Wandering Rocks' takes Bloom's concerns about the Dedalus children and dramatises them in some of its most vivid passages. Dilly Dedalus already appears ravaged by the effects of malnourishment, as even her father notices her weak posture: 'Stand up straight, girl, he said. You'll get curvature of the spine.'[22] Meanwhile Dilly's sisters come home from school totally famished: 'Boody cried angrily: Crickey, is there nothing for us to eat?'[23] There is, it turns out: peasoup begged from the Sisters of Charity in Upper Gardiner Street; 'Boody sat down at the table and said hungrily: Give us it here.'[24] The child's biological body speaks here and neither Boody's hunger nor the yellow thick soup she devours are denatured or abstracted.

Boody eats peasoup, not potatoes and marge on this day, and the ecological connection between the earth, its crops and human and animal sustenance is not specifically addressed at this moment. The potato famine does receive another earlier gloss when Mr Deasy's alarm about the possible effects of foot and mouth disease on the Irish cattle industry prompts him to write a letter to the newspapers that he enjoins Stephen Dedalus to place for him. But Deasy's concern is purely economic rather than ecological: 'You will see at the next outbreak they will put an embargo on Irish cattle.'[25] The boys who attend his Dalkey school are in little danger of hunger and malnutrition. However, another set of half-orphans are as potentially vulnerable as the Dedalus girls, namely the five Dignam children whose father has just left them a mortgaged life insurance policy. To be sure, young Patrick Dignam is still going to have porksteaks on this day of his father's funeral, and his mother and her friends and neighbours still enjoy cups of sherry to sip and cottage fruitcake to share.[26] And, to be fair, Father Conmee is abroad on the boy's behalf this very afternoon to see if he can be placed in a Christian Brothers institution where he is unlikely to starve. Except for Boody Dedalus and her sisters, the Irish children of 'Wandering Rocks' are not yet experiencing an ecological crisis and, indeed, they harbour their own anti-ecological perceptions. Although Dilly Dedalus ultimately gets some money out of her father for 'a glass of milk for yourself and a bun or a something',[27] her response is to buy a French primer rather than food for her underfed body. She is clearly following her brother's example of putting hunger of mind ahead of hunger of body. Stephen is less gratified than dismayed by her intellectual priority, which deepens his pity for her misery: 'She is drowning,' he thinks, presumably referring to the hopelessness of her general condition. 'She will drown me with her, eyes and hair. Lank coils of seaweed hair around me, my heart, my soul.'[28]

Drowning is a metaphor of suffocating misery for Stephen, and he deploys ecological metaphors elsewhere in the play of his imagination. One of these could be read as a curious gloss on the poetic name for Ireland, often called 'The Emerald Isle'. The name derives from the poem 'When Erin First Rose' by William Drennen, which grounds the jewel reference in the attributes of the island's natural environment.[29] While watching a lapidary at work behind a dusty window, Stephen remembers the origin of precious metals, bronze, silver, as well as crystals ('cinnabar') and rubies in the earth: 'Born all in the dark wormy earth, cold specks of fire, evil, lights shining in the darkness.'[30] The natural image is quickly denatured and retroped – 'Where fallen archangels flung the stars of their brows' – before being naturalised once more: 'Muddy swinesnouts, hands, root and root, gripe and wrest them.'[31] Even in the midst of metaphoric play, Stephen here actually 'grounds' the wandering rocks of gems that have found their way into culture and commerce back in the ground from which they are excavated with difficulty by dirty miners. However, 'Wandering Rocks' takes the image of the imperilled miners and transposes it to the urban landscape. The incident evoking urban miners involves a story discussed by Lenehan and M'Coy about Tom Rochford, that echoes earlier stories about

Mulligan and a boatman who saved men, including Reuben J. Dodd's son, from drowning. Rochford's heroic feat was the rescue of a man stuck in a sewer drain: 'One of those manholes like a bloody gaspipe and there was the poor devil stuck down in it, half choked with sewer gas.'[32] Rochford seems to have had himself lowered into the manhole with a rope around his 'booky's vest' which he tied around the imperilled worker, allowing both men to be hauled to safety. Even in a 'paved civilisation' like Dublin's, men are obliged to engage with the urban transmogrifications of nature. Instead of rocks shaken loose from the seabed, here men are sucked into crevices like wandering rocks returned home, in danger of suffocation by sewer gas rather than seawater.

Father Conmee, too, offers a surprising gloss – not on miners, per se – but nonetheless on workers who dig in the earth. His comments have an ecological bent to them, in the sense that he pictures a dependent and harmonious relationship between the earth, its products, and the human beings and animals who transform them into means of survival. A turfbarge is moored under the poplar trees of Charleville Mall, accompanied by 'a towhorse with pendant head, a bargeman with a head of dirty straw seated amidships, smoking'.[33] The image invokes in him a pastoral sentiment: 'It was idyllic: and Father Conmee reflected on the providence of the Creator who made turf to be in bogs whence men might dig it out and bring it to town and hamlet to make fires in the houses of poor people.'[34] Father Conmee, like the *General Slocum*, is a historical figure who, indeed, authored an actual 'little book *Old Times in the Barony*'.[35] Anne Fogarty describes the pamphlet, which was published in 1895 and reissued in 1900, 1902 and 1907, as 'an idiosyncratic but heartfelt meditation on a traditional rural world' which she identifies as Athlone:[36] 'Conmee depicts the forgotten locality in idyllic terms as a self-sufficient feudal economy, an epitome of Celtic civilisation, and an organic community undisturbed by class divisions and populated by local figures, survivors from a bygone age.'[37] The priest's vision of an Irish past is reflective of what Lawrence Buell terms 'pastoral ideology':[38] 'the idea of (re)turn to a less urbanized, more "natural" state of existence'.[39] Indeed, Anne Fogarty points out that the priest's thoughts 'consistently gravitate to the outskirts of Dublin, whether to Malahide, the shore of Lough Ennel, or Rathcoffey, a village in the vicinity of Clongowes Wood College'.[40] We last see him walking through stubble in a field, which tickles his 'thinsocked ankles' as he reads his breviary, the sky bedecked with 'a flock of muttoning clouds' and 'cabbages, curtseying to him with ample underleaves'.[41] These sentimental perceptions and perspectives offer at least an implicit critique of the effects of urbanisation on both the landscape and on the people and their children who occupy the new paved civilisation.

However, Father Conmee's ecological bent is subverted from attention to nature by his interest in aristocracy and the role of gentry in rural life, on the one hand, and on the other by his religion which complicates the secularism conducive to an ecocritical sensibility. Yet 'Wandering Rocks' may be making an even larger and more sophisticated artistic point by demonstrating Timothy Morton's provocative argument in *Ecology Without Nature* that perhaps 'nature give us the slip' in art.[42] The trope, evocative of 'wandering rocks' which give boats and sailors the slip, suggests that nature is not in any case capable of being represented per se in literature, and is inevitably denatured by the need to conceptualise, to form into images, to resort to metaphors when dealing with it. 'Wandering Rocks' makes a much more specific point than this when it represents the city and demonstrates the way the urban imagination of its citizens is obliged to contend with ecological issues. Maritime disaster, hunger and malnutrition, urban and cultural usurpation of the earth, even pastoralism reduced to nostalgia and sentimentalism, all are dealt with in ways that draw our attention to the way nature, landscape, the body all slip away even when they are imperilled and in need of attention. This point would be magnified and elaborated if it were contrasted with other conceptualisations of sea, earth, landscape, geography, the body, the animal, plant life, weather and so on, in other parts of *Ulysses*, particularly in Molly Bloom's imaginings of the solid and un-wandering rock of Gibraltar in 'Penelope'. But because 'Wandering Rocks' encompasses a much larger picture of Dublin in its purview – with the reader removed and poised at a distance that makes it possible to assess relationships and interdependencies not only among characters but also between their perspectives and that of the narrative as trained on their environmental situation – an ecocritical view of the episode's anti-ecological visions offers a valuable, contrasting insight. 'Wandering Rocks' may be a view, and indeed an overview, of the city of Dublin. But in its evocation of maritime disaster, of hunger and famine, of the mining of gems and jewels and the repair of sewers, of nostalgia for pastoral idylls, its vision rises above Ireland to envision a larger country and a larger world suffering from people's problematic relationships to their environment.

Joyce Beyond the Pale

BRANDON KERSHNER

Ecological readings of Joyce's works have not exactly flourished over the past decades, as the field was establishing itself, and for an obvious reason: unlike, say, Thomas Hardy or even George Moore, Joyce is a deeply and determinedly urban writer. His stories are entitled *Dubliners*, referring in the first place to the characters, who are mainly distinguished by the fact that they belong to a metropolitan area, a capital city even if it only sometimes assumes that status as a 'mask'.[1] In the second place the term 'Dubliner' might refer to the urban setting that is itself sketched in each story, as if any characters were secondary to the space they inhabit. *Ulysses*, famously bounded temporally by a single day, also takes place within the enclosure of Dublin – within the Pale, as it were – with only a few sketchy recollections, such as Molly's memories of Gibraltar, to evoke a different locale. It is notoriously difficult to 'place' the action of *Finnegans Wake*, but at least on one level much of the book transpires in a public house in Chapelizod. This evasion of the natural world reflects the fact that Joyce's personal experience was first suburban and then urban. Still, as Michael Bennett and David Teague point out in the introduction to *The Nature of Cities: Ecocriticism and Urban Environments*, an important critical task 'is to point to the self-limiting conceptualisation of nature, culture and environment built into many ecocritical projects by their exclusion of urban places'.[2] Joyce's limited deployment of the natural world reflects the fact that in some ways he was consciously resisting the rural/pastoral ideology that had been developed by Yeats and Æ to undergird the Irish literary renaissance. Finally, it reflects his political conviction that, for better or worse, the future of Ireland would be inseparable from the fate of her major city.

Still, this does not mean that Joyce's writing simply ignored or denied nature. To appreciate Joyce's relationship to the 'natural world' in Ireland it is important to understand that country's paradoxical attitude toward 'nature'.[3] Partially because of cultural tradition, partly for reasons connected with a reliance on tourism, the Irish have for centuries imagined their country as fundamentally rural, a place of picturesque ruins, small farms, and gorgeous landscape. Obviously, Fáilte Ireland exploits that image to this day. And yet the country – early deforested during the eighteenth century and in economic depression for most of the nineteenth and twentieth centuries – has been historically unable or unwilling to undertake action toward recovery of the very natural environment on which it depends so heavily for income and food. Today's situation is not much better. Tim Wenzell points out that

> statistically, Ireland has been ranked near the bottom in Europe on the environment, and urban sprawl is growing faster in Ireland than anywhere else in Europe. This is mainly because people can no longer afford to live in the cities of Dublin or Cork . . . and the amount of urbanised land is expected to double in twenty years. As a result, Ireland has been transformed into one of the most car-dependent countries in the world.[4]

Wenzell suggests that with the potato famine in the 1840s, a 'deep disconnection between the Irish and the natural world' arose, severing whatever organic relationship had originally existed between people and their environment in the primarily rural country. Elaborating on this idea, Catherine Maignant claims that 'in the nineteenth century, the reign of almighty History began, irrevocably putting an end to the traditional Irish social mode based on the reproductions of patterns of behavior within a dull and uniform temporal frame'.[5]

But at least from a British standpoint, the place of nature in the image of Ireland was never that straightforward. Eóin Flannery observes: 'While never civil or metropolitan, the physical and cultural topographies of Ireland did oscillate between the anemic aesthetics of the picturesque and the degeneracy of "strangeness".'[6] Of these alternatives, Yeats, Æ and their followers chose the aesthetics of the picturesque and tried to infuse it with mystery and vigour enough to inspire creative works. Both poets sought to assert a nostalgic pastoralism that was rather oddly blended with Eastern spiritualism; both Yeats and Æ believed that the key to the great mysteries could be provided through the discovery of a peasant figure from the West, perhaps a fisherman.[7] Yeats' and Lady Gregory's adaptations and translations of Gaelic poems and folk-tales similarly were meant to point the way to a kind of cultural production that would not be indebted to and thus compromised by the English literary tradition. Indeed, simply to invoke the rural West became an ideologically charged gesture. As Wenzell states:

> The importance of landscape and the natural world, for Yeats and the Irish Literary Revival, cannot be understated. For while it is generally perceived that this movement was meant primarily as a means to distinguish the Irish culture from a persistent British presence, it was the loss of a connection to the natural world that became of paramount importance for those poets who sought to reclaim that connection.[8]

Under Yeats' influence the Abbey Theatre began to project the image of a pastoral country, rooted in the romantic past. As Oona Frawley observes, 'The Abbey Theatre . . . subscribed heavily to the ideal of the landscape as the site of the glorious Irish past in its production of "peasant plays", and the peasant became the icon of real Ireland.'[9]

This rather simplified ideology was one to which Joyce could not assent. But we should note that in his poems Yeats developed a more ambiguous, less didactic version of nature, connecting it with the land of Faerie and thus with a realm of magic, the land of the dead, a world of potential unlimited self-development, self-expression, freedom from worldly responsibility and from the passage of time. This other world is also a space of transmutation between the animal and the human; in short, a place of Otherness that defines daily existence by presenting a dangerous alternative to it. The simplest and most domesticated version of this space is in poems like 'The Lake Isle of Inisfree', where the speaker asserts that he will arise and go to this microcosm of the natural world, where with bees and linnets he will lead a self-sufficient life eating beans and honey, peacefully embraced by the natural world rather than exploiting it. Of course on a realistic level Yeats is perfectly aware that the actual lake isle barely has room for a campsite, let alone agricultural space to make him self-sufficient. Still, that other space exists for him as an imaginative alternative, a counter-weight to the daily urban world of 'pavement'. Another allotrope of this visionary world is evoked in poems such as 'Who Goes with Fergus', in which the choice of joining the world of Faerie is imaged through 'deep woods', 'level shore' and the 'sea', all of which are ruled by Fergus. Again the vision is one of ultimate escape from the trials of love, hope and fear, a passage to a space in which one would be immune to the issues that inevitably plague the merely human condition.

Curiously, in Yeats' vision of Faerie, that land is more or less coterminous with the daily world, like a parallel universe that is entered through a psychological movement rather than a physical one. Still, the point of entry into the alternative world, when it is not 'going under the hill', can be through 'natural', rural actions. In 'The Song of Wandering Aengus' the speaker, in an inspired state, makes contact with a representative of the other world through a ritualistic version of fishing and catches a silver trout that changes into a 'glimmering girl'. When she calls his name, runs and fades away, Aengus begins a pursuit that will never end until he finds and kisses her in an Edenic vision of direct access to the mystical cosmos. He walks through long grass forever, harvesting

> The silver apples of the moon,
> The golden apples of the sun.[10]

This, it seems, is the 'loveliness which has long faded from the world' (mediated by a female figure) that Yeats, through Michael Robartes, desires to embrace and that Joyce explicitly rejects, through Stephen Dedalus: 'Not this. Not at all. I desire to press in my arms the loveliness which has not yet come into the world.'[11] Politically, Joyce was opposed to idealising a life that springs from the natural world, but that is nostalgically identified with the Irish past and its rural identity. In a somewhat different context, Declan Kiberd explains how essentialising a 'pure' Irish quality is regressive: '[The nationalists'] search for a pristine "Ireland" was a quintessentially English search, because it involved them in the search for a corresponding "England" as well, if only so that they might repudiate it.'[12] To a considerable degree, Yeats' vision of a mystical, de-Anglicised Ireland fell into this epistemological trap and it was one that Joyce, for all his nationalist sympathies, was determined to avoid, thus his quintessential modern Irishman, the Jewish son of an immigrant, Leopold Bloom.

So what was Joyce's vision of what Yeats and the Revival saw as the 'natural world' in Ireland and where is it found in his writing? At first glance one is tempted to deny that it has any significant role, but on further examination it appears that this is not the case. Although the stories of *Dubliners* are undeniably urban and concentrate on human actors within social situations rather than within the natural world, a number of them evoke the natural world as a kind of horizon to their action or vision. This realm is never directly confronted, but is omnipresent as a boundary to merely human actions and desires, a kind of parentheses that presents a far larger and rather darker perspective upon the various plots. Indeed, I would argue that the natural world inevitably affects the world of Joyce's stories whether or not he makes specific reference to it, much as Toni Morrison argues in *Playing in the Dark* that the inescapable presence of racial blackness in American culture has an effect even in books that make no explicit reference to it. One way or another, she argues, all 'white' American literature has no choice but to respond to the dark and abiding Africanist presence.

Whether or not the individual stories of *Dubliners* include a vision of the natural world, Joyce's 'scrupulous meanness' in presentation always suggests an amoral, animal world in which naked survival is the constant issue. In 'Eveline', for instance, Eveline's thoughts are only sporadically about Frank, the sailor who offers a potentially dangerous alternative to her miserable existence. Much more often they focus on her fear of physical abuse from her father – 'Even now, though she was only nineteen, she sometimes felt herself in danger of her father's violence'[13] – and her fear of abandoning even a dead-end job that provides her with food and shelter. Family loyalty and affection proves to be a thin veneer over the world of Darwinian struggle that haunts Eveline without ever rising to her full consciousness. It is as if the moment Eveline thinks of leaving the dull round of her daily existence and the shelter of her father's house, she will be surrounded by ravenous animals and an alien wilderness. Nor is she necessarily exaggerating the danger. This may be a dark interpretation of the 'natural world' studied by ecocriticism, but for a fearful protagonist it is an inescapable one. The clay in the story 'Clay' works similarly, however small a representative of the cold inhuman world outside it may be. Unlike all the other tokens in the game, it is 'natural', and therefore the adults all rush to suppress it and its brutally honest prognostication of Maria's future.

The two stories that I think evoke the natural world most directly and powerfully are 'A Painful Case' and 'The Dead', two of the pieces in the collection where Joyce's focus is the widest and the closest to his own intellectually informed view. Mr Duffy lives in Chapelizod, a western suburb, 'because he wished to live as far as possible from the city of which he was a citizen'.[14] He is not in the countryside, but is within reach of it, because he wants to avoid the sort of social emotional entanglement that in fact he experiences during the story. After reading the newspaper account of Mrs Sinico's death, Duffy stares out his window at a 'cheerless evening landscape',[15] including the Liffey and the abandoned distillery, both markers of the edge of civilisation and a liminal position between the urban and the rural. Duffy leaves his house, stops in a pub for a protracted drink and then wanders out to the local park. He climbs Magazine Hill, from where he can see the bodies of lovers against the park wall, taking advantage of the domestic wilderness that separates city from countryside and the licence that location affords. But instead of sexual licence, which he never sought, the darkness and the trees offer him a brutal epiphany of how far he has diverged from the path of ordinary human desires. The train with its 'fiery head winding through the darkness obstinately and laboriously'[16] certainly doesn't strike Duffy as phallic, but as a wormlike symbol of the natural decay that awaits him. By locating himself fastidiously on the edge of things, Duffy has wound up an 'outcast from life's feast',[17] unable to disguise from himself that he is subject to all the natural processes that reign over the countryside around him.

'The Dead', unique among the stories in many ways, is the tale that renders a vision of nature most concretely and powerfully. It invokes very directly the 'nativist' ideology elaborated by Yeats in the position espoused by Miss Ivors, who gently berates Gabriel for publishing in a unionist, 'West Briton' newspaper and preferring to take his holidays in Europe rather than to visit the West of Ireland. Finally, annoyed by her teasing and unable to mount a rational defence against her position, he snaps, 'I'm sick of my own country, sick of it.'[18] For his sins Gabriel will be drawn to confront a vision of the West, inspired most powerfully by his wife Gretta's memory of a boy who courted her in her youth and her romantic belief that, singing outside her gate in the cold, he died for her'. But long before this, Gabriel's attention is drawn to the outside by the ghostly tapping of snowflakes at the window. As if in response,

> Gabriel's warm trembling fingers tapped the cold pane of the window. How cool it must be outside! How pleasant it would be to walk out alone, first along by the river and then through the park! The snow would be lying on the branches of the trees and forming a bright cap on the top of the Wellington Monument. How much more pleasant it would be there than at the supper-table![19]

This is clearly a city-dweller's version of nature, a wild space that has been colonised by the urban just as his own country has been colonised by the British. But it is nevertheless constructed here in Gabriel's consciousness as a natural alternative to the superficial sociality of the party: it is cold, empty, quiet, with all the irregularities of the scene smoothed out by the omnipresent snow. Later in the evening he imagines people standing outside in the snow listening to the music from the window above: 'The air was pure there. In the distance lay the park where the trees were weighted with snow. The Wellington Monument wore a gleaming cap of snow that flashed westward over the white field of Fifteen Acres.'[20] An element of wildness has begun to creep into this description: the snow is more insistent and heavier, and the cap mysteriously flashes westward – perhaps catching the last rays of the setting sun – to the real country outside the city's borders, beyond the pale.

The climactic version of this vision comes at the story's end, after Gabriel has been confronted by his wife's love for a dead boy who represents all the passion and intensity that Gabriel lacks. He lies in bed, realising that 'One by one they were all becoming shades. Better pass boldly into that other world, in the full glory of some passion.'[21] He imagines he sees the forms of the dead, and feels his own identity fading out. The tapping at the window makes him watch the snow falling and he imagines it covering 'every part of the dark central plain, . . . the treeless hills, falling softly upon the Bog of Allen and, further westward, falling into the dark mutinous Shannon waves'.[22] At this vision 'his soul swooned slowly' and he is clearly in an altered, visionary state.[23] Certainly he has experienced an epiphany, but more than that, he has experienced a vision of raw nature in its lyrical beauty and its infrahuman coldness. Like Mr Duffy but even more intensely, his visionary experience of the natural world, linked to youth, romance, purity and even patriotic nostalgia, is also linked to the dead. It brutally presses on him the knowledge of all that is different from him and will remain so. Surely this is an example of the 'strangeness' that Ireland's cultural topography can take on when it is not seen through the lens of the picturesque.[24]

That this passage is the only extended meditation on the natural world in *Dubliners* is significant, for the finale of 'The Dead' stands as a border to the urban stories that precede it and a transitional space marking the beginning of the countryside. Gabriel's vision starts with the Wellington Monument, located near the entrance to Phoenix

Park, which for many years was the largest urban park in Europe, and is located to the west of Dublin. It ends with the snowflakes falling into the Shannon River, which traditionally marks the beginning of the West of Ireland: 'The time had come for him to set out on his journey westward.'[25] But the role of the Phoenix Park as a mediator between the purely urban and the natural is important throughout Joyce's writing. Andrew Ross points out that 'Gardens, parks, and green spaces were considered to be civilising agents, even when they were designed to evoke "wilderness", which in pre-Romantic times was associated with barbarism'.[26] For Gabriel the Phoenix Park, the site of a brutal assassination, is a transitional space before the frightening wilderness of his own country begins. And the West itself is a site both of desire and fear – the need to escape even if only through death – and of responsibility, the demand to join Miss Ivors in affirming the purity and connection with the earth attributed to the peasants. Further, as typifies urban visions of nature, it is also constructed as female, the great mothering space of earth, and thus is a fourth female figure to defeat Gabriel that evening.

A Portrait of the Artist as a Young Man Stephen does a remarkable amount of walking around Dublin but seldom even explores its borders. The references to the natural world beyond the city sometimes come in talks with his friends, as when Davin tells of returning through the countryside one day and speaking with a young woman who invites him in, thus underlining the association of the natural world with sexuality and with a female figure. In his diary, Stephen speaks of another friend travelling in the west who meets an ignorant old red-eyed peasant whom Stephen identifies as his antagonist, though he means the old man no harm.[27] But I feel that the main vision of nature is Stephen's confrontation with the 'bird girl' as he stands at the edge of Dublin Harbour watching his schoolfellows playing in the water. He looks at the river's mouth, where the Liffey joins Dublin Bay, and walks barefoot up a rivulet in the strand until he sees the girl standing midstream before him. This is all unusual for Stephen, who on this occasion wades in the water he fears and dislikes even though 'his flesh dreaded the cold infrahuman odour of the sea'.[28]

In *Portrait* Stephen's visions of transcendence tend to involve birds: the girl seems 'a strange and beautiful seabird' during this flash of intense inspiration, a girl with whom he identifies in preference to the boys swimming in the bay, and who is found midway between city space and ocean. But equally intensely, at the end of his diary, without directly invoking the idea of a bird he hears a flock of mysterious figures around him and feels that 'the air is thick with their company as they call to me, their kinsman, making ready to go, shaking the wings of their exultant and terrible youth'.[29] In both cases of transfiguration, the bird-girl and Stephen, the characters are made half-animal by verbal means rather than by the physical magic invoked in fairy tales, but the result is much the same; when Joyce means to convey the sheer power of Stephen's visions and emotions he calls upon animal imagery. Animals, especially birds, are of course an ancient means of picturing transcendence of any sort, and Irish writers such as Joyce's feminist follower Edna O'Brien often rely upon animal imagery in dramatic situations.[30] There is no space here to explore the well-worn topic of what the bird imagery implies, but I think it is important to point out from an ecocritical perspective that the 'real' girl is undoubtedly collecting mussels and cockles, and is thus intervening gently in a natural cycle; indeed, half-bird as Joyce describes her, she appears to be part of a natural cycle herself, and so inspires some jealousy in Stephen along with his erotic response and his aesthetic celebration. He has locked eyes with a figure that evokes the greater world beyond Dublin a beautiful woman who is part of nature. As such, she offers an alternative to the mystically informed old peasant sought by Yeats and Æ, with whom Stephen fears he must struggle.[31]

Cheryll Glotfelty has asserted that 'all ecological criticism shares the fundamental premise that human culture is connected to the physical world, affecting it and affected by it. Ecocriticism takes as its subject the interconnections between nature and culture, specifically the cultural artifacts of language and literature.'[32] This is exactly what we have observed Joyce representing in *Dubliners* and *Portrait*, and what he enacts more explicitly and variously in *Ulysses*. Greg Garrard rather expands this definition, arguing that 'the widest definition of the subject of Ecocriticism is the study of the relationship of the human and the non-human, throughout cultural history and entailing critical analysis of the term "human" itself'.[33] In this broader definition of ecocriticism, an analysis of *Ulysses* would certainly have much to offer. For example, the chapter 'Aeolus' explores the urban systems that sustain humanity – the trams and trains, the roads and modes of goods delivery, the sewage system through which human waste is carried to the Liffey – and all the other interfaces between the human and the non-human in Dublin 1904. The telephones and newspapers themselves could probably be fruitfully analysed as a circulation system dealing with knowledge and opinion. But here I will restrict my discussion to the interaction between characters and representations of nature in some form.

Probably the most memorable scene of 'nature' in *Ulysses* is the one on the hill of Howth, where Molly speaks her life-affirming 'yes' among the rhododendron bushes and near the stumbling nannygoat, with the sea below stretching to the horizon. Here the natural scene harmonises with the couple's erotic urges, both their sense of blossoming and their feeling of elevation above ordinary concerns, as no doubt Bloom had intended in bringing Molly there in the first place. In the book's present time, Molly in bed thinks first of the natural scenery of her native Gibraltar:

> God of heaven there's nothing like nature the wild mountains then the sea and the waves rushing then the beautiful country with the fields of oats and wheat and all kinds of things and all the fine cattle going about that would do your heart good to see rivers and lakes and flowers all sorts of shapes and smells and colours springing up even out of the ditches primroses and violets nature it is . . .[34]

Molly's thoughts turn to the idea that with so much natural beauty in the world there must be a creator, then drift to her childhood when she saw the Alameda gardens and finally to Bloom on Howth Head calling her a flower of the mountain. Not only Molly's men, but her experiences of nature tend to meld together and her intense appreciation of natural beauty is intertwined with her sense of her own sexual ripeness – past and present – and also, perhaps paradoxically, with her spirituality. Her belief that as a girl she 'was a Flower of the mountain'[35] is evidence that her boundaries of selfhood are far more permeable than Bloom's, and that she has tacitly absorbed a strongly romantic sense of potential union with nature.

In this she is far more flexible in her selfhood than is either Bloom or Stephen. Both of the men usually seem to be temporary tourists in natural scenes, whether it be Bloom remembering a school outing or both exploring the beach of Sandymount Strand. Stephen in 'Proteus' is so engaged with his speculations and other mental activity that it is difficult to determine which of his experiences are empirically 'real'. Although he does not visit his uncle Goulding in actuality, he imagines the visit so vividly that he might as well have done so; in a way, this mental visit suggests the limits of his earlier demonstration that the world is 'there all the time without you: and ever shall be, world without end'.[36] When he sees the old woman and the cockle-pickers, instead of engaging in interpersonal relations with them he is driven into elaborate fantasies about them, just as the beach itself triggers visions of Viking invaders and such. Perhaps the only natural object he confronts directly is the live dog, whom he fears, because the dead dog is merely more fodder for his symbolic imagination. Stephen converts everything else he sees around him to symbols – the sea to his mother's bile, the sand to dead language – perhaps because only here, on the border of the wild, do things hold still long enough for him to work on them. Nature is his poetic victim in 'Proteus', and the famous transmutation sentence, 'God becomes man becomes fish becomes barnacle goose becomes featherbed mountain', is a demonstration of his power rather than evidence of his engagement with the natural world.[37]

Bloom's visit to the beach is heavily mediated by the presence, both physical and narrative, of Gerty MacDowell, and this mediation affects the deployment of the natural world in the chapter. The chapter begins with the narrator (whom we soon suspect of reflecting Gerty's sensibilities) describing a scene in which the natural is intertwined with the human:

> The summer evening had begun to fold the world in its mysterious embrace. Far away in the west the sun was setting and the last glow of all too fleeting day lingered lovingly on sea and strand, on the proud promontory of dear old Howth guarding as ever the waters of the bay, on the weedgrown rocks along Sandymount shore and, last but not least, on the quiet church . . .[38]

In this world all the parts of nature love and protect one another, and they have the same attitude toward the human world as well. This is a portrait of the natural world that is nearly opposite to that of *Dubliners*, and one that would be alien to Bloom as well. One of the difficulties of evaluating the attitude of a modernist author such as Joyce is his use of multiple narrators; in this case his use seems parodic, although we are given no direct knowledge of what the author's picture of nature would be if it were independent of Gerty's narrative filter. Surely most readers will identify this vision as sentimental, nostalgic and oddly anthropomorphic in the way nonhuman objects like the sun and mountain are given human emotions and motivations. But in any case, we soon realise that any natural presence in the chapter is arranged so as to highlight Gerty herself, who is striking a pose designed to inflame Bloom and capture his attention.

We have relatively little access to Bloom alone on the beach. Like Stephen, much of what we experience in Bloom is a stream of thoughts and memories and only seldom does he interact with his environment. He does take the stick and write on the beach 'I AM A', and then decides to 'let it go'.[39] This is a nice image of the natural world as *tabula rasa,* with the additional implication that whatever man writes upon the face of nature in an effort at self-definition will in any case soon vanish. Again, Bloom's relationship to the world of the beach seems almost exactly opposite to Gerty's smug certainty of its affectionate feelings toward her. The chapter closes with a fascinating opposition between the highly artificial cuckoo clock in the priest's house and the little bat flittering about, a bat already saturated with Stephen's associating it with vampire lovers. Bloom has no powerful confrontation with the natural world here, although the encroaching sea and the strange bats haunt the borders of his thoughts and vision, darkening the tone of his otherwise matter-of-fact mulling over social things.

Stephen has a few significant confrontations with the natural world, although far fewer than we might expect of a poet, with all the romantic baggage that term carries. Bloom is more the urban man, a product of the city for whom nature is a peripheral detail, almost unnoticed. Gerty created her own sentimental version of nature as a chorus for her sexual drama. And paradoxically enough Molly, who virtually never appears outside her bed, much less her house, has a far more powerful and positive relationship to nature, even if she shares some of Gerty's tendencies to identify with its beauty and to assign it to the female gender. A novel as internal as *Ulysses* gives little direct evidence of the attitude of Joyce, as opposed to that of any of his characters, toward the natural world. The novel is mainly concerned with the city, to such an extent that nature virtually never appears unmediated in the work. But like Dublin, bounded to the south by the Wicklow mountains, to the east by the Irish sea, to the north by fields, and to the west by Phoenix Park, *Ulysses* is bounded by the natural world on all sides and we cannot read its version of the modern city without realising what all along has framed that unusual space.

It has become clear in the course of the preceding discussion that the relation between the human and the natural as Joyce presents it is often heavily gendered. In her essay 'New Directions for Ecofeminism: Toward a More Feminist Ecocriticism', Greta Gaard explores some of the critical dimensions such an ecocritical reading might entail. In particular, she suggests that 'a feminist ecopsychology would build on the early work of feminist psychologists . . . and explore the ways that a feminist relational identity is developed in conjunction with connections not just to humans but also to places, plants, and species alike'.[40] It is surely not coincidental that the climactic moments of *Dubliners*, *Portrait* and *Ulysses* all involve a male figure moving or wishing to move toward a state that he reads as feminine, and which simultaneously presents itself as linked to the natural world. As I have argued elsewhere, in 'The Dead', 'Gabriel's final "epiphany" is in fact an act of self-abasement, an extremity of Schadenfreude that enables him to identify with his wife, to take her position, and simultaneously to join the hosts of the dead'.[41] Having been seriously confronted by three women during the party and continued the confrontation with Gretta, whom he sees as 'country cute' and who is strongly linked with the Irish countryside to the west, he has surrendered his masculinist urban presumptions and moves semiconsciously to become something other. In *Portrait*, Stephen's famous epiphanic moment with the 'bird-girl' is quite explicitly framed as simultaneously a woman and an animal, and for the first time in the book her femininity has little to do with the social construction of womanhood. Stephen's confrontation is less sexual than transcendent, and he clearly regards it as a change in himself before which he is a passive celebrant. Finally, the scene with Bloom and Molly on Howth Hill (a place that ironically is now part of an urban park) mixes Bloom's rather passive sexuality with Molly's more active acts of assent, the nanny goat strewing the 'currants' of its elimination, the 'seedcake' traded from one mouth to the other and then eaten, and especially the wild surroundings and the waters of the bay far below, as Bloom calls her 'a flower of the mountain'.[42] In Joyce, the female is something that begins with the traditional association with Nature, but an ecofeminist reading might help to establish some of the ways in which the identification is dramatically different as well, in which the acts of digestion, elimination, sexuality, masculinity and womanhood wildly combine.

'Aquacities of Thought and Language': The Political Ecology of Water in *Ulysses*

GREG WINSTON

> The availability of water is the symbol of a civilized society.
>
> Charles Fishman, *The Big Thirst*

> Water does not divide; it connects. With simplicity it links all aspects of our existence.
>
> David Rothenberg, *Writing on Water*

> What in water did Bloom, waterlover, drawer of water, watercarrier, returning to the range, admire? Its universality: its democratic equality and constancy to its nature in seeking its own level . . .
>
> James Joyce, *Ulysses*

A noticeable dearth of contemporary ecocritical writing about water belies the significant presence and role of the substance in our daily lives. Water covers more than two-thirds of the surface of the globe and comprises more than half the human body.[1] The vast majority of people live in communities set in close proximity to rivers, lakes or oceans and those bodies of water have long been essential for drinking, bathing, agriculture, transportation and industry. For most citizens of contemporary, industrialised nations, water has become so ubiquitous and varied enough in its uses as to become invisible in more than just a literal sense. Most do not recognise how, directly or indirectly, water is deeply intertwined in not only the biological, but also most of the industrial and technological processes taking place at any given moment, to such an extent that even the most mundane water usage, as Alex Prud'homme aptly describes, 'sets off a ripple effect with wide and deep consequences'.[2] Simple acts like taking a drink or washing hands have far-reaching and sometimes complicated environmental impact. This is increasingly the case given the rapid, parallel shifts into a global economic climate and a global climate change, both of which cast uncertain shadows over future water access and availability in many places.

Water has become a major topic in current environmental reporting and long-form journalism. Several recent studies consider the fundamental role of water throughout history and how it will be particularly instrumental in shaping social, political and economic circumstances in the coming decades.[3] These works generally suggest that as water moves from being an abundant resource to a scarce commodity, it could exert the same level of geopolitical influence on this century as oil did in the last. Nevertheless, water has received less attention from the branch of literary and cultural studies that has emerged to address humans' relationships to their surroundings and natural resources. Despite its position at the root of many hotly debated environmental issues, it remains mostly unseen or largely taken for granted by contemporary environmental scholarship. The burgeoning subfield known as 'blue ecology' could eventually fill the gap, but to date this promising direction remains relatively underdeveloped.[4] Where it has taken shape, the aquatic dimension of ecocriticism tends to focus on maritime issues and environments rather than the decidedly less exotic issue of urban water supply.[5]

To be sure, the oceans and their resources merit attention for being, as Lawrence Buell observes in *Writing for an Endangered World*, 'the closest thing on earth to a landscape of global scope. They are also incomparably the largest commons; if there is to be "tragedy of the commons", this will be the biggest.'[6] At the bioregional level, however, the notion of the watershed has emerged as a primary identifier of local ecology and human community, and, in a true ecological sense, the interdependence of the two. All watersheds are, of course, always inextricably linked to the greater marine commons by the global water cycle. Nearly all (97%) of the 1.4 billion cubic kilometres of the hydrosphere is salt water in the oceans, of which about half a million cubic kilometres annually evaporate, desalinate and precipitate back to earth as rain and snow.[7] Joseph Conrad asserts such hydrological global interconnectedness when he has the narrator of *Heart of Darkness* ultimately characterise the Thames as 'the tranquil waterway leading to the uttermost ends of the earth'.[8] In his critical analysis of riparian fiction and nonfiction writings, Buell emphasises a key role that creative literary imagination plays in 'making watershed consciousness a potent force'.[9] While his focus is mostly on twentieth-century American regional nature writing, Buell concludes his readings of 'Watershed Aesthetics' with notable reference to one modernist Irish writer, concluding the ultimate goal for all bioregional, river writing is to honour the environmentalist's wish and 'Make the whole watershed cry out, as Joyce makes Dublin's River Liffey'.[10] As Buell notes, *Finnegans Wake* 'grandiosely mythicizes its landscape' through its multi-layered 'transfiguration' of the Liffey waters.[11] Indeed, the riverine personification of Anna Livia Plurabelle suggests the dynamic, many-voiced nature of water as a foundational substance of human life and literary expression.

The cry of the watershed can issue in various tones – from mythic to political, from cultural to spiritual – but fundamental to them all is the notion of water as a physiological necessity and key indicator of socioeconomic condition. Environmental criticism has barely begun to address the topic of water on and beneath the land, especially issues of its availability and use in urban communities. Water was the topical focus for the journal *Concentric* in March 2008, an issue that juxtaposed literary criticism with creative non-fiction journalism and memoirs. In his segment of the editors' introduction, Scott Slovic remarks on the importance of environmental scholarship 'not only . . . about water as water, but about how water expresses itself in the world and in doing so satisfies the needs of human beings and other beings'.[12] The five critical essays included in the issue engage in meaningful interpretations of literature but keep mainly to the established parameters of blue ecology that privilege marine and riparian environments and considering water chiefly as psychological or cultural signifier. Ecocriticism might venture further in considering some of the important questions of water as a common public resource and, increasingly, an economic commodity. Issues of water access, distribution and consumption are closely tied to those of justice, equity, human rights and environmental sustainability. Writing from diverse periods and places can provide an effective frame for seeing water in this context. Given the water crises now confronting many areas of the globe, from Atlanta to Australia, from Baja to Bahrain, an environmental literary scholarship concerned specifically with questions of water resources would appear essential and timely for the early twenty-first century.

A logical starting point for such a critical project is the literature that straddled the turn of the twentieth century, when public availability and access to water had become a defining feature of urbanism and modernity. Massive public reservoirs, diversion canals and transport systems ushered in what Charles Fishman dubs the 'golden age of water' starting in the late nineteenth century, as the resource became relatively inexpensive, readily available and seemingly limitless in most industrialised nations.[13] To gain an understanding of water as a key social and political factor both today and a century ago, it is worthwhile to revisit classic literary texts whose own creation coincided with or followed closely upon those of the first large-scale water works. Seeing what this new access and convenience meant to some of those consumers can help us recapture the meaning of water and render it more visible in our daily lives. Tracing water's course through literary works that have previously benefited from scant ecological interpretation, or none at all, can contribute to an expanded awareness of the world, the text and the resource in question.

Reading water resources in this way can also contribute to the evolving critical project of literature-and-environment studies. To revisit familiar and canonical, yet also environmentally neglected, texts in this manner is to follow Glen Love's recommendation to apply an ecocritical approach to 'memorable literature' by 'shifting attention from the anthropocentric to the biocentric'.[14] A number of critics in the last decade have begun to reconsider canonical works not previously considered nature writing or predominantly about environmental issues, marking the emergence of a second wave of ecocriticism.[15] The expanded scope is underscored by Robert Kern's assertion that 'ecocriticism becomes most interesting and useful . . . when it aims to recover the environmental character or orientation of works whose conscious or foregrounded interests lie elsewhere'.[16] Perhaps those interests appear to lie elsewhere due to longstanding critical trends and perceptions. In this sense, it is worth considering how Buell explains his own shift to a second-wave approach:

> Once I thought it helpful to try to specify a subspecies of 'environmental text', the first stipulation of which was the fact that the nonhuman environment must be envisaged not merely as a framing device but as an active presence, suggesting human history's implication in natural history. Now, it seems to me more productive to think inclusively of environmentality as a property of any text – to maintain that all human artifacts bear such traces, and at several stages, in the composition, the embodiment, and the reception.[17]

The temporal markers 'Once' and 'Now' delineate the shift from first- to second-wave approaches embodied in Buell's studies *The Environmental Imagination* (1995) and *Writing for an Endangered*

World (2001). The premise of the latter book, that an environmental stamp can be detected 'on all human artifacts', offers an encouraging challenge for environmental critics to apply their thinking to hitherto unlikely texts.

Modernism – often regarded as a cosmopolitan literary movement distanced from or even antagonistic to nature, more concerned with man's place in the metropolis than his role in the biosphere – offers a compelling array of creative works for the urban orientation of second-wave ecocriticism. One ideal text in the modernist canon to reconsider through an environmental lens is Joyce's *Ulysses*. As environmental criticism encourages expanding the scope of the field to works with less overt environmental content, Joyce's novel of the city offers a prime opportunity. Buell considers the book, or parts of it at least, alongside Whitman's 'Crossing Brooklyn Ferry' and Woolf's *Mrs. Dalloway,* as belonging to a 'still relatively scant and fragmented' genre of 'urban bioregional imagination'.[18]

Urban nature, if previously an oxymoron, for second-wave ecocriticism has become increasingly fertile critical ground.[19] Karla Armbruster and Kathleen R. Wallace argue, 'One way ecocriticism can and should widen its range of topics is to pay more consistent attention to texts that revolve around . . . less obviously 'natural' landscapes and human attempts to record, order, and ultimately understand their own relationships to those environments.'[20] Tuning in to this reality of nature in its complex relation with the built environments and altered landscapes of human development has, for a planet facing environmental crisis, become arguably more important than experiencing nature in a pristine or romanticised wilderness setting. It is at the interface of urban growth and natural resource use that ecocritics can consider how literature depicts the interconnectivity of people, their surroundings and their environmental resources that are the essence of ecological awareness.

Among its many feats of imagining nature and city ecology, *Ulysses* reflects upon the novelty and importance of supplying water for large-scale urban use as well as the social and economic disparities that can flow with it. This occurs, following a myriad of watery images and associations through the course of the day, with Leopold Bloom's turning of his kitchen tap in 'Ithaca'. The action triggers a sustained meditation on the specifics of the Dublin city water system as well as the general physical properties of water. It is one of many moments in which Joyce's fiction concerns itself with water but arguably the most pragmatic and political for its concern with questions of human water use. Among other things, the moment explores how the dissemination of water conveys notions of power and community, and in doing so, brings to the surface some of the pressing social and moral questions that defined early twentieth-century Dublin, if not all cities and societies everywhere.

Joyce scholarship has viewed water in *Ulysses* as an aesthetic trope or metaphoric conceit as well as a source of historical and cultural insight.[21] Most recently, considering Joyce's writing in the context of public infrastructure and political economy, Michael Rubenstein argues how the 'Ithaca' waterworks passage 'struggles . . . to transcend disconnectedness' in the postcolonial modernisation of the Irish Free State.[22] Along with city sewers, gas lines and electricity grids, the public water system in the novel establishes a mimetic description of a 'social sublime' that embodies an integration of art and engineering in the province of public works to which the modernist novel and the modern city waterworks belong.[23] Still, beyond the notion of infrastructure and social connectivity, there is the water itself. The rest of this essay will consider how Joyce's depiction of an essential resource and a disputed urban commodity constructs an ecological perspective on water that subsumes its diverse biological, socioeconomic and legal significations. Among numerous natural-resource topics in *Ulysses*, including forestry, agriculture and energy production, the description of water in 'Ithaca' emphasises the technological achievements, political divisions and social cohesion surrounding the public water supply in early twentieth-century Dublin. *Ulysses* encourages a comprehensive perspective on the natural resource, a sense of political ecology that resonates a century later, as water availability becomes one of the most pressing global concerns in our own time.

Joyce and Water

Water is general all over Joyce. It occurs in its free-flowing, natural state, as rainfall, river and ocean, and in harnessed form, as civil-engineering marvel and kitchen convenience. Water in Joyce's fiction is physical and pragmatic, technical and scientific, social and political; it is also spiritual and mythic, represented for its powers to preserve life and to take it away. Water courses through his works as setting and character, image and symbol, style and form. It even gives rise to the phrase most often used to describe Joyce's revolutionary narrative technique: stream of consciousness. Indeed, water is so ubiquitous in Joyce that there is hardly the space here to contain every allusion to it, but the following samples will give a sense of its abundance. In frozen form, water falls faintly over the Irish landscape and taps hauntingly at the windows of the Gresham hotel in 'The Dead'.[24] Earlier in that story, water is behind Gabriel's nagging insistence that Gretta wear galoshes to protect herself from the winter damp and part of Gretta's sad recollection that Michael Furey might 'get his death in the rain' of Galway.[25] Water also figures prominently in *A Portrait of the Artist as a Young Man*, in the childhood of Stephen Dedalus, who learns early the connection of a wet bed with warm life and cold mortality.[26] It is there in his schooldays, in the rat-infested moat beside the playing fields, whose cold slime ultimately lands Stephen in a feverish state in the infirmary, and in the more tranquil association with the springtime sounds of Clongowes cricket bats, which Stephen's onomatopoetic mind likens to a melodious tone of water: 'pick, pack, pock, puck: like drops of water in a fountain falling softly in the brimming bowl'.[27]

The experimental language of *Finnegans Wake* begins with the portmanteau word 'riverrun', a compound that – orthographically, grammatically and syntactically – depicts the dynamic chemical and physical properties of water.[28] The unpunctuated ending of the book sends the reader back to the beginning, not unlike a molecule of water tracing a structural loop in the eternal return of the water cycle. The most vocal element in that cycle resonates in the ten instances of one-hundred-letter words for thunder that appear across the work.[29] By the final section of Part I, water is essential for the mythic washerwomen, transformed to tree and stone 'beside the rivering waters', and of course in the spirit of the Liffey and final monologue of Anna Livia Plurabelle, which embody the multi-dimensional and sacred nature of the substance credited by ancient myth and modern science alike with the power to originate and sustain life.[30]

Water also figures prominently in *Ulysses,* as befits the modernist reworking of a Homeric epic that revolves around the realm of Poseidon. As Joyce distils Odysseus' decade of ocean wandering to a day in the life of the modern city, liquid references abound. Water remains an essential fact of human life spanning the gulf of four millennia that separates Joyce from Homer, and a chemical compound of both practical and poetic concern to Leopold Bloom, Stephen

Dedalus and other Dubliners. The seaside perspective of 'Telemachus' sets the parameters of water as human origin and ultimate end. Buck Mullligan and Stephen Dedalus regard the sea variously as 'snotgreen', 'scrotumtightening' and, recalling the Algernon Charles Swinburne poem 'The Triumph of Time', as 'great sweet mother'.[31] Soon after, to Stephen's mind, Dublin's 'ring of bay' becomes a 'dull green mass of liquid' that triggers a memory of the bile-filled bowl next to his mother's deathbed.[32]

In 'Proteus' – the very title suggests the divine, transformative nature of an ocean deity – the sea is associated with maternity as well as mortality. As Stephen walks the dynamic littoral zone of Sandymount Strand, seeing midwives and corpses, his imagination is driven by the cycles and detritus of the tides while offshore a coast guard ship tacks across the bay in search of a drowning victim. Thoughts of what T.S. Eliot in *The Waste Land* calls 'death by water' are suffused with nautical terms as well as poetic allusions to Shakespeare and Milton: 'Five fathoms out there. Full fathom five thy father lies. At one he said. Found drowned. High water at Dublin bar. Driving before it a loose drift of rubble, fanshoals of fishes, silly shells. A corpse rising saltwhite from the undertow, bobbing a pace a pace a porpoise landward. There he is. Hook it quick. Pull. Sunk though he be beneath the watery floor. We have him. Easy now.'[33]

'Calypso', by contrast, shows water as integral to making life bloom on land. Reading the promotional flyer for Agendath Netaim planters' company, Leopold Bloom thinks of water scarcity and the need for 'artificial irrigation' in the 'waste sandy tracts' of the Levant, then imagines the inhospitable conditions of 'the dead sea: no fish, weedless, sunk deep in the earth'.[34] In the next episode, he seeks out the physical comfort and meditative tranquillity of water in the 'mosque' of the Turkish bathhouse: 'Enjoy a bath now: clean trough of water, cool enamel, the gentle tepid stream. This is my body.'[35] At the Holles Street hospital in 'Oxen of the Sun', water suggests life and procreation, when the theme of gestation culminates in the meteorological description of air 'impregnated with raindew moisture, life essence celestial, glistening on Dublin stone'.[36] Later in the episode, the chemical formula for water appears in the barroom request of 'Some H_2O for a gent fainted'.[37] The holy chemical trinity of two atoms of hydrogen linked to one of oxygen mirrors the bond shared by the three main characters in the novel, as well as the tripartite division that makes their stories and identities distinct yet connected.

Of all the aquatic moments in *Ulysses*, however, the most direct and sustained comes with Bloom's simple act of turning the tap to wash his hands and make two cups of 'Epps' soluble cocoa' in the early hours after Bloomsday.[38] The action bookends with his morning tea-making in 'Calypso', yet, beyond mere structural symmetry, this ordinary gesture prompts an extraordinary reflection on water and the modern city that remains as relevant now as when it was written. Filling the iron kettle at his kitchen sink, Bloom utilises a technological innovation that was at the time a novelty for most Dubliners. As we know from the presence of outhouse and chamber pots, Eccles Street does not have indoor flush-toilets, but it does have the relatively recent luxury of an indoor water tap. At thirty-eight, Bloom belongs to a generation that would remember the time before water became directly available inside most middle-class Dublin houses. Therefore, it is not surprising that Bloom's thoughts turn to extended meditation and admiration of the source of the water coming from the faucet:

> Did it flow?
>
> From Roundwood reservoir in county Wicklow of a cubic capacity of 2400 million gallons, percolating through a subterranean aqueduct of filter mains of single and double pipeage constructed at an initial plant cost of £5 per linear yard by way of the Dargle, Rathdown, Glen of the Downs and Callowhill to the 26 acre reservoir at Stillorgan, a distance of 22 statute miles, and thence, through a system of relieving tanks, by a gradient of 250 feet to the city boundary at Eustace bridge, upper Leeson street . . .[39]

While the passage speaks of water, in Joyce's typically self-reflexive fashion, the question of its flow might apply just as readily to the writing on the page as to the water in the pipe. In the ensuing response, Joyce's prose most certainly *does* flow unimpeded, redirected only by the occasional comma, much like the city water supply cascading down the Wicklow Mountains via catchment basins, pipes, tunnels and tanks. The detailed course Bloom traces for Dublin water was the city's first modern project for water storage, treatment and transport. Its construction in the 1860s was unprecedented in size, scale and expense for Ireland at the time. Joyce's sustained allusion to the Vartry waterworks shows respect for the engineering feat while confronting some of the political tensions, social inequities and civic responsibilities that flowed along with this essential natural resource.

Liquid Assets: The Vartry Scheme

Throughout the medieval and early-modern periods, Dublin, like other cities, drew its water directly from the many area rivers and streams, including the Liffey, Dodder, Tolka, Camac and Poddle. The earthworks and quays of Viking-era Dublin contained Liffey flooding and diverted several lesser streams. By the late eighteenth century, an elaborate canal-and-basin system had taken shape, built primarily for drainage, transportation and trade, but also to serve the drinking and bathing needs of area residents. The advent of bacteriology in the mid-nineteenth century brought awareness of the importance of clean municipal water to public health.[40] Increased demand in Dublin led city officials to seek out a supply from more distant sources. Following passage of the Dublin Corporation Water Bill in Westminster on 21 July 1861, the Corporation considered several options for building a reservoir and aqueduct system. Geographic proximity and political pragmatism made the River Vartry in the Wicklow Mountains the optimal choice. The Corporation obtained 550 acres near Roundwood, County Wicklow, about seven and a half miles from the Vartry headwaters, and the following year began construction on the so-called Vartry Water Scheme, whose course and cost are so precisely recounted by Bloom in 'Ithaca'.

The Vartry Scheme began with construction of two Pennine-style earthen dams to create the Roundwood Reservoir, into which the waters of the Vartry were first diverted through an eduction tunnel in June 1863. Two distributing reservoirs covering an area of twenty-six acres and containing forty-three million gallons were built on the outskirts of the city at Stillorgan, from which water flowed to Dublin through a twenty-seven-inch diameter main, entering the city centre at Eustace Bridge on Leeson Street. Over the twenty-two miles from Roundwood to Stillorgan, the water travelled the course Bloom describes, through filtration beds and multiple relief (or surge) tanks designed to prevent the dangerous pressure buildup known as a water hammer. At Roundwood, the water entered thirty-three- and forty-eight-inch pipes, the first being the city water supply, the second serving as an emergency drainage sluice for managing the reservoir level. Water moving through the thirty-three-inch pipe flowed first through the treatment system consisting of initially seven, and later ten, sand-lined filter beds designed to catch large particles of suspended debris. The slow-sand filtration system, rare for cities and towns at the time, turned out to be effective as well in trapping some microbial forms even before much was known about their role as agents of disease.[41]

From the filtration beds, the water travelled two and a half miles underground to Callowhill through a tunnel six feet high by five feet wide that took three and a half years to build. The Roundwood–Callowhill tunnel was by far the most ambitious segment of the Vartry project. Using the best technologies available, the tunnel miners averaged less than four feet of progress per week chiselling and drilling the hard granite to connect a series of twenty-one vertical shafts set at intervals of 600 feet along the route.[42] At Callowhill the thirty-three-inch pipe resurfaced to bring the water down from the mountains seventeen miles to the distributing reservoirs at Stillorgan. It entered the city through two twenty-seven-inch mains to Eustace Bridge, Leeson Street and a series of valves at the city centre for subsequent local distribution. In addition to serving city water needs, the Vartry Scheme supplied the southern suburbs including Dalkey, Bray and Kingstown (Dun Laoghaire). By completion of this initial infrastructure in 1868, Dublin boasted a public water system that, both for its engineering achievement and benefits to public health, rivalled many found in Europe or America. Leopold Bloom was certainly not alone in his admiration of this civil engineering feat.

The Vartry Scheme was due in large part to the efforts of Sir John Gray, who served as chairman of the Dublin Corporation Waterworks Committee from 1863 until his death in 1875. During that time Gray was both politically instrumental and financially integral to the success of the project. As Waterworks Committee chairman and a former MP with strong political connections, he advocated legislation for public water and helped mount a defence against parliamentary opposition to the Water Bill at Westminster. Once the political ground was prepared, he quickly purchased the land for the Roundwood reservoir and deeded it to the Corporation 'at no profit to himself', moving on it before land speculators could act on news of the project and drive up the price of the acreage.[43] A Dublin physician, Gray no doubt took a medical interest in the benefits clean water would have for preventing further outbreaks of cholera and typhus, water-borne diseases which had ravaged the country during the Famine. He was a moderate nationalist, with ties to Daniel O'Connell as well as William Smith O'Brien and the 1848 Young Ireland movement; from 1841, Gray was also owner and publisher of the *Freeman's Journal*, where of course Joyce has Bloom employed as an ad canvasser. Thus, in more than one sense, Sir John Gray is responsible for the liquidity of Joyce's main character.

In 1879, a statue of Gray by Sir Thomas Farrell, a sculptor of the Royal Hibernian Academy, was raised on the median of Sackville (now O'Connell) Street, near the intersection with Abbey Street, close by the offices of the *Freeman's Journal*. It is one of the public landmarks by which the mourners pass in their carriage ride to Paddy Dignam's funeral.[44] The statue also appears in 'Aeolus' where Joyce suggests Gray's association with water by referring to its location as 'sir John Gray's pavement island'.[45] The inscription on the base of the monument reads in part: 'Erected by public subscription to Sir John Gray Knt. M.D. J.P., Proprietor of The Freeman's Journal; MP for Kilkenny City, Chairman of the Dublin Corporation Water Works Committee 1863 to 1875 During which period pre-eminently through his exertions the Vartry water supply was introduced to city and suburbs'.[46] City engineer Michael Moynihan said of the statue in 1931 that 'the citizens of Dublin have raised a noble monument to the memory of Sir John Gray. It was nobly earned, for to him is due the Vartry supply of water to our city.'[47] He was honoured at the starting-point of the Vartry works as well: in 1881, to commemorate the twentieth anniversary of the Water Bill, a bust of Gray, also by Farrell, was unveiled at the Vartry Lodge, beside Roundwood reservoir, in the heart of the land he had helped secure for the project.

While Gray's philanthropic real estate deal undoubtedly helped make the Vartry project possible, it also illuminates the dependency of society on private wealth and charitable work in order to serve one of its most basic needs. Gray's part in the project is a reminder of the socioeconomic challenge of allocating a natural resource like water, particularly when that resource and the land on which it is found are increasingly regarded as commodities guided by the forces of the marketplace. Parke Neville, MP, sponsor of the Water Bill and author of *A Description of the Dublin Corporation Waterworks* (1875), remarked at the completion of the Vartry Scheme that 'every part of the city is now effectively supplied with water, and the service affords universal satisfaction'.[48] Yet, in reality, the benefits were not felt as universally as Neville's statement would suggest.

The Vartry scheme, along with dozens of similar nineteenth-century urban water projects, belonged to what Charles Fishman calls the 'first water revolution'.[49] It marked the start of a period that saw improved public health and extended life spans, and that accelerated industrial growth and technological innovation.[50] *Ulysses* salutes such benefits with its lengthy account of the versatile nature and diverse applications of water. Bloom's admiration is couched in terms that are as much social and political as they are chemical and biological. Alongside a litany of scientific facts – for instance, the volume and density of water as well as its proportional presence on the surface of the earth and in the human body – Bloom's admiration of the substance assumes a number of subjective and anthropomorphic expressions.[51] The 'waterlover' loves it for a number of qualities that suggest proper social interaction and just political representation, the same causes he articulated a few hours earlier for the hostile audience in Barney Kiernan's. Among the list of appealing qualities Bloom attributes to water are: 'Its universality: its democratic equality and constancy to its nature in seeking its own level.'[52] As Ariela Freedman argues, 'water is anything but universal here. It belongs to a particular time, place, and mode of passage, is measured and collected, transmitted and received.'[53] The word choice also offers a striking similarity with Parke Neville's early claim about the indiscriminate social benefits of the Vartry scheme.

At the same time, it raises concerns as to whether such goals are tenable or compromised by the social and political disparities that emerge around this public water supply intended to afford in Neville's words 'universal satisfaction'. Despite this equitable aim, water tended to amplify economic differences. In this regard, Dublin was much like other European and American cities completing the first large-scale modern municipal water systems around the same time. In his environmental history of the twentieth century, J.R. McNeill notes the increasing socioeconomic disparities around the new public water systems:

> The uneven history of the provision and treatment of urban water after 1880 was a case of escalating distinctions between the haves and have-nots. Those who had clean water and good sewerage got it because they were comparatively rich, and getting it made them healthier and richer still. Those who lacked it, lacked it mainly because they could not afford it, and lacking it made them sicker and poorer still. Economists use the

> term 'increasing returns' to describe situations in which the more you have the more you get. The increasing returns generated by investment in clean water helped to create, and widen, the cleavages in wealth and health that characterize the world today.[54]

In this regard, it is worth noting how Bloom's reflection on water also features personifications of some less egalitarian tendencies. Like human beings, water can demonstrate a kind of overzealous political ambition, as seen in 'its *indisputable hegemony* extending in square leagues over all the region below the subequatorial tropic of Capricorn' or a distorted theocratic egoism, via 'its *infallibility* as paradigm and paragon'.[55] Both of these traits might find self-correcting remedy in 'the *multisecular stability* of its primeval basin'; even the description of water's chemical formula, emphasising 'the simplicity of its composition, two constituent parts of hydrogen with one constituent part of oxygen', sounds as though it were lifted from a political science lecture or committee-room strategy session.[56] In absorbing the social shocks of anti-Semitism and adultery, Bloom admires as well some physical traits of water that speak to psychological turmoil, fortitude and resilience, including 'the *restlessness* of its waves and surface particles', 'its *subsidence after devastation*', and 'its *imperturbability* in lagoons and highland tarns'.[57] Water represents an ideal and desirable chemistry for human society, a hope for mending the imperfect or unsatisfactory relations Bloom has experienced through the course of the day.

Water Pressures

Alongside this gushing account of water's remarkable properties comes the paradoxical sense in 'Ithaca' that water, now a newly available public resource, has become a more legalised and commoditised property. While Bloom praises the human expertise that can supply water to his city, he also sees the socioeconomic tensions that flow with it. These are made particularly prominent through Joyce's account of a fictional water shortage described in conjunction with an actual lawsuit concerning excessive water consumption by residents of a housing facility for the poor. The narrative voice of 'Ithaca' imagines a shortage (the summer of 1904 was in fact fairly typical as far as rainfall) and conflates it with an actual legal action by Dublin Corporation, when

> from prolonged summer drouth and daily supply of 12½ million gallons the water had fallen below the sill of the overflow weir for which reason the borough surveyor and waterworks engineer, Mr Spencer Harty, C.E., on the instructions of the waterworks committee had prohibited the use of municipal water for purposes other than those of consumption (envisaging the possibility of recourse being had to the impotable water of the Grand and Royal canals as in 1893).[58]

As the seemingly infinite supply from the Roundwood Reservoir reached its limit, those in charge of the Vartry waterworks were faced with enforcing strict domestic water rations. Joyce's parenthetical reference to a summer 1893 shortage recalls the decision of the Waterworks Committee in that year to augment public supply by having the fire brigade draw from the Fifth Lock works of the Grand Canal on the south side and from the Blessington Street Basin of the Royal Canal on the north side. The use of water from these sources harkened back to mid-century when they served as the regular city supply. Still, public awareness of the safer, filtrated water suggested a reluctance to revert to prior sources whose cleanliness seemed to be in doubt. While the Committee deemed the canal water 'safe and unexceptionable',[59] clearly the narrative voice of 'Ithaca' disagrees, regarding it as 'impotable', as presumably did a number of city residents who had come to trust and depend on the Vartry supply.

Even apart from shortages real or fictional, public water was a tightly controlled business for the city of Dublin. Domestic water usage was monitored by City Engineer Spencer Harty (named in the 'Ithaca' waterworks passage) and his team of inspectors whose task it was to verify that households stayed within prescribed limits by ensuring that all homes were equipped with regulation half-inch fittings. The latter ensured safe pressure levels for the new system and also limited the quantity delivered to each house, especially in times of water scarcity. In addition, during the 1904 shortage the Corporation set a daily ration of eighteen gallons per person for domestic use. The typical daily draw from the Vartry system was 12,500,000 gallons for approximately 330,000 city residents, or about forty-two gallons per person.[60] Everyone in Dublin would have felt the impact of such a required cutback in usage. Along these lines, the Corporation's authority to dictate water usage led to controversial legal action against a charitable organisation, the

South Dublin Guardians, who operated the South Dublin Union, a workhouse and residence for the area's poor.

Prior to the Vartry scheme, the Canal Companies provided water free of charge for the several thousand workhouse residents. Upon completion of the Vartry works, the Dublin Corporation Waterworks Committee required revenue from all users to help absorb the cost of construction, which totalled £620,000, or £1 17s 6d per person in the Dublin region. In addition to water rates for city residents, the Committee opted to assess usage and levy fees for the poor by charging the non-profit organisations that housed them. It negotiated a contract with the Guardians board for the South Dublin Union at the rate of 4d per thousand gallons, which by 1897 amounted to £510 per year.[61] The growing financial burden for the Guardians set the stage for hostile litigation.

The case referenced in *Ulysses* shows how a public utility could be just as ruthless as a private enterprise in its management of water resources. In the spring of 1904, the Dublin Corporation accused the South Dublin Union of overconsumption by maintaining a six-inch pipe in the facility from as early as 1898. The Corporation filed suit to collect damages for what it deemed excessive usage by the Guardians. For their part, the Guardians countered that a half-inch pipe, sufficient for households, even if left running day and night could only supply the needs of 312 persons, or fewer than one-tenth of the 3,500 to 4,000 people in residence at the workhouse. The case was heard by the Lord Chief Baron and the Judges of the King's Bench Division, and ultimately reached the nius prius Court of Appeals in the first week of June 1904. The *Irish Daily Independent* reported that after three days of argument concluded, a verdict was reached on 8 June ordering the Guardians to pay the Corporation 'for damages to be calculated on the difference between the amount allowed for domestic purposes, estimated at eighteen gallons a head for the time being, and the amount actually ascertained by meterage, the period to be calculated from the 1st January '98 to the present date'.[62] The settlement was to be carried out 'without prejudice to the future rights of the parties', and the presiding judge, Justice Gibson, sought to re-establish their cooperation by suggesting 'it would be a good thing if the Corporation and the Guardians, by a small Committee of three or four gentlemen on each side, would have a conference and try to adjust the matter for the future'.[63]

Even after the verdict was in, the two sides continued to argue the case in the court of public opinion. In a letter to the editor that ran in the *Irish Independent* on 10 June, Gerald Fitzgerald, solicitor for the South Dublin Union Guardians, blasted the coverage in the paper the previous day, saying it 'was calculated to produce a false impression as to the result of . . . the costly litigation between the Corporation and the defendants'; he pointed to the total cost of £1,200 to the Corporation in order to recoup damages from the Guardians, an amount that far exceeded the £700 owed for excess water consumption.[64] Five days later the Corporation Law Agent Ignatius Rice would counter that the Guardians had put the entire city water supply at risk through its action. The rhetoric of his response seized on the very notion of guardianship, public responsibility, and civic authority:

> The Corporation are the guardians of the public water supply and, if the other public bodies and persons were to act as the Guardians have done, supply to the inhabitants would be seriously injured, as well as the supplies to the Corporation for public purposes and to the townships.[65]

The *Irish Independent* literally undercut this high-minded claim by following Rice's letter with an editor's note that blasted Rice for failing to address 'the astounding charges' of wasting taxpayer money: 'As this correspondence cannot be prolonged we think it right to point out that the above letter appears to us to be no answer at all to that of the solicitor of the Board of Guardians so far as the unfortunate ratepayers of Dublin are concerned.'[66] The editor put the issue to rest with a defence of taxpayer interests that spared little for either side: 'It is surely time to put an end to this shocking waste of public money. The notion that anyone except the lawyer can profit by it is too ludicrous for refutation.'[67]

This legal dispute surfaces in the water passage of 'Ithaca', including overt mention of Rice himself:

> particularly as the South Dublin Guardians, notwithstanding their ration of 15 gallons per day per pauper supplied through a six inch meter, had been convicted of a wastage of 200,000 gallons per night by a reading of their meter on the affirmation of the law agent of the corporation, Mr Ignatius Rice, solicitor, thereby acting to the detriment of another section of the public, self-supporting taxpayers, solvent, sound.[68]

While Bloom's figure for the daily water ration is off by a few gallons, the rest of the account is accurate in its listing of facts and public figures. It offers an insightful, artful assessment of the case when, for instance, the description of taxpaying public puns cleverly on the physical, financial and geographic significance of water. As common fiscal and legal descriptors, the paired terms 'solvent, sound' double as aquatic terminology to reference a major chemical function of water as well as a geographic feature formed by it. Furthermore, the extended flow of the final lengthy modifying clauses generates a telling grammatical ambiguity, one that leaves the reader to wonder whether it is Ignatius Rice and the Corporation, or the South Dublin Guardians, or both, who have been 'acting to the detriment of . . . taxpayers' in the case. Is it worse to overuse public water to support the poor or to squander public money in prosecuting such use? Siding with the ratepayers above either party in the dispute, the voice of 'Ithaca' resembles that of the *Irish Independent* editor. The Corporation might have won the lawsuit, but the true costs and damages in this rift, financial and social, are borne by the people.

Joyce's depiction of the controversy around management of the water supply anticipates issues about the control and distribution of water. It also raises fundamental questions about the basic political and ecological nature of water, including whether it should be considered a commodified resource or a public right. In *The Ripple Effect*, Alex Prud'homme asks, 'Is water just another article of commerce, a "commodity" like oil or natural gas to be extracted from the earth, processed, and traded in the global marketplace? Or is it a "common", a basic human right, like the air we breathe?'[69] Texas businessman T. Boone Pickens' move to control the Ogallala Aquifer in the American West represented a prominent example of the privatisation and corporate control of water. More recently, and with broader global reach, the controversy surrounding remarks by Nestlé chairman Peter Brabeck-Letmathe has prompted debate about the role of companies in the distribution of municipal water supplies and about the future status of water as a universal right.

The Vartry Water Scheme placed the water supply of Dublin residents nominally under city control. Overall, it provided greater access to clean water to more people than ever before. It could be counted among the highest civil-engineering and public-health achievements for Dublin, if not for all Europe, but at the same time it revealed the tendency for water to escalate political tensions and deepen economic fault-lines in the city. As Michael Corcoran notes, Joyce's account of the Vartry scheme conveys his admiration of its engineering success while at the same time articulates 'the terrible inequalities of Dublin life'.[70] The tensions between private property and public health, capitalist commodity and shared resource, remain unresolved. *Ulysses* certainly makes this apparent as its treatise on water shifts suddenly from the infrastructural wonders to the social consequences of the new water supply.

In this regard, 'Ithaca' shifts from an initial fascination with the remarkable engineering facts of the Vartry water system to recognition of the social differences and class divisions that it reinforces. The remainder of the episode shows how water can be not just a source of power and conflict but also a levelling factor for a more cohesive and unified community. Through the main characters' awareness of water and their connection to it, and to each other, Joyce suggests the potential for restoration of social unity and ecological harmony.

Such a redirection is evident primarily in the reconciliation of contrasts that water helps to achieve between Stephen and Bloom. As far as water is concerned, the two men could not be more different, as evidenced by their thoughts and conversation. Bloom is 'waterlover' and 'watercarrier', benefiting even at this late hour water's two primary uses, drinking and washing.[71] By contrast, Stephen is repelled by everything to do with water. He declines his host's offer to wash his hands under the tap, confessing that he is a 'hydrophobe' who took his last bath eight months earlier.[72] The aversion is not surprising, perhaps even appropriate for one whose mythic namesake plunged into the sea from the lofty heights of art and invention. Stephen therefore dislikes artifice that bears resemblance to water, such as 'the aqueous substances of glass and crystal', and is described as 'distrusting aquacities of thought and language'.[73] Learning this, when Bloom contemplates advising Stephen as to the best techniques and hygienic benefits of contact with water, he thinks better of it and decides to hold his tongue, recognising 'the incompatibility of aquacity with the erratic originality of genius'.[74]

This question of incompatibility emerges through the interplay of individuals like Bloom and Stephen and organisations like the Dublin Corporation and the Guardians, as the novel represents the city itself as shaped by the geographic presence, public allocation and economic availability of water. *Ulysses*, Joyce's own aquacity of thought and language, effectively reconstitutes Dublin as *aqua city*, showing how life in the Hibernian metropolis is defined, for better and worse, by its safe and immediate access to water. It documents the fascination with the substance by one citizen and his city at the beginning of the twentieth century, and with new methods of ensuring a vaster, cleaner and more constant supply for more people. *Ulysses* also shows how that public improvement is inevitably linked with questions of political conflict and social inequity. It proves for Edwardian Dublin a socio-historical truism stated more overtly by Steven Solomon in his recent study, *Water: The Epic Struggle for Wealth, Power, and Civilization*:

> That control and manipulation of water should be a pivotal axis of power and human achievement throughout history is hardly surprising . . . Through the centuries, societies have struggled politically, militarily, and economically to control the world's water wealth: to erect cities around it, to transport goods upon it, to harness its latent energy in various forms, to utilize it as a vital input of agriculture and industry, and to extract political advantage from it.[75]

The latter part of 'Ithaca' imagines a way out from such manipulation and control, back to a more beneficent allocation of water resources. This arrives in the practical and symbolic action of water during Bloom and Stephen's after-hours visit at 7 Eccles Street. Together, the two men consume and process water, showing their intimate relation to the substance and to one another. The 'current issue of the *Freeman's Journal* and *National Press*' that Bloom handed Bantam Lyons earlier in the day outside Sweny's chemist shop included an advertisement for the very cocoa he now mixes with the water from his kettle.[76] The actual ad copy reads in part: 'Epps' Cocoa. Grateful and Comforting, Nutritious and Economical. The Original Cocoa for Breakfast and Supper, The finest flavoured, the most nutritious, The best suited *for all ages and classes*, The greatest invigorator for the fagged . . .'.[77] The advertising copy promises a social unity and restorative energy that the advertising canvasser and his guest both desire after the many divisive and exhaustive interactions of the day. In this sense, the simple, transformative act of dissolving 'Epps's soluble cocoa' into water suggests the potential resolution – or re-*solution* – in the troubled lives of Bloom and Stephen, between the feuding factions of the Dublin Corporation and South Dublin Guardians, and indeed, for any individuals or social groups ('for all ages and classes') that have somehow lost their place and seek a restored connection with the world.

The 'democratic equality' of water, then, can be a cause of social conflict or legal dispute, but it can also be a catalyst for social accord and communal cohesion. In the end, the late-night connection forged by Bloom and Stephen is supported from start to finish by the public resource of the Vartry works. As the naturalist-philosopher David Rothenberg writes: 'Water does not divide; it connects. With simplicity it links all aspects of our existence.'[78] Stephen and Bloom feel something of this simple and sublime connectedness when, towards the end of 'Ithaca', they move from drinking to making water together. As much as the voice of the chapter recalls how water divided the city managers from the workhouse residents, the affluent from the poor, it reflects as well how water joins Bloom to Stephen as surely as culture, language or the arts. After the two have talked of such matters as music, of Irish and Hebrew language – all connective media in their own right – just prior to Stephen's departure the two participate in that timeless ritual of homo-social bonding known as simultaneous urination. The action quite literally extends the Vartry waterworks even as it emphasises the men, socially and biologically, as distinct and complementary beings by showing how 'the trajectories of their, first sequent, then simultaneous, urinations were dissimilar'.[79] Stephen's stream is the higher, but Bloom's is the longer (we even learn that he outdistanced his entire high school class in just such a competition). Even in passing water, the two embody, respectfully, the Wandering Jew and Greek artificer. Their distinct yet concurrent streams represent the individual distinction and social attraction that, like a molecule of water, brings together distinct elements into one compound: Jewgreek and Greekjew. Bloomstephen and Stephenbloom. It suggests the continuity of the water cycle that begins at Roundwood Reservoir, flows down to the city, and eventually through each and every Dubliner.

In essence, *Ulysses* combines the biological and mechanical, political and economic, psychological and social aspects of water into a vision that might best be termed ecological. It provides a kind of literary forerunner to the interdisciplinary field of political ecology that has taken shape in more recent decades to assess the impact of social, political and economic factors on the environment. Political ecology is rooted in the idea that human institutions, class structures and political histories shape the world in profound ways; as Paul Robbins writes, it is a perspective predicated on the notion that 'any tug on the strands of the global web of human-environment linkages reverberates throughout the system as a whole'.[80] It considers as well how the inequalities within a human community, such as Joyce's Dublin, can both affect and be exacerbated by that community's exploitation of natural resources.

Beyond its reconstruction of the water issue for early twentieth-century Dublin, *Ulysses* points to the potential to reimagine the resource for human society in all times and places. Its reconstituted vision of a political ecology for water begins with individual awareness. A century later, how many people can tell as explicitly and precisely where their water comes from as Leopold Bloom? Few know the natural source or technological course that brings it to their household tap. Fewer still think about the many ramifications of that local supply or the universal cycle to which it belongs: 'One of the hallmarks of the twentieth century, at least in the developed world, is that we have gradually been able to stop thinking about water. We use more of it than ever, we rely on it for purposes we not only never see but can hardly imagine, and we think about it not at all.'[81] *Ulysses* recalls a time before we took water for granted; doing so, the novel asserts the central role of water in the modern city. As we proceed further into a century that seems likely to test the limits of water resources in many places, the admirations, tensions, curiosities and controversies surrounding water in *Ulysses* have much to teach us. For now, we live again in a time when we cannot afford to take water for granted.

The final, fluid connection and cohesive bond between Joyce's central characters subtly implies the more overt assessment given a century later by Charles Fishman: 'The availability of water is the symbol of a civilized society.'[82] Fishman's remark comes amid increasing scarcity and competition for water among states and multinational corporations operating at a geopolitical level that dwarfs Joyce's depiction of a single municipal water system. Even as he has Leopold Bloom ponder the massive numbers of people on the planet, the birth and death of every minute, 'Cityful passing away, other cityful coming',[83] could he have imagined a world population exceeding seven billion, nearly seven times that of 1904? Nevertheless, Joyce depicts water in its marvellous depth and mundane detail, showing how water is tied inextricably to the political, social and economic contexts of human experience. Fostering such a blend of perspectives, it looks to restore a sense of wonder and instil a realistic awareness of water, all the while asking us to reorient our relationship to it, and to each other. To read *Ulysses* in the early twenty-first century is to face the urgent and recurring question of whether water is to be a common natural resource that will continue to symbolise the best of human civilisation, or a restricted capital commodity that divides individuals and societies.

'Clacking Along the Concrete Pavement': Economic Isolation and the Bricolage of Place in James Joyce's *Dubliners*

CHRISTINE CUSICK

Critics concerned with the socioeconomic forces that shape human relationships with nonhuman nature have found an academic home within the fields of environmental justice, urban ecocriticism and the intersection of the two, which is often termed social ecology. While contemporary studies in this field explore literary texts that give voice to the more obviously environmentally charged issues of watershed supplies and air pollution, a study of an early twentieth-century text such as *Dubliners* is a helpful reminder that especially since the industrialisation of European cities, economic place has always shaped the human perception and understanding of built and natural environments. Situated within the broader theoretical framework of place studies as communicated through the work of scholars such as Michael Begnal, this study explores *Dubliners* through the more focused lens of urban ecocriticism. Specifically, this essay examines the human ambulatory interaction between the characters of *Dubliners* and the cityscape of Dublin, an urban landscape that failed to sustain human needs of economic viability. This essay argues that the characters' economic isolation is more than merely reflected in the physical terrain of their stories; it is the lens through which they perceive their relationship to their built environment, thus shaping all processes of self-actualisation.

As an ecocritic, my experience with literary texts is largely defined by my connection to their material preoccupations, the way the characters swallow the air and the force of their boots upon the riverbank. I'm interested in the way that plot evolves in relation to its changing environment, how the metaphors embody a human conception of the land and enact the confluence of culture, nature and imagination. As a scholar of Irish studies, my preoccupations are inevitably bound to island topography, to colonial and postcolonial identities, and to how cultural inscriptions represent and invade human experience and interactions. For most of my professional career, the dialogue of these interests has meant that I study the Burren and the Connemara strands through the verse of gifted poets such as Moya Cannon and Mary O'Malley, the limestone and the lore of the Aran Islands and Connemara through the cartography and nonfiction of writers such as Tim Robinson, and the visual frames upon the Donegal landscape through photographers such as Rachel Brown. For artists such as these, the materiality of experience and of historical resonance is undoubtedly negotiated by nonhuman nature, by ecological environment, which of course includes human movement and interaction but which in comparison is rightfully and clearly viewed in the context of its ecological magnitude.

And so, I am in one sense surprised that I find myself writing about a figure such as James Joyce, a writer whose legacy I admittedly find daunting and whose concern with 'environment' is, on the surface, largely removed from my critical and imaginative sensibilities as a scholar and as a writer. And yet, when I examine more closely how my conceptions of Irish place studies have evolved, I see that Joyce's work and topographies have lingered as an inarguable force. It is hardly surprising that Joyce is the first Irish writer that I encountered, by way of an ambitious high-school English teacher who entrusted *Portrait of the Artist as a Young Man* to sixteen-year-olds. Joyce's construction of scene and place were secondary to my fascination with his stylistic narrative ambition, his psychological precision and of course his unabashed literary talk of sex. When years later I encountered *Dubliners* for the first time, it was, as for so many readers, the haunting glow of the gas lamps and the gritty honesty of human characters passing one another along concrete paths that became a part of my understanding of how language shapes place. And while I left *Dubliners* as a subject of critical engagement, it continues to enter my classroom in various forms. A year ago, while I was teaching *Dubliners* to a seminar of upper-class English majors, a student asked me how James Joyce, an urban writer largely concerned with human nature rather than with nonhuman nature, influences my work in Irish ecocriticism, and I was given reason to pause. As the good ones always do, this student's question stayed with me, forcing me to examine what it is about Joyce that I hold onto, that I return to, in my work. His philosophical questions enter my critical analyses and his images have surfaced in my creative nonfiction. What lingers for me is the way his fiction asks fundamental epistemological questions about how humans come to know a place. For Joyce, place knowledge is necessarily knowledge of urban, largely built, environments. Not because he negates or demonises the rural, but because city life, Dublin life in particular, is the environment to which he, and perhaps consequently his characters, have access. At the same time, for Joyce, place knowledge is inherently tied to self-knowledge, both frustrated and realised. In this way, long before any formal critical discourse was named 'ecocritical', his work was asking the essential questions about the intersections of environment, culture, politics and identity. Contemporary ecologist Neil Evernden argues that 'preservation of the non-human' demands 'a rejection of the homogenisation of the world that threatens to diminish all, including the self. There is no such thing as an individual, only an individual-in-context, individual as a component of place, defined by place.'[1] One only has to perform a simple word search of Joyce criticism and see how many times the word 'Dublin' appears in essay titles and analyses to understand the centrality of the embeddedness of person and place in Joyce's fiction.

The origin of ecocritical praxis, as it is now realised, is rightly linked to Western Studies in North America, the first conversations originating in the late 1980s and early 1990s. As such, as a body of criticism, it has historically been concerned with representations of nonhuman nature as it exists in the open and unadulterated spaces such as the tundra, the prairie, or the forest. Of course this makes good sense, as it is a criticism interested in human representation of nonhuman life. There have been clear delineations between what is called 'nature writing', 'environmental writing', and 'place writing'. Writing about nonhuman nature in the nature essay, for example, is not necessarily the same gesture as writing about the human degradation of nature through poetic metaphor. The evolution of ecocriticism has afforded scholars the opportunity to polish these distinctions and to define these parameters, and through these discursive exercises we have deepened our philosophical engagement with place-based epistemologies.

Urban ecocriticism is the product of these conversations and is inherently suggestive of the implicit reverberations of our social and ecological lives. In distinguishing writing about cities, Lawrence Buell writes:

> an urbanist concentrates especially on a district rather than envisaging the locale on macro-organismic terms. The city as

> environment, both the built and the natural spaces, generally presents itself in pieces to literary and critical imagination . . . For ecocriticism to recognise 'the city' as something other than non-place is itself a great and necessary advance.[2]

Buell's observations suggest that an ecocritical turn to include more urban writing as the subject of analysis invites new reading practices, practices that value the fragmentation of a city narrative that often inscribes place through specificity rather than expanse. A reader of Joyce's *Dubliners* can undoubtedly relate to such process, the city of Dublin captured with photographic precision of scene and experience like that which we see in 'An Encounter' when the possibilities of 'a day's miching' are captured in the young narrator's description of the cityscape:

> All the branches of the tall trees which lined the mall were gay with little light green leaves and the sunlight slanted through them on to the water. The granite stone of the bridge was beginning to be warm and I began to pat it with my hands in time to an air in my head. I was very happy.[3]

This moment of innocence is quickly thwarted in the story as the young boys' ramblings lead them to a predatory stranger whose questions and monologue ultimately shape the cityscape as much as the slanted light upon the water. With precision and acuity, Joyce aligns the fragments of urban experience and often makes them whole.

Like Lawrence Buell, Glen Love argues for the necessity of a more expansive ecocritical criticism. In *Practical Ecocriticism: Literature, Biology, and the Environment*, he argues that if ecocritical praxis is to reach its full potential, it must take as its subject not just nature and environmental literature but all cultural texts as products of an ecological world:

> As a cultural activity . . . English teaching and research goes on within a biosphere . . . In some of the literary texts that we study and discuss, this enveloping natural world is part of the subject on the printed page before us. But even when it is not, it remains as a given, a part of the interpretive context.[4]

For Love, contemporary environmental crises stir an ethical imperative to bring an ecological consciousness to all teaching and scholarship. By extension, it would seem that this means that even, or perhaps especially, texts that have the metropolis as their guiding metaphor are ripe for ecocritical scholarship.

In his Introduction to *The Philosophy of Social Ecology: Essays on Dialectical Naturalism*, Murray Bookchin illuminates what he describes as the possibility for an '*objectively grounded* ethical meaning' for nature, claiming that 'The social can no longer be separated from the ecological, any more than humanity can be separated from nature'.[5] Urban spaces offer an illuminating paradigm by which to understand these intersections. Human conceptions of nonhuman nature are inevitably shaped by urban experiences, and so to exclude cities from the domain of ecocritical consideration is to negate the material reality of human *and* nonhuman nature. With unprecedented rates of urban growth in the twenty-first century, it is undeniable that for most humans, experiences of place are ultimately bound to cityscapes. If ecocriticism is to effect a change in ecological consciousness then we must study the places that so many humans inhabit.

* * *

Dubliners has of course received a formidable amount of critical attention, including debates over its use of naturalism, the rightful epiphanic moment, the landmark maps of Dublin city streets and narrative unity, and the paralytic tension to name just a few of scholars' pervading preoccupations. And while many critics acknowledge the integrality of the Dublin scape, its value is often positioned as the subject of Joyce's commentary or as the backdrop of his characters' dilemmas. This essay argues for a more integrated approach to the primacy of the material containment of Dublin and the self-actualisation of Joyce's characters. It explores what the theoretical compass of an urban ecocriticism might uncover about Joyce's construction of Dublin's cityscape as it is positioned against the seeming stagnation of its stifled characters.

At the same time, this essay is interested in what Joyce might teach critics about the praxis of urban ecocriticism, arguing that the epistemology of Joyce's Dublin mapping might in fact offer critics a model for how to study human nature's psychological and physical embodiment of urban space. In his Introduction to *Joyce and the City: The Significance of Place*, Michael Begnal incisively describes the essence of this dialogue:

> To Joyce, on the one hand space meant urban space – the city – and it was the hustle and bustle of modern life in close quarters that fed his imagination. On the other hand, he was concerned with the spaces of the mind, and this outer-inner tension is central to the convolutions of his work.[6]

This essay seeks to explore how economic position mediates this tension as economic place within one's social and political structure ultimately becomes the lens through which she understands and mediates the physical paths and boundaries of her city place.

John Wilson Foster argues: 'In Joyce, nature is absorbed – to the point of invisibility – into cultural scheme in the manner of literary modernism, which tends to the urban and international.'[7] *Dubliners* is inarguably an urban text and while nature may in fact be consumed 'into cultural scheme' as Foster notes, ecocriticism reminds us that even in this invisibility it bears a presence. As much as Joyce's mapping of the Dublin streets may suggest that the city exists in a vacuum, apart from the rest of Ireland, there are in fact inherent implications of a world beyond its streets, and that beyond begins with the rest of Ireland. The often-noted exchange between Miss Ivors and Gabriel Conroy in 'The Dead' is perhaps the most powerful illustration of this tension. What begins as a seemingly gentle invitation to accompany his friends to the Aran Islands turns into the verbal positioning of Dublin against Connacht, Ireland against the continent, the Irish language against French and German until the point of Gabriel's mental exhaustion: 'O, to tell you the truth, retorted Gabriel suddenly, I'm sick of my own country, sick of it!'[8] Despite the ideological and political burden of these preoccupations, for Gabriel Conroy, imagining and, more importantly, experiencing places beyond Dublin is permitted because of his place within Dublin's social class. This is, of course, not the case for many of the Dubliners of these stories. One's access to this beyond was, above all things, mediated by one's hope for economic agency. Moreover, movement from the urban to the rural and the rural to the urban held different connotations depending upon one's starting point. Joseph Brady, for example, points out that at the turn of the century, 'While the better off fled [Dublin city], the poor, in contrast, had flocked to the city from an impoverished countryside. Most probably intended taking ships for other countries, but many stayed even if this condemned them to a life of poverty.'[9] And so while Miss Ivors was calling Gabriel to rural Ireland for holiday and leisure, a sign of an evolving Irish elite, she is calling him to a place that many of Dublin's poor had sought to escape because a landscape ravished by imperial territories had ceased to sustain them.

* * *

The theme of thwarted escape recurs throughout *Dubliners* but is perhaps most haunting in Joyce's character, Eveline. The narrative continuity of the collection carefully takes the reader from the moment of epiphanic anguish in 'Araby' to the reflective opening lines of 'Eveline': 'She sat at the window watching the evening invade the avenue. Her head was leaned against the window curtains and in her nostrils was the odour of dusty cretonne. She was tired.'[10] In this moment, the city street is shaped not by human step or building shadows but by the liminal space of day meeting night, the creeping of time. The window serves as a tenuous lens between the domestic interior space that has a hold on Eveline through obligation and promises to a deceased mother, and the exterior space of the urban environment. The scent of the tainted curtain fabric cradles her weariness, and yet the details suggest that this is not the first time that she has been so attentive to the scene: 'Few people passed. The man out of the last house passed on his way home; she heard his footsteps clacking along the concrete pavement and afterwards crunching on the cinder path before the new red houses.'[11] Joyce's use of sound in this passage maps the city man's actions, a decrescendo from knocking of the pavement to the softer step upon the cinder, the earth's built surface shifting from the impenetrable strength of concrete to the dusty surface of slag. In these simple glimpses of Eveline leaning against the window, interpreting the city scene of a man pressing against the ground at the end of the working day, we see humans inhabiting physical place, present against the material earth not simply because of flesh against earth but also because of perception placing order upon the cityscape, recognising neighbours, scripting the social ecology of person against place through memory and imagination.

Even with the prospect of a future lingering on the other side of the windowpane, Eveline's view takes her into the past, inscribing a deserted street with the scenes of memory: 'One time there used to be a field there in which they used to play every evening with other people's children. Then a man from Belfast bought the field and built houses in it – not like their little brown houses but bright brick houses with shining roofs.'[12] Eveline's memory of this physical space is defined by what once was, by the openness of a field that allowed for neighbourhood play, a field that was turned into a commodity for an outsider. Terence Brown's note to this passage identifies a crucial detail for this scene, suggesting that 'a man from Belfast' indicates 'a man from the industrial and largely Protestant city in the north of the country. The commercial aggressiveness and philistine bumptiousness of the stereotypical Belfastman is perhaps suggested in this reference.'[13] Martha Fodaski Black makes a similar point when she writes: 'the man who destroyed the natural environment of Eveline's family is from Belfast. His urban renewal is really a form of English usurpation and exploitation of Dublin's poor.'[14] In this juxtaposition of natural environment against political context, the narrative enacts the underlying premise of social ecology; that is, the inherent confluence of social and ecological effect. In this detail we see the compelling connections between childhood loss and an urbanised landscape. Moreover, this physical space is also defined by layers of imperial presence; the coloniser, even if just by association, is defining what will become of this physical space, and in this case it is transformed into 'bright brick homes with shining roofs' which are contrasted to Eveline's 'little brown' house.[15] The new built environment that has taken away the field is not for those of Eveline's economic status; the glimmer of modernity is in sight but not within reach. Attention to the materiality of this built environment presents a new lens through which to interpret Joyce's implication of modernity, a lens that diffuses emphasis on the alienated individual and gives voice to the reciprocal relationship between the situated human life and its material and social environment.

And yet, Eveline remembers the time before the 'bright brick houses' and thinks: 'Still they seemed to have been rather happy then. Her father was not so bad then; and besides, her mother was alive.'[16] The memory is short-lived, however, and ends with a litany of the dead and disappearing characters of the past followed by the final conclusion: 'Everything changes. Now she was going to go away like the others, to leave her home.'[17]

The possibility of this new life is explicitly determined by Eveline's economic freedom. Despite the fact that she has a steady job as a store clerk, escape from the domestic space of her family home would not be possible without the prospect of marriage. And so her deliberations are, in kind, focused on the practical matters of shelter and care:

> She had consented to go away, to leave her home. Was that wise? She tried to weigh each side of the questions. In her home anyway she had shelter and food . . . Of course she had to work hard both in the house and at business.[18]

Despite being the primary caretaker of the domestic space of her home, Eveline has no agency. Her brother Harry attempted to care for her interests but he was 'nearly always somewhere in the country'.[19] Her abusive father takes even her hard-earned pay, forcing her to quarrel for any change for herself: 'the invariable squabble for money on Saturday nights had begun to weary her unspeakably. She always gave her entire wages . . . but the trouble was to get any money from her father.'[20] But as Catherine Whitley points out, even when Eveline manages to get some money from her father her connection to the very wages she earns is defined by her obligation to care for the interior space of the home, but only after braving the threatening space of the city streets: 'she must "elbow" through crowds, "holding her black leather purse tightly in her hand" in order to buy provisions for her younger siblings, on a tense, rushed shopping trip'.[21] Whitley reads Joyce's positioning of characters against the Dublin cityscape as 'a sort of litmus test, because the city allows us to read the characters as consumers and judge their financial abilities by their actions, noting whether they are harried in search of provisions or leisured and in search of pleasure'.[22] In this way, we again see that the characters' perception of the urban landscape is inevitably bound by their financial position against it. And this position is undoubtedly mediated by gender. The dialogic nature of social ecology and ecofeminism is a helpful tool in creating meaning for the character of Eveline in this instance. Serenella Iovino reminds us that this lens is necessarily bound to pervading cultural hierarchies:

> Social ecologists and ecofeminists see ecological crisis as rooted in the tendency, which has progressively grown in industrialised societies, to conceive of nature as an element to be conquered . . . in line with a dualistic hierarchy that opposes nature to a dominating and conquering humankind. On the historical and social level, this hierarchy has also implied the subjection of humans to other humans. Such an interpretation aims, therefore, at demystifying . . . the conceptual architectures of domination, by the same token showing the mistakes of historical and economic phenomena such as colonialism, industrialism, liberalism, and consumerism.[23]

In Eveline's simple gaze into the moment of the city street beneath her window, we see her situate her own agency against the forces of colonialism, industrialism and patriarchy, all of which rely upon hierarchies of dominance. Her capacity to subvert these structures of power is directly correlated to her economic independence. And so, her perception and relation to the material place of Dublin evolves as a consequence of these competing forces which simultaneously alienate her from and confine her to the urban landscape.

At the same time, this positioning demonstrates the specificity of Joyce's construction of his Dublin cityscape. As Desmond Harding observes:

> The modern city James Joyce presents in *Dubliners* (1914) constitutes a signal shift in urban ideology. The old idea of the spiritual city, founded on a consecrated burial place with a centrally located sanctuary, has given way to the vision of a rationally organised metropolis radiating out from the Duke of Wellington Monument, the heart of imperial and commercial Dublin.[24]

The materiality and historicity of this cityscape is always present for Joyce's Dubliners, and in this presence economic place is essential to both the perception and construction of the built environment.

Eveline's deliberations about her planned journey are interrupted and, to a degree, quieted, by a narrative return to time against space. 'The evening deepened in the avenue' and her worry seems tempered by genuine fondness for her family:

> Her father was becoming old lately . . . he would miss her. Sometimes he could be very nice . . .when their mother was alive, they had all gone for a picnic to the Hill of Howth. She remembered her father putting on her mother's bonnet to make the children laugh.[25]

As in the beginning of the story, glimpses of childhood contentment are positioned against open space and nonhuman nature. But again these memories are short-lived as she soon returns to gazing out the glass against a dusty curtain.

There is no evidence that Eveline's desire to escape is directly related to a desire to leave Dublin as a city except for what it represents of her disintegrating family. And her impulse to leave remains a pragmatic one. It is not wedded bliss that Eveline necessarily seeks in Frank or in Buenos Ayres: 'He would give her life, perhaps love, too.

But she wanted to live.'[26] Even love is secondary to Eveline's desire to escape, to exist in a new way, to, as she repeats, *live*. When read against these lines, the story's ending, Eveline's paralysis against the iron railing, her act of staying, is all the more haunting because they suggest that she knew what the consequences of staying would be. As Whitley reflects:

> Joyce's female characters are generally portrayed as physically occupying interior spaces, yet these spaces serve as deadly traps for both women and men. Home for Eveline represents a lifetime of abuse; her decision to stay instead of fleeing for a potentially better life elsewhere is an act of self-immolation.[27]

As a narrative sequence in Joyce's *Dubliners*, 'Eveline' offers a glimpse into a young woman's domestic space, the hauntings of a deceased mother's life and expectations, and the cycles of paralysis spun by abuse and economic control. From a critical perspective, Joyce's character of Eveline also offers us a paradigmatic example of the intersections of social ecology and ecofeminism. This dialogue offers us a helpful lens through which to understand Joyce's critique of institutional hierarchies such as colonialism, patriarchy and industrialism, revealing an inextricable link between female and economic agency.[28]

Joyce's situation of the individual against the urban experience is necessary for what can be defined as a quintessentially Modernist preoccupation with the cultural evolution of cityscapes. Garry Leonard examines the cultural specificity of these interests: 'For the purposes of isolating and examining "Irish" modernity in Joyce, I would define modernity as the historically specific lived experience of twentieth century culture on the social, psychological and economic level. This experience is both stimulated and shaped by the increasing complexity of the urban environment.'[29] *Dubliners* is evidence enough that Joyce's concerns with the individual's purview of urban experience enacts modernism's creative impulse. This resonance is perhaps most compellingly articulated in Joyce's rendering of the middle-class working man's life through the character of Little Chandler. As in the opening scene of 'Eveline', Joyce positions Chandler against a windowpane in the beginning of 'A Little Cloud'. Anticipating the visit of an old friend who has found success and wealth in a career working for the London press, Little Chandler disrupts the routine of his own office job:

> He turned often from his tiresome writing to gaze out of the office window. The glow of a late autumn sunset covered the

> grass plots and walks. It cast a shower of kindly golden dust on the untidy nurses and decrepit old men who drowned on the benches; it flickered upon all the moving figures – on the children who ran screaming along the gravel paths and on everyone who passed through the gardens.[30]

The almost idyllic description of the quiet autumn light is quickly tempered by human characters and activity. The cityscape is filtered by the glass of an office window, through the fragments of sunlight, and by the movement of urban routine.[31] Watching the elements of place shuffle beneath his window: 'he thought of life; and (as always happened when he thought of life) he became sad. A gentle melancholy took possession of him. He felt how useless it was to struggle against fortune, this being the burden of wisdom which the ages bequeathed to him.'[32] The urban landscape again becomes the lens through which the character examines their position within the social structure of literal and, more so in this case, figurative wealth, thereby accentuating the connection between work, social class and human relation to physical place.

Little Chandler's reverie is broken by the end of his workday, the gateway by which he carefully becomes a part of the scene he was observing: 'When his hour had struck he stood up and took leave of his desk and of his fellow-clerks punctiliously. He emerged from under the feudal arch of the King's Inns, a neat modest figure, and walked swiftly down Henrietta Street.'[33] Now an actor in the cityscape that he had been observing from his office window, the scene is darker, the streets a bit grittier:

> The golden sunset was waning and the air had grown sharp. A horde of grimy children populated the street. They stood or ran in the roadway or crawled up the steps before the gaping doors or squatted like mice upon the thresholds. Little Chandler gave them no thought.[34]

Unlike when Chandler observed the street paths from his office, as he walks to meet Gallaher at Corless', a high end Dublin restaurant, his expectation of the evening filled him with 'a present joy'.[35] The joy, it seems, stems from anticipation of time with an old friend who had escaped the mundaneness of middle-class Dublin life and of the thought of being among the wealthy socialites of Dublin, the sort that 'eat oysters and drink liqueurs'; he was walking *to* the scenes that he typically 'walked swiftly *by* at night'.[36] In this case, even a momentary encounter with an elevated social class transforms Chandler's way of existing in place.

Little Chandler's inhabitation of the Dublin city streets is embodied in the pace and tenor of his walking gait. He is aware of the social scene that he is about to enter, recalling details of powdered faces and 'noisy dresses', even though 'He had always passed without turning his head to look'.[37] He is simultaneously engaged and disengaged with the urban backdrop of his daily life: 'It was his habit to walk swiftly in the street even by day and whenever he found himself in the city late at night he hurried on his way apprehensively and excitedly'.[38] 'Swiftly', 'apprehensively', 'excitedly': Little Chandler is a restless actor against the city streets, his restlessness invading the measure of his step. And yet, at the same time, he is self-aware enough to court 'the causes of his fear', pushing the limits of his own comfort: 'He chose the darkest and narrowest streets and, as he walked boldly forward, the silence that was spread about his footsteps troubled him, the wandering silent figures troubled him; and at times a sound of low fugitive laughter made him tremble like a leaf.'[39] In wilful tests of courage, Little Chandler 'boldly' challenges the hauntings of his discontent only to be defeated by a self-imposed stranger status.

And yet, on the evening of his reunion with Gallaher, just as he turns onto Capel Street, which Terence Brown reminds us 'gives on to Grattan Bridge over the Liffey', he reflects on his friend's success, 'Ignatius Gallaher on the London Press! Who would have thought it possible eight years before?'[40] Little Chandler's experience of the city streets changes:

> Little Chandler quickened his pace. For the first time in his life he felt himself superior to the people he passed. For the first time his soul revolted against the dull inelegance of Capel Street. There was no doubt about it: if you wanted to succeed you had to go away. You could do nothing in Dublin.[41]

It is only through Little Chandler's reimagining of his social status through the vicarious celebration of Ignatius Gallaher's success that his relationship to the city streets, and the people who roam them, is elevated. Gallaher's escape to wealth and notoriety now becomes Little Chandler's windowpane to the Dublin pathways, and in this reflection his sense of self-worth is affirmed.[42]

This momentary, elevated sense of self moves Chandler to see the built environment of Dublin's texture as a part and particle of his introspection, the contrasts of dusty, pewter-hued structures against the evening light:

> As he crossed Grattan Bridge he looked down the river towards the lower quays and pitied the poor stunted houses. They seemed to him a band of tramps, huddled together along the river-banks, their old coats covered with dust and soot, stupefied by the panorama of sunset and waiting for the first chill of night to bid them arise, shake themselves and begone.[43]

In this personification of the meager, poor houses, life is provoked not by the light of the evening's turn but by the sharpness of the 'first chill', spurring them to action. In a similar way, this scene moves Little Chandler to his most engaged response to his physical space:

> He wondered whether he could write a poem to express his idea. Perhaps Gallaher might be able to get it into some London paper for him. Could he write something original? He was not sure what idea he wished to express but the thought that a poetic moment had touched him took life within him like an infant hope. He stepped onward bravely.[44]

Again, Chandler's gait enacts his intellectual processing of his surroundings, his body propelled by a mild recognition of his artistic self, of the possibilities that filled the pages of the books on his bookshelves, of the poems that he was too shy to read to his wife.

The movement of this scene draws Chandler closer to Gallaher, but also nearer to the possibilities that Gallaher's success represents. Joyce writes: 'Every step brought him nearer to London, farther from his own sober inartistic life.'[45] These steps spur Chandler to become lost in a moment of self-invention, admitting his hunger to give verse to the world, even if only to a small corner of it, wondering how his Irishness might distinguish his contribution:

> He tried to weigh his soul to see if it was a poet's soul. Melancholy was the dominant note of his temperament, he thought, but it was a melancholy tempered by recurrences of faith and resignation and simple joy. If he could give expression to it in a book of poems perhaps men would listen . . . The English critics, perhaps, would recognise him as one of the Celtic school by reason of the melancholy tone of his poems; besides that, he would put in allusions.[46]

In this moment, Little Chandler's self-actualisation remains reflective of place, if only to the extent that it creates in him a desire to escape it for a life of expression and humble recognition. And yet, even in the ideal hope of his imagination, this recognition is acutely attached to place identifiers, simplifications of association that craft a caricature of the wet-eyed Irishman. Through Chandler's processes of self-actualisation it is clear that like so many of Joyce's urban dwellers he confronts the inherent crisis of a modern life. As Leonard reminds us:

> At the level of the individual, 'modernity' means new modes of consumption, new styles of self-presentation, new attitudes toward crowds and urban spaces, new definitions of public and private spaces . . . 'Modernism' is the aesthetic response to this lived experience, and it, too, is historically specific in that modernist artists felt the need to depict the 'everyday' quality of life.[47]

Critical consideration of this modern experience of these 'new modes' has historically been preoccupied with its resulting psyche and aesthetics at the cost of a close study of the material places that create them. An ecocritical lens, specifically one grounded in social ecology, illuminates the confluence of these forces and invites closer examination of how this human experience is not only shaped by its environment but also how it effects responsive changes to the contour of its landscape.

For Joyce's work, these changes are first enacted through his humans' mapping and traversing of city streets. In Chandler's imaginings of literary fruit, he becomes lost within Dublin, missing landmarks and turns: 'He pursued his revery so ardently that he passed his street and had to turn back.'[48] Like the 'first chill of night' that 'bid [the band of tramps] arise', this turning back jarred Little Chandler into his present moment and 'As he came near Corless' his former agitation began to overmaster him and he halted before the door in indecision'.[49] When faced with the details of the Corless scene, Chandler's uncertainty and his own sense of outsider status returns midst a sea of affluence:

> The light and noise of the bar held him at the doorway for a few moments. He looked about him, but his sight was confused by the shining of many red and green wine-glasses. The bar seemed to him to be full of people and he felt that the people were observing him curiously.[50]

Throughout 'A Little Cloud', Joyce constructs a series of scenes that position Little Chandler as simultaneous observer and inhabitant of his physical place. He fades in and out of engagement with the

Dublin streets and architecture, his own flesh and tenuous manner of movement reflecting the tenor of his inhabitation. He is stifled by his own self-alienation from the despair of the poor as well as the indulgence of the elite, while at the same time is trapped by the routine of his middle-class existence as worker, husband and father. As a statement of social ecology, the character of Chandler articulates the crisis of the lone city worker whose constant negotiations between his social role and urban landscape define his Dubliner status. In some ways, Little Chandler is perpetually at the pane of his office window looking onto the Dublin streets. Desmond Harding writes:

> At one level Joyce's Dublin represents a predatory urban space in which the presence of and interaction with strangers contribute to the worst aspect of urbanism: the estrangement of the individual from the self and from the city. At the same time, Joyce's naturalistic vision poeticises the entropy of Irish life, and in so doing creates a space of where life and art combine to both celebrate and resist the city.[51]

While Chandler seems to fall short of actually celebrating the city, it is clear that his estrangement from both Dublin and self is shaped by the intricacies of the entrenchments of class and both personal and imperial conquest. In her study of gender construction of Joyce, Catherine Whitley reminds us that:

> James Joyce abhorred institutions, and over the course of his career his fiction explored and undermined the institutions of colonialism, nationalism, gender politics, and narrativity, among others . . . Joyce experimented with various ways to interrogate these power relations by playing with the concepts of interiority, both of people and places.[52]

Through characters like Little Chandler and Eveline, it is clear that the interiority of a person in relation to place has watery boundaries, one often a refraction of the other.

* * *

Michael Bennett argues that 'Social Ecologists have not . . . simply accepted cities as they are; they frequently offer a critique of the ways in which metropolitan culture transforms urban environments'.[53] Implicit in such critiques is an understanding that physical place is infused by the economic disparagement, political context and existential crises that embody it. *How* humans reflect and affect the air that they breathe and the slag that they crunch beneath their feet is as much a part of their environment as the material earth itself. Whether it is the bogland of Connemara or the Liffey Quays, it is the *way* that we inhabit place that has consequences for what it will become. Joyce understood this relationship long before critics began articulating the discourse that illuminates it.

In Heyward Ehrlich's essay 'James Joyce's Four-Gated City of Modernisms', he notes that the only portrait in Joyce's Paris flat was Vermeer's well-known 'Portrait of Delft', which Arthur Power tells us Joyce admired simply as 'the portrait of a city'.[54] At first glance, this description seems almost reductive, simplifying the image as a mere reflection upon the water, but if one is attentive to Joyce's achievement in *Dubliners* it is clear that such a portrait requires both excavation and construction; it demands a sensitivity to the economy of how humans survive or fail to do so. On some streets this is about earning a wage to put food in the kitchen for one's younger siblings, and upon a bridge across town it is about finding even fleeting hope in an old friend's escape to London. Through a narrative form that pieces together cinematic city scenes and through content that problematises the boundaries of interiority, *Dubliners* in fact enacts this relationship, mapping a bricolage of place, a piecing together of the material ruins that define the physical and philosophical contours of the spaces we inhabit.

Joyce the Travel Writer:
Space, Place and the Environment in James Joyce's Nonfiction

DEREK GLADWIN

Every story is a travel story – a spatial practice.[1]
Michel de Certeau

Joyce, Travel Writing and Ecocriticism

During the years 1907–1912, James Joyce wrote nine articles for the Italian-language newspaper *Il Piccolo della Sera*. These articles were journalistic pieces intended for *Il Piccolo*'s local Triestine readership, but Joyce composed them with the ambition to later develop them as a book for wider European readership with the Genoese publisher Angelo Fortunato Formiggini. The aim of these articles, according to Joyce, was quite simple: to make a case for Ireland to a broader audience. Due to the powerful influence of the British press, Joyce believed the world had been systematically misinformed about the colonial relationship between Ireland and England.[2] Such a belief was, in part, the reason Joyce left for Trieste, and it is within this context that he wrote the nine articles for *Il Piccolo*. Although Joyce has been predominantly celebrated for his fiction of *Dubliners* and *Ulysses*, this essay explores another side to Joyce illuminated by his non-fiction articles: Joyce the travel writer.

In two particular articles published in the summer of 1912, 'The City of the Tribes: Italian Echoes in an Irish Port' and 'The Mirage of the Fisherman of Aran: England's Safety Valve in Case of War', Joyce, while satisfying the strictly journalistic demands of his Irish-themed contributions for *Il Piccolo*, nevertheless presented a subtle and subversive commentary on travel writing as an ecocritical examination of place. Travel writing, when it includes a depth of cultural, environmental, historical or geographical analysis, is well positioned to provide a recognisable form of environmental criticism. In both articles, Joyce approaches the geographical region of western Ireland in such a way that we can read his articles as an historical atlas containing a repository of cultural memory. This repository contains a long history of the region's residents, their relationship to both the rural and urban landscape, and the impacts of Empire, all of which are framed by the distinctive place of Galway. Some critics have considered these articles simply as Joyce's pragmatic foray into journalism; I want to suggest, however, that he goes beyond this classification, functioning as a travel writer in order to probe the deeper historical and cultural geographies within his Irish itinerary by using a spatial and ecocritical practice called place-attachment: accessing place through personal and cultural experience in a landscape. Joyce explores the region's underlying cultural and environmental currents, at times controversial and conflicted, revealing his deeper emerging interest in the land's cultural geography. At the heart of these two essays, then, is Joyce's ability to see the cultural history of Galway and the Aran Islands connected to the landscape, while also highlighting issues of space and place within this region.

Joyce's nonfiction writings have, for good reason perhaps, been read strictly as journalistic pieces. In the introduction to *James Joyce: Occasional, Critical, and Political Writing*, Kevin Barry places the Triestine articles in a section titled 'Journalism and Politics'.[3] Even Joyce himself admitted to his brother Stanislaus, 'I may not be the Jesus Christ I once fondly imagined myself, but I think I must have a talent for journalism.'[4] In contrast, A. Nicholas Fargnoli and Michael Patrick Gillespie refer to 'The City of the Tribes' as 'a short travel piece' in *James Joyce A to Z: The Essential Reference to the Life and Work*,[5] while Richard Ellmann and Ellsworth Mason also describe them as 'travel pieces' in which Joyce 'changes his tone and writes deftly and attractively about Galway and about the Aran Islands'.[6] However, while Fargnoli, Gillespie, Ellmann and Ellsworth briefly recognise travel motifs in Joyce's articles, they do not explicate the process in any great detail. In what follows, I aim to track more deeply the role of the travel writer as a way for Joyce to engage with a sense of place-attachment through the lens of ecocriticism, which is a critical methodology that examines the relationships among literature, culture, geography and the environment.

Travel writing acutely observes how 'space' and 'place' may implicate various tensions that pervade a landscape, whether they are geographical, historical or political. Functioning as geographical concepts, place and space are both synonymous and distinctive terms. 'Place', as Lawrence Buell articulates in *The Future of Environmental Criticism*, 'entails spatial location, entails a spatial container of some sort. But space as against place connotes geometrical or topographical abstraction.'[7] Unlike space, place contains meaning rooted in experience. While the quality of place attracts the traveller to a specific region, the lineaments of space supply the fundamental and physical framework to the region. Travel photographs, as an illustration, usually show people experiencing a specific place – exhibiting an emotional association to a specific geography made familiar through story or personal connection – while also being in a physical space. The relationship between space and place is by no means oppositional; any space, such as bog or a wooded thicket, may be transformed into place depending on the actions or experiences occurring in that location. Ultimately, place holds cultural and personal currency while space is often defined through denotative identifications; place connotes emotive valence while space is often considered a 'topographical abstraction'.[8]

By looking into how these two concepts are negotiated, we can then turn to Joyce's use of geography as an exploration of space and place within culture and the environment.[9] I intend to argue that the environment, like any material space, becomes a repository of personal and cultural memory through the practice of what Buell calls 'place-attachment'.[10] In other words, place carries meaning because it reflects the emotional, historical and cultural attachment of people to an existing space. Not only is place 'associatively thick' and 'defined by physical markers as well as social consensus', it also demonstrates a collective history where the histories of space become place through the 'quotidian idiosyncratic intimacies that go with "place"'.[11] As a consequence, place-attachment, unlike the non-attachment of an abstract space, firmly roots one in a specific environment and can be seen most vividly in the genre of travel writing.

Irish travel writing and Irish nature writing have followed similar trajectories. Indeed, at one time they were lumped together as the same genre of writing, and it is still the case that many people read travel writing as a form of nature writing. European readers were typically more interested in adventure and intrigue than in species of trees or the local fauna, but early travel writers still conventionally accompanied their holidays with biological observation. Eóin Flannery contends, 'just as Romanticism mutated physical wildness into passive scenic for consumption by urban constituencies, so travel writers began to mediate Ireland as a playground for sumptuous and unpolluted rustic leisure'.[12] In the late eighteenth century, Arthur Young's multi-volume *A Tour of Ireland* catalogues his 'tours', but many of his travel accounts also focus on the Irish landscape, in addition to his perceptions of Irish culture as an outsider.[13] Young's *Tour* – along with other travel accounts written and documented in a similar style, scope, and tone written by Thomas Campbell, Richard Pococke and Coquebert de Montbret – was written in the period between 1775 and 1850, which is generally considered to be the high period of Irish travel writing.[14] However, Heinrich Böll's *Irisches Tagebuch* (1957) is the major exception, continuing to serve as the most popular of all Irish travel writings.[15] Even today, nature writing and travel writing attract similar readers, a market that has steadily increased in Ireland due to its robust tourism industry. Yet in Ireland, due to a history of colonial occupation that lasted centuries, nature writing continues to exist in tandem with politically and culturally inflected travel writing, particularly in topographical accounts of these contested landscapes.[16]

At this stage, it seems necessary to briefly outline ecocriticism and its inclusion in Irish studies. Since its inception over thirty years ago, ecocriticism has significantly expanded in an attempt to engage with what Cheryll Glotfelty recognises as 'the interconnections between nature and culture, specifically the cultural artifacts of language and literature'.[17] Greg Garrard extends this definition a bit further and maintains that 'ecocriticism is the study of the relationship of the human and the non-human, throughout human cultural history and entailing critical analysis of the term "human" itself'.[18] Since Glotfelty and later Garrard helped to develop and expand the field, ecocriticism has begun to reach a critical mass where theorists have suggested implementing new terminology to more clearly disseminate its theoretical discourse. In other words, ecocriticism is more than simply writing about so-called 'nature' in literature and culture. Rather, it engages with extensive forms of built and non-built environments that extend to both human and non-human in all forms of cultural praxis. In fact, Lawrence Buell's proposed term 'environmental criticism'[19] was adopted in order to accommodate the many far-reaching disciplines outside literary studies. Drawing from some of these recent moves in ecocritical theory, I intend to investigate the relationship between Joyce's human cultural history and the critical analysis of place, while also combining connected ideas from post-colonial and critical geography studies.

It is important to recognise that Irish cultural and literary studies, up until the last few years, adopted a less 'eco'-centric terminology when attempting to examine the environment. Irish geographers, such as William Smyth, Kevin Whelan, Catherine Nash and Patrick J. Duffy, have been addressing environmental concerns similar to those of ecocritics in North America for a couple of decades. And even though they speak from a different disciplinary and theoretical perspective, they frequently address salient literary, cultural and historical issues related to the environment in Ireland. In this sense, then, the recent ecocritical movement in Ireland owes a great deal to the work compiled by earlier Irish geographers, and because of this critical history it is difficult to deploy ecocriticism within an Irish context without also including some of the critical work from geographers in Ireland.

It is, moreover, Gerry Smyth who has most effectively contextualised the perceived ambiguity between Irish studies and environmental criticism in his book *Space and the Irish Cultural Imagination*. He argues:

> Geographical peculiarity and historical discontinuity produced a situation in Ireland in which questions concerning space, landscape, locality, gender, urban and rural experience, nature, and so on became central to both the cultural and the critical imagination (Carpenter 1977; Harmon 1984; Duffy 1997). When the Irish writer describes a landscape in terms of gender, therefore, or when a critic addresses the ambivalent overlapping of public and private spaces in an Irish text, they are in fact 'doing' ecocriticism. They are doing it, moreover, in concrete situations which realise the abstraction of a discourse which, by the nature of its subject matter, is obliged to focus on the bigger picture and thus risk much of its affective potential.[20]

It is fair to say, therefore, that Joyce's travel writing remains ambiguous for the present-day ecocritic since Joyce did not develop a clearly articulated environmental discourse within it; after all, he is not typically considered a nature or environmental writer. He does, however, bring issues of urban and rural experience, landscape and locality to the fore throughout his entire corpus, which, according to Smyth's assertion, demonstrates that Joyce fosters an environmental imagination and is in fact 'doing' ecocriticism. In 'The City of the

Tribes' and 'The Mirage of the Fisherman of Aran', Joyce looks at the cultural artefacts of language, history and geography within Galway and the Aran Islands, exposing these essays as ecocritical writings. To put it another way, his environmental impulse lies within the fabric of the cultural representation of place. In 'Blues in the Green: Ecocriticism Under Critique', Michael Cohen indicates that one of the three directions where ecocriticism should grow as a critical theory is in its 'focus on place and region'.[21] Joyce, in this instance, is a travel writer who magnifies the cultural and natural landscapes of the Galway region through place-attachment – or, the emotional, visceral and internal connection to a geographical space.

Joyce's 'Other' Irish City

The city as a specific travel motif does not often evoke the picturesque landscapes frequently associated with travel writing, especially within this genre in Ireland. There is already a clear sense that urban landscapes are significantly equated with Joyce's writings because they are where the modernist writer can construct a multivalent sensibility through differing narratives and cartographic complexities. Both of these articles are set in County Galway (which includes the city of Galway and is located in the West of Ireland, about two hundred kilometres from Dublin). In Joyce's two articles, Galway functions as an equivalent urban setting to that of Dublin, but he arrived at its character in an entirely different manner. In 'Fellow Travellers: Contemporary Travel Writing and Ireland', Michael Cronin states that 'cities and particularly Dublin are largely either ignored or condemned on account of what is perceived as their visual poverty'.[22] Galway city, which is even smaller than Dublin and considered insignificant from a Triestine point of view, represents Cronin's description of a visually impoverished location because of its urban and colonial history in contrast to the surrounding scenic beauty of Galway Bay and the Aran Islands. Joyce's decision to spotlight Galway is remarkable for two reasons: first, he focuses mostly upon an urban setting in a region that is far more celebrated for the charms of its natural landscape; second, he concentrates on a city not characteristically associated with his more recognisable achievements in *A Portrait of the Artist as a Young Man*, *Dubliners* and *Ulysses*. Galway is not only a city centre, but also a county that forms a larger regional identity of both the urban and the rural environment. And since

Joyce tends, in the words of Buell, 'to favor literary texts orientated toward comparatively local or regional levels of place-attachment',[23] his focus on Galway in 'The City of the Tribes' and 'The Mirage of the Fisherman of Aran' enables an ecocritical reading to unfold by examining both built and non-built environments.

By investigating the natural and cultural factors in the Galway landscape, Joyce magnifies the interplay between nature and culture that contributes to what Buell calls 'place-making'. Travel writing, as a method of place-making, conflates two quintessential and multivalent elements of environmental criticism – nature and culture. It also situates the nature-culture link in a specific place. Buell argues that one of the ways in which environmental criticism needs to move forward is through examining this very relationship between nature and culture with regards to place. He remarks,

> the emergence of contemporary environmental criticism is in part the story of an evolution from imagining life-in-place as deference to the claims of (natural) environment toward an understanding of place-making as a culturally inflected process in which nature and culture must be seen as a mutuality rather than as separable domains.[24]

This raises the question, is the environment natural or cultural? After all, both 'nature' and 'culture' are socially constructed and notoriously difficult terms to define. According to the geographer Robert Sack, the circuits and networks of place are what link nature and culture together in a specific geography.[25] Joyce establishes place in these two articles by integrating the inherent connections among landscape, culture and nature, which are all inseparable and part of a larger interconnected network. In *Landscape and Memory*, Simon Schama argues that 'while we acknowledge (as we must) that the impact of humanity on the earth's ecology has not been an unmixed blessing, neither has the long relationship between nature and culture been an unrelieved and predetermined calamity'.[26] Joyce avoids the 'sentimental environmental determinism'[27] of aestheticising nature, which is often associated with accounts of place-focused ecocriticism, by demonstrating the influence of culture and history in relation to the environment.

One could say, however, that Joyce's concentration on an urban centre would seem to run counter to an ecocritical perspective. If we look at Joyce's use of urban representation in terms of bioregionalism, which, according to Mitchell Thomashow, attempts to 'integrate ecological and cultural affiliations within the framework of a place-based sensibility',[28] then urban (or built) spaces can be just as significant to the ecology of a region as the topographies of forests, bogs or mountains. Unlike a broadly defined term such as 'environment', the term 'bioregion' signifies a place where the 'populace is a collectivity of ethnically and economically diverse stakeholders'[29] and where the geography is shaped through the inhabitants 'who have made a long term commitment to living there'.[30] By the same token, Buell remarks, 'So far the new environmental criticism's most distinctive contribution to the taxonomy of place-scales may be the concept of the bioregion.'[31] Joyce accentuates the uniqueness of Galway city as an urban centre that shares the same bioregion with the rural County Galway (which includes the Aran Islands among other notable topographies such as Connemara). As he leaves by boat for the island of 'Aranmor' (*Árainn Mhór*) in 'The Mirage of the Fisherman of Aran', he notices how the little boat 'leaves the little port of Galway and enters open water, leaving behind on its right the village of Claddagh, a cluster of huts outside the walls of the city. A cluster of huts, and yet a kingdom.'[32] And because of the ongoing cultural development of the city, its historic relationship with the environment blurs the boundaries of the traditional rural/urban divide. In this regard, Joyce measures the place-scale of the bioregion by drawing a kind of 'map' that depicts the networks of culture and nature.

In 'The City of the Tribes', Joyce draws attention to this very interplay between rural and urban space in Galway when describing the contents of a document from an Italian traveller of the sixteenth century later found in the parish house of St Nicholas. It states, 'although he had travelled throughout the world, he had never seen in a single glance what he saw in Galway – a priest elevating the Host, a pack chasing a deer, a ship entering the harbour under full sail, and a salmon being killed with a spear'.[33] The diversity of activities, by both human and non-human agents, demonstrates that the urban centre of Galway existed as both a functioning international port and a thriving bioregion. There is also a clear sense of place-attachment for the Italian traveller who, upon merely experiencing Galway for a brief period of time, was surprised by the apparent paradoxes of this geography. For example, the traveller noticed that ships were once entering this international port while deer were simultaneously running nearby on the banks overlooking the bay. Cultural ceremonies (taking the communion) or activities upon the landscape (hunting and fishing) also establish examples of place-attachment. In addition, Joyce plants figures that appear to grow out of the organic fabric of landscape. In 'The Mirage of the Fisherman of Aran', for instance, he describes how 'the fishermen kneel down and uncover themselves, and the friar, uttering prayers of exorcism, shakes his aspergill on the sea, and divides the dark air in the form of a cross'.[34] These activities frame the identity of this region and provide an internal imprint drawn from viewing the external activities upon the landscape and the surrounding sea. In this regard, the bioregion of Galway inscribes an identifiable attachment to place upon the traveller's memory.

At the same time, it is this sense of place-attachment that drives the narrative in these two travel pieces. Geography impacts the travelogue in such a way that each character depicted in the travel stories – whether it is the fisherman of Aran, St Brendan, James Lynch Fitz-Stephen or the Duke of Lorraine – is equally implanted into the geography. These characters are, in Joyce's words, 'the hum of bees around a hive' that is called Galway.[35] Bees experience autonomy insofar as they can exist outside of their place-attachment to the hive. The hive, as a significant symbol conflating nature and culture, not only sustains life but also serves as a community of place that extends from a material space. Joyce draws upon geographical allusions to stitch together seemingly random events and characters in order to attach everything, like an interconnected ecosystem, through history and circumstance in a specific place.

Fortunately for Joyce, *Il Piccolo* was a nationalist publication designed to deride the Austro–Hungarian Empire that ruled the Italian city of Trieste in the midst of great local contention. This provided Joyce with the freedom to incorporate politics related to Irish nationalism into these essays; indeed, at this time in the early twentieth century Irish nationalists were busy promoting the Third Home Rule Bill as a modified form of Irish independence vis-à-vis Westminster. Such a move came in contrast to Joyce's focus in previously published essays, namely the ones published in the *Daily Express* between 1902 and 1903. Due to the *Express'* neutral opinion on the colonial situation in Ireland, Joyce had to voice a more moderate view of Ireland's relationship with Britain.[36] According to Joyce's retelling of history in these pieces,[37] Ireland's empowerment would not only come through resistance to Britain, but through forging alliances as an equal with, not as a subordinate to, other empires. The cultural geographer Catherine Nash asserts:

> In the context of Ireland's colonial history, the West functioned as a primitive 'other' against which the superiority of the colonial power could be measured. Yet the West continued to function as an internal 'other' through which to articulate difference, a difference valued in the national context, its cultural and racial purity and health, considered lost or declining in the rest of the country.[38]

By using colonial history as a backdrop, Joyce repositions the West of Ireland, and more specifically the bioregion of Galway, as a legitimate international port, functioning as an 'internal "other"'. He notes, 'Oliver Cromwell's correspondence shows that the port of Galway was the second most important harbour in the United Kingdom, and the prime market in the entire Kingdom for the Spanish and Italian trade.'[39] In this respect, Joyce is able to represent Galway as a geographical centre attracting cosmopolitan Europeans on a global scale, while also maintaining the intimate sense of place containing nature and culture. It is, the connections between place and colonial history which Joyce sews together here that are the integral elements in understanding Ireland's relationship with the environment.

Looking at Joyce's relationship with the Galway bioregion more specifically, it is important to highlight the both/and relationship found in his writing in order to understand some of the oppositional and simultaneously connective forces at work in these travel pieces. Joyce, like other modernist writers, utilises both/and relationships to syncretise discrete or opposite ideas and images in order to produce a rich and complex unity. We can then frame Joyce's relationship to Galway in terms of the both/and relationship of both an outsider and an insider. He is an outsider because of his Dublin upbringing and later exile in Trieste, but he is also an insider as someone originally from Ireland. Although his intended readership for these essays resided in Trieste, Joyce was also writing for an Irish audience. He was even in exile on the occasions he wrote for the *Daily Express* (while living in Paris) and *Il Piccolo*. Yet, as Eric Bulson observes, these two articles for *Il Piccolo* 'read like the nostalgic ramblings of a local'.[40]

As both/and an outsider/insider, Joyce accesses the local by illustrating a history that generates place-attachment to a particular environment, while at the same time demonstrating a distance of perspective. Joyce, for example, positions himself in the both/and relationship as a Dubliner and a Galway local. He is not, of course, a local of Galway (Nora, his wife, was a local of Galway). But for the Triestine audience at the time, he could have easily passed as one. In this way he offers another feature of travel writing that connects a reader to place: exporting the exotic as recognisable and intimate rather than vague and abstract. Smyth maintains that 'the rhetoric of travel discourse is the manner in which these exotic locations are described and oriented in terms of more familiar landscapes'.[41] Familiarity of place generates emotional attachment to the environment; it also provides greater cultural and historical understanding.

Unlike his contemporaries, Joyce did not agree with the cultural Revival's image of the exotic West as the quintessential Ireland. Instead, Joyce positions the West as a viable area with political and cultural legitimacy on a European scale, not simply for tourism, but for greater cultural capital. Galway contains the both/and relationship within other similar paradoxes, such as nature/culture, rural/urban, local/European, and modern/Western. Pascale Casanova maintains, 'Joyce's exclusive concern with Dublin and urban life signaled his rejection of the peasant folklore tradition and his determination to bring Irish literature into European modernity.'[42] For a brief moment, Joyce focuses on the 'other' Irish city as a way to access *both* European modernity *and* a local connection with place. By situating Galway's bioregionalism within a larger environmental and geographical history, Joyce legitimises its broader European tradition. He also maintains the notion of the local by demonstrating what the pastoral tradition, also with an emphasis on place, often failed to do: celebrate the environment while also painting a picture of the land's contested history.

Contested Environments

Joyce's articles in *Il Piccolo* were largely intended to confront forms of imperial rule in Ireland and Trieste. Ellmann and Ellsworth point out that Roberto Prezioso commissioned all nine pieces written for *Il Piccolo* because he wanted a 'display of evils of the British imperial rule in Ireland' in order to 'have its lesson for the imperial ruler of Trieste'.[43] Despite the fact that 'The City of the Tribes' and 'The Mirage of the Fisherman of Aran' appear to be the least political of the Triestine articles,[44] Joyce's portrayal of Galway demonstrates tensions between the environment and political exploitation, thereby pinpointing the cultural connection to place-attachment. Joyce reads the ecological elements of the bioregion against the colonial apparatus of the British state as though they should share a similar conversation. He describes Galway, or what he calls 'the Spanish city', 'scattered among innumerable little islands, cut by rivulets, cataracts, conduits, and canals, at the lower end of a vast gulf of the Atlantic Ocean in which the entire British navy could anchor'.[45] When explicating Joyce's articles in relation to place, it is necessary to examine his frequent references to a colonial history that entails contested geographies. After all, colonial occupation is, as Edward Said argues, 'an act of geographical violence'.[46] Such a history of violence suffusing the geography manifests itself in the place of a region, thereby politicising the surrounding environment.

The impact upon the environment within the colonies of the Spanish and British Empires reveals fierce tension between the demands for imperial development and the need for a colony's natural sustainability. In *Postcolonial Ecocriticism*, Graham Huggan and Helen Tiffin identify many shared concerns between colonialism and the environment. They argue, 'Postcolonial studies has come to understand environmental issues not only as central to the projects of European conquest and global domination, but also as inherent in the ideologies of imperialism.'[47] Within this framework we can read Joyce as a writer interested in exploring and commenting on Ireland's history of British imperialism in these two articles, a history that magnifies the geographical element of the land. Eric Bulson acknowledges, 'Joyce was not simply interested in playing the role of Irish tour guide for his audience of Triestine readers'; he has more interest in 'the coded discussions of British imperialism in Ireland'.[48]

In 'The Mirage of the Fisherman of Aran', Joyce intimates that the landscape forms both environmental and anti-colonial barriers that resist control and exploitation. He comments that just outside of Galway Bay the 'entire British navy could anchor'. He goes on to say: 'At the mouth of the gulf, the three Aran islands, lying on the grey waters like a sleeping whale, form a natural breakwater and take the force of the Atlantic waves.'[49] Joyce implies that the islands not only provide a naturally occurring archipelagic barrier for Galway Bay, but they also function as an obstacle for the British navy. The Aran Islands, therefore, are not isolated and jettisoned from civilisation;

instead, they are at the centre of Galway's cultural and environmental history. For Joyce, these islands trigger a colonial memory embedded in the landscape. He writes, 'beneath the waters of this bay and along its coast lie the wrecks of a squadron of the unfortunate Spanish Armada' (after their defeat in the sixteenth century by the British navy).[50] As distinctive and strategically placed landforms, the islands outside of Galway city form material barriers to occupation. Joyce recalls, 'you have only to close your eyes to this bothersome modernity for a moment to see in the twilight of history the "Spanish city"'.[51] The ruins of an alternative history, as if the Spanish Armada had never been defeated, are transparent in the surrounding environment of the city. Joyce juxtaposes this colonial history against the 'bothersome modernity' of the 'suburbs – new, gay, and heedless of the past'.[52] It is as if modernity has no recollection of the past because it may hinder development of the future. On the one hand, the material and symbolic decay of the 'Spanish city' foreshadows an eventual deterioration of British power. On the other hand, it indicates the decline of the bioregion resulting from colonial expansion, urbanisation and industrialisation.

Joyce's historical 'Spanish city' implies an alternative future in which Ireland's geography might belong to the Irish. As a critic of colonial rule, Joyce brings together a discussion of colonisation and the environment in 'The City of the Tribes' and 'The Mirage of the Fisherman'. The larger issue here is that, as Nash argues, 'the development or recovery of an effective relationship with place, after dislocation or cultural denigration by a supposedly superior cultural and racial colonial power, becomes a means to overcome the sense of displacement and crisis of identity'.[53] The cultural effect of colonisation directly impacts any sense of place-attachment to a specific geography. Regarding the geographical relationship of the colonised and coloniser, the Marxist geographer David Harvey remarks, 'The world's spaces were deterritorialised, stripped of their preceding significations, and then reterritorialised according to the convenience of colonial and imperial administration.'[54] While the British attempted to reappropriate topographies of place through deterritorialisation, Joyce reinscribes meaning in this place of colonial encounters through a form of reterritorialisation that involves place-attachment, by connecting local meaning and culture with an otherwise oppressive history of the environment. Due to the coloniser's inevitable influence, according to Said, topographies of place are only recoverable through the imagination.[55] In this sense, then, Joyce attempts recovering and re-imagining the occupied landscape through exploring historical examples of place-attachment in Galway.

Furthermore, contested space is a concern for Joyce in these two articles because it represents a colonised geography where place-attachment is confronted with the possibility of displacement. Brian Graham tracks this tension in his introduction to *In Search of Ireland: A Cultural Geography*: 'If landscape can be depicted as a contested text or narrative, it is clearly implicated in a people's identity, itself embedded in particular intellectual, institutional and temporal contexts.'[56] Galway establishes itself as part of the people's identity in this bioregion, particularly with the Spanish and British in the forefront, but also among the fourteen tribes in the background.[57] One of the points Joyce makes in these two articles is that Galway is as much a contested space as Dublin, or even Ireland for that matter. Such spaces contain not only contested geographies, but also contested histories. Specific historical events are often what determine the boundaries of a geographical space or establish its identity, just as cultural developments unfold at particular locations within the landscape that then evoke its character. Historical accounts often appear through story, which is also a way to inscribe place in a particular space. Indeed, there has been what is referred to as 'a problem-centred tradition of English travel writing about Ireland' that exploded in the eighteenth century and lasted all the way into the nineteenth century.[58] These non-Irish voices produce a different and often contesting version of environmental history and, consequently, re-appropriate any sense of Irish place.

Joyce, in contrast, weaves history through an Irish travel narrative to recover these contested landscapes. In doing so, he offers an alternative place in the past and, therefore, foregrounds the future. In the introduction to *Contested Landscapes*, Barbara Bender maintains, 'Landscapes contain the traces of past activities, and people select the stories they tell, the memories and histories they evoke, the interpretative narratives that they weave, to further their activities in the present-future.'[59] Drawing from Bender's assertion, I want to claim that Joyce similarly recounts the traces of past activities of this landscape in order to retell a different history. Recasting place as story in the shadow of the British imperialism during the time Joyce wrote these pieces also differentiates place-attachment for both the coloniser and the colonised, albeit for vastly different ends. As Said argues, what 'distinguishes the imagination of anti-imperialism' is 'the primacy of the geographical element'.[60] With this in mind, Joyce frames an alternative historical geography of Galway in order to foster an anti-imperialist sensibility through his version of Galway's past and present. His ability to attach a sense of place merges with the project of decolonialisation by developing the 'primacy' of a specific environment in contradistinction to colonised spaces.

The Mirage of Mapping and Memory

In 'The Mirage of the Fisherman of Aran', Joyce provides the account of the 'fisherman of Aran' as an accessible entry into establishing place-attachment by integrating the fisherman's experience into the larger fabric of the Galway bioregion. In the article, the Aran Islands are integral to Galway's environmental and cultural history because they extend back to St Brendan's era when the islands were not remote bastions of unrecognised peoples, language and culture. Joyce uses the geography of 'Aran' to peel back the layers of history in order to draw attention to the undergrowth of the landscape and its cultural memory. He writes,

> From the new world, wealth and vital energy would run through this new artery of an Ireland drained of blood. Again, after about ten centuries, the mirage which blinded the port fisherman of Aran, follower and emulator of St. Brendan, appears in the distance, vague and tremulous on the mirror of the ocean.[61]

When identifying place-attachment, the mirage is the memory of history, infused, entangled, connected, and remembered in the landscape. The phrase 'vague and tremulous on the mirror of the ocean' reflects the memory of a once-vital period when the geographic arteries contained vitality, not an insipid existence where the Spanish houses in Galway are overtaken with the overgrowth of weeds and grasses. In ecocritical accounts of Irish travel writing, as Flannery claims, 'the landscape is purged of its historical details and an aesthetic picturesque displaces traumatic memory'.[62] Joyce, however, embellishes historical details of the local people and culture to disrupt the trail of a traumatic memory and envision another way to view Galway. Instead of elevating the picturesque or exotic accounts of the Aran Islands, Joyce materialises the mirage as an alternative history.

Or, as Barry acknowledges, Joyce 'thinks *with* history'.[63] In so doing, Joyce covers a vast area of record infused with personal history and experience. The mirage of history offers another way of perceiving the Aran Islands, one that connects the same topography of place for the fisherman and St Brendan with two different points in history. Therefore, Joyce's purpose as a travel writer, with what I am suggesting contains an ecocritical sensibility, is to evoke the meaning of place and to provide one possible vantage point for peering into an alternative history of this region.

Reimagining history as though it were a mirage on the horizon also suggests how landscape can function for Joyce. The word landscape, via the Dutch, came to the English language in the sixteenth century. *Landschap*, later converted to colloquial English as *landskip*, represented a place for human occupation and jurisdiction.[64] Joyce expands this denotative definition of landscape pertaining to occupation and control into representational space. The eventual attachment to place, then, occurs through history, language and culture, thereby fostering a sustained relationship with a bioregion as a representational space. By this way of viewing landscape, the Aran Islands evoke perhaps the strongest sense of place-attachment for Joyce. While 'Aran, it is said, is the strangest place in the world',[65] it also serves as an historical landscape that connects travellers to this place through its sense of the Irish locale, whether they are readers of Joyce's articles or tourists who travel to the Aran Islands. To this effect, Joyce takes the reader to the Aran Islands in order to witness the local fisherman with 'sure feet' because he wears locally made shoes called 'pampooties', which are a 'rough sandal of untanned cowhide'.[66] Through these details of locality Joyce implants an emotional attachment to the place of Aran without relying on strict observation or abstract analysis of the space. Joyce also explains that 'around the stunted shrubs which grow on the hills of the island his [the fisherman's] imagination has woven legends and tales which reveal the depths of his psyche'.[67] The fisherman's direct relationship with the landscape relates to a collective cultural unconscious, where the fisherman accesses the cultural memory of his people 'woven' through legends and deposited in his psyche. The connection to place is not only through a collective history, but also through a shared landscape that can be felt in the depths of a person's interior. Landscape, therefore, is both external, as a spatial jurisdiction, and internal, as an emotional register of place-attachment.

A case could be made that forms of mapping, along with memory and landscape, contribute to the development of place-attachment. Travel writers map through prose, as well as through technical maps, and identify topographical and cultural signposts. The specificity of the cartographic coordinates does not matter as much as the metaphoric existence of such topographies, colouring the cultural nuances that make up various bioregions. Although a map is open and its signposts are seemingly transparent, the ambiguities of a map and deciphering its signposts can be limited to the viewer's own subjective experience. A map is also a claim, quite literally a claim upon the land as an appropriation for a given power and figuratively an argumentative interpretation of a land's identity. To map, then, is to claim and name, or rename, a territory and ultimately define ownership. When looking at the map from a different angle, the cartographer Tim Robinson, who mapped the Aran Islands in the 1970s, claims that mapping can also function as a prose map of descriptive geography and cultural identification. He goes on to say in an interview with Christine Cusick that the 'cartography of particular places can imply something on that general theme, but ultimately only prose, land prose at length, recursive and excursive, can begin to map it and act out the building-up of the overarching, underpinning, encircling realities of sky, land and sea out of uncountable glints of detail'.[68] These signposts connect a reader through place-attachment, navigating a sense of place through personal encounters within a specific geography.

Joyce describes this cartographic process of prose writing about particular places in 'The City of the Tribes':

> Thus, the map maker enumerates and depicts fourteen bastions, fourteen towers on the wall, fourteen principal streets, fourteen narrow streets, and then, sliding down into a minor mode, six gardens, six altars for the procession of Corpus Domini, six markets, and six other wonders. Among these last, in fact, the last of the last, the worthy Dean enumerates 'the old pigeon house located in the southern part of the city'.[69]

The Dean's remark regarding the pigeon house at the end of the quotation is quite telling, despite the obscurity of it on the surface. One reading could demonstrate Joyce's ironic humour by describing the quaint, archaic relic of the pigeon house. Yet, this last sentence illustrates that every point on this cultural map represents an aspect of Galway's history, symbolically ordering both the human and non-human worlds that exist in this landscape. The pigeon house may be old and located in a less desirable part of the city, but the Dean recognises its importance and integrates it into the larger cartographic description of the city where built and non-built environments exist congruently. It also reveals another example of place-attachment since such a personal and minor detail resonates as an emotional signifier. The pigeon house represents something built and cared for by a local inhabitant, thereby connecting the human and non-human within the bioregion. The pigeons, in contrast, are clearly non-built, non-human parts of the environment that are equally cared for and supported. By culturally codifying the memorable elements of the Galway landscape, Joyce establishes a viable method for non-cartographers to view, as John Wilson Foster proposes, 'the "real" three-dimensional landscapes of Ireland'.[70]

Joyce's closing lines in 'The Mirage of the Fisherman of Aran' perhaps best encompass his overarching approach to these environmental articles, bringing together themes of mapping, memory, and the history of place.

> In the twilight the names of the ports cannot be distinguished, but the line that leaves Galway and ramifies and spreads out recalls the motto placed near the crest of his native city by a mystic and perhaps even prophetic head of a monastery: *Quasi lilium germinans germinabit, et quasi terebinthus extendans ramos suos* [It will grow like a sprouting lily, stretching out its branches like the terebinth tree].[71]

While the actual port names contain less significance for the traveller than the feeling acquired in this place, the connection to Galway and the rest of the world underscores both the local and its connection to Ireland's larger diaspora. The West of Ireland does not represent the end of the Irish frontier; rather, it is the beginning of an entire network of histories and genealogies, extending its tree branches out to many geographical regions across the Atlantic. The tree metaphor provocatively ends the essay for two reasons. First, it signifies the extension of both a tree and a map as a limitless form of record forged from the environment. Second, it conflates 'nature' and 'culture' together in order to establish that place-attachment exists at the heart of Joyce's two environmental articles. In a fitting end, Joyce extends his own prose branches in order to guide the reader through this variegated geographical forest.

Lost and Found

Even though Joyce is a writer known more for developing an urban rather than ecological sensibility, he effectively addresses landscape, geography, locality and the environment through an analysis of place-attachment. In fact, Joyce's repeated interplay between place and space reveals a key aspect to his environmental imagination. My task here has been to present Joyce as a travel writer in order to examine his overlooked nonfiction with specific attention to its critical environmental subtext. In doing so, I argue that place-attachment exists in Joyce's cultural readings of Irish geographical history and thus demonstrates that he is in fact 'doing ecocriticism' of a certain kind.[72] Unlike other environmentally engaged writers focused on activism, Joyce does not explicitly call his readers to take some sort of action in environmental preservation. Instead, he recognises the emergence of place-attachment within a given geography that unmasks various cultural and historical codes. Consequently, Joyce calls Ireland to action by recalling a geographical history of place in the West rather than rewriting a history solely for the consumption of tourists and travellers. When approaching travel writing in this way, Joyce is able to underscore the primacy of the environment, where the relationships between geography and cultural history are fundamental to appreciating the confusions and contestations of Ireland's identity.[73]

Throughout 'The City of the Tribes' and 'The Mirage of the Fisherman of Aran' Joyce provides not just 'another explanation of what we have lost', as Simon Schama reminds us, but 'an exploration of what we may yet find'.[74] Finding cultural and environmental understanding in a complex geography is possible through writing that encourages personal connection to place. Joyce assumes the role, in a rare but important moment, of a travel writer who directs the reader toward a distinctive cultural and geographical history of the West of Ireland. Joyce's environmental imagination locates the contested territory of Galway, and the West, through his unique lens as a travel writer in order to retell a version of history that establishes place-attachment as a vital element to understanding Ireland's cultural and environmental landscapes.

III

Joyce, Somatic Ecology and the Body

'Can excrement be art . . . if not, why not?'

Joyce's Aesthetic Theory and the Flux of Consciousness

EUGENE O'BRIEN

In the fifth chapter of James Joyce's *A Portrait of the Artist as a Young Man*, Stephen is having a detailed conversation on aesthetics and beauty with his friend Lynch. He is in the process of defining his aesthetic theory, and is explaining how this came about:

> To finish what I was saying about beauty, said Stephen, the most satisfying relations of the sensible must therefore correspond to the necessary phases of artistic apprehension. Find these and you find the qualities of universal beauty. Aquinas says: *ad pulcritudinem tria requiruntur integritas, consonantia, claritas.* I translate it so: *three things are needed for beauty, wholeness, harmony, and radiance.*[1]

Stephen is quoting Thomas Aquinas and is defining art in very intellectual terms. The rationalistic division and partitioning of aesthetic experience has been very much the norm in Western thinking on beauty and at this juncture, the quotation mirrors this through a suasive rhetorical sleight of hand. The word 'apprehended', a term that is bound up with sensuous experience of the world, is denuded of its corporeal dimensions through its sub-division into the Thomistic tripartite qualities of '*integritas, consonantia, claritas*'.

The division of a single quality into intellectual abstractions means that the mind/body duality was enforced through a redefining of perception. Thus, the mind is the agency of perception, while the body becomes one of the objects of perception; the mind is the active creator of our sense of beauty, while it is no longer an active participant in its agency. As Umberto Eco puts it:

> The beautiful object is an object that by virtue of its form delights the senses, especially sight and hearing. But those aspects perceivable with the senses are not the only factors that

> express the Beauty of the object: in the case of the human body an important role is also played by the qualities of the soul and the personality, which are perceived by the mind's eye more than by the eye of the body.[2]

This sense that the mind, and not the body, is the sole actant in the apprehension of beauty has a long intellectual history. Since, in Plato's view, the body is a 'dark cavern that imprisons the soul', then the 'sight of the senses must be overcome by intellectual sight, which requires a knowledge of the dialectical arts, in other words philosophy'.[3]

While it is Aquinas who is cited, there are definite hints of Cartesian dualism at work in Stephen's early formal discussion of beauty. The Australian ecofeminist Val Plumwood makes the point that Descartes, as part of a project of making the body less of an agent in thinking, took the 'mental activities which involve the body, such as sense perception, and which appear to bridge the mind/body and human/animal division' and reinterpreted them in terms of 'consciousness', which he saw as a 'purely mental operation'.[4] Greg Garrard, in his overview of ecocriticism, sees this as a Cartesian hypersaturation of mind and body, and he traces the mind/body split back to Descartes, who denied to animals not only the 'faculty of reason, but the whole range of feelings and sensations that he had associated with thought'.[5] In this chapter, I will argue that art, and specifically that of *A Portrait of the Artist as a Young Man*, offers a corrective to this dualism, and that Joyce's aesthetic theory, which is worked out through this book, is a holistic one which values all aspects of experience as part of the aesthetic. I will also suggest homologies between Joyce's thinking on art and that of a number of philosophers and thinkers. The politics of such a view have strong implications for a criticism which sees the world not as an object to be used and mastered, but rather as a partner in aesthetic apprehension and experience.

Martin Heidegger critiques the *Cogito* from precisely this perspective of a disassociated certainty, noting that: 'the absolute "Being-certain" [*Gewisssein*] of the *Cogito* exempted him from raising the question of the meaning of the Being which this entity possesses'.[6] Maurice Merleau-Ponty would agree, noting that 'consciousness is in the first place not a matter of "I think that" but of "I can"'.[7] Both thinkers see the detachment of the mind from the body and the environment as flawed and both also see art as a way of restoring that sense of connectedness. This separation encourages a view that sees the 'I' as self and the environment as other, which can lead to that discourse of mastery and use which has little consideration for and appreciation of the environment. However, the 'understanding of the earth granted by art' challenges this view that:

> does not let the matter be, but seeks to master it, to overpower it by subjecting it to human measures . . . To be open to the reality of things is to be open to that dimension of things that will always resist human mastery. It is this dimension Heidegger calls the earth. Art recalls us to the earth.[8]

Heidegger has been identified as a predecessor of 'deep ecology', and the figure of the 'Green Heidegger' is a familiar one in textbooks on his philosophy.[9] In their seminal book *Deep Ecology*, Bill Devall and George Sessions have written that 'Heidegger called us to dwell authentically on this Earth, parallel to our call to dwell in our bioregion and to dwell with alertness to the natural processes'.[10] His ongoing critique of 'anthropocentric humanism, his call for humanity to learn to "let beings be", his notion that humanity is involved in a "play" or "dance" with earth, sky and gods' makes his work central to the concerns of ecocritical thinking, and helps to 'support the claim that he is a major deep ecological theorist'.[11] As we will see, Joyce's sense of the aesthetic has a similar imperative of connectedness and relatedness of the self and the world.

Jacques Derrida has also referenced Descartes as a source of the mind/body dualism. He notes how in the famous phrase *Cogito ergo sum* (I think, therefore I am), Descartes abstracts from the 'I am' his own 'living body, which, in a way, he objectivises as a machine or corpse (these are his words); so much so that his "I am" can apprehend and present itself only from the perspective of this potential cadaverisation'.[12] The use of the term 'cadaverisation', a typically Derridean quasi-neologism, is interesting as Derrida is signifying not that the body is separate from the mind, but rather that the body has been made a cadaver and that its agency and influence have been diminished by this sense of Cartesian separation of mind and body. For Descartes, in order to define access to a pure 'I am', it is necessary to suspend or, rather, detach, 'precisely as detachable, all reference to life, to the life of the body, and to animal life'.[13] Derrida has had a long association with the works of Joyce. He explicitly discusses his links with Joyce in his essay 'Two Words for Joyce', in which he claims, 'every time I write, and even in the most academic pieces of work, Joyce's ghost is always coming on board';[14] while in 'Ulysses

Gramophone: Hear Say Yes in Joyce', he refers to 'the book of all books, *Ulysses* or *Finnegans*'.[15]

The detachability of which Derrida speaks is, I would argue, the origin of the attitude of the Western *mentaliteé* to the environment and to the living world in which we have our being. It has allowed reason to separate itself from the environment and to take on a dominant and exploitative role. Extrapolating from the dualism of mind and body and from the hierarchical structure set up wherein mind is the greater and body is the lesser term, one can trace the progression to viewing the mind as dominant over the body and over the living world which the body inhabits. One of the negative consequences of Enlightenment rationality is precisely this privileging of instrumental reason which saw the body, the world, the environment and everything outside of rational inquiry as in some way less important. Theodor Adorno and Max Horkheimer, in their *Dialectic of Enlightenment*, have offered a telling critique of such instrumental reason, where they speak of how 'instrumentality' has led to 'the blind mastery of nature'.[16] They trace this dialectic of mastery and use-value through what they see as the methodical extirpation of all natural traces 'due to the sublimation into a transcendental or logical subject, which forms the reference point of reason, the legislating authority of action'.[17] I would argue that the aesthetic is a counter-discourse to this hegemonic view as, unlike technology, art 'signals the site of a true dwelling on earth', because art 'begins with the world as this unfamiliar, uncanny phenomenon, which it does not seek to reduce, but to deepen, to "understand" in a way that is radically different from its rational–scientific conquest',[18] and in this chapter, I will be looking at the aesthetic very much in this light.

Derrida has also commented on the Cartesian attenuation of the role of the body in the realm of thinking. Indeed, the title of his book *The Animal that Therefore I Am* is both a parody of and an *homage* to Descartes' *Cogito*. Joyce, too, has been influenced by Cartesian thought, but like Derrida, it is an influence with which he takes issue and with which he has a complex relationship. In a punning phrase that has echoes of Derrida's own title, Joyce also parodies the *Cogito*: 'Cog it out, here goes a sum',[19] and goes on to refer to Descartes again in *Finnegans Wake*:

> All moanday, tearsday,
> wailsday, thumpsday, frightday, shatterday till

> the fear of the Law. Look at this twitches!
> He was quisquis, floored on his plankraft of
> shittim wood. Look at him! Sink deep or
> touch not the Cartesian spring![20]

Normatively, the days of the week rationally divide our experience into equal temporal units, thereby symbolising the intellection of our apprehension of the world through rational thought. In this novel, however, orthographic representations of the days of the week are haunted by the body and by emotion. As well as being signifiers of time, each word also signifies the lived emotions of people in time: 'moan'; 'tears'; 'wails'; 'thumps'; 'fright' and 'shatter' are all redolent of a lived experience of time. They exemplify the depth of living as opposed to the rational structures of thought. To achieve a perspectival depth, to 'sink deep', then the Cartesian spring must be avoided and I argue that, despite Stephen's initial swerve towards the intellectualisation of the apprehension of beauty which we have noted, Joyce's more developed aesthetic theory is, in fact, a deconstruction of the mind/body duality, and acts as a call for the primacy of bodily sensation in the aesthetic as a whole.

In this sense, there is a strong correlation with the ideas of Maurice Merleau-Ponty on the phenomenology of the aesthetic and of perception. His notion of 'intentionality', which is distinguished from the Kantian relation to a possible object, is that the 'unity of the world, before being posited by knowledge in a specific act of identification', is 'lived' as 'ready-made or already there'.[21] He feels that 'in experiencing the beautiful, for example, I am aware of a harmony between sensation and concept, between myself and others, which is itself without any concept'.[22] He posits a perceptual 'synergic system', where the experience of the external world involves 'the synchronisation of my body with it'.[23] Merleau-Ponty speaks of a 'co-existence or communion',[24] which is centred at a 'nexus of living meanings'.[25] This sense of a unified perception, unified in terms of mind and body and in terms of an 'already there' relationship with the world, is contiguous to what Joyce is attempting to set out as an aesthetic theory, or, to be more exact, an aesthetic process in this book. Indeed, 'a nexus of living meanings' and a 'synergistic experience' could both be used to describe the list of weekdays in the above quotation.

It is no accident that his desire to avoid the Cartesian spring is prefaced by the phrase 'shittem', a variant of the slang term for excrement. As his aesthetic theory develops in *A Portrait of the Artist as a*

Young Man, excrement will again feature in his discussion of the value of the aesthetic:

> I have a book at home, said Stephen, in which I have written down questions which are more amusing than yours were. In finding the answers to them I found the theory of esthetic which I am trying to explain. Here are some questions I set myself: *Is a chair finely made tragic or comic? Is the portrait of Mona Lisa good if I desire to see it? Is the bust of Sir Philip Crampton lyrical, epic or dramatic? Can excrement or a child or a louse be a work of art? If not, why not?*
>
> Why not, indeed? said Lynch, laughing. – *if a man hacking in fury at a block of wood*, Stephen continued, *make there an image of a cow, is that image a work of art? if not, why not?*[26]

In this discussion, the italicised examples foreground the inclusivity of his aesthetic theory in terms of the human body. His questions take in all of human form, not just the traditional objects that are seen as beautiful. The discussion moves from the traditional objects of intellection, the Mona Lisa and a bust of Sir Philip Crampton (both portraits in different ways), through to the key questions as to whether excrement or a child or a louse can be a work of art. I would suggest that this has some significance in terms of ecocriticism, as Joyce is suggesting that there is no split between mind and body in terms of the aesthetic. An enigmatic smile, or the head of an aristocrat, or a piece of excrement, or a louse, or a child can all, he suggests, become a work of art and if not, why not?

The example of the wooden cow is interesting, especially in the light of its similarity to a programmatic point made by Martin Heidegger:

> A cabinetmaker's apprentice, someone who is learning to build cabinets and the like, will serve as an example. His learning is not mere practice, to gain facility in the use of tools. Nor does he merely gather knowledge about the customary forms of the things he is to build. If he is to become a true cabinetmaker, he makes himself answer and respond above all to the different kinds of wood and to the shapes slumbering within wood-to-wood as it enters into man's dwelling with all the hidden riches of its nature. In fact, this relatedness to wood is what maintains the whole.[27]

Both writers see a value in the response of the artist to his material, and while one expresses this in the interrogative, the other,

Heidegger, is more certain. For Heidegger, the relationship between the creator and the material of creation is a bodily one, where there is a harmony and a connection between mind, body and world. Heidegger expresses this sense of holistic unity in a resonant phrase – 'poetically man dwells'[28] – which stresses the relatedness between the human and his or her environment. It can be shown that excrement is a signal part of this relatedness. As food taken from the environment is processed by the body, so excrement is returned to the environment and this is an aspect of our inter-relatedness that is ongoing and necessary; given that excrement can also be used as fertiliser to nourish new growth, it is also an example of environmental recycling before this term became part of the lexicon of ecocriticism. And of course, it is an example of the external being internalised and then returned to the external again, as well as the presencing of an item of our lives that is normally occluded and is seen as almost a somatic opposite to the intellect. So Joyce is taking a part of experience that has been hitherto seen as separate from thinking and aesthetic creation and bringing it to the fore. It is by taking these and unpacking the occluded elements of value that they can become 'grafted onto a "new" concept of writing',[29] which is the emancipatory aim of the exercise. In Heidegger's view the artist represents his medium, as opposed to mastering it, and thereby makes it conspicuous: 'according to Heidegger the work moves the earth itself into the Open of a world. In the world it asserts the usually passed over earth.'[30]

However much traditional rationality would like to excise the bodily functions from our humanity, by stressing the idea of 'intelligible extension as a denuded body',[31] the artist will always stress the inter-relation between the human and his or her environment, the 'dwelling' of which Heidegger speaks. For him, the separation of mind and body is not tenable: 'in order to say what he must say, reporting what he sees, relaying what he hears, the author has to speak of the gods, mortals, the earth, shoes, the temple, the sky, the bridge, the jug, the fourfold, the poem, pain, the threshold, the difference, and stillness as he does'.[32] This would parallel Joyce's own views about the importance of the integration of body, mind and soul in the creation of aesthetic experience. As he describes his first game of rugby, he stresses the bodily dimension of the experience: 'he felt his body small and weak amid the throng of the players and his eyes were weak and watery'.[33] When he is being teased about whether or not he kisses his mother, his reaction is again an integrated one: 'he felt his whole body hot and confused in a moment'.[34] As he goes on to ponder the notion of kissing, again, we see the integrated and undetachable nature of his aesthetic musings:

> Was it right to kiss his mother or wrong to kiss his mother? What did that mean, to kiss? You put your face up like that to say good night and then his mother put her face down. That was to kiss. His mother put her lips on his cheek; her lips were soft and they wetted his cheek; and they made a tiny little noise: kiss.[35]

Here there is intellection and rational exploration of sensation, but there is also sensation for its own sake, a core part of the aesthetic experience.

In the infirmary, we see this aesthetic fusion come to fruition. Lying in bed, having caught cold from the square ditch,[36] he hears a bell and:

> He said over to himself the song that Brigid had taught him.
> Dingdong! The castle bell!
> Farewell, my mother!
> Bury me in the old churchyard
> Beside my eldest brother.
> My coffin shall be black,
> Six angels at my back,
> Two to sing and two to pray
> And two to carry my soul away.
> How beautiful and sad that was! How beautiful the words were where they said Bury me in the old churchyard! A tremor passed over his body. How sad and how beautiful! He wanted to cry quietly but not for himself: for the words, so beautiful and sad, like music. The bell! The bell![37]

Here we see the power of words over the body and the way in which apprehension is an embodied trait; the fusion of the life of the mind and 'the life of the body'.[38] The words have a somatic effect on his body and provoke a reaction: in a nutshell, this is the core of Stephen's aesthetic portrait and of Joyce's aesthetic theory, as it explores the interconnection and relatedness of all aspects of life from the aesthetic perspective. This is what Heidegger terms a 'primal oneness' through which 'the four – earth and sky, divinities and mortals – belong together in one'.[39] Joyce's aesthetic theory foregrounds this sense of belonging and oneness. Stephen's reactions to the sound of the bell, and his synthesising of sound, mind and body, can be seen as an example of art as presencing.

For Heidegger, presencing is 'luminous self-concealing'. It is the 'sheltering of what is present within the intangible nearness of what remains in coming – that coming which is an increasing self-veiling'.[40] In connection with the intentionality already spoken of, the work of art, rather than mastering its material, instead allows the material to presence itself. So, 'the work as work, in its presencing, is a setting forth, a making';[41] it is an 'urgent' readiness for action,[42] and this readiness is the readiness to see the connectedness between self, mind, body and earth through aesthetic perception.

For Stephen, the body is a crucial dimension in the aesthetic experience, and the connections between sexual and aesthetic feelings in the book are a testament to this. From the outset, his synaesthetic relationships with the environment and with women (as evidenced by his pondering on kissing) have been central, and this theme will climax in the apotheosis of the bird-girl on Sandymount Strand in Chapter Five. In this example, in Chapter Four, he remembers the touch of a girl's hand, and it is a memory that is synaesthetic:

> Then in the dark and unseen by the other two he rested the tips of the fingers of one hand upon the palm of the other hand, scarcely touching it lightly. But the pressure of her fingers had been lighter and steadier: and suddenly the memory of their touch traversed his brain and body like an invisible wave.[43]

The foregrounding of the touch of the hand is interesting as again, there are Heideggerian resonances at work here. For Heidegger, all thinking is a craft, a 'handicraft', and he sees thinking as 'something like building a cabinet', a task that fuses mind, body and the element of wood. Heidegger focuses especially on the hand, and his teasing out of the epistemology of the hand:

> In the common view, the hand is part of our bodily organism. But the hand's essence can never be determined, or explained, by its being an organ which can grasp. Apes, too, have organs that can grasp, but they do not have hands. The hand is infinitely different from all grasping organs – paws, claws, or fangs – different by an abyss of essence. Only a being who can speak, that is, think, can have hands and can be handy in achieving works of handicraft.[44]

For Joyce, the relationship between feeling, thought and expression is very similar to that proposed by Heidegger: mind and body are fused in their reaction to and aesthetic expression of the world in which they exist.

Interestingly, Joyce mentions hands some one hundred and eighty five times in *A Portrait of the Artist as a Young Man*, with references to Eileen's hands being crucial to the very young Stephen's gradual understanding of the concept of metaphor. He recalls how Dante reminds him that Eileen Vance was a Protestant and that when Dante was young, she used to hear Protestants making fun of 'the litany of the Blessed Virgin': '*Tower of Ivory*, they used to say, *House of Gold*! How could a woman be a tower of ivory or a house of gold?'[45] In pondering this question, a question which arises in his mind in the midde of the tense Christmas Dinner episode, Stephen is once again attempting to see how language connects with reality, and to understand the connection between word and world. He is, far from detaching mind and body, intent on fusing them in order to understand the Heideggerian primal oneness and interconnectedness of place, transcendence, mind and body:

> Who was right then? And he remembered the evening in the infirmary in Clongowes, the dark waters, the light at the pierhead and the moan of sorrow from the people when they had heard. Eileen had long white hands. One evening when playing tig she had put her hands over his eyes: long and white and thin and cold and soft. That was ivory: a cold white thing. That was the meaning of TOWER OF IVORY.[46]

The fusion of mind and body here demonstrates the importance of the body in terms of language and expression, as well as the relationship between the body and its environment. It is through touch that the aesthetic apprehension of the meaning of metaphor becomes real in Stephen's mind, and this is the interrelation of which Heidegger spoke in terms of how man [*sic*] dwells poetically. It is this sense of dwelling, of being part of the world, of being a creature of the world, that is at the core of Joyce's sense of the aesthetic, and his use of hands is a metaphorical connection with the Heideggerian sense of a hand as an organ whose meaning is dependent on the mind and speech of the person as human.

That the hand is the organ of written expression, of inscribing language on blank sheets of paper, is also a strong factor, and it is noteworthy that this sense of Stephen as physically writing is made overt in the final chapter, where the style of the book is now that of a diary, where each entry is handwritten and where each date is redolent with the emotions that are experienced on that date (in a manner proleptic of the days of the week already quoted from *Finnegans Wake*). It is also interesting that when he takes communion after the purification of his retreat, again it is a fusion of body and soul that expresses his sense of joy: 'his hands were trembling and his soul trembled as he heard the priest pass with the ciborium from communicant to communicant'.[47] The use of 'trembling' to describe a movement of the soul is very much in line with Joyce's sense of a fusion that is aesthetically sanctioned, just as before his first sexual encounter with a prostitute, it is described how her 'tinkling hands' ran through his hair.[48] His description of his first sexual experience, again in terms of touching the other and in terms of a related experience, is replete with this sense of relatedness:

> He closed his eyes, surrendering himself to her, body and mind, conscious of nothing in the world but the dark pressure of her softly parting lips. They pressed upon his brain as upon his lips as though they were the vehicle of a vague speech; and between them he felt an unknown and timid pressure, darker than the swoon of sin, softer than sound or odour.[49]

The connection of brain and lip here, through the word 'press', is another example of his aesthetic sense where experience is loaded with meaning and with a sense of aesthetic connectedness. There is no mastery here but rather surrender.

The same is found when he hears a woman singing *Rosie O'Grady*, and Cranly responds with the Latin phrase:

> *Mulier cantat.*
> The soft beauty of the Latin word touched with an enchanting touch the dark of the evening, with a touch fainter and more persuading than the touch of music or of a woman's hand.[50]

Once again, the sense of touch is both intellectual and physical, and that fusion is at the core of Joyce's thinking. Here touch affects the 'dark of the evening' and is compared to the 'touch of music' or to the touch of a woman's hand. In this sense, one could apply a Heideggerian tag that would be appropriate:

> the sail
> of thinking keeps trimmed hard to the
> wind of the matter.[51]

Joyce's portrait explores how the aesthetic sensibility has grown and developed in Stephen's grasp of the interrelation between self, other and the world. Stephen's rootedness underscores Heidegger's point that 'what maintains and sustains even this handicraft is not the mere manipulation of tools, but the relatedness to wood',[52] as he, too, is related to his environment:

> Stephen Dedalus
> Class of Elements
> Clongowes Wood College
> Sallins
> County Kildare
> Ireland
> Europe
> The World
> The Universe.

That was in his writing: and Fleming one night for a cod had written on the opposite page:

> Stephen Dedalus is my name,
> Ireland is my nation.
> Clongowes is my dwellingplace
> And heaven my expectation.[53]

Here, there is a very strong sense of Heideggerian dwelling as Stephen is located within his world and on the earth. The fusion between the local and the global; the present and the future; the immanent and the transcendent is clear in the location of Stephen as part of the fourfold and as part of his environment, and it is an index of Joyce's own integrative and syncretic aesthetic processes.

I mention Joyce here, as opposed to Stephen, because I suggest that Joyce's aesthetic theory is one wherein the body (be it of excrement, child or louse) is at the centre of his aesthetic and epistemological theoretical paradigm. Throughout *A Portrait of the Artist as a Young Man*, the human body is at the core of his aesthetic experience. The title is significant here as it is a portrait of the artist, when he is a young man. It is a development, not just of the subjectivity of Stephen Dedalus, but of his aesthetic subjectivity. As Colin McCabe has noted, 'central to the discourse of literary criticism is the philosophical category of the subject',[54] and in terms of Irish writing, the *Bildungsroman* (a narrative of growth from childhood to maturity), has long been a staple in Irish writing, across the genres of short story and poetry but especially in the case of the novel. A kind of subset of the *Bildungsroman* is the *Künstlerroman*, the story of an artist's growth to maturity, and this necessitates a focus on the senses and the body, and from the outset, the body is foregrounded in this book. As art is synaesthetic, he is providing, throughout *A Portrait of the Artist as a Young Man*, a deconstruction of the Cartesian dualism and he reinscribes the role of the perceiving, or intentional, body (in the phenomenological sense) as an agent of knowledge and experience.

In this book, it is not mind or body, but the relation between mind and body, which is the subject of the portrait in question. He takes 'balanced binary oppositions of classical philosophy,'[55] and disrupts this balance through a writing that demonstrates that such oppositions, while seemingly underpinned by a logic of 'neither/nor', can be deconstructed to reveal a logic of 'both this and that'.[56] As Derrida notes, one 'never accedes to a text without some relation to its contextual opening and that a context is not made up of only what is so trivially called a text';[57] in this case, the text of the mind as mastering the body, and by extension nature, needs to be examined in the context of its dwelling in nature. This is very much what Joyce does by demonstrating the connectedness of mind, body and environment in his developing aesthetic theory in this book.

The final example of this can be seen in the opening of the book, where the dawnings of an aesthetic consciousness are to be found in the infant Stephen's recollections of his early encounters with the world. These encounters are significant in the development of subjectivity. Jacques Lacan notes that the 'little man' at the *infans* stage manifests 'the symbolic matrix in which the *I* is precipitated in a primordial form, prior to being objectified in the dialectic of identification with the other, and before language restores to it, in the universal, its function as subject'.[58] In other words, it is the conflation of the infant with language that is creative of subjectivity, and it is the initial stages of this conflation that are the focus of the opening pages of the book. The opening section is a series of sense impressions where all of the senses are involved. The narrator *hears* the story: 'once upon a time'; he *sees* his father: 'he had a hairy face'; he *feels* the touch of the cold urine in bed: 'When you wet the bed first it is warm, then it gets cold'; he *smells* the oilsheet: 'it had a queer smell', while taste is indexed in the fact that Betty Byrne 'sold lemon platt'.[59] These sensory impressions of the world are recalled in language but they refer to sensations which the infant Stephen is attempting to express in language. That this language is incipient and nascent is very clear from the mispronunciation of 'the green rose blossoms' as 'O, the green wothe botheth'.[60] These are infant recollections and they involve the incipient stages of expression speech (song):'he sang that song. It was his song.'[61] The Italian philosopher Giorgio Agamben makes some interesting points about the development of language. He sees early experiences as wordless and feels that the human need to acquire language acts as a form of limit on infancy:

> On the contrary, the constitution of the subject in and through language is precisely the expropriation of this 'wordless' experience; from the outset, it is always 'speech'. A primary experience, far from being subjective, could then only be what in human beings comes before the subject – that is, before language: a 'wordless' experience in the literal sense of the term, a human *infancy [in-fancy]*, whose boundary would be marked by language.[62]

Infancy is a term that, for Agamben, is intimately linked to potentiality, and in many ways this is the thematic and narrative core of *A Portrait of the Artist as a Young Man*.[63] As Agamben makes clear, speech and infancy are linked in the most substantial way.[64] From the beginning, where there is a mimetic presentation of baby talk and of the beginnings of an interaction between the infant Stephen and his world and its words, there is a teleological progression at work which culminates in his resonant declaration of aesthetic purpose towards the conclusion of the book:

> The soul is born, he said vaguely, first in those moments I told you of. It has a slow and dark birth, more mysterious than the birth of the body. When the soul of a man is born in this country there are nets flung at it to hold it back from flight. You talk to me of nationality, language, religion. I shall try to fly by those nets.[65]

I would suggest that there is a double logic at work here. The word 'by' can be read as an adverb, signifying a movement past, suggesting that he will fly past or around those nets. This meaning would suggest that the nets are traps that aim to catch him and inhibit his free movement. But the word can also be read as a preposition, meaning a mode of propulsion, suggesting that he will use those nets to fuel his flight. The interesting thing about this statement is the swerve from the mind to the body, with the soul seen as incorporeal, but either attempting to fly around, or else using as a means of propulsion, the very material nets of nationality, language, religion.

Even if Stephen were to try to fly around these or to escape from them, he is incapable of so doing as he is Irish and writes about his Irishness to a huge extent, in the shape of Parnell, the Irish language and its relationship with English, and the cultural politics of the time. The same can be said for religion, because even as he attempts to sublate religion through aesthetics, his frame of reference is suffused with religious terminology: he sees himself as 'a priest of the eternal imagination, transmuting the daily bread of experience into the radiant body of everliving life'.[66] I would suggest that what is at work here is a double logic, where each meaning interweaves with the other to create a layered structure, a structure which parallels the days of the week that we saw in *Finnegans Wake*, where the rational and the emotional informed each other. For this 'double logic is the order of both "this and that" and, simultaneously, "neither this nor that"',[67] and it exemplifies the Heideggerian relationship with the artistic material. By dwelling in the complexities of nationality, language and religion, he allows the aesthetic to view each of these differently. It is not accidental that he uses 'nets' as the metaphor for these three structures. In Chapter Three, when he was contemplating his sense of sin during the retreat, he also mentions nets:

> His soul was foul with sin and he dared not ask forgiveness with the simple trust of those whom Jesus, in the mysterious ways of God, had called first to His side, the carpenters, the fishermen, poor and simple people following a lowly trade, handling and shaping the wood of trees, mending their nets with patience.[68]

We return to the idea of the craftsman and the cabinetmaker and his relationship to his material. Nets will be broken and will be mended again and again. Whether they are broken by the Daedalan figure flying through them or whether they are broken by being used as fuel for those flights is not of huge importance. The importance is that the nets, a fusion of the material and the immaterial, will be remade again and again. What we see here is what has been gradually developing throughout the book as a whole; it is a 'flux of consciousness', which is 'beyond any "lived experience" or any prior psychic reality'.[69] It is that relatedness to material of which Heidegger spoke; it allows that presencing of the earth in language, of the world in the word. So, to answer the question whether, for Joyce, excrement can be a work of art, the answer is yes it can. As part of the body and of the earth, excrement has as much right to aesthetic value as has any other property of the mind, the body or the world: it too is part of the flux of consciousness.

Environment and Embodiment in Joyce's 'The Dead'

ROBERT BRAZEAU

> It is in a country unfamiliar emotionally or topographically that one needs poems and maps.
>
> Clifford Geertz

This essay argues that James Joyce's 'The Dead' engages fundamentally with theories of evolutionary biology, and that this previously unconsidered aspect of the story offers important insights into how we might profitably approach this and other works by Joyce. I reference the work of contemporary ecocritics in order to draw out the discussion that Joyce stages in 'The Dead' regarding the relationship between knowledge and embodiment on the one hand, and, concertedly, the relationship between space, culture and the inescapable biologism of our existence on the other. For Joyce, as for contemporary evolutionary biologists and environmentally engaged critics, knowledge evolves, in large measure, out of a dialectic relationship with the world around us – including the natural, physical environment – and even the most complex social and informational circuits have to be worked through a cognitive apparatus that is both knowable and unknowable, that is produced in the present and in an irretrievable past, that is conscious and unconscious and that represses at least as much as it acknowledges. Joyce, I argue, structures the closing scenes of 'The Dead' compellingly around the relationship between embodiment and cognition. However, it is not simply the case that Joyce is trying, in this story, to confirm the validity of arguments about evolution; nor is he suggesting that we are animals before we are humans (whatever that might mean). Rather, 'The Dead', especially in its concluding stages, works to show, through Gabriel, that human consciousness is produced by, and is also productive of, a variety of concerted and discordant desires, pulsations, affects and compulsions.

In her essay '"The Esthetic Instinct in Action": Charles Darwin and Mental Science in *A Portrait of the Artist as a Young Man*', Sandra Tropp demonstrates that Joyce was well versed in the fields of biological and evolutionary science, was himself a reader of Darwin and, further, that he was aware of the works of contemporaries like Bain and Allen, both prominent evolutionary theorists and philosophers of psychology. Tropp's detailed exegesis of Joyce's explicit reference to, and implicit discussion with, the works of these thinkers in *Portrait* is compellingly argued and thoroughly researched. For Tropp, in fact, the theory of beauty espoused in *Portrait*, which is, of course, central to the text, derives primarily from intertextual references to Darwin, Bain and Allen. As Tropp convincingly argues, 'the entire conversation with Lynch about aesthetics is suffused with allusions to Darwinian science, beginning with the perception of man's animal nature'.[1] She then goes on to chronicle the numerous ways in which Darwinism and evolutionary science suffuse themselves into *Portrait*, including, and this will be significant for my purposes here, Joyce's rendering of people in animalistic imagery.[2]

Tropp's argument resonates throughout my reading of 'The Dead', which, by drawing attention to Joyce's interest in the biological substrate or rhythm of human behaviour and knowledge, rests on a reading of Joyce as not simply interested in the sciences of evolution and cognition, but, rather, as interested in these in a way that we could now call ecocritical. There are, in fact, a number of arguments about time, subjectivity and the environment explored in 'The Dead', where Joyce thematises many of the behaviours associated with species survival: eating, drinking, procreation, living in groups and, as I will show, wayfinding, cognitive mapping and seeking out preferred environments. My focus here will be on the evolving cognitive demands that modern culture and society force upon Gabriel Conroy and how, in Joyce's story, all knowledge emerges, first and foremost, out of our cognition of, and embodied experiences within, space. Throughout the story, we see Gabriel managing the informational demands of his various environments poorly, but the cause of this may not be personal shortcoming so much as the shifting complexity of the social and cultural terrain. He has no way of knowing what the evening will hold for him as he shakes the snow off his shoe tops in the entryway to his aunts' house in Usher's Quay, but he does reveal a strong antipathy to change and a relatively poor ability to adapt as the challenges of the evening present themselves. In 'The

Dead', Gabriel remains very much out of step, or out of rhythm, with his own time, his wife, his extended family and his nation. It is, at the story's close, unclear if he will ever bridge that gap, but at the very least, the closing scene of 'The Dead' alerts him to the dissonance between the reality that he has constructed for himself and the rhythmical vitality of the world around him from which he has, wittingly or unwittingly, become detached.

In 'The Dead', then, Joyce is interested in nothing less than the manner in which we exist in our world as social, political and cultural entities on the one hand, and in how much of our behaviour and desire is firmly rooted in our status as biological beings on the other. A number of ecocritics have, similarly, offered sharp critiques of the supposed 'nature/culture' binary. In *Space and the Irish Cultural Imagination*, Gerry Smyth asserts 'the premise underpinning ecocriticism is that all human activity is fundamentally rooted in the physical environment, but that this dimension has been systematically marginalised' by Western cultures.[3] In fact, working to disrupt the fixed distinction between these terms is the foremost concern of Lawrence Buell's ecocriticism.[4] Buell was among the first ecocritics to take seriously the notion that, even while nature obviously exists beyond the human perception of it, nature is, like culture, a human construct, and an environmentally based ecocriticism that posits the 'naturalness' of nature as supposedly unassailable would likely falter before it began.[5] Dana Phillips, in two important articles but somewhat more concertedly in *The Truth of Ecology*, sounds a similar note, albeit in a way that is far more critical of existing ecocriticism than is Buell.[6] Finally, Greg Garrard has offered what I would say is a consistently engaging foray into this sometimes polemical discussion. Garrard's *Ecocriticism*, while clearly intended as a primer for an undergraduate readership, nevertheless instructively works through many of the thorniest issues in ecocriticism including the nature/culture dyad. Early in his work, Garrard states that one of its chief mandates will be 'to balance a constructionist perspective with the privileged claims to literal truth made by ecology. Ecocritics remain suspicious of the idea of science as wholly objective and value-free, but they are in the unusual position as cultural critics of having to defer, in the last analysis, to a scientific understanding of the world.'[7] Not all ecocritics would agree with the final assertion here, but Garrard's overarching point is simply that, even while nature is indeed a cultural construct, even if we were to stop constructing it (in literature, painting, scientific manuals, music, conscious and unconscious reflection on it, etc.) it would not suddenly evaporate before our eyes. That is, nature is simultaneously given and mediated. In these works and, more recently, in Kate Soper's *What is Nature?* and Timothy Morton's polemical *Ecology Without Nature*, the ability of ecocriticism to articulate a positive political or theoretical agenda is perceived to inhere in its capacity to demystify the unassailable objectivity of the natural world even while it must posit that nature remains, for all of our beneficial and, at times, destructive attention to it, somehow outside of human cultural activity. Nature, it would seem, is simultaneously real and constructed, given and mediated, attentive to our needs and oblivious to them.[8]

Aside from ecocritics, ecopsychologists have similarly begun to explicate the myriad ways in which cognition, personality and even mental disorder may emerge out of our conflicted relationship with the natural world. According to Andy Fisher, a leading figure in the movement, the still-emerging field of inquiry seeks to synthesise 'ecology and psychology, placing human psychology in an ecological context, and mending the divisions between mind and nature, humans and earth'.[9] Equally of interest in the context of my essay is Fisher's claim that ecopsychology works 'to describe the human psyche in a way that makes it *internal* to the natural world or that makes it a phenomenon of nature'.[10] This relatively new field of study has, predictably enough, a fairly wide remit, but there are a number of ways in which this work speaks to literary and cultural practices.[11] In *Mourning and Modernity*, Isaac Balbus combines a reading of contemporary culture that engagingly intertwines psychology, environmentalism and a critique of consumer and technological culture to diagnose what Balbus sees as a contemporary malaise that emanates primarily from our separation from the natural world and our vital, physical being.[12]

Rather than attempt to assay all of the ways in which Joyce's 'The Dead' works through ecological or even ecopsychological themes, I have chosen to focus my discussion on what I see as the most fundamental aspect of Joyce's environmentalism in 'The Dead'. As the story concludes, Joyce looks at wayfinding and cognitive mapping as structuring not only how we engage with nature, but also how nature engages with us. To put it another way, 'The Dead' suggests that culture and prevailing modes of subjectivity do not somehow get us away from nature even though culture, at least in the West, persistently works to suppress the relationship between our biological selves and the natural world on the one hand, and our minds on the other. Throughout 'The Dead', we see Gabriel's ego very much at odds with his non-rational (that is, biological) self, and are offered a view of how, for Joyce, this may well represent the endemic condition of modern life. As the story moves into its concluding movements, Gabriel's ego emerges and recedes, determines and impedes his behaviour, compels his connection to others and obstructs him socially. In all of this what emerges is that, for Joyce, our belonging to our bodies and to the natural world represents an inalienable aspect of our subjectivity, despite how fulsomely we may want to regard this aspect of our being as incidental, accidental, or burdensome. 'The Dead' does not provide anything like a roadmap for living better or more vitally, but it does explicate the consequences of living inattentively to the rhythms of nature and embodiment.

Evolutionary Psychology and the Condition of Living in Nature

In a series of cogent and tightly conjoined articles and books, Stephen Kaplan has argued for the existence of what he calls 'evolutionary psychology'. According to Kaplan, evolutionary studies have tended to focus almost exclusively on physical and biological changes to a species over time, charting the competitive or adaptive advantages to be gained by (almost exclusively) biomorphic change. Kaplan's view is that human psychology has, similarly, adapted over time and, indeed, that our view of the world needs to be contextualised from the point of view of adaptive changes that the species has undergone psychologically. In an early position paper on this new approach, Kaplan asserts the following: 'I am convinced that man has very strong biases concerning knowledge and information and that these are central both to his current plight and to possible remedial measures.'[13]

According to Kaplan, the study of evolution needs to take more seriously the evolutionary advantage gained from being able to process more, and more complex, information. As well, the cognitive sciences also need to investigate the affective aspects of information gathering and possessing far more coherently. Aside from needing vast amounts of it, humans also tend to enjoy having information. *Finnegans Wake* arguably brings human cognitive capacity to the precipice, especially in terms of its frustrating severing of voice, language and sense (for most readers, the *Wake* represents information that we resolutely do not enjoy), but already in 'The Dead' Joyce is engaged with the issue of how astutely we read our environment for clues on how the friendly or unfriendly forces in it may impact us.

Pre-eminent in Kaplan's theory and investigated at length by Nancy Easterlin is the role of wayfinding in the evolution of human information-gathering practices. As the scope of our physical efficacy expands and our ability to navigate a terrain that is more vast becomes relatively easy, the species has developed a complex set of hermeneutic tools to assist in the daunting imperative to gather information quickly about new spaces. According to Kaplan, as we manage information about various places, we develop strategies for determining the benefits or threats in that place. Kaplan summarises his research findings as follows:

> Increasingly, we have come to see [environmental] preference as an expression of an intuitive guide to behaviour, an inclination to make choices that would lead the individual away from inappropriate environments and toward desirable ones. As we have seen, the centrality of information in these decisions is quite appropriate. If humans are indeed organisms whose survival through the course of evolution required the construction and use of cognitive maps . . . then being attracted by information would seem thoroughly adaptive. In particular, people should be enticed by new information, by the prospect of updating and extending their cognitive maps.[14]

What Kaplan terms 'environmental preference' is, of course, central to 'The Dead'. The Conroys live in Monkstown, County Dublin, and while they would no doubt be renters rather than owners, this detail nevertheless marks them as part of the administrative and middle-management sector that left the city in the late 1880s and into the early 1900s to settle in what is now called suburban Dublin (Monkstown, Chapelizod and the coastal suburbs including Blackrock, Sandycove and Dalkey are all important sites in Joyce's fiction). Very little has been written on the coastal suburbs and their import in Joyce's work, but it is worth noting that the out-migration that the electrification of the tram made possible was constituent of a broader and what is generally seen as a deleterious demographic change in the city's life. Recall that in 'The Dead' Mary Jane's students belong to 'better-class families on the Kingstown and Dalkey line' which suggests the economic impact that this out-migration has had on the city itself.[15] As Mary Daly notes, 'in 1851 Dublin was still the second largest city in the United Kingdom. By 1871 she had declined to sixth place and in 1891 had suffered the final indignity of losing her position as Ireland's largest city to the upstart Belfast . . . The realisation that Belfast had a larger population provoked near-hysteria in nationalist circles.'[16] Belfast had eclipsed Dublin by incorporating its suburbs into the city itself and by the time of the next census Dublin had followed suit, so if you were a resident of Bray, Dalkey or Monkstown you were now a Dublinite again.[17]

But the choice to settle in Monkstown is only one example of Joyce's treatment of the theme of environmental preference in the story: Molly Ivors expresses a preference for the West of Ireland (Connaught) over the city; notwithstanding this, however, she lives in the city or its environs. Gretta desires to visit Galway, which is a more deeply felt instance of a character in the story expressing a preference for one environment over another. Even the otherwise unreadable Mrs Mallins would rather be in Scotland.[18] These references are, of course, resonant with implications for the discussion of Irish cultural nationalism that the story offers. Lastly, and importantly, Gabriel books a room at the Gresham for himself and Gretta, planning to woo his wife in this upscale hotel rather than drive back to their house in Monkstown: the house is, of course, symbolic of what their lives together have become, and Gabriel prefers the hotel because it is, at least in his mind, redolent with new and liberating possibilities.

Before focusing on the final scene of the story, I want to explicate the transitional moment between the end of the evening at Usher's Quay and the arrival at the Gresham. The final moments in the doorway at the home of Gabriel's aunts inaugurates a transition in the story from the world of culture and sociality to that of individual desire. We will come to see Gabriel repeatedly stifled in his attempts to make the closing events of the evening conform to a notion of success that he has built up in his mind, and Joyce will use the navigation through Dublin's city centre to allegorise Gabriel's search for happiness. Throughout, we are going to also see Joyce turn to a pattern of diction marked by references to Gabriel's biological being, quasi-animal sexual desire, and his sense of vitality and thriving in nature to signify Gabriel's erotic desires as the story reaches its anticlimax. Gabriel's attempts to connect with the vital forces of nature that he wants to believe are pulsing in his body are treated ironically by Joyce, not because Gabriel is not a desiring, physical being, but rather because he is too mired in his egocentric desires to successfully engage with those around him, most notably Gretta. The moments of the story that I wish to explicate in some detail begin with the following passage:

> Gabriel advanced from the little pantry behind the office, struggling into his overcoat and, looking around the hall, said:
> – Gretta not down yet?[19]

We should note Gabriel's hurried nature here, still getting into his coat as he leaves the pantry. We should note that syntax is highly reflective of the action, almost mimicking it, in fact. The participles 'struggling' and 'looking' begin clauses that serve to impede the completion of the sentence. Similarly, Gabriel seems impeded in a small space struggling with his overcoat, in his desire to come forward into the foyer. It is possible, of course, that he is trying to distance himself from Lily as quickly as possible. The earlier difficulty between them was purely Gabriel's creation, of course, but he is possibly still feeling slighted by her earlier comment. However, I suspect that rather than read this scene as anchored in the past dispute with Lily, we read it as explicitly revealing Gabriel's desire to move the evening, where he will be alone with Gretta, forward as quickly as possible. In fact, it is plausible that Gabriel is hurrying in hopes that Gretta is doing the same, since he must realise that Mrs Mallins will have the most compelling claim to the first cab that comes by. At this time of the morning, the first cab may well be the only cab and Gabriel, anxious to move events toward the Gresham with Gretta, attempts to beat a hasty retreat from the house.

In the passage above, it is significant, then, that the word 'advanced' is used rather than 'came from'. 'Advanced' is one word, so is arguably quicker than two (and therefore suggests Gabriel's desire to speed events forward), but the word also suggests not simply that Gabriel was in one place and is now in another, but that the movement from one to the other represents an improvement, at least in his mind. He advances (his desire? his prospects?) by moving into the foyer, closer to the door, closer to the Gresham. Also, the word is part of a more general pattern of signification that Joyce writes into the story from about this point forward: Gabriel is 'advancing' towards his prey, Gretta.

From his earliest entrance into the story, through the toast he makes at dinner and, now, into the closing moment of the story,

Gabriel is nearly obsessed with the passage of time, with scheduling and with keeping events moving forward. Recall his opening line in the story: 'I wager they did, but they forgot that my wife takes three mortal hours to get herself dressed.'[20] This highly characterising aspect of Gabriel's personality reveals for us the phobia that he has developed regarding the encroachment of the past into the present. Learning that Gretta has not yet come down, Gabriel embarks on a lengthy retelling of the story of Patrick Morkan's horse, Johnny, who circles around the statue of King William, compulsively repeating a pattern that makes eminent sense to the horse, but is not, ultimately, productive. The story that Gabriel recounts here concludes as follows:

> Round and round he went, said Gabriel, and the old gentleman, who was a very pompous old gentleman, was highly indignant. *Go on, sir! What do you mean, sir? Johnny! Johnny! Most extraordinary conduct! Can't understand the horse!*[21]

This vignette and its import for a reading of the wider cultural or historical debates at work in the story has been thoroughly glossed by Joyce's critics, and to those analyses I would add only the observation that Gabriel, like his uncle Patrick, imagines that he is on a journey that holds out the hope of progress through time and space, only to find out that he is compelled to compulsively repeat the past. Gabriel, we know, believes that his wife should already be down and ready to leave and fills the moments until her arrival with a verbose retelling of the story. All the while, of course, he must be aware that Gretta has not arrived, that his desire to move the evening to the Gresham has stalled and that another 'pompous gentleman' is not in control of the larger mechanism that governs whether his life will move forward or will remain in its rut.

When Gretta does reappear in the story, we see the strength with which Joyce structures the narrative along the lines of presence and absence, the familiar and the unknown, the past and the present, movement into the future and movement back into the past. All of these are central to wayfinding and, I argue, help form the cognitive map that readers of 'The Dead' should have in mind as the story nears its conclusion:

> Gabriel had not gone to the door with the others. He was in a dark part of the hall gazing up the staircase. A woman was standing near the top of the first flight, in the shadow also. He

> could not see her face but he could see the terracotta and salmonpink panels of her skirt which the shadow made appear black and white. It was his wife. She was leaning on the banisters, listening to something. Gabriel was surprised at her stillness and strained his ear to listen also. But he could hear little save the noise of laughter and dispute on the front steps, a few chords struck on the piano and a few notes of a man's voice singing.[22]

The scene is a complicated one: Gabriel, confused by the voices from the street, which here symbolise the movement into the present, into motion, out of this space and into the one which awaits, cannot comprehend the power that the past has to impede or perhaps prevent the arrival of the future that he desires. Gabriel, that is, wishes to embark on a journey into what he sees as a new future with his wife, whereas Gretta is surveying the past from which she has come and judging the present against it. As they leave Usher's Quay and migrate toward the city centre, they come to embody these mutually exclusive orientations toward the present. This sense of separation between the two structures the scene of wayfinding that follows and, read in view of the conclusion of the story, would seem to mark the moment where Gabriel and Gretta are clearly on distinct and perhaps irreconcilable paths in terms of their mutual desires.

Wayfinding, the ability to navigate an unknown or little-known environment by reading obvious and subtle clues, or by relying on experience and familiar spatial and geographic markers, becomes thematised in the story as it moves toward the Gresham Hotel. Gretta and Gabriel (along with Bartell D'Arcy and Miss O'Callaghan) are literally navigating the terrain of Dublin's city centre, but, more importantly, Gabriel and Gretta are also navigating within Irish social and cultural realities, their own marriage, their expectations of each other and, of course, their hopes for the future. Joyce treats all of this in terms of the physical navigation of an actual, knowable terrain. But more than this, 'The Dead' suggests the way in which our knowledge of, and engagement with, the environment structures all manner of cognition.

Embodiment, Impediment and Finding Your Way

Nancy Easterlin's cognitive ecocriticism combines an interest in human cognitive evolution with an environmentalist view that stresses the connection between emplacement, subjectivity and cognitive capacity. Easterlin argues persuasively that 'human cognitive dispositions support our wayfinding, knowledge-seeking, and highly social nature, having evolved to solve environmental challenges in our evolutionary past'.[23] She offers as an example that the human capacity to think in terms of binaries most likely evolved from a desire to simplify inputs, 'especially in terms of severing the *self* from the *other*'.[24] She goes on to argue that these dichotomies become subsumed within narratives of the past with the goal of facilitating 'future effects' that bodies will have on each other; this process is essential in planning a future, but also 'binds the individual to the social group and to the physical environment through a causal sequence of events'.[25] Narrative, then, binds the individual to both the social group and the environment, and also 'impose[s] order on the group's past, providing information, meaning, and identity amid the contingencies of existence'.[26] While Easterlin does not emphasise this, it becomes clear that our knowledge of the environment and others has to be highly flexible and fluid, yet also reasonably self-certain and decisive.

It is, as I have been suggesting, in the movement between Usher's Quay and the Gresham where we see Joyce engage with these numerous and subtle aspects of wayfinding, self/other relations, the flexibility of our knowledge as it is demonstrated in our ability to accommodate others and, finally, the power of narrative to help us order the present and the past and to bind the social group into a reasonably cohesive unit. Because of Joyce's narrative point of view, we see this most clearly from Gabriel's perspective, but we also realise intuitively that Gretta has been engaging in a form of wayfinding on both a personal and what we would call a socio-economic level. She has, for reasons both obvious and recondite, chosen to marry Gabriel, who, then as now, would have been regarded as a safe, capable, upwardly-mobile provider.[27] Unlikely to imperil his family or its finances, Gabriel was a safe but perhaps uninspired 'catch' for the young Gretta, who, it is likely, wanted to close the door on a painful history in Galway with Michael Furey by choosing his antithesis as a partner.[28] Clearly, much has gone into Gretta's choice to marry Gabriel, and not all of it is positive. Despite this, she has (at least up until now) made her peace with her choices and has tried to live happily with Gabriel, even though it is clear that much divides them in terms of beliefs and aspirations.

However compelling this discussion may be, it remains speculative, largely because, as I suggest above, we essentially occupy Gabriel's mind during this phase of the story, and much of what Joyce discloses about knowledge of the self and other (including society at large) and knowledge of the environment is mediated through his consciousness. A close reading of key textual details elucidates the centrality of knowledge, prediction, embodiment and emplacement at this point in the text, and while Joyce is satirising Gabriel at times here, he nevertheless works to confirm the significant link between cognition, wayfinding and embodiment. For example, as Gabriel, Gretta, Bartell D'Arcy and Miss O'Callaghan walk east along the quay, Gabriel, presumably in conversation with Miss O'Callaghan, thinks the following:

> She was walking on before him with Mr Bartell D'Arcy, her shoes in a brown parcel tucked under one arm and her hands holding her skirt up from the slush. She had no longer any grace of attitude but Gabriel's eyes were still bright with happiness. The blood went bounding along his veins; and the thoughts went rioting through his brain, proud, joyful, tender, valorous.[29]

Like an animal or hunter stalking its prey, Gabriel trails Gretta, and Joyce even has Gabriel focus on key details of his prey, especially details relating to her mobility. Gabriel as literal hunter would want to know how quickly Gretta might be able to flee, and so he astutely notes impediments related to the speed of her movement (her dress is tucked up in one hand, and she is holding a parcel, both of which, would impede her flight). More than that, though, Joyce allegorises Gabriel's physical desire for Gretta in terms of the ready-made connection between sexuality and other predatory behaviours. It can hardly escape our attention here that Gabriel's erotic drives toward Gretta emerge from a desire to dominate and symbolically consume her, neither of which suggest a healthy reciprocity between loving partners. In fact, one might argue that by having Gretta walk ahead of Gabriel, Joyce is suggesting that the two are fundamentally out of step with each other in terms of their immediate desires for this evening and, more generally, in terms of their aspirations for their lives together.[30] That Gabriel is in mock pursuit of Gretta also suggests that the hunter will remain thwarted as the evening progresses.

As Nancy Easterlin confirms, behaviours associated with hunting form the basis of our wayfinding knowledge, and Joyce's characterisation of Gabriel as a hunter is meant to draw out the connection between him, his environment and his wife. As the story's geographical terrain expands (from house to city to nation), the connection between Gabriel and those around him will be drawn in ever greater complexity, but in the early stages of this thematisation in 'The Dead', Joyce explicitly and ironically, models Gabriel on the archetype of the hunter. As Easterlin asserts, early humans were generally home-based but also hunters, which meant that they needed to be able to assimilate stores of knowledge about the environment, other humans and animals. As well, early weapons had a limited range of attack, which meant that if you were hunting something with the capacity for aggression, you needed to be observant about its mobility and capacities for self-defence. Of necessity, this implies a deep and affective knowledge of our surroundings and the species with which we share it. Easterlin remarks that without this 'emotional connection to the environment' we would likely lack the necessary interest in it to form and retain the kinds of complex knowledge we need to survive.[31] As well, it is not the case that wayfinding was only important to our hunter-gatherer ancestors, or that modern technologies delimit the importance of wayfinding for contemporary peoples as, according to Easterlin, 'we would not be able to make maps, give directions, or ride a bike round-trip to the store without our wayfinding disposition'.[32]

In the passage cited above, we should also note the connection that Joyce forges between physicality and cognition: the blood bounds through Gabriel's veins in the same way that thoughts riot through his brain. Interestingly, Joyce chooses 'brain' over 'mind' in this passage, I would argue, to emphasise Gabriel's physical and biological self rather than his distinct subjectivity or personality. He desires his wife in a purely physical way here, and Joyce's pattern of signification suggests the biological over the 'higher orders' of human intelligence. Interestingly, the words 'bounding' and 'rioting' in the passage above could be exchanged for each other: the blood, of course, could just as easily be 'rioting' and the thoughts 'bounding'. In this, again, Joyce implies not simply a connection between our biological being and our cognitive capacity, but the causal effect that our biology has on thought. Joyce is, I contend, working explicitly with a detailed understanding of the relationship between our hunting-gathering past and how it has conditioned us, on a very deep level of cognitive capacity, to read our environments and those in them. It is not that information about the environment is simply more important to us than other types of information, but rather that knowledge of our environment both structures and grounds all knowledge, including knowledge of the other.

But the references to Gabriel's rushing and coursing blood also signal the emergence of a new set of codes that will dominate the narrative from this point forward, and they relate to Gabriel's bodily and erotic drives and processes. Of course, discourses of our embodied connection to the earth and to those around us are central to ecocriticism and signal another important way in which 'The Dead' works through an ecocentric consciousness in its treatment of Gabriel as a frustrated and alienated (and, of course, alienating) subject. His blood, breathing, 'dull aches', all come to be emphasised as the story reaches its culmination. Here, however, we need to be mindful of the fact that Gabriel is probably not simply experiencing what is happening to his body as much as he is attempting to will a sense of 'deeper' vitality into existence. My view is that this does not change the fundamentally ecological reading of the story, but only complicates it somewhat, since, in trying to tap into some sense of himself as a vital, desiring body, Gabriel is less responding to the real forces at work on him than he is trying to master them consciously. In fact, this may be the predominant way in which the character is revealed to be at odds with himself and his surroundings. Frederic Jameson is no doubt correct to remind us that 'vitalism is also an ideology',[33] and a careful reading of Gabriel's thoughts and actions at this point in the story can only confirm this view. This does not mean, however, that Joyce is discounting that we are able to experience a vital connection with something outside of ourselves (whether that is another person or the environment more generally) but only that Gabriel himself is not yet capable of effecting these connections in his own life because it is dominated by egocentric concerns emanating from mastery of the environment and those in it. Gabriel's vitality here is not so much illegitimate as it is performative. He is not 'tapping into' some life-force of vital existence (although he feels that he is) and becoming one with his biological drives: rather, he is trying to convince himself that he is doing this, or that he is capable of doing this, or that the situation calls for him to be more physically present and expressive. Of course, it is not working and it is only destined to fail again, and with greater consequence, at the Gresham.

While I do not have the time to investigate this at length in the present essay, I want to suggest here that the critique of vitalism proffered through Gabriel here does a kind of double-duty in 'The

Dead', since it also speaks directly to the ideology of the Revival, as represented by Molly Ivors, and its attempt to similarly will itself into a greater sense of engagement with Ireland's rural past and folk or peasant cultures. Joyce was, as is well known, critical of the Revival, and in 'The Dead' offers, through Gabriel, a clear indication of the impossibility of simply willing yourself into a deeper connection to the land or the past, especially when these come to stand in for some cryptically or ill-defined nascent and sustaining life-force. However, this does not mean that Joyce is an anti-environmental writer, but only that, as a critic of the Revival, he was attentive to ways in which doctrines of self-overcoming were more wish fulfilment than actuality. By my reading of 'The Dead', as I have said, Gabriel could be more embodied and present in his world, but his egocentrism precludes this. Similarly, Molly Ivors wishes to be more attached to the land, but is similarly unable to effectuate this move to a more presentist or vital state. In no way does this discount the ways in which people legitimately belong to nature, as is explored in other ways in 'The Dead', but only that in the context of Gabriel and Molly Ivors, these performative impulses clearly miss the reality of their lives.

This sense of Gabriel's living at a distance from his own reality is only magnified as he and Gretta arrive at the Gresham. The Gresham Hotel represents the final and most significant of the 'preferred environments' in 'The Dead'. One of the evolutionary advantages associated with wayfinding and seeking out preferential environments is that such environments have a relatively high degree of predictability to them. Knowing what is likely to happen, or even what is possible, however remote, is a keen skill to nurture as early people attempted to survive and thrive in a sometimes hostile terrain. Gabriel, of course, hopes that the evening will unfold very much in the manner that he anticipates, and that the poshness of this upscale hotel will assist him in his overtures toward Gretta. Of course, he is wrong in this assumption and his romantic overtures toward Gretta are famously unsuccessful.

As I have been suggesting, the migration across the physical space of the city parallels a more resonant aspect of the ways in which wayfinding functions as a central trope in 'The Dead'. As the story moves toward the Gresham, it becomes clear that Gabriel and Gretta are psychologically wayfinding through the past and present as both individuals and as spouses. Gretta, we will come to learn shortly, has decided to embrace the past rather than continuing to repress it and move forward into the future fully in possession of a new and more complete cognitive map of her circumstances. That is, she is becoming aware of the consequences of her choice to leave Galway and marry Gabriel, and of the sacrifices that this has entailed. It may also be the case that she has been aware of all of this for some time but has been unwilling to confront her personal history fully, perhaps because of the changes to her life that will likely ensue from her conscious awareness of the unhappiness that has accompanied her choices. Gabriel is reverting to simple nostalgia of their lives together, and has receded into a past that may be just as much fiction as reality, or may be some combination of nostalgic projection and real events. Regardless of how we read the specific details of the trajectories that both characters are on here, and I admit that my sketch is hardly definitive, what is important is that they manage to miss each other completely as they work to locate themselves in terms of their personal and cultural histories.

Significantly for the present discussion, at the Gresham Hotel the story maintains its emphasis on Gabriel's body and its biological pulsations or rhythms, but what comes more clearly into focus here, even for Gabriel it seems, is that his status as embodied subject does not offer a way out of his stifling reality, but becomes the locus of his greatest frustration. As the two arrive at the Gresham, Gretta rests on Gabriel's arm as she exits the cab and this sends a 'keen pang of lust'[34] through Gabriel. Ensuing references to 'the wild impulses of his body' and 'the thumping of his own heart against his ribs'[35] only build up the expectation for both Gabriel and the reader, but as the scene wears on we perceive a slow admixture of desire and frustration, the latter coming to supplant the former as the predominant register of Gabriel's embodiment. For example, when Gabriel tells Gretta that Freddie Mallins has repaid a debt he owed to Gabriel, he uses what the narrative refers to as 'a false voice'.[36] This highlights, of course, the distance between his desire and his behaviour, but since the voice remains, within both metaphysics and popular understanding, so keenly marked as an index of presence, the falseness of Gabriel's voice here suggests the depth of his self-difference, of what I have been calling his living at a distance from his real drives and desires. This is made clear in the following passage:

> He did not know how he could begin. Was she annoyed, too, about something? If she would only turn to him or come to him of her own accord! To take her as she was would be brutal.

> No, he must see some ardour in her eyes first. He longed to be master of her strange mood.[37]

Here, Gabriel seeks to blame Gretta for his lack of impulsiveness and his general inability to initiate physical contact. Gabriel here sees his wife and his environment as a source of frustration, as the cause of his shortcomings, rather than as the occasion to try to move beyond his own stultifying preconceptions of himself and his life with Gretta.

Interestingly, just before Gretta tells Gabriel about her past in Galway and her affections for Michael Furey, he sees himself in a full-length mirror, noting 'his broad well-filled shirt-front' and 'the face whose expression always puzzled him when he saw it in a mirror'.[38] As Gretta recounts her past with Michael Furey, we see his confusion and anger registered explicitly on the level of the body: 'The smile passed away from Gabriel's face. A dull anger began to gather again at the back of his mind and the dull fires of his lust began to grow angrily in his veins.'[39] Note here that Gabriel's 'mind' is engaged rather than his brain, as we saw earlier, suggesting the emergence out of the brief period of affected or performative capitulation to a sense of vital embodiment, and back into the world of identity, difference, argument and strife. What becomes perhaps more compelling as the story concludes is that Gabriel, feeling his defeat on the level of the body, comes to see 'some impalpable and vindictive being . . . coming against him, gathering forces against him in its vague world. But he shook himself free of it with an effort of reason and continued to caress her hand. . . . Her hand was warm and moist: it did not respond to his touch but he continued to caress it just as he had caressed her first letter to him that spring morning.'[40] The being gathering force against him is not necessarily the ghost of Michael Furey, although we can certainly read the text as suggesting this. My sense is that this 'other being' is a mental projection, by Gabriel, of his own abject body at which he feels very much at war. This is also implied, I would argue, by the closing scene of the story: when Gabriel steps to the window in response to 'a few light tappings', some apparition of his body reflected in the window would appear to float in space outside of him.[41] The strong suggestion at the end of the story is that Gabriel is very much haunted by the spectre of his own body, by the condition of his embodiment and by his inability to forge a connection to those in his immediate and, as the frame of the story broadens in the final paragraph, within his distant, national environment.

In his seminal work *The Long Revolution*, Raymond Williams argues that cultural studies needs to explore the relationship between 'the evolution of the human brain [and] the particular interpretation [of cultural objects] carried by particular cultures'.[42] Williams sustains an argument about the interconnection between cultural studies and the cognitive sciences over many pages of the text, and the former clearly occupied a foundational place in his understanding of the origins and efficacies of cultural studies. Despite the argument in that foundational work and Williams' place in the canon of cultural studies, very little attention has been focused on evolutionary and cognitive science as at all relevant within the domain of cultural studies. This is not to say that all studies need explicitly work through the mechanics of evolutionary biology or cognition before proffering their arguments about specific works. However, where a writer or artist appears to be engaging specifically with themes in cognitive science, that material needs to be explicated as part of a thorough reading of the work. 'The Dead' explicitly engages with the evolution of human cognitive capacity as a product of our necessary and sustained emplacement within our various environments. Joyce takes up two discussions in cognitive ecocriticism by ordering his story around the themes of wayfinding and its relationship to cognition and, later in the work, by drawing out the relationship between embodiment, affect and the resonant somatic sources of human knowledge. In the story, we see Gabriel persistently at odds with his body and his environment, stifled by the former and persistently confused in and by the latter. For Joyce, Gabriel's conscious attempts to overcome himself as well as his various environments and those within them all prove vexatious and serve to increase his personal frustration and social isolation. Gabriel's difficulties, however, do not necessarily remain insurmountable and the story, despite its sombre conclusion, may well point the way for Gabriel to restore a sense of vitalism and possibility to his life, not through the cracked looking glass of nostalgia, but as a product of a deeper knowledge of the places and people around him.

'Sunflawered' Humanity in *Finnegans Wake*:

Nature, Existential Shame and Transcendence

JAMES FAIRHALL

Critics have long been aware of the near-clinical interest that James Joyce, a former medical student, invested in his descriptions of bodily processes. Indeed, the body as a major theme in Joyce's writing is a well-established area of inquiry.[1] Yet Joyceans and other literary critics, even some ecocritics,[2] appear to share a deep-seated Western philosophical ambivalence about the relationship between the natural and the human. As Kate Soper observes: 'We have thought . . . of humanity as being a component of nature even as we have conceptualised nature as absolute otherness to humanity.'[3] This ambivalence is emotionally and intellectually fraught. It is a way of acknowledging yet repressing the fact that humans, in spite of our drive to transcend nature, are continually pulled back into our physical selves by natural laws whose impingement we feel to be, in varying degrees, alien and shame-provoking.[4] In this essay I will take a trans-corporeal approach,[5] derived from Stacy Alaimo's theories and phenomenology, to understanding Joyce's concern with the locus of the human experience of nature: the body. In conjunction with that experience, Joyce, most notably in *Ulysses* and *Finnegans Wake*, explored the poles of transcendence and shame. By shame, I mean the feeling aroused by the vulnerability, limitations and necessities of our existence as spirit-like minds tethered to animal-like bodies. What I will discuss as 'transcendence' differs from the phenomenological definition of that term; it arises out of aspects of experience that Joyce depicted as rising above time's quotidian flow and the imperfectibility of relationships between people.

In Merleau-Ponty's phenomenology, our bodies interact with nature through the modality of the senses and co-create the physical world,[6] as Stephen Dedalus demonstrates at the outset of the 'Proteus' episode in *Ulysses*.[7] In doing so the body endows us with pleasure and delight; yet it also generates what the ecologist William

Jordan III calls 'existential shame'.[8] He contrasts this universal, many-sided shame with guilt:

> [It] may arise from wrongdoing, but it is not associated only with moral failure. It is rather a sense of existential unworthiness, the painful emotion a person naturally feels on encountering *any* kind of shortcoming or limitation . . . [G]uilt is the emotional register of a debt that might be repaid, or . . . a failing for which we are responsible . . . Shame . . . is the emotional register of our natural, radical, existential dependency and a debt for which we are not responsible.[9]

At heart, we owe this debt to nature and it is our condition as self-reflective yet organic creatures that are born, suffer and die which is the root cause of existential shame.

Two related ideas stem from existential shame: the notion of the birth of humanity as original sin, and the need to compensate and atone for that sin. Natural imperfection is a product of culture that signifies a rupture between nature and human nature. Metaphorically, it is born of the tumble of Adam and Eve from unreflective, animal-like yet perfect existence – in a garden whose creatures do not exert themselves, suffer or change – into both nature and nature-transcending self-consciousness in the same instant.[10] The vehicle of their fall is the body, which comes into being at that instant as something that is them and not-them,[11] both animal and human. Their appetite for the forbidden fruit marks the body as an alienated vessel of desire – the desire of a body that is not one with nature. In this sense, the fall is the awakening of individual human consciousness and the experience of shame insofar as becoming human entails a confrontation with limitations: the constraints of the lone individual, rising above yet circumscribed by nature, whose desire is defined by its inevitable frustration. I take Adam and Eve's fall in *Genesis* to be a parable of the process in evolutionary history that led to the creation of big-brained, self-aware human beings, and in this essay I conflate the Biblical and evolutionary events, both of which result in schism and shame.

Jordan examines creation myths and rituals that, in many societies, account and compensate for humanity's imperfection. The primary mode of atonement is the enactment in ritual of a god's death or self-sacrifice leading to his resurrection. Broadly defined, the ritual performance is comedy, as derived from the fertility god Comus, a symbol of life perpetually renewed through rebirth.[12]

The philosopher Susanne Langer views it as an art form that arises 'wherever people are gathered to celebrate life' and embodies 'human vitality holding its own in the world'.[13] The transcendence for which the comedic ritual serves as a vehicle, lifting participants psychically out of the flow of profane time, comes into being only in the context of that flow. The comedy of the restoration of human oneness with the world and its cycles, therefore, defines the tragedy of human alienation and vice versa. Together these binary oppositions – reconciliation and alienation – form the necessary poles between which the human apprehension of life oscillates. Like the categories of fair and foul in Yeats's poem 'Crazy Jane Talks with the Bishop', the uplift of transcendence and the lowness of the mortal body need each other. In his mature fiction, especially the respective epic and cosmic comedies of *Ulysses* and *Finnegans Wake*, Joyce creates a sustained dialectic between these seeming contraries.

East of the Garden: Imperfection and Nature's Cycles

> The oaks of ald now they lie in peat yet elms leap where askes lay.
> Phall if you but will, rise you must.[14]

The theme of existential shame and aspiration toward transcendence runs from the first version of 'The Sisters' to the final paragraphs of *Finnegans Wake*. As a lapsed Catholic of philosophical bent whose writing explores the human condition, Joyce could hardly help investing with significance the fact that our bodies are imperfect. More often than not, his characters' physical flaws reflect nature's shame-inducing infringement of desire.

This theme plays out less elaborately in Joyce's early fictions than in *Ulysses* and *Finnegans Wake*, partly because the latter are written on an epic scale. In *Ulysses* the fall from nature into humanity is primarily a subtext, albeit a crucial one, which only Stephen ponders directly. In the *Wake*, in contrast, the fall occurs and recurs and is always current news. The author of the *Wake* explores the endlessly iterated, forever flawed state of the world that his writing prior to *Ulysses* touches on but does not grapple with as a major theme. Repeatedly, human history comes into being through the fall in the guise of Viconian cycles, conflated with the master narratives of Christianity and other belief systems, which are announced by thunder words:

> The fall (bababadalgharaghtakamminarronnkonnbronntonnerronn tuonnthunntrovarrhounawnskawntoohoohoordenenthurnuk!) . . . is retaled early in bed and later on life down through all christian minstrelsy.[15]

This 'great fall' leads to the death-dealing tumble from a ladder of Tim Finnegan. His return to life is swiftly foreshadowed by a reference to 'the park',[16] that is, the Phoenix Park, named for its spring of clear water (Irish, *fionn uisce*) but suggesting through its sound and Anglicised spelling the mythological bird that dies and is resurrected. Allusions and images relating to cyclical birth, death and rebirth – especially of the resilient putative hero,[17] the many-sided Humphrey Chimpden Earwicker (HCE) – abound. Unlike *Ulysses*, however, there is no predomination of light over darkness.[18] HCE's theatre of action within nature and history, resembling that of famous male figures into which he sometimes morphs, seesaws bewilderingly between creation and destruction. Insofar as he is linked to the Duke of Wellington and other phallic overreachers, he is implicated in history's violence. His deepest shame, notwithstanding, appears to derive from his physical role within the family circle as both agent and victim of fallen human nature.

Above all, the *Wake* is a book of the body, as many critics – such as John Bishop, in his wonderful *Joyce's Book of the Dark* – have explicated. It revolves around a dreaming mind in a sleeping body, which for convenience I will treat as HCE's. The sleeper's dream encompasses his own and the world's histories, and his body is the medium through which history expresses itself in symptoms of humankind's radical imperfection. Imperfection is passed on through the generations since the fall: 'He does not know how his grandson's grandson's grandson's grandson will stammer up.'[19] HCE's own stuttering, a Freudian sign of repressed material, is tied up with his mysterious sin or crime in the park. The crime may be the act of exposing his bottom, a highly cathected part of the body throughout the *Wake*. In Book III, Chapter 2 the exposure of this act (through the sense of sight, shameful exposure flows both ways: 'We are all eyes')[20] awakens punitive anger: a combination of his son Jaun's (Shaun's), a policeman's, and his own anger (projected onto Jaun). The angry one expresses a prurient desire to bring, through corporal punishment, 'the poppy blush of shame to your peony hindmost'.[21] Given the tendency of dreams to reify wishes that have not been enacted, HCE may not be guilty of perverse misdeeds; nevertheless, his floating existential shame attaches itself to any failure to 'stammer up': a failure to measure up to standards of conduct, for instance, or to the aspirations of desire. The modality of vision expresses his longing for taboo things, in particular his daughter Issy. Bishop writes: 'A goodlooking looker with "looks"',[22] 'Isabelle' 'is a belle'[23] and, as such, the object of HCE's specular desire.'[24] The modality of vision also expresses his drive toward higher things and rebirth at sunrise, as Bishop argues; yet, though he is a heliotropic 'sunseeker', he remains 'sunflawered'.[25] The first part of these two portmanteau words, 'sun', enfolds the earth's star, the Son and sin: the original sin redeemed by Christ's crucifixion and resurrection, but equally the innate sense of being flawed that is one of the prices of our unique human consciousness bequeathed to us by evolution.

The *Wake* alludes many times to Darwin ('Charley, you're my darwing!') and his theories ('naturel rejection', 'the assent of man').[26] Although relativised by the jostling of other ideas and by the veil of parody cast over famous personages, evolution is a tantalising motif in the *Wake*. Most likely, it did not offer Joyce enough poetry and thematic richness to displace Viconian philosophy or Christian cosmology as structuring devices; and perhaps, like many European intellectuals born toward the end of the Victorian era, he viewed it as a scientific hypothesis from which the glamour of the shock of the new had evaporated. He adapted Vico's notion that each new cycle of history is inaugurated by an original sin committed by God and communicated in the thunder word.[27] Still, Darwin slips through the door anyway inasmuch as Vico's *New Science*, as Bishop notes, foreshadows evolutionary theory:

> [M]en in a state of nature [were] semi-bestial clods who had barely thrown off their fur [and were] speechless giants . . . This was a conception of history that needed a Darwin before it could become at all generally accepted . . . To discover the genesis of rational consciousness in 'our family furbear'[28] is one whole struggle of *The New Science*, which tries scientifically to determine how beasts driven into caves by the sound of thunder happened to make themselves over generations into learned Enlightenment thinkers.[29]

In *The New Science*, even the greatest thinkers cannot escape the sin of creation and their bestial origins. So, notwithstanding Vico's precedence over Darwin as an influence on Joyce, the world dramatised in *Finnegans Wake* is unthinkable without the fact that a long line of evolutionary development culminated in Homo sapiens, a transcendent yet naturally imperfect ('sunflawered') creature.

* * *

The opening/continuation of *Finnegans Wake* – 'riverrun, past Eve and Adam's, from swerve of shore to bend of bay, brings us by a commodious vicus of recirculation back to Howth Castle and Environs' – braids together several sorts of flow.[30] As the renewed river of time, ALP carries a new cycle of history in which ALP and HCE are reborn as human actors; the river runs in tandem with the bloodstream and the digestive process, connoted by 'recirculation' and the commode or chamber pot in 'commodious'.[31] The Christian fall reverberates in the first five words, and the Viconian divinity's original sin echoes soon after in the thunder word. The human history initiated in both cycles is subsumed by the broader framework of a Godless, post-Darwinian world. In this world, '*homines sapientes*'[32] (as Joyce referred scathingly in a 1934 letter to the supposed end result of evolution) inevitably aspire or pretend to transcendence, in cycles grand and small, and inexorably fall/fail. Although some critics question Bishop's theory of HCE's sleeping body as the key to the *Wake*, it remains a novel in which physical functions furnish the touchstone for understanding overarching events of natural and cultural history. The River Liffey's flow embodies the cyclical flow of Viconian time but has no meaning except in the context of human experience such as ALP's sense of *durée* – her Bergsonian awareness of her life flowing through time – and the body's various flows and cycles.[33]

Unlike *Ulysses*, the *Wake* focuses on the daughter's menstruation rather than the mother's. John Gordon identifies the tortured medical histories of Joyce and his daughter Lucia – each of them a victim of biological chance in the form of disease-driven half-blindness and schizophrenia respectively – as the basis of the relationship between HCE and his daughter Issy. Issy's menarche marks her splitting into two characters, one innocent and the other seductive, an event that suggests humanity's fall into its divided selfhood, at once unconsciously natural and unnaturally self-aware. In turn, her self-division precipitates one of HCE's great falls, his own binary fission. Gordon explicates the biographical-fictional links:

> Issy's menarche and ('mensuration makes me mad'[34]) schizophrenic madness . . . corresponds to Lucia Joyce's decline into madness and coincides with the onset of the author's glaucoma . . . [B]oth events are identified with the . . . splitting of the father into a similarly paired clear-eyed Shaun and purblind Shem [his sons].[35]

The repeated Viconian fall, the sequence of reproduction and cell division, a woman's monthly production of eggs, all these cycles are aspects of the overall circulation of ALP as life force. The fall of human beings into themselves as self-consciously mortal and ashamedly limited creatures is encapsulated in Issy's mensuration, which involves on the one hand her initiation (menarche) into the biological cycle of sexuality and reproduction, and on the other hand her ability to think (*mens*, Latin for 'mind'). Although ALP in her role as nature recirculates, natural forces don't care about individuals; thus the tragedy, the necessary obverse of life's comedy, of Issy and HCE, of Lucia and Joyce.

For Joyce there could have been nothing humorous about Issy/Lucia's moving away from childhood and biological initiation into womanhood. In contrast, the spectacle of Molly Bloom, a mature, healthy woman annoyed at being driven by her late-night period onto her chamber pot, plays a part in the comedy of *Ulysses*. The analogous vignette features her husband moving his bowels in the outhouse; in both scenes the actors respond to bodily necessity without shame (though Bloom needs privacy and a little time to relax in making the transition from culture to an animal function which humans are taught early to repress). In the *Wake*, urination is natural for children and potentially shameful for adults who fill or (like the charwoman and midden-minder, Kate) empty chamber pots. In the case of Issy's pissing, the sound – innocent in itself as transmitted by the modality of hearing – is transmuted by the modality of culture into a phenomenon that excites and consequently shames HCE, who in another episode is the 'Dirty Daddy Pantaloons' caught spying on four girls urinating in the park.[36] For young children, urination is a form of body language, which Gordon connects with Issy's lisping.[37] The fact that her childish lisp also excites her father points to the provenance of voiced language as a gendered product of the body in which nature and culture intersect, sometimes shamefully: 'He fell for my lips, for my lisp, for my lewdspeaker.'[38] (Bloom's recalled arousal when listening to a streetwalker is analogous: 'Whew! Girl in

Meath Street that night. All the dirty things I made her say.')[39] Earlier urinary references in Joyce's works oscillate between the titillation of males listening to the sexual-shameful (and artistically inspirational) tinkling of nubile females – thus the double entendre of his first volume of poems, *Chamber Music* – and the matter-of-factness of males relieving themselves: for instance, Stephen and Bloom in the latter's back garden.

Although urination and urine provide little humorous entertainment in *Finnegans Wake*, much of the *Wake*'s low comedy is digestive and scatological. Unlike bathroom humour, it debunks rather than mocks bodily lowliness, in keeping with Joyce's life-affirming art, while at the same time it acknowledges cultural taboos against exposure of certain body parts and functions. HCE's vehement denial of violating taboo by dropping his trousers (and perhaps defecating) in the public space of the park, for example, works in three ways. It is funny; it implicates the reader insofar as we recollect our own dream experiences of shameful exposure; and in its ridiculousness (we must assume that HCE is more everyman than sociopath), it puts into perspective the difficulties of balancing the binaries of our combined human and animal nature.

The burlesque episode of Buckley and the Russian general is similarly a parable of the permutations of cultural responses to bodily lowliness. Ellmann recounts the source of this episode, a pub tale of Joyce's father:

> Buckley . . . was an Irish soldier in the Crimean War who drew a bead on a Russian general, but when he observed his splendid epaulettes and decorations, he could not bring himself to shoot . . . [A]live to his duty, he raised his rifle again, but just then the general let down his pants to defecate. The sight of his enemy in so . . . human a plight was too much for Buckley, who again lowered his gun. But when the general prepared to finish the operation with a piece of grassy turf, Buckley lost all respect for him and fired.[40]

Analysing the episode in light of another source,[41] Rabelais' *Gargantua and Pantagruel*, William Sayers relates Gargantua's obsession with methods of anal cleansing to the general's making a convenience of a humble earth-clotted plant.[42] The young giant's preferred choice of bumfodder turns out to be a live gosling with which he sodomises himself. Sayers argues that Buckley grows sexually excited when the general introduces 'a foreign body, the grass, into his own' and, firing his rifle, penetrates him.[43] This is certainly right and implies the castigating Irish private's identification with the offender (a version of HCE, in the *Wake*'s shape-shifting drama of interchangeable selves). In the context of nature and existential shame, the following simplified sequence plays out. The general steps out of culture and the war by partly removing his uniform. No longer an enemy officer, he is a human being, responding to a call of nature, with whom the Irishman empathises. When the Russian inserts the still-living grass into his backside, à la Gargantua, he moves so shamefully close to nature that Buckley's identification with him becomes intolerable. Outrage replaces empathy:

> For when meseemim . . . beheaving up that sob of tunf for to claimhis, for to wollpimmsolff, puddywhuck . . . At that instullt to Igorladns! Prronto! I gave one dobblenotch and I ups with my crozzier! Mirrdo! With my how on armer and hits leg an arrow cockshock rockrogn. Sparro![44]

On one level, the Irish soldier is furious over an excremental insult (*merde*: shit) to Ireland (paddywhack, a racist epithet for an Irish person, is associated with spanking a low part of the body, the buttocks, thus offering added offence to the 'tunf' or turf of 'Igorladns'/Ireland[45]). On another level, he seems to take umbrage on behalf of Russian soldiers (Igor lads) and human dignity in general; thus his rifle is also a bishop's crozier, a symbol of spiritual-moral leadership. What he shoots is not just the enemy's posterior but a culturally conditioned vision of the split-off animal side of humanity. What his aim misses is the totality of the human condition, which includes in a continuum both beast-like lowliness and angelic aspiration to higher things. Unknowingly, Buckley's alter ego Butt, prosecuting Taff (the general and HCE), wears a version of Oscar Wilde's buttonhole carnation. His '*sunflawered beautonhole*' is an emblem of flawed heliotropic reaching-up for higher beauty linked to the bodily hole whose lower beauty, to the moral outrage of British philistines, also attracted Wilde.[46]

The Paradox of Creation

> [S]ensation that drives desire that adheres to attachment that dogs death that bitches birth that entails the ensuance of existentiality.[47]

If *Ulysses* is Joyce's bright book of life, *Finnegans Wake* is an equally animated but darker book. It takes place at night in a dream mode – perhaps in HCE's dreaming mind-body, as Bishop argues – and obscures the lines, clear enough in the daytime of consciousness, between creation and destruction, between one dissolving, recombining creature and another. Nighttime, the unconscious, and dying (if only to be reborn) link the *Wake* to magic. Marcel Mauss remarks: 'Magical beings and magical things notably include the souls of the dead and everything associated with death. Witness the eminently magical character of the universal practice of evoking the dead.'[48] Death enters Joyce's earlier works as an uncanny intrusion, the transformation of a once-familiar living body – Isabel Daedalus, Father Flynn, Mrs Sinico, May Dedalus – into the other: one that was a human, to paraphrase *Hamlet*'s gravedigger. The audience participates, as when Stephen and his mother, in *Stephen Hero*, are transfixed as they contemplate Isabel's dissolution. Mauss explains the communal nature of a rite that attempts to ward off or encapsulate a taboo event which threatens the watchers by contagion:

> [N]egative sympathetic rites . . . are public activities, supported by mental states which are shared by the community . . . A circle of impassioned spectators collects around the action being performed. They are . . . absorbed, hypnotised by the spectacle. They become as much actors as spectators in the magical performance.[49]

The *Wake* is a rite – Tim Finnegan's 'grand funferall' – which blurs Mauss's line between negative and positive through its continual performance of metamorphoses, magical returns to and emergences from the matrix of nature.[50] Its shape-shifting actors share mental states as they watch, overhear, talk about and enact the mysteries of birth, life, death and rebirth. They are, in fact, inseparable from the seemingly magical transformations of the natural world. What they perceive in it is, in spite of their dreaming minds' evasions and distortions, themselves.

Among the *Wake*'s four elements – air, earth, fire, water – water is the most transformative and therefore the most magical and closest to creation and destruction. In various forms, from the amniotic fluid of the womb to the ocean, water pervades the *Wake*. Experiencing the intrauterine regression of deep sleep, HCE is a fishlike, boat-like 'waterbaby' floating on 'majik wavus' (magic waves) 'backtowards motherwaters'.[51] Yet as an embryonic human[52] he is already marked by the fall – 'O, foetal sleep! Ah, fatal slip'[53] – and defined by his trans-corporeal relationship with all the waters of nature (he is 'a bairn of the brine'[54]), not only maternal fluids. 'Motherwaters' suggests the feminised watery 'deep' of Genesis as well as the primordial ocean in which organic life and evolution began. His newborn daughter and 'the little love apprencisses' who are her alter egos, like the seductive sea grasses in 'Proteus' ('the writhing weeds lift languidly and sway'[55]), sexily populate 'the curliest weedeen [earliest Eden] old ocean coils around'.[56] But this undersea garden exists in time, that is, after the fall, which begot our awareness of time. Through the modality of vision, HCE's briny wet dream both creates and draws him incestuously to his own child, whom his gaze unclothes in the likeness of newborn Venus: '[F]or the love of goddess . . . I reveal thus my deepseep daughter which was bourne up pridely out of medsdreams unclouthed when I was pillowing in my brime.'[57] Thus he is 'increaminated' in the scandal of creation that gives birth to appetency and, admitting his guilt as the short-of-breath 'catasthmatic old ruffin' who coexists with HCE as foetus, makes a confession that he signs/designates as '[f]all stuff':[58] Shakespeare's desire-driven Falstaff and material relating to the fall.

Issy's use of Pond's vanishing cream ('[t]hree creamings a day') may be one reason why her father feels 'increaminated',[59] but the deeper significance of Pond's relates to the Narcissus-like near-loss of her identity as she admires herself in a watery mirror that, like Thoreau's Walden,[60] looks back and absorbs her: 'Sure she was near drowned in pondest coldstreams of admiration forherself . . . making faces at her bachspilled likeness in the brook after and cooling herself in the element.'[61] Like Narcissus, she cannot separate her reflection from the element in which it is bathed. Her desire for herself draws her down through her own image to nature, which is both her and not-her and so threatens to drown the inverted conception of herself to which she gives birth ('Nircississies are as the doaters of inversion').[62] The tempter (desire), the tempted (Issy), and the temptation (the reflected self) are all aspects of nature and human nature, split off from each other after the fall while remaining at the same time interwoven in a mutually constitutive, trans-corporeal relationship. In her incarnation as Eve and Isis (the Egyptian goddess of motherhood, magic, and – as prime mover of generations of children – beginnings), Issy is implicated in the creation of humanity and thus of nature as perceived and sensorily co-created by humans. As John Gordon observes, she is 'identified with apples, especially the apple of the fall',[63] and also (through her role as the *Wake*'s sibilant temptress) with the serpent in the garden. Sliding down a tree bearing 'epples' and 'pommes', she is a sinuous snake, vine clad in a fascinating satanic dress of leaves:[64]

> [a] downslyder in that snakedst-tu-naughsy whimmering woman't seeleib such afashionaping sathinous dress out of that exquisitive creation and her leaves . . . sinsinsinning since the night of time . . . in their new world through the germination of its gemination from Ond's outset till Odd's end . . . Evovae![65]

Here, as the serpent, naked Eve, and sensual desire – a 'snakedst' woman moved by a whim to fashion herself in an act of self-creation from ape to human being – Issy unites the tempter, the tempted and temptation in a moment that germinates the time-driven human drama of shame (the sinful senses) and death. As evolution, she ushers in and embodies the new world of natural-unnatural, fleshly-spiritual ('seeleib'), uniquely self-regarding humanity. Throughout the *Wake* her narcissistic gaze takes in nature as an epiphenomenon of herself, and she remains blinkered against the fact that her efforts to achieve transcendence through self-enhancing artificial means (such as clothing and cosmetics) will not keep her from vanishing, against the backdrop of geological time, as fast as Pond's cream or a reflection in water.

Among the many waters in *Finnegans Wake*, rivers are the most important. The ocean is primarily an intra-European pathway for invaders and returning lovers; its deepest point is dismissed ('Challenger's Deep is childsplay')[66] in comparison with the depth of the novel's soundings of the unconscious. The emergence of life from the intercourse of the ocean and primordial lightning storms is acknowledged – '[c]umulonubulocirrhonimbant heaven electing, the dart of desire has gored the heart of secret waters' – and at the end 'the old man of the sea',[67] seen by Anna Livia as her 'cold mad feary father',[68] symbolises engulfment and death. In contrast, rivers are feminine, nurturing the earth with their 'affluvial flowandflow'.[69] They are a 'safety vulve' and a 'constant of fluxion, Mahamewetma':[70] references to the re-creation of the earth through the Vedic world cycle ('mahamavantara'), as Bishop explicates, and to maternity and birth ('vulva', 'wet', 'ma[ma]').[71] Flowing unceasingly from source to mouth, rivers are also ancient metaphors for unbounded time; yet because they flow from beginning to end, they can stand as well for bounded human life.

These antithetical riverine metaphors point to the central paradox of *Finnegans Wake*. When identified with the macrocosmic fluxes and refluxes of nature, our self-renewing chain of being – Stephen's 'strandentwining cable of all flesh',[72] the umbilical cord he imagines in 'Proteus' as linking humankind to Eve – seems to align us with virtual immortality. Thus ALP is the Liffey and nearly a thousand other rivers, more or less ever-circulating as part of a larger cycle of discharge and replenishment. The cycle, when it absorbs an observer and temporarily removes her/him from the everyday concerns of the individual self, is beautiful and uplifting, as in the biologist Tyler Volk's description of the movement of carbon atoms:

> A carbon cycle unfolds, repeatedly, and in a grand chorus: Plant detritus is consumed by a worm, which releases carbon dioxide, which dissolves into groundwater that flows into river and then ocean, and from there diffuses as a gas back into the atmosphere. Then photosynthesis brings it back again into a plant's tissue . . . A fallen leaf from this second plant is caressed and consumed by the searching hyphae of a fungus.[73]

Life as experienced in *durée* – 'between all the goings up and the whole of the comings down and the fog of the cloud in which we toil and the cloud of the fog under which we labour'[74] – flows in a different way. It moves through happiness, troubles and uncertainty to dissolution. A once-young, nubile, Issy-like temptress, ALP, in her incarnation as a descendent/alter ego of the first mother, rushes toward death as the consequence of orgasm/'dying': 'Die eve, little eve, die!'[75] She mingles memory with regret as she mourns HCE, herself, all humanity: 'First we feel. Then we fall . . . I thought you the great in all things, in guilt and in glory. You're but a puny . . . My leaves have drifted from me. All.'[76] She is not a river; she is not a plant caught up in the carbon cycle, painlessly yielding fallen leaves to nature for consumption and metamorphosis. Swirled away by old age, she faces the direst of existential limitations and feels terror and shame.[77] The *Wakean* universe, being as fundamentally irreligious as the rest of Joyce's fiction, does not provide for individual rebirth. Hence she can take no consolation from the new cycle of history with which the novel recommences. Further, the *ricorso* is post-Edenic from the outset (except perhaps in infancy when '[w]e are once amore as babes awondering in a wold made fresh') because its actors are human beings struggling to transcend the limits of nature that are within and outside them.[78] It is '[t]he seim anew':[79] renewed life, with its pleasures and occasional joys, but also renewed shame.

* * *

In closing, I quote an Irish naturalist's comments on the River Liffey as a biological entity:

> The water of the Liffey, even in its purest state before humans ever settled by its banks, has – like all rivers – always carried a substantial burden of organic material. Dead leaves, the excrement of fish and the last mortal remains of all kinds of animal life are carried downstream in suspension. In due course the human settlements added to the quantity and variety of this material. From the moment of death, plant and animal remains begin to be broken down by bacteria into simple chemicals.[80]

The Liffey is not a person, but Christopher Moriarty's description of its recycling of organic matter makes clear its trans-corporeal relationship to other entities, including people. The constant metamorphoses of the river and what it carries form a microcosm of the natural processes from which the *Wake*'s actors, in life, dissolution, or death, are inseparable.

The development of Joyce's fiction most famously reflects his increasing interest in form; but it also reflects his increasingly passionate meditation on the body as the omphalos of human experience, embracing nature as it manifests itself through (and is co-created by) the senses as well as through a spirit-like mind. Caliban (limitation) joined at the hip to Ariel (transcendence) appears to sum up the mature Joyce's view of the human condition in a world encompassed, ultimately, not by God but by nature. He acknowledges the alienating 'monstrosity of the just-so of the world':[81] biological necessity as a personal impingement, not a graceful external process such as the carbon cycle evoked by Volk. But he sets against it the transcendence of reconciliation through the sacred moment (that is, heightened connectedness with the other) and through art. In *Ulysses*, Bloom and Molly's shared transcendent memory of their courtship on Howth affectively suspends time. Although divinity cannot redeem nature's voraciousness, as Stephen avers at the maternity hospital,[82] the epic art of *Ulysses* and the *Wake* – art framing nature within nature's flux, like Breughel's *The Fall of*

Icarus in Auden's poem 'Musée des Beaux Arts' – does redeem time and nature, temporarily, reader by reader.

Before *Finnegans Wake* got well underway, Joyce was a prematurely aging man beset by natural shocks in the form of his eye disease and his daughter's schizophrenia. He did not need to venture out into wilderness to experience '[t]he shock of the real';[83] nature was battering him. It is not surprising that he should have been writing a darker book than *Ulysses*, a tragicomedy about the fall: a comedy because of its humorous affirmation of the creative life force, a tragedy because of its acknowledgement of the obverse, destructive face of that force, which brings pain and terminates the one-way flow of the individual's life. Part of the genius of the *Wake* is its comprehensive vision of the natural and the human, of 'every person, place and thing in the chaosmos of Alle anyway connected'.[84] Bodies of all kinds interpenetrate and define each other in its portrayal of 'this timecoloured place where we live';[85] and while Joyce was far from being a naturalist or a nature-lover, he became something of a philosopher of nature, that is, a philosopher of the trans-corporeal interweaving (a continuous, feminine process rather than a fixed masculine property) of nature and human nature. In both the *Wake* and *Ulysses*, his artistic-philosophical explorations of the deepest relations among people, bodies and things strike a balance between existential shame and transcendence, as if he were heeding Pascal's warning not 'to show man . . . how much he resembles the beasts, without showing him his grandeur'.[86] In spite of the two novels' formal intricacy, neither embodies an impulse to flee from the biological realm into the Byzantium of art. Their 'sunflawered' main characters reach up, like the lotus or the tree of life, while remaining grounded in a web of natural relationships.

Ineluctable Modality of the Visible: 'Nature' and Spectacle in 'Proteus'

GARRY LEONARD

> Dead breaths I [Stephen Dedalus] living breathe, tread dead dust, devour a urinous offal from all dead.[1]

> Most of all he [Leopold Bloom] liked grilled mutton kidneys which gave to his palate a fine tang of faintly scented urine.[2]

Joyce's fiction has always been a purifying fire purging various critical approaches of any hyperbole their unexamined assumptions might allow. To put this another way, while all critical approaches seem to find resonance with Joyce's work, it is a quite separate question as to what Joyce might have thought of various critical approaches. Ecocriticism, to be sure, might have appealed to him because it is, quite literally, 'grounded'. So much of Joyce's stated intent, as indicated in his letters to Grant Richards about *Dubliners*, for example, was to 'get behind' appearances. Joyce takes a denied essence – for example, 'the soul of that hemiplegia or paralysis which many consider a city'[3] – and renders it as a 'special odour of corruption which . . . floats over [his] stories'.[4] The 'epiphany' itself, 'a sudden spiritual manifestation . . . in the vulgarity of speech or of gesture',[5] seems to be about whiffs of this denied essence constantly emanating – sometimes incrementally, sometimes explosively – from both the pungent streets of Dublin and the fetid consciousness of its inhabitants.

The 'odour' of an acute essence behind a suspiciously rosy exterior concerns the narrator of Joyce's first story 'The Sisters': 'There was a heavy odour in the room – the flowers.'[6] Is it really the flowers? Or *just* the flowers? Or is it the smell of the flowers masking the odour of a corpse? Thus Joyce gives us an olfactory correlative for some hidden but nonetheless disconcerting truth about Father Flynn that festers behind all the adult discourse wafting its way towards him. The figure of the gnomon he recalls offers a geometric equivalent of a figure of a parallelogram with a corner missing, in other words a 'complete' figure whose very completeness draws attention to an apparent absence: '[The word paralysis] had always sounded strangely in my ears, like the word gnomon in the Euclid.'[7] That which is unrepresented in what purports to totalise it often remains elusive to thought, *but therefore becomes more constitutive of affect.*

Depression, for example, is an effect produced by the dialectical tension between the un-thought that is also, and despite this, still known, if only in an affective register. Gabriel 'knows' he is distant from Gretta, but he refuses to think it until the impalpable presence of Michael Furey becomes more palpable than the specious quality of his own existence: 'A vague terror seized Gabriel . . . some impalpable and vindictive being was coming against him, gathering forces against him in its vague world.'[8] In his attempt to recover a sense of presence, it is the very *ground* of Ireland that seems to ground his thoughts: '[S]now was general all over Ireland. It was falling on every part of the dark central plain, on the treeless hills, falling softly upon the Bog of Allen and, farther westward, softly falling into the dark mutinous Shannon waves.'[9] We can say this background that restores him to himself is 'nature', and, so it is, but it is Joyce's Nature, not Wordsworth's. The landscape in 'The Dead' does not wait to impart wisdom to an expectant viewer as it does in Wordsworth's 'The Solitary Reaper'; instead it menaces Gabriel's wilful ignorance, presses in upon his self-deceptions, confuses his various strategies of self-preservation, and urges him toward a self-revelation both unwelcome and unanticipated. The Romantic Nature of Wordsworth awaits one like a patient lover, while Joyce's Nature ambushes like a lover spurned. After all, both the rain falling on the Lass of Aughrim in the song Gretta remembers, and the rain falling on Michael Furey of Galway who sang it to her long ago, manages to kill both of them – dark and mutinous indeed.

To employ a different metaphor, Nature seems to manifest itself in Joyce the way a 'correction' alters the stock market. It comes from a 'nowhere' that clearly becomes a 'somewhere' as its presence takes irrevocable effect on what now suddenly becomes, in a way that can no longer be ignored, a nowhere only imagined as a somewhere: 'I lingered before her stall, though I knew my stay was useless, to make my interest in her wares seem the more real.'[10] In this essay, I will compare Stephen Dedalus as he experiences two 'corrections' from the natural environment. The first, from his so-called 'bird girl' epiphany in *Portrait*, is a corrective that prompts him to ecstatically banish all nagging thoughts of perhaps entering the priesthood (which enticed him in the first place primarily because he would get to hear the confessions of girls his age), stirring him instead to announce his vocation as a 'a priest of the eternal imagination'.[11] The second correction, also on a beach (Sandymount Strand), occurs in the 'Proteus' episode of *Ulysses*, after Stephen has crash-landed, yet again, in true Icarian fashion, from his previously over-hyped flight 'to forge in the smithy of [his own] soul the uncreated conscience of [his] race'.[12]

In doing this, I hope to avoid setting Joyce up as an ecologist and suggest he is 'green' in a profoundly radical way: Nature is what your body smashes up against if you persist long enough in self-serving, self-delusion. In this sense, the original Dedalus employs a radical form of ecocriticism when he advises Icarus not to fly directly toward the sun. His warning stages a by-now classic mismatch of biology and technology. Yes, the technology of the wings permits flight – an apparent triumph over the natural restrictions against people flying – but it does not thereby grant immunity from all laws of physics: fly too high, the wings will melt, the machine will fail and the Nature you imagined you transcended will kill you. Or, burn fossil fuels without respite, destroy the ozone layer, raise the earth's temperature, and the Nature you imagined you controlled will kill you. These days, we are all Icarus, heading straight for the sun, unless we heed the warning of Ovid's Dedalus, a warning expressed with elegance and vigour by the best ecocriticism.

Many ecocritics use their various insights to debate 'nature' as a linguistic construction in the hopes of restoring Nature. But, as Soper concisely noted, 'it is not language that has a hole in its ozone layer; and the "real" thing continues to be polluted and degraded even as we refine our deconstructive insights at the level of the signifier'.[13] Perhaps it is on this point Joyce will help us move forward. After all, it is the early narrator of 'The Sisters' who sees language as fascinating *and* destructive: 'It filled me with fear, and yet I longed to be nearer to it and to look upon its deadly work'.[14] Joyce's great talent as a wordsmith should not blind us to the fact he also persistently warns us to beware 'its deadly work'. My reading of 'Proteus' will show how Stephen seems increasingly aware that if mankind destroys itself, it will be by mistaking the protective power of the Symbolic Order as absolute. But as Soper's comment suggests, no symbolic representation, however sophisticated it might be, is going to do a single thing to patch up the hole in the ozone layer. 'Modelling' the degradation of the natural environment, if it does not prompt behavioural change, is actually dangerous since it is easy to mistake technological mapping as a solution in itself when it can only be a warning that a solution needs to be found.

Stephen's search for the overlap between 'eco' and 'ego' – for a literal nature and not a representation of it – is evident in the opening line of 'Proteus': 'Ineluctable modality of the visible: at least that if no more, thought through my eyes'.[15] What exactly is it that is ineluctable? Is it visibility? No, ineluctable means 'unavoidable', and yet, if you shut your eyes, you're in the dark. True, it is still 'there' when you open them again, but haven't you managed to avoid it, if only for a little while? And besides, Stephen's eyesight, like Joyce's, is quite bad. Ineluctable modality of the blurry? He couldn't do his work at Clongowes when his glasses broke, and got pandied for it, a fate he would have avoided if he could, but he couldn't see to see. Wouldn't smell be closer to ineluctable? You can smell with your eyes opened or closed. You could 'stop smelling', but really only if you didn't breathe. Stephen's gloss on seeing is 'thought through my eyes'. But sight and thought are not at all the same thing, necessarily, although it may be 'thinking' that opens up and stabilises the 'visual field' of what it is possible to register as 'having been seen'.

But what is ineluctable about this relationship of seeing and thinking? Think a different thought, see otherwise than before; or, conversely, see unexpectedly and think differently. The very word 'ineluctable' seems out of place in a chapter devoted to shape-shifting. Unless what is ineluctable, in fact, is not the shape, but the shifting – even the slippage – between the thought and the seen. As Stephen says of his snatch of poetry, we must 'pin down' the otherwise eternally restless flotsam and jetsom of the continually shifting real: 'Here. Put a pin in that chap, will you? My tablets'. Significantly, this bit of poetry, and the urge to jot it down, follows from seeing the midwife glance his way and noting the tide behind her is indistinguishable from the tide within her: 'A tide westering, moondrawn, in her wake. Tides myriadislanded, within her'.[16] The midwife assists the separation of child from mother just as Stephen's line attempts to be a poetic 'midwife' separating, via language, 'nature' from Nature.

This delivery process pins down a reality consisting of 'signs' and it provides a welcome clarity, but brings to him as well a lingering sense of something sinister: 'I throw this ended shadow from me, manshape ineluctable, call it back. . . . Who watches me here? Who ever anywhere will read these written words? Signs on a white field'.[17] This is a feeling already noted in the narrator of 'The Sisters' who thinks of the effects of language as 'a sinful and maleficent being' that he nonetheless wished to be 'closer to' in order to 'look upon its deadly work'. After all, in Homer's version, we are specifically told the God Proteus will take shapes that are frightening and therefore one must hold on, regardless, until he finally assumes 'his' shape and answers the questions one seeks to have answered.

Even when you do think about what you are seeing, the thoughts have no inherent origin in what is seen. William Blake's Los will make a brief appearance in this chapter, and it is Los who is charged by Blake to 'smash' the fatally restricted vision of Urizen, whose very eyeballs have 'shrunk' to make it seem ineluctable to Urizen that what he can measure is the full panoply of all that can be seen. The result is that it is not only his eyeballs that shrink, but the world itself they claim to behold in all its totality. The constriction of both eye and world must occur simultaneously and equally if the constriction is to be plausibly denied and the constitution of each is to be claimed as mutually constitutive.[18] The irony of totalitarianism is that it can only be achieved through reductionism. Whatever purports to explain 'everything' has already shrunk that everything to only a part of the whole. For Urizen, everything can and should be measured, but what this really means is that he can only see what can be measured – not at all the same thing. From that point on, everything Urizen's meta-narrative purports to explain is an explanation of a part separated from a whole masquerading as all-inclusive – a total world view that is in fact a gnomon: that is to say only possible because of actualities that must remain missing, and so can not even be allowed as possibilities.

* * *

II

Stephen's Jesuitical hyper-intellectualism, so long accepted as a part of Stephen, is often seen as evidence of arrogance, but it seems more accurate to see it as evidence of fear, insecurity and loneliness; it is self-protective, not self-assured, more symptomatic than pedantic.[19] Stephen's relentless theorising, like his earlier fantasy of building the cave of *The Count of Monte Cristo* out of tin foil and imagining Dublin as 'sunny Marseille', is his way of not acknowledging his father's alcoholism, or his family's poverty. As I have argued elsewhere, in his long aesthetic discussion with Lynch, he demonstrates that theorising is his way of not inhabiting his own life: 'Indeed, Stephen's studied indifference when recounting his aesthetic theory is routed in an instant, not by the clamoring city, which it is designed to keep at bay, but by Lynch's remark: "Your beloved is here". Instantly he is flooded with bitterness brought on by having seen her flirt with a real priest instead of confiding her sinful thoughts to him: "Lynch was right. His mind, emptied of theory and courage, lapsed back into a listless peace".[20]

So it is not the visible *per se* that Stephen finds ineluctable, but rather the *modality* through which that which is visible is in fact seen. Without modality there is no visibility. Visibility takes place 'through' modality. It is the *modality* – the nature of one's question, not the question of Nature – that grabs hold of Proteus and then hangs on to him, while he furiously shape-shifts until he is forced to, in essence, take on the shape of your question in order to answer it. The dominant visual modality of modernity is the Cartesian objectivity that permits modern scientific inquiry. You first have a question, an hypothesis, and then you 'grab hold' of the protean world all around you, grip it tight, oblivious to any alternatives that manifest themselves as a result of your grip, until your reductive view of 'nature' settles down into an approximation of what your question requires in the form of an answer.

Proteus is quite stingy with the responses he is forced to give. He makes sure it strictly conforms to the scope of the question asked. This means that while his response is true, it is also, always, incomplete. Even when he deigns to prophesise, what he foresees is really no more than what your own modality will bring about; a view of the future, yes, but a future that is the only one remaining after one's own modality forecloses on all others. It is easy to prophesise when one understands someone else's 'way of seeing' because knowing *how* they see makes clear what they are *able to see* – and what they are not – and this predetermines choices and outcomes that are likely to occur in a 'future' that is already pre-ordained by what one's modality brings forth as 'evidence'.[21]

What is seen, then, is not the equivalent of all that is potentially visible. What is seen is that which both stimulates thought, and that which then progressively, in 'the blink of an eye', reduces itself to the circumference of the thought, transforming and shrinking as it does so, in order to conform to the implicit direction of the thought, culminating in a 'discovery' that is actually a visible organisation of primal matter that apparently proves an initial hypothesis, thus earning the status of 'fact' and serving as a building block for subsequent hypotheses. It is a paradox right up there with Stephen's theory (according to Mulligan) that Hamlet is his own grandfather: 'He proves by algebra that Hamlet's grandson is Shakespeare's grandfather and that he himself is the ghost of his own father'.[22] Without a modality, one cannot get a grip on the shape-shifting Proteus, but with a modality, the fully sublime chaos of the possible is shrunk to the merely measurable in order to bring forth a consistency and standardisation of observation that can then be used to determine what is 'significant', which is really to say 'statistically significant' – only that which meets the threshold of a particular modality of 'evidence' – thereby permitting it to become 'visible'.[23]

Not only is everything visible *not* all there is to be seen, to 'see' at all requires that one also not see, and the resulting 'blind spot' of what is significant, what one does not see, is the modality, the intellectual apparatus, that permitted the production of 'significance' in the first place.[24] The 'matter' from the natural world provided an ocular stimulus alerting us to the physical context within which our bodies flourish or die, but this stimulus gets suppressed so the body can be separated (or remembered only as a source of corruption and decay).

Even as I fine tune this essay, I see on the front page of my Toronto newspaper the headline 'Physicists a step closer to "God"'.[25] This is so, I am informed, because 'scientists have drawn tantalisingly close to finding the elusive "God Particle" that explains the existence of mass in the universe'. And this is significant, one physicist goes on to say, because 'the whole world *we live in* is based on the science of electromagnetism. *Our whole society* has evolved from that: *iPads, cameras, lights, computers*' (my emphasis). First, the whole world is reduced to 'the whole world we live in'; then the physicist lists various *consumerist* items that use non-renewable energy sources to reorganise an unpredictable Nature into data that can be manipulated in such a way as to give it an apparently predictive capacity, while ignoring that these various predictive machinations use non-renewable energy sources and thereby contribute to the growing problem of sustaining the biosphere of the *actual* world. 'The world we live in' is about *us*, not the actual world. In the formula outlined in these remarks, the 'God particle' will permit such 'advances' as better apps for our Iphones. Society does not 'evolve' *from* these inventions, it adapts *to them* and around them. We shape our tools, and then the tools shape us, or rather they give shape to dominant ways of conceiving self/other relationships as separate from Nature and thus exempt from any of its contingencies.

Furthermore, what is not seen in order that one might see must also continue to not be seen – if one is to continue seeing, to see 'further', and then construct theorems and build models designed to actualise and maximise predictability. What Stephen seems to be intuiting (or 'almosting' as he puts it) is that his relationship of 'seen' to 'not seen' has an historical dimension, which means vision and visuality also have an historical dimension, which means, implicit in both, is the realisation and the rationale for historically specific cultural, social and economic dimensions. The scientific modality is a way to quantify 'nature' so that its future incarnations can be plotted and graphed in a way calculated to maximise its use value. Of course, such a modality, as Heidegger noted, converts nature from source to 'resource'; any remainder after the process is complete is viewed as 'waste'.

The cameo in 'Proteus' of midwives bringing some integral part of the biological imperative back to the ocean – a miscarriage? an abortion? a still birth? – effectively undercuts all of Stephen's arid musings about the 'source' of the visual; all he is really surveying is the reiteration of the same modality of viewing nature as a resource, a view traceable throughout the history of Western philosophy. Stephen is just the latest thinker trying to catch the bone thrown by the ape in the opening scene of Kubrick's *2001*. In the famous 'jump cut' in this scene, Kubrick 'leaves out' four million years as the turning bone 'becomes' a space station orbiting the moon. Has nothing else happened in four million years? From the perspective of a scientific modality, much would seem to have occurred. From a biological perspective, the 'tribe' of the United States and the 'tribe' of the USSR are still fighting over a waterhole: the bone is now a nuclear missile. Various myths of modernity conflate technological innovation with the 'progress' of the human race toward some vaguely imagined perfection.[26] Stephen employs these same sorts of 'jump cuts' as he moves restlessly from one philosopher to another, all the while keeping a wary eye on the midwives and an unpredictable dog ebbing and flowing toward him like the waves on the strand.[27]

What Jay Martin calls (after a term coined by Christian Metz) 'the scopic regime of modernity' consists of a complex tension between two modern perspectives that underwrite scientific modality: Cartesian perspetivalism 'with its faith in a geometricalised, rationalised, essentially intellectual concept of space' and Baconian empiricism, which 'casts its attentive eye on the fragmentary, detail, and richly articulated surface of a world it is content to describe rather than explain'.[28] Both these regimes underwrite modernity and nominate scientific discourse as the hegemonic discourse of modern life: the Cartesian with its valorisation of hierarchy, objectivity, possession and domination (the viewer is positioned as lord of all he surveys, ownership is conflated with mastery and manipulation is conflated with knowledge), and the Baconian with an equal, though different objectivity devoted to the sleek lines of the manufactured and mass-produced commodity as object of desire. Both Caertesian and Baconian perspectives, despite their fundamentally different emphases, share a capacity to place the viewer in an apparently chosen and active, but actually quite constructed and passive 'position' relative to the visual field that is thereby permitted. Cartesian and Baconian perspectives establish alternating, yet fully correlated, visual fields; the Cartesian world view of 'mathematically regular spatio-temporal order filled with natural objects' intersects with a more leisurely observational capacity to note 'the surface of objects, their colors and textures . . . rather than their placement in a legible space'.[29]

To historicise this, the nexus point of these alternating scopic regimes situates the viewer as a modern consumer. First, the Cartesian perspective visualises all of nature as what Heidegger has called 'standing reserve' – as a resource to be 'developed' – a view that permits the presumed 'advance' of technology, as well as the design of the factory and the assembly line, and the creation of the modern economic structure based on energy consumption that converts the 'standing reserve' of Nature first into product, then into distribution; in short, the 'industrial revolution'. The train is an apt invention that shuttles back and forth between these two, first bringing 'Nature' to the factory, then leaving the factory to bring 'product' to the consumers. This advance is given further weight by becoming embedded in a 'myth of progress' so ably expressed by Mr Deasy where 'history' is reduced to a predictive formula: 'All human history moves towards one great goal, the manifestation of God'.[30] It turns out it is technology, not cleanliness, that is next to Godliness.

But such an industrial revolution, converting Nature with maximum efficiency from 'resource' into 'commodity', thereby producing profit in the form of capital, would have no chance of success without a modern scopic regime that also taught us to 'see' objects as objects of desire, as forms that complete a modern sense of self; in other words, commodities.

To bring Lacan into the discussion alongside Heidegger, Lacan argues that modern 'self' is predicated on a misrecognition of its own sovereignty, This misrecognition is based on a perceived sense of 'wholeness' (the mirror image) that initiates a sense of lack experienced as 'desire', and hands us over to the imagined gaze of the Other, where henceforth our capacity to 'see' is actually driven by our sense of how we are being 'seen' by this Other, and how yearningly we solicit it to confirm a sense of wholeness which is, to go back to the beginning of this 'self'-induced mirage, already a fiction. Commodity objects can not only now be set up as that which completes our lack and that which appears as the object of our desire, they can do so with a perpetual slippage where the manufactured object of desire, corresponding to our produced senses of self, becomes not *what* we desire, but what *causes* us to desire. Therefore the act of 'possessing it' simultaneously de-cathects it as a fetish object which had, prior to our possessing it, appeared capable of authenticating our own (fictitious) totality.[31] In other words, Cartesian and Baconian perspectivalism come together to produce a perfect storm: the modern consumer. The modern consumer requires accumulation, rather than mere one-time-only acquisition, because it is the *dynamic* of consuming – the interface it provides between resourced Nature and constructed self – not the outcome – shopping, not purchasing – which stabilises the chronic failure of the modern self to authenticate its own spurious 'wholeness' as something independent from, outside, and, most importantly, therefore *apart from* 'nature'.

Of course, Joyce has documented this before, most notably in 'Araby', where the boy sets off to the Araby bazaar – a British-owned emporium of cheaply manufactured objects set-up underneath the exhilarating novelty of electric lights – designed, in fact, with admirable efficiency to fleece a few more coppers out of impoverished Dubliners. In the event, he hasn't enough for what he was never even able to imagine getting (he only could tell Mangan's sister it would be 'something') and he promptly falls apart in a manner that not only wipes out his presumption of a masterful subjectivity, but also registers primarily as a blurring of his ability to see: '*Gazing up into the darkness* I *saw myself* as a creature driven and derided by vanity; and *my eyes* burned with anguish and anger' (my emphasis). [32]

Even more germane to Stephen in 'Proteus' is the Stephen of *Portrait* who also tried, quite briefly, and sporting the same euphoria as the narrator of 'Araby', to be a consumer and found, while his thirty pound essay prize lasted, that it was quite a solid fortress, but only so long as he had a fresh influx of cash to keep it going. The 'fortress', rather than being anything concrete or sustainable, was merely a force field maintained by the dynamic of shopping and consuming:

> For a swift season of merrymaking the money of his prizes ran through Stephen's fingers. Great parcels of groceries and delicacies and dried fruits arrived from the city . . . In his coat pockets he carried squares of Vienna chocolate for his guests while his trousers' pocket bulged with masses of silver and copper coins . . . When he could do no more he drove up and down the city in trams. Then the season of pleasure came to an end . . . How foolish his aim had been! He had tried to build a break-water of order and elegance against the sordid tide of life without him and to dam up, by rules of conduct and active interest and new filial relations, the powerful recurrence of the tides within him. Useless. From without as from within the waters had flowed over his barriers: their tides began once more to jostle fiercely above the crumbled mole.[33]

This is a portrait of the uncertain artist as a confident consumer – an early practitioner of 'retail therapy' – who returns, once the money runs out, to his previous uncertainty. The abrupt termination of his ability to buy things leaves him with an overload of consumerist impulse that rebounds as sexual desire, and so then he 'shops' in the street, converting girls that he sees into avatars of an implausibly excessive lust:

> He turned to appease the fierce longings of his heart before which everything else was idle and alien . . . A figure that had seemed to him by day demure and innocent came towards him by night through the winding darkness of sleep, her face transfigured by a lecherous cunning, her eyes bright with brutish joy. Only the morning pained him with its dim memory of dark orgiastic riot, its keen and humiliating sense of transgression.[34]

If we strip away Stephen's uniquely Catholic capacity to exaggerate the magnitude of his transgression in order to amplify his lust, this morning-after regret is a sexualised form of buyer's remorse 'jostling fiercely' (to stick with Stephen's 'ocean' metaphor) from the realm of the marketplace over into the realm of a ferociously acquisitive sexual desire. Later, this same consumerist attitude will be concretised further when he approaches the prostitutes as if they were commodities on the shelf, and he the shopper looking for the precise object that will complete him:

> The whores would be just coming out of their houses making ready for the night, yawning lazily after their sleep and settling the hairpins in their clusters of hair. He would pass by them calmly waiting for a sudden movement of his own will or a sudden call to his sin-loving soul from their soft perfumed flesh.[35]

This guilt-ridden and ecstatic Stephen will be sublimated, by the end of *Portrait*, into the artist on the verge of his career. The 'soft perfumed flesh' of 'the whores' will become the 'thighs, fuller and soft-hued as ivory' of the girl in the surf whose 'eyes turned to him in quiet sufferance of his gaze, without shame or wantonness'.[36] Because the Romantic sublimation of Nature is not the consumption of it (even if it does permit a spurious superiority of a different sort), it can urge Stephen toward more and more idealised expression:

> Her image had passed into his soul forever and no word had broken the holy silence of his ecstasy. Her eyes had called him and his soul had leaped at the call. To live, to err, to fall, to triumph, to recreate life out of life! A wild angel had appeared to him, the angel of mortal youth and beauty, an envoy from the fair courts of life, to throw open before him in an instant of ecstasy the gates of all the ways of error and glory. On and on and on and on![37]

Well, yes, 'on and on' indeed; but, just like the soaring sunward of Icarus, Stephen's enthusiasms are never sustainable. Down he plunges in the next extended scene; there he abandons nature all together in his aggressive promotion of a sort of athletic aestheticism that has Lynch nimbly ducking and bobbing by his side:

> – You say that art must not excite desire, said Lynch. I told you that one day I wrote my name in pencil on the backside of the Venus of Praxiteles in the Museum. Was that not desire?

– I speak of normal natures, said Stephen. You also told me that when you were a boy in that charming carmelite school you ate pieces of dried cowdung. . . .

– As for that, Stephen said in polite parenthesis, we are all animals. I also am an animal.

– You are, said Lynch.

– But we are just now in a mental world, Stephen continued.[38]

And this is where Stephen dwells at the close of *Portrait*, islanded on his own mental world, working on a new pair of wings. In the gap from *Portrait* to *Ulysses*, he has taken yet another Icarian flight and crash-landed back in dear, dirty Dublin. When thinking of visiting his Aunt Sarah's, he hears his father's ready-made taunt: 'Couldn't he have flown a bit higher than that, eh?' [39] Stephen is no less harsh with himself:

> Reading two pages apiece of seven books every night, eh? I was young. You bowed to yourself in the mirror, stepping forward to applause earnestly, striking face. Hurray for the Goddamned idiot! Hray! No-one saw: tell no-one. Books you were going to write with letters for titles. Have you read his F? O yes, but I prefer Q. Yes, but W is wonderful. O yes, W. Remember your epiphanies written on green oval leaves, deeply deep, copies to be sent if you died to all the great libraries of the world, including Alexandria? Someone was to read them there after a few thousand years, a mahamanvantara. Pico della Mirandola like. Ay, very like a whale. When one reads these strange pages of one long gone one feels that one is at one with one who once . . .[40]

But Stephen's self-critique differs from his father's. While both mock his youthful pretensions, his father merely notes his failure to 'get on'; while Stephen's own rumination focuses on his absurd faith in the 'mental world' to somehow affect fundamental change in the actual world, putting his scribbled epiphanies on the same level as the *Magna Carta*, perhaps. Pico della Mirandola's 'Oration on the dignity of Man' is often cited as a foundational text for the Renaissance and Humanism, particularly for the way it grants man a separate destiny from his environment, one where he can choose his status through the exercise of sheer will:

> I have placed you at the very center of the world, so that from that vantage point you may with greater ease glance round

> about you on all that the world contains. We have made you a creature neither of heaven nor of earth, neither mortal nor immortal, in order that you may, as the free and proud shaper of your own being, fashion yourself in the form you may prefer. It will be in your power to descend to the lower, brutish forms of life; you will be able, through your own decision, to rise again to the superior orders whose life is divine.[41]

This is actually God speaking to Adam. As a 'free and proud shaper of [his] own being', Adam is clearly receiving a mandate from God to be a free and proud shaper of his environment, independent from it, and above any interrelationship with it. In a letter to the *MLA*, Louise Westling, then President of the Association for the Study of Literature & Environment, specifically named Mirandola's work as a legacy that must be challenged:

> The need for change must be defined against the basic notions of human superiority we inherited from Renaissance humanism. Pico della Mirandola's Oration on the Dignity of Man articulated a confident vision of human possibility transcending 'the fermenting dung heap of the inferior world'. According to Pico, we can withdraw from the body into 'the inner chambers of the mind' and become 'neither a creature of earth nor a heavenly creature, but some higher divinity, clothed with human flesh.' Cartesian philosophy and Newtonian mechanics of the Enlightenment era grew out of such notions, but the mechanistic model of the universe was thoroughly debunked in the earliest decades of the twentieth century, even though dominant rhetorics fail to move away from it. An ecological humanism would restore appropriate humility, absorbing the lessons of quantum physics and emphasizing cooperative participation within the community of planetary life.[42]

Certainly we can see the attraction for Stephen of a philosophy guaranteeing a capacity for him to transcend 'the fermenting dung heap of the inferior world', something he has been attempting to do at least since he was revolted by the cow pastures of his childhood. However, his dismissive tone here suggests Stephen may have ascended and crashed for the last time. Although still wary of his natural environment and still afraid of immersion in water, he seems resigned to walking the Earth – or at least Sandymount Strand – as a somewhat bewildered, somewhat resentful part of it.

We can also see nascent in Mirandola's work a philosophical basis for the disavowal of the body which is a mainstay of Cartesian perspectivalism. It is this disavowal at the epicentre of Cartesian objectivity Beckett notes when he tweaks Decartes' cogito 'I think therefore I am,' to read instead 'I suffer therefore I may be'. Stephen has always been particularly ferocious in his denial of every aspect of the body, except the sinful cravings of the flesh for sexual release, and this aspect he has alternately scourged or compulsively over-indulged. He associates his alarmingly reactive body with his father's inexorable economic downward spiral, conducted with agonising inevitability, over the course of his entire childhood. His fear of the abject causes him to think of sewage and shit whenever his 'mental world' appears to falter:

> [H]e felt his forehead warm and damp against the prefect's cold damp hand. That was the way a rat felt, slimy and damp and cold. Every rat had two eyes to look out of. Sleek slimy coats, little little feet tucked up to jump, black slimy eyes to look out of. They could understand how to jump. But the minds of rats could not understand trigonometry. When they were dead they lay on their sides. Their coats dried then. They were only dead things.[43]

The sewage into which Wells had shouldered him had been the site where a student once saw a plump rat jump in, so rats are very much on his mind when he falls ill. But years later, reacting to Father Arnall's highly corporeal hell sermons (the body prominently featured, albeit only as a vessel permitting eternal torture), he has his own personal version of hell, and again it is a creative melange of the abject, the only difference a substitution of goats for rats:

> Creatures were in the field: one, three, six: creatures were moving in the field, hither and thither. Goatish creatures with human faces, hornybrowed, lightly bearded and grey as indiarubber . . . their long swishing tails besmeared with stale shite, thrusting upwards their terrific faces . . .
>
> Help![44]

Nature, for Stephen, had not always been thus:

> Once upon a time and a very good time it was there was a moocow coming down along the road and this moocow that was coming down along the road met a nicens little boy named baby tuckoo . . . When you wet the bed first it is warm then it gets cold. His mother put on the oilsheet. That had the queer smell.[45]

But the darling cow, and the warmth of wetting the bed, at first a source of curiosity, soon gets inextricably linked with the abject:

> But when autumn came the cows were driven home from the grass: and the first sight of the filthy cowyard at Stradbrook with its foul green puddles and clots of liquid dung and steaming bran troughs, sickened Stephen's heart. The cattle which had seemed so beautiful in the country on sunny days revolted him and he could not even look at the milk they yielded.[46]

The vision of the sweet moocow, of course, emanated from the voice of his idealised father: 'His father told him that story: his father looked at him through a glass: he had a hairy face'. But the father's economic decline causes them to move year after year to worse and worse dwellings, with less and less room. In such a downward spiral, 'the queer smell' of an oilsheet would be accompanied by far more, and far stronger smells, and it is this that drives Stephen to reduce the natural to the merely abject. His disgust at the decay and smell of nature gone bad parallels his disgust with the way his idealised father reading to his 'nicens little boy' mouldered into a self-involved alcoholic and bankrupt.

But the Stephen on the beach of 'Proteus' is not the Stephen on the beach of *Portrait*. In *Portrait*, his repeated attempts to fly above sewage ditches, smelly goats and dung-eating acquaintances always end up with him plopping right back down into the middle of it. Interestingly, the only time he was comfortable with the abject, indeed driven to 'experiment with it,' was when he had insulated himself from feeling any connection with it by entirely devoting his every thought to constant prayer and physical mortification:

> So entire and unquestionable was this sense of the divine meaning in all nature granted to his soul that he could scarcely understand why it was in any way necessary that he should continue to live . . . Each of his senses was brought under a rigorous discipline . . . To mortify his smell was more difficult as he found in himself no instinctive repugnance to bad odours . . . He found in the end that the only odour against which his sense of smell revolted was a certain stale fishy stink like that of long-standing urine; and whenever it was possible he subjected himself to this unpleasant odour.[47]

Stephen's sense of detachment here, though discussing his body's odours and excretions, is so absolute he is able to even recall 'many curious comparisons and experiments' he conducted. Fortunately, we are spared detail, but 'experimenting' and 'comparing' your bodies various excretions is a triumph of both Cartesian objectivity and the Baconian impulse to catalogue. Stephen's body has been entirely converted into a scientific curiosity. But the experiment fails because, in the end, his 'unquestionable . . . sense of the divine meaning in all nature' leaves seething within him not only a fury and contempt for his own bodily excretions, but for those of others as well: 'His prayers and fasts availed him little for the suppression of anger at hearing his mother sneeze'.[48]

Stephen's modern reduction of his sense of wonder ('when you wet the bed first it's warm then it's cold') to mere calculation ('comparisons and experiments')[49] leaves him scurrying back and forth, this way and that, inside the glass box of his 'mental world', able to see nature as only sinful, fallen and abject, rather than a model of successful sustainability, much less as an invitation to reciprocity, affection and gratitude. Stephen is still a skilled intellectual gymnast in 'Proteus', and many commentators on this chapter have chronicled his rapid-fire philosophical allusions, but there is a sense that even Stephen is bored with his own considerable aptitude for what his friend Lynch correctly identified as 'the true scholastic stink'.[50] Stephen is full of it. In every sense of the word. And the result is he is isolated and lonely. It is painful to watch Stephen gravitate to the beach, to walk amidst its array of unpredictable breezes, of ephemeral waves, uncountable grains of sand, even random garbage, and then gloss over all of it with his perpetual cataloguing: 'Signature of all things I am here to read'.[51] Why must nature be translated? Why must it be 'read' at all? Stephen's personal alienation is emblematic of the alienation guaranteed by the enlightenment 'project' which stripped nature of its sublimity, declared it the opposite of God's goodness, and thus left it as nothing more than an uncatalogued wasteland, knowable only through formulation, quantification and measurement – but unknowable as the ineluctable physical context for our bodies; ironically, it is *logic* that permits us to *imagine* our bodies as separate.

More than this, the first category of knowledge (Nature as that which awaits use) requires that the second remain unknown (the body as an extension of its physicality). Much of Stephen's sparring with absent and long-dead philosophers serves to mask his current shrivelled state of being. The futility of this strategy, heralding as it does the dire necessity of meeting Bloom, is at least as meaningful as any philosophical content. Stephen's often irreverent, impatient tone with the likes of Aristotle and company betrays his restlessness toward his own task: he seeks to abolish the radical discontinuity of the human body from nature but knows, even as he does so, he is using the same kind of reductionist thought that created it in the first place. The motivating force behind the clarity of his predicament seems nowhere alluded to in this walk on the strand, which is the death of his mother and the nightmare of her coming to him as a freshly buried corpse, urging him to repent. If a memory trace of his mother is in his ruminations, it would be in this poignantly physical and uncharacteristically bodily interlude: 'Touch me. Soft eyes. Soft soft soft hand. I am lonely here. O, touch me soon, now. What is that word known to all men? I am quiet here alone. Sad too. Touch, touch me'. [52] As this is the only fully physical passage in 'Proteus', I will trace its emergence from Stephen's relentless musings on the objectivity of perspective.

Stephen first presents this yearning for touch as, partly, his imagining what a woman in a Grafton street bookstore thought when their eyes met: 'The virgin at Hodges Figgis' window on Monday looking in for one of the alphabet books you were going to write. Keen glance you gave her'. [53] If the dominant modality of visibility has been 'thought through my eyes', this, by contrast, is 'feelings through my eyes'. It is not a welcome intrusion for Stephen as it threatens to jolt him out of his 'mental world' where he is most comfortable. This sudden thought of woman interrupts his attempt to review, yet again, how perspective formulates itself: 'Hold hard. Coloured on a flat: yes, that's right. Flat I see, then think distance, near, far, flat I see, east, back. Ah, see now! Falls back suddenly, frozen in stereoscope. Click does the trick'.[54] How would this objective, scientific thought lead to memories of a woman he exchanged glances with, but then failed to follow up, in a Grafton street bookstore? The segue would appear to be in the phrase 'click does the trick', thus identifying this creation of perspective as photographic and stereoscopic, a technique used alike for travel pictures and erotic postcards. The snapshot and the erotic have already been alluded to in the opening chapter when Bloom's daughter Milly gets mentioned as a 'photo girl', prompting Mulligan's locker-room jibe 'Snapshot, eh? Brief exposure'. [55]

From there, it is a short hop back to Stephen's earlier memories in *Portrait* of his masturbatory stash of pictures hidden behind a brick in the family fireplace: 'The soot-coated packet of pictures which he had hidden in the flue of the fireplace and in the presence of whose shameless or bashful wantonness he lay for hours sinning in thought and deed'. [56] In typical rhythm, he moves from deliciously foul abasement to impossible sanctification where the Virgin Mary joins his hand with that of Emma:

> Take hands, Stephen and Emma. It is a beautiful evening now in heaven. You have erred but you are always my children. It is one heart that loves another heart. Take hands together, my dear children, and you will be happy together and your hearts will love each other. [57]

A similar progression occurs after 'click does the trick', where he imagines, or remembers himself saying, perhaps to an interested but bewildered young woman: 'You find my words dark. Darkness is in our souls do you not think? Flutier. Our souls, shamewounded by our sins, cling to us yet more, a woman to her lover clinging, the more the more'. [58] But here he is self-conscious, urging himself to more stylised rhetorical exhortations ('flutier') to lure her closer: 'She trusts me, her hand gentle, the longlashed eyes. Now where the blue hell am I bringing her beyond the veil? Into the ineluctable modality of the ineluctable visuality. She, she, she. What she?' [59]

And it is from this point he finally conjures up an actual woman: the virgin at Hodges Figgis' window. Here, too, he denigrates his physical attraction to her by designating the encounter as a pick up: 'She lives in Leeson park with a grief and kickshaws, a lady of letters. Talk that to someone else, Stevie: a pickmeup. Bet she wears those curse of God stays suspenders and yellow stockings, darned with lumpy wool'. [60] This seems dismissive, but let's not forget 16 June 1904 is Bloomsday because of a certain 'pick up' between James Joyce and Nora Barnacle, a pickup where Joyce claimed her 'touch' changed him from a boy to a man. The reference to Stevie takes us back to *Portrait* yet again, this time to Davin, to the country-Irish boy Stephen suffered to call him that, because of his undoubted sincerity. At that earlier time, Stephen is forcibly struck by Davin's story of a refused chance sexual encounter. Davin had missed any possibility of a getting a ride back to town from a hurling match. On his long trek back, he knocks on a cottage for a drink:

> And all the time she was talking, Stevie, she had her eyes fixed on my face and she stood so close to me I could hear her

> breathing. When I handed her back the mug at last she took my hand to draw me in over the threshold and said: 'come in and stay the night here. You've no call to be frightened. There's no one in it but ourselves . . . I didn't go in, Stevie.[61]

Stephen's musings about how we look at a landscape and create depth and distance has been collapsed by an unsolicited memory of a story featuring the sensation of unexpected, intimate touch – refused by Davin on the road back to Dublin, and by Stephen in a Dublin bookstore.

Stephen never recovers the presumed mastery of his philosophical perspective; thoughts of a trusting intimate touch lead to thoughts of love ('word known to all men'), and this scatters his attempts at constructing perspective for the remainder of the chapter. Instead, he has fragmentary glimpses, first of himself, then of the beach, followed by a frank awareness of his complete lack of any plan for his life, or even for where he will spend the night. Not a masterful position, to be sure, but at least grounded, literally, in his actual life, his actual surroundings. His one final dwelling on corporeality is related to the drowned man they expect to find surfacing sometime today. His initial imagining of the drowned corpse shows the typical fixation of Stephen on evidence of physical decay as a horror:

> Bag of corpsegas sopping in foul brine. A quiver of minnows, fat of a spongy titbit, flash through the slits of his buttoned trouserfly. God becomes man becomes fish becomes barnacle goose becomes featherbed mountain. Dead breaths I living breathe, tread dead dust, devour a urinous offal from all dead. Hauled stark over the gunwale he breathes upward the stench of his green grave, his leprous nosehole snoring to the sun.[62]

But couched in this Poesque recital is a curious celebration of natural sustainability, unrelated both to visibility and to various Cartesian and Baconian constructions of perspective: 'God becomes man becomes fish becomes barnacle goose becomes featherbed mountain'. God–Man–Fish–Bird–Feather. Circularity and interdependence supersede isolation and alienation. It would seem to be 'feather' that takes us full circle to 'God'. There is no 'self' in the equation, no decay, sin, corruption or stench. It does not seem likely this opening to the creative chaos of nature will hold for long; Stephen's pre-occupation with and dependence upon the false certainty of Cartesian perspective to shield him from shame and confusing gusts of physical desire runs deep; but it is significant that the 'dead breaths' he breathes take us back to the life-affirming humility felt by Gabriel in 'The Dead', who also realised the world he lived in had been lived in by them. The breathing of 'urinous offal' certainly sounds unpleasant, but there was an earlier moment in *Portrait* where Stephen did not find the smell of urine either conveniently mortifying or unremittingly disgusting. The occasion is the conclusion of the Whitsuntide play. His family waits for him, but he does not see someone he hoped to see – presumably Emma – and the result is unbearable disappointment:

> [H]e ran across the road and began to walk at breakneck speed down the hill. He hardly knew where he was walking. Pride and hope and desire like crushed herbs in his heart sent up vapours of maddening incense before the eyes of his mind. He strode down the hill amid the tumult of sudden-risen vapours of wounded pride and fallen hope and baffled desire. They streamed upwards before his anguished eyes in dense and maddening fumes and passed away above him till at last the air was clear and cold again.[63]

We might notice the focus on eyes and sight, the 'vapours' rising up 'before the eyes of his mind'. Once again, he is blinded, all perspective lost. The 'tears of anguish' felt by the boy of 'Araby' return, 'they streamed upwards before his anguished eyes'. Without having planned his flight, he finds himself before 'the sombre porch of the morgue'. The ineluctable modality of the visible – a false mastery that is really a constriction – is disabled by this random path, and the sense of smell asserts itself in a far more expansive manner: 'That is horse piss and rotted straw, he thought. It is a good odour to breathe. It will calm my heart. My heart is quite calm now. I will go back'.[64] Both urine and urinating will provide the primary segue from Stephen to Bloom. Here in *Portrait* a young Stephen uses the pungent earthiness of urine to calm himself. At the close of 'Proteus', he urinates and makes a sound that is not a 'sign', but which nonetheless foretells of the coming of Henry Flower (Bloom): 'And spent, its speech ceases. It flows purling, widely flowing, floating foampool, *flower unfurling*'. In the scene immediately succeeding 'Proteus', the 'urinous offal from all dead' will, through a *natural* metampsychosis, become, not simply calming, but actually quite tasty!:

> Mr Leopold Bloom ate with relish the inner organs of beasts and fowls. He liked thick giblet soup, nutty gizzards, a stuffed roast heart, liverslices fried with crustcrumbs, fried hencods' roes. Most of all he liked grilled mutton kidneys which gave to his palate *a fine tang of faintly scented urine.* [65]

And moments before parting at the close of 'Ithaca', the two steams finally converge: 'At Stephen's suggestion, at Bloom's instigation, both, first Stephen, then Bloom, in penumbra urinated'. The ocean inside of each converging on planet Earth, a union blessed by celestial manifestation:

> What celestial sign was by both simultaneously observed?
>
> A star precipitated with great apparent velocity across the firmament from Vega in the Lyre above the zenith beyond the star group of the Tress of Berenice toward the zodiacal sign of Leo.[66]

The ecocritic Lawrence Buell listed various characteristics a text ought to evince in order to be considered 'nature writing'. The first, from which the others follow, is that 'the nonhuman environment is present not merely as a framing device but as a presence that begins to suggest that human history is implicated in natural history'.[67] From the grains of sand in 'Proteus' to the meteor in 'Ithaca', bridged by Bloom's longer trajectory of urination and Stephen's more sibilant one, Joyce's texts answer to definitions of 'nature writing', echoing as well that proto-modern nature writer, William Blake, who urged us 'To see a world in a grain of sand / And a heaven in a wild flower, / Hold infinity in the palm of your hand / And eternity in an hour'.[68]

Notes and References

FOREWORD (FOGARTY)

1 'The Day of the Rabblement', *Occasional, Critical and Political Writing*. Ed. Kevin Barry (Oxford: Oxford University Press, 2000), pp. 50–2.
2 Raymond Williams, *The Country and the City* (London: The Hogarth Press, 1985).
3 On second-wave ecocriticism, see Lawrence Buell, *The Future of Environmental Criticism: Environmental Crisis and Literary Imagination* (Oxford: Blackwell Publishing, 2005), pp. 17–28 and for an overview of current critiques of pastoralism and arguments for a post-equilibrium ecology, see Greg Garrard, *Ecocriticism*. Second Edition (London: Routledge, 2012), pp. 36–92.
4 Timothy Morton, *Ecology Without Nature: Rethinking Environmental Aesthetics* (Massachusetts: Harvard University Press, 2007), pp. 1–28.
5 'Tilly', *Poems and Exiles*. Ed. J.C.C. Mays (London: Penguin, 1992), p. 42.
6 On the function of animal motifs in *Ulysses*, see Maud Ellmann, "*Ulysses*: Changing into an Animal", *Field Day Review*, ed. Seamus Deane and Breandán MacSuibhne 2 (2008): 75–110.
7 *A Portrait of the Artist as a Young Man*. Ed. John Paul Riquelme (New York: Norton), p. 5.
8 'Calypso', *Ulysses*. Ed. Hans Walter Gabler with Wolfhard Steppe and Claus Melchior (London: Bodley Head, 1986), pp. 45–57.
9 See J.M. Synge, *The Aran Islands* (London: Penguin, 1992), p. 33.
10 *A Portrait of the Artist as a Young Man*, pp. 149–50.
11 "Nausicaa", *Ulysses*, pp. 284–313.
12 *Finnegans Wake* (London: Penguin, 1992), pp. 593–628.
13 Bonnie Kime Scott, *In the Hollow of the Wave: Virginia Woolf and the Modern Uses of Nature* (Charlottesville: University of Virginia Press, 2012).

INTRODUCTION (BRAZEAU AND GLADWIN)

1 Seamus Heaney, Eamonn Wall, Maeve McGuckian, and Patrick Kavanagh, all suggest themselves immediately, but the list is much, much longer. In this volume, Bonnie Kime Scott looks at Joyce and Eavan Boland together.
2 William Rueckert, 'Literature and Ecology', in Cheryl Glotfelty and Harold Fromm (eds.), *The Ecocriticism Reader: Landmarks in Literary Ecology* (Athens, Georgia: University of Georgia Press, 1996), p. 121.
3 Lawrence Buell, *The Future of Environmental Criticism: Environmental Crisis and Literary Imagination* (Malden, MA: Blackwell Publishing, 2005), pp. 12–13.

4 Cheryll Glotfelty, 'Introduction: Literary Studies in an Age of Environmental Crisis', in Cheryll Glotfelty and Harold Fromm (eds.) *The Ecocriticism Reader: Landmarks in Literary Ecology* (Athens, Georgia: University of Georgia Press, 1996), p. xix.

5 Contributors to this collection will be using some of these terms interchangeably. Because ecocrtitical theory has expanded so rapidly in the last twenty years, it is would be impossible to outline the theory here in greater depth. We rely mainly on the use of ecocriticism because it is still the most widely recognised term. For more on recent trends and subsequent texts in ecocriticism see Lawrence Buell, Stacy Alaimo, Greg Garrard and Timothy Morton, as well as going to ASLE's website at www.asle.org.

6 Buell, *The Future of Environmental Criticism*, pp. 22–23.

7 See Liam Leonard, *The Environmental Movement in Ireland* (New York: Springer, 2008), pp. 45–49, and Mark Boyle, 'Cleaning Up After the Celtic Tiger: Scalar 'fixes' in the Political Ecology of Tiger Economies', *Transactions of the Institute of British Geographers* 27:2 (2002), pp. 172–194, as well as the writings of the Irish environmentalist Michael Viney.

8 Gerry Smyth, *Space and the Irish Cultural Imagination* (London: Palgrave, 2001), p. 10.

9 Smyth, 'Shite and Sheep: An Ecocritical Perspective on Two Recent Irish Novels', in 'Contemporary Irish Fiction', special issue, *Irish University Review* 30: 1 (2000), p. 164.

10 John Wilson Foster, 'Preface', in John Wilson Foster (ed.) *Nature in Ireland: A Scientific and Cultural History* (Montreal: McGill-Queens University Press, 1997), p. xi.

11 It is also important to note that Foster was the keynote speaker at the 'Ireland and Ecocriticism: An Interdisciplinary Conference' in June 2010, where he examined the tensions and successes in defining and subsequently constructing an Irish ecocriticism in his presentation, 'The Challenges to an Irish Ecocriticism'.

12 See Marisol Morales Ladrón, 'James Joyce's Early Writings and Ecocritical Theory: A New Turn?', pp. 197–210 and Margarita Estévez Saá, 'Could We Speak About an Eco-Feminist Joyce? in Universidad de Deusto (ed.) *New Perspective on James Joyce* (La Rioja: Dialnet, 2010), pp. 211–224.

13 Sean Latham, 'Twenty-first-century Critical Contexts', in John McCourt (ed.), *James Joyce in Context* (Cambridge: Cambridge University Press, 2009), p. 156.

14 Edward Said, *Culture and Imperialism* (New York: Vintage, 1993), p. 225.

15 Timothy Clark, *The Cambridge Introduction to Literature and the Environment* (Cambridge: Cambridge University Press, 2011), p. 111.

16 Bonnie Kime Scott, *James Joyce* (Sussex: The Harvester Press, 1987), p. xiv.

17 Derek Attridge, 'Reading Joyce', in *The Cambridge Companion to James Joyce*, ed. Derek Attridge (Cambridge: Cambridge University Press, 1990), p. 28.

18 James Joyce, *Ulysses* (New York: Random House, 1986), pp. 1267–69.

JAMES JOYCE, CLIMATE CHANGE AND THE THREAT TO OUR 'NATURAL SUBSTANCE' (BECKET)

1 Slavoj Žižek, 'Žižek: the lecture', University of Leeds, 18 March 2008.

2 Kate Soper, *What is Nature? Culture, Politics and the non-Human* (Oxford: Blackwell, 1995), pp. 110–11.

3 James Joyce, *A Portrait of the Artist as a Young Man* (St Albans: Triad/Panther

Books, 1977), p. 12. Hereafter *PAYM*.

4 Karl Marx, *Capital* (Oxford: Oxford University Press, 1999), p. 297. Hereafter *C*. In some versions this reads as the 'metabolism' of man and soil, a metaphor which unites the body of man and the body of the earth.

5 I especially like Terry Eagleton's account of the commodity in Marx described as 'transgressive, promiscuous, polymorphous; in its sublime self-expansiveness, its levelling passion to exchange with another of its kind, it offers paradoxically to bring low the very finely nuanced superstructure – call it "culture" – which serves in part to protect and promote it', in *The Ideology of the Aesthetic* (Oxford: Basil Blackwell, 1990), p. 374.

6 Timothy Clark, 'Some Climate Change Ironies: Deconstruction, Environmental Politics and the Closure of Ecocriticism', *The Oxford Literary Review* 32.1 (2010), pp. 131–149.

7 Timothy Clark, *The Cambridge Introduction to Literature and the Environment* (Cambridge: Cambridge University Press, 2011).

8 Dana Phillips, *The Truth of Ecology: Nature, Culture, and Literature in America* (New York: Oxford University Press, 2003); Timothy Morton, *Ecology without Nature: rethinking environmental aesthetics* (Cambridge, Massachusetts and London: Harvard University Press, 2007).

9 Clark, 'Some Climate Change Ironies: Deconstruction, Environmental Politics and the Closure of Ecocriticism', pp. 144–5.

10 Clark, 'Some Climate Change Ironies', p. 142.

11 Clark, 'Some Climate Change Ironies', p. 146.

12 Clark, 'Some Climate Change Ironies', p. 133; 147.

13 Seamus Deane, 'Joyce the Irishman', in *The Cambridge Companion to James Joyce* edited by Derek Attridge (Cambridge: Cambridge University Press, 1990 rpt. 1997), pp. 31–53; p. 53.

14 Clark, 'Some Climate Ironies', p. 144.

15 Ursula K. Heise, *Sense of Place and Sense of Planet: the environmental imagination of the global* (Oxford: Oxford University Press, 2008), p. 79.

16 Heise, *Sense of Place and Sense of Planet*, p. 81.

17 Slavoj Žižek, *Looking Awry: an introduction to Jaques Lacan through popular culture* (Cambridge MA: MIT Press, 1991), pp. 35; 39.

18 Richard Kerridge, 'Introduction' in *Writing the Environment: ecocriticism and literature*, edited by Richard Kerridge and Neil Sammells (London and New York: Zed Books, 1998), pp. 1–9; 3.

19 Slavoj Žižek, 'Žižek: the lecture', University of Leeds, 18 March 2008.

20 Terry Eagleton, *The Ideology of the Aesthetic* (Oxford and Cambridge, MA, 1990), p. 376.

21 Eagleton, *The Ideology of the Aesthetic*, pp. 317–319.

22 Heise, *Sense of Place and Sense of Planet*, p. 79.

23 Chris Williams, *Ecology and Socialism* (Chicago: Haymarket Books, 2010), p. 179.

24 Clark, 'Some Climate Change Ironies', p. 134.

25 Eagleton, *The Ideology of the Aesthetic*, p. 90.

26 Eagleton, *The Ideology of the Aesthetic*, pp. 93–94

27 Morton, *Ecology without Nature*, p. 108

28 John Cowper Powys, *Wolf Solent* (London: Penguin, 1964; rpt 2000). Hereafter *WS*.

29 This is an echo of Lawrence's assertion that 'in the tension of opposites all things have their being', D.H. Lawrence, *The Complete Poems*, edited by Vivian de Sola

Pinto and F. Warren Roberts (London: Penguin, 1977, rpt 1993), p. 348.
30 J.G. Ballard (1962) 'Which Way to Inner Space?', qtd in *A Companion to Science Fiction*, edited by David Seed (Malden MA and Oxford: Blackwell, 2008), p. 208.
31 J.G. Ballard (1962) *The Drowned World* (London: Millennium, 2000). Hereafter *DW.*
32 Heise *Sense of Place and Sense of Planet*, 209.
33 Robert Pogue Harrison, 'The Forest of Literature', in *The Green Studies Reader: From Romanticism to Ecocriticism*, edited by Laurence B. Coupe (London and New York: Routledge, 2000), p. 217.
34 Phillips, *The Truth of Ecology*, pp. 141–2.
35 Gilles Deleuze and Félix Guattari, *A Thousand Plateaus: Capitalism and Schizophrenia*, translation and foreword by Brian Massumi (London: The Athlone Press 1988; rpt 1992), p. 5. Hereafter *TP.*
36 Gilles Deleuze and Félix Guattari, *Anti-Oedipus: Capitalism and Schizophrenia*, translated by Robert Hurley, Mark Seem and Helen R. Lane, preface by Michel Foucault (London: The Athlone Press 1984, rpt 1990), pp. 4–5.

JOYCE AND THE EVERYNIGHT (HERR)

1 See, for instance, *Papers by Command*, vol. 31, p. 113 for testimony about old pipes with bad cement. Great Britain. Parliament. House of Commons, 'Royal Commission on Sewage Disposal', p. 1903.
2 *Papers by Command*, p. 115.
3 *Papers by Command*, p. 116.
4 *Papers by Command*, p. 121.
5 *Papers by Command*, p. 122. Further quotations in the paragraph derive from pages 121 and 122.
6 Letter to Grant Richards, 15 October 1905, *Selected Joyce Letters*, ed. Richard Ellmann (New York: Viking, 1975), p. 79.
7 Letter to Grant Richards, 23 June 1906, pp. 89–90.
8 Similar opinions can be gleaned from the *British Medical Journal*, large portions of Hansard, *The Sanitary Record*, the *Transactions of the Sanitary Institute of Great Britain* and, of course, the indispensable book by Joseph V. O'Brien, *Dear, Dirty Dublin: A City in Distress, 1899–1916* (Univ. of California Press, 1982) and the more recent volume by Jacinta Prunty, *Dublin Slums 1800–1925: A Study in Urban Geography* (Dublin: Irish Academic Press, 1998). The best and most recent work to treat these issues is Michael Corcoran's *Our Good Health: A History of Dublin's Water and Drainage* (Dublin: Dublin City Council, 2005).
9 H.G. Wells, 'James Joyce', *New Republic*, 10 March 1917.
10 Paul Mariani, *Gerard Manley Hopkins: A Life* (New York: Viking, 2008), p. 159.
11 Mariani, *Gerard Manley Hopkins*, p. 198.
12 Mariani, *Gerard Manley Hopkins*, p. 319.
13 Mariani, *Gerard Manley Hopkins*, p. 320.
14 Norman White, *Hopkins: A Literary Biography* (Oxford: Oxford Univ. Press, 1995), p. 459.
15 Michael Rubenstein, *Public Works: Infrastructure, Irish Modernism, and The Postcolonial* (Notre Dame: Univ. of Notre Dame Press, 2011).
16 Rubenstein, *Public Works*, pp. 1–2.

17 Rubenstein, *Public Works*, p. 68
18 Rubenstein, *Public Works*, p. 68.
19 Rubenstein, *Public Works*, pp. 68–69.
20 Rubenstein, *Public Works*, p. 69.
21 Rubenstein, *Public Works*, p. 70.
22 Rubenstein, *Public Works*, p. 71.
23 Lawrence Wright, *Clean and Decent: The Fascinating History of the Bathroom and the Water-Closet* (London: Penguin, 1960), p. 4.
24 Wright, *Clean and Decent*, p. 5.
25 Wright, *Clean and Decent*, p. 7.
26 *Papers by Command*, p. 114.
27 B. Seebohm Rowntree's *Poverty: A Study of Town Life* (London: Macmillan, 3rd ed, 1902).
28 Rowntree, *Poverty*, pp. 154–55.
29 James S. Atherton, *The Books at the Wake: A Study of Literary Allusions in James Joyce's Finnegans Wake* (Carbondale: Southern Illinois Univ. Press), p. 76.
30 Atherton, *The Books at the Wake*, p. 76.
31 National Archives of Ireland, 'Ireland in the Early Twentieth Century', *http://www.census.nationalarchives.ie/exhibition/dublin/main.html* (accessed 1 September 2011).
32 Rowntree, *Poverty*, p. 51.
33 George Peck, 'The Night Soil Men', 'George Peck's Memories of Stafford Street', *http://www.localhistory.scit.wlv.ac.uk/articles/GeorgePeck2/NightSoilMen.htm*
34 In the context of labour history, it is interesting to recall that James Connolly (b. 1868) while still in his teens, followed in his father's footsteps when he became a manure-carter and night soil man.
35 Joseph V. O'Brien. *Dear, Dirty Dublin: A City in Distress, 1899–1916* (Berkeley: Univ. of California Press, 1982), pp. 120–121.
36 *Papers by Command*, p. 122.
37 *Papers by Command*, p. 123.
38 O'Brien, *Dear Dirty Dublin*, p. 121.
39 A. Walton Litz, *The Art of James Joyce: Method and Design in Ulysses and Finnegans Wake* (New York: Oxford Univ. Press, 1961), p. 142.
40 Louis O. Mink, *A Finnegans Wake Gazetteer* (Bloomington and London: Indiana Univ. Press, 1978), p. 55.
41 Mink, *A Finnegans Wake Gazetteer*, pp. xvi–xvii.
42 Mink, *A Finnegans Wake Gazetteer*, p. xvii.
43 Patrick A. McCarthy, 'Making Herself Tidal: Chapter I.8', in *How Joyce Wrote Finnegans Wake: A Chapter-by-Chapter Genetic Guide*, ed. Luca Crispi and Sam Slote (Madison: Univ. of Wisconsin Press, 2007), p. 176.
44 W.L. White, 'Pare Lorentz', *Scribner's Magazine*, vol. 105, no. 1 (January 1939), p. 11.
45 Pare Lorentz, *FDR's Moviemaker: Memoirs and Scripts by Pare Lorentz* (Las Vegas and London: Univ. of Nevada Press, 1992), p. 41.
46 Lorentz, *FDR's Moviemaker*, p. 73.
47 Lorentz, *FDR's Moviemaker*, p. 52.
48 Lorentz, *FDR's Moviemaker*, p. 57.
49 See Kelly Anspaugh, 'Death on the Missisliffi: Huckleberry Finn and *Finnegans Wake*', *Colby Quarterly* 28 (September 1992), pp. 144–154.

50 Timothy Morton, 'Ecology as Text, Text as Ecology,' *Oxford Literary Review*, 32 (2010), p. 3.
51 Timothy Morton, 'Here Comes Everything: *The Promise of Object-Orientated Ontology*', *Qui Parle* 19.2 (Spring/Summer 2011), pp. 163–190'.
52 Morton, 'Here', p. 165.

JOYCE, *ECOFEMINISM AND THE RIVER AS WOMAN* (KIME SCOTT)

1 Feminist interpretations of modernism have called into question many of the dismissals of specific practices as modernist. These include sentimental, performative, queer and mythical representations that brought women writers in particular literary recognition and success in their own time. See Suzanne Clarke, *Sentimental Modernism: Women Writers and the Revolution of the Word* (Bloomington: Indiana University Press, 1991) and Carrie J. Preston, *Modernism's Mythic Pose: Gender, Genre, Solo Performance* (New York: Oxford University Press, 2011).
2 For early interest in this area, see Margot Norris, *Beasts of the Modern Imagination: Darwin, Nietzsche, Kafka, Ernst and Lawrence* (Baltimore, MD: Johns Hopkins University Press, 1985). Recent work can be found in Marianne DeKoven, 'Guest Column: Why Animals Now', *PMLA* 124.2 (2009), pp. 361–69 and Keri Rohman, *Stalking the Subject: Modernism and the Animal* (New York: Columbia University Press, 2009), which treats the work of Joseph Conrad, H.G. Wells, Djuna Barnes and (most extensively) D.H. Lawrence. Hemingway receives considerable attention in Cary Wolfe, *Animal Rites: American Culture, the Discourse of Species, and Posthumanist Theory* (Chicago: University of Chicago Press, 2003).
3 For more, see Stacy Alaimo, *Bodily Natures: Science, Environment and the Material Self* (Bloomington: Indiana UP, 2010).
4 See Val Plumwood, *Feminism and the Mastery of Nature* (London: Routledge, 1993).
5 See Catriona Sandilands, *The Good-Natured Feminist: Ecofeminism and the Quest for Democracy* (Minneapolis: University of Minnesota Press, 1999).
6 For a discussion of the ways ecofeminism has been under-represented in mainstream ecocritical studies, as well as new connections and directions for ecofeminist analysis, see Greta Gaard, 'Toward a Queer Ecofeminism', in Rachel Stein (ed.), *New Perspectives on Environmental Justice* (New Brunswick: Rutgers University Press, 2004), pp. 21–44.
7 James Joyce, *A Portrait of the Artist as a Young Man* [1916] (New York: Viking, 1964), p. 7.
8 James Joyce, *Selected Letters of James Joyce*, (ed.) Richard Ellmann, (New York: Viking, 1975), p. 285.
9 See Friedhelm Fathjen, 'Horses versus Cattle in *Ulysses*', *Joyce Studies Annual* 12 (2001), pp. 172–75, who argues for the greater importance of the moocow strain; in this genre one could also cite Vincent Cheng, 'White Horse, Darkhorse: Joyce's Allhorse of Another Color', *Joyce Studies Annual* 2 (1991), pp. 101–28.
10 Donna Haraway, *When Species Meet* (Minneapolis: University of Minnesota Press, 2008), p. 20.
11 Cheryl Herr, 'Art and Life, Nature and Culture, *Ulysses*,' in Robert D. Newman and Weldon Thornton (eds.), *Joyce's Ulysses: The Larger Perspective* (Newark: University of Delaware Press, 1987), pp. 19–38 (27). Herr introduces a definition of natural that parts ways with the word as employed by

ecologists, and demonstrates the power of Western norms for the 'natural', but supports this sort of attachment: 'the stream-of-consciousness technique appeals to our sense of what is natural – to life, particularly the unconscious life, that we seem to share' (p. 20).

12 James Joyce, *Ulysses*, (ed.) Hans Walter Gabler (New York: Vintage, 1986), 4.10–11.
13 Ibid., 4.24–25.
14 Ibid., 4.26–27.
15 Ibid., 4.30–31.
16 Ibid., 4.33, 4.35.
17 Ibid., 4.27–28.
18 Joyce, *Portrait*, p. 172.
19 Joyce, *Ulysses*, 12.1262–3.
20 Ibid., 12.1267–9.
21 Ibid., 3.288.
22 James Joyce, in Robert Scholes and A. Walton Litz (eds.), *Dubliners: Text Criticism, and Notes* (New York: Viking, 1969), p. 22.
23 Ibid., pp. 21–22.
24 James Joyce, *Finnegans Wake* (New York: Viking, 1939), p. 627.
25 Ibid., p. 619.
26 Ibid., p. 622.
27 Ibid., p. 626.
28 Ibid., p. 628.
29 Eavan Boland, 'James Joyce: the Mystery of Influence', in Karen Lawrence (ed.), *Transcultural Joyce* (Cambridge: Cambridge University Press, 1998), pp. 11–20 (18).
30 John Eglinton, *New Statesman*, 12 July 1913, p. 10.
31 Eavan Boland, *New Collected Poems* (New York: W.W. Norton, 2008), pp. 261–262.
32 Boland, 'James Joyce', p. 18.
33 Eavan Boland, 'The Woman, the Place, the Poet', *Georgia Review* 4.44 (Spring/Summer 1990), pp. 97–109 (99).
34 Ibid., p. 100.
35 Boland, *New Collected Poems*, p. 230.
36 Ibid., p. 231.
37 Ibid., p. 230.
38 Ibid., p. 231.
39 Ibid.
40 Ibid.
41 Ibid., p. 232.
42 Boland, 'The Woman', p. 104.
43 Boland, *New Collected Poems*, p. 235.
44 Ibid.

WORD AND WORLD (WALSH)

1 Samuel Beckett, *Murphy* (New York: Grove Press, 1957), p. 65.
2 See for example Margot Norris' discussion of the portmanteau word as an example of the Freudian principle of condensation in dreams (Norris, *The Decentered Universe of* Finnegans Wake*: A Structuralist Analysis* [Baltimore: The Johns Hopkins University Press, 1976], p. 108.) and Derek Attridge's dis-

cussion of the portmanteau word as forcing the reader to continually evaluate the boundaries of each word, compelling a more productive reading process (Attridge, 'Unpacking the Portmanteau or Who's Afraid of *Finnegans Wake*?', in *On Puns: The Foundation of Letters,* ed. Jonathan Culler [New York: Blackwell, 1988], pp. 140–155).

3 Ruben Borg, 'Neologizing in *Finnegans Wake*: Beyond a Typology of the Wakean Portmanteau', *Poetics Today* 28.1 (2007), p. 146.

4 Louis Gillet, 'The Living Joyce', in *Portraits of the Artist in Exile*, ed. Willard Potts (Seattle: University of Washington Press, 1979), p. 198.

5 James Joyce, *Ulysses* (New York: Vintage, 1986), 5.244–46. Hereafter cited in text.

6 The importance of 'the letter' to Joyce is further suggested in a recollection by a friend, Oliver St John Gogarty: '[Joyce] would often excuse himself "to write a letter", which was his way of recording any turn of phrase he heard, or any one of my "epiphanies", by which he meant unconscious "giveaways"' (Oliver St John Gogarty, 'James Joyce: A Portrait of the Artist', in *James Joyce: Interviews and Recollections,* ed. E.H. Mikhail [New York: St. Martins, 1990], p. 27).

7 Gregory Bateson, *Steps to an Ecology of Mind* (Chicago: The University of Chicago Press, 2000), p. 466. Hereafter cited in text.

8 Wiener's definition appears in the subtitle of his seminal work, *Cybernetics: Control and Communication in the Animal and the Machine* (New York: MIT Press, 1961).

9 Fritz Senn, 'A Reading Exercise in *Finnegans Wake*' in *Critical Essays on James Joyce's* Finnegans Wake, (ed.) Patrick A. McCarthy, (New York: G.K. Hall & Co., 1992), p. 50.

10 See the American Society of Cybernetics' page on 'Defining 'Cybernetics' for such jokes, including perhaps the most famous, 'Use the word "cybernetics", Norbert, because nobody knows what it means. This will always put you at an advantage in arguments' (attributed to Claude Shannon in a letter to Norbert Wiener, 1941), *http://www.asc-cybernetics.org/foundations/definitions.html* (accessed 28 September 2011).

11 As cybernetics has been historically linked with military precision, systems of state control and other technologies of Foucauldian biopower, its ethical viability, as the ethical viability of Darwinism and its offshoots more generally, remains contentious.

12 James Joyce, *Finnegans Wake* (New York: Penguin, 1976), 18.17–19. Hereafter cited in text.

13 William York Tindall, *A Reader's Guide to* Finnegans Wake, (Syracuse: Syracuse University Press, 1996), p. 39. Hereafter cited in text.

14 John Marvin, '*Finnegans Wake* III.3 and the Third Millennium: The Ghost of Modernisms Yet to Come', *Hypermedia Joyce Studies.* 6.1 (Jul. 2005), *http://www.geocities.com/hypermedia_joyce/marvin.html* (accessed 1 August 2008).

15 Kimberly J. Devlin notes this pun as well, characterising the 'absentminded' reader as one who has 'forgotten history', and whom the text thus instructs to read the archaeological language of the *Wake*'s 'claybook' (Kimberly J. Devlin, 'Alphabetic Archaeology in *Finnegans Wake*'. Presented at California Joyce Redux, Irvine, CA, January 2010. [MP3 audio file], http://replay.uci.edu/public/winter2010/Panel_2_-_Web_%281024x768%29_-_20100130_04.37.34PM.html).

16 It is important to note that Bateson explicitly characterises his shift to mind as

the unit of evolutionary change as moving away from a Darwinian model of evolutionary change based on hierarchical taxonomic organisation and the notion of the evolutionary unit as set apart from and against the background of the environment (p. 466). Though Bateson legitimately constructs his theory of ecological mind against a Darwinian model, a fundamental continuity between Darwinian and Batesonian thought is apparent in their common emphasis on process over essence. Darwinian natural selection is the conceptual forebear of Bateson's ecological mind.

17 Umberto Eco, *The Limits of Interpretation* (Bloomington: Indiana University Press, 1990), p. 141. Hereafter cited in text.

18 Joseph Campbell and Henry Morton Robinson, *A Skeleton Key to* Finnegans Wake*: Unlocking James Joyce's Masterwork* (Novato, CA: New World Library, 2005).

19 The *Wake*'s word-world-wood correspondence also evokes the language of ogham, the earliest extant form of Irish writing, whose alphabetical characters corresponded to specific trees. The characters of ogham were inscribed as a series of line-cuts on wood or stone slabs. The tree language of ogham thus presents a refusal to distinguish between material and semiotic phenomena, word and world originating in ancient Celtic culture. George Cinclair Gibson's *Wake Rites: The Ancient Irish Rituals of* Finnegans Wake (Gainesville, FL: University Press of Florida, 2005) suggests that Joyce incorporated references to ogham: 'all the Irish signics' (223.4) of her 'helpabit' (223.4) came from 'Father Hogam' (223.4). See also Maria Tymoczko, 'The Broken Lights of Irish Myth' in *The Irish Ulysses* (Berkeley: University of California Press, 1994), pp. 221–276, for a discussion of Joyce's knolwedge of early Irish history and literature and his incorporation of Irish sources into the early works and *Ulysses.*

20 Sandra Tropp,'"The Esthetic Instinct in Action": Charles Darwin and Mental Science in *A Portrait of the Artist as a Young Man*', *James Joyce Quarterly* 45, no. 2 (2008), pp. 221–244.

21 Ibid., p. 238.

22 Charles Darwin, *On the Origin of Species* (New York: Penguin, 1968), pp. 115, 116. Hereafter cited in text.

23 For the former, see the work of Evelyn Fox Keller, Steven Shapin and Nancy Cartwright; for the latter see Gillian Beer, George Levine, and John Glendening, in particular.

24 I will retain the antiquated term 'Indian' here, for consistency with the quoted material.

25 Roland McHugh, *Annotations to* Finnegans Wake (Baltimore: The Johns Hopkins University Press, 1991).

26 Joyce described his *Work in Progress* as a squared circle in a 1927 letter to Harriet Shaw Weaver: 'I am making an engine with only one wheel. No spokes of course. The wheel is a perfect square. You see what I am driving at, don't you? I am awfully solemn about it, mind you, so you must not think it is a silly story about the mouse and the grapes. No, it's a wheel, I tell the world. *And* it's all *square*.' James Joyce, *The Letters of James Joyce*, ed. Stuart Gilbert (New York: Viking, 1957), p. 251.

27 This reading (and all readings) of the *Wake*'s 'decentering' qualities are indebted to Margot Norris' foundational work in *The Decentered Universe of* Finnegans Wake (Baltimore: The Johns Hopkins University Press, 1976).

28 The onomatopoeic lisps of this passage, particularly the injunction to 'Lispn!', also present a speech impediment. Speech impediments, most memorably the stutter, from which HCE and one of his doubles, Parnell, suffer, suggest a fallen state throughout the text.

29 'Eve and Adam's' alludes to the church on the Liffey's Merchant's Quay, Adam and Eve's, a site along the river's progress towards the bay presided over by 'Howth Castle and Environs' (Joyce, *Finnegans Wake*, p. 1.3).

30 Adolph Hoffmeister, 'Portrait of Joyce', in *Portraits of the Artist in Exile: Recollections of James Joyce by Europeans*, ed. Willard Potts (Seattle: University of Washington Press, 1979), p. 131. Hereafter cited in text.

31 Alessandro Francini Bruni, Joyce's friend and fellow teacher at the Berlitz school, recalls the importance of the Apostle John for Joyce: 'Two cardinal points dominate Joyce's star-studded sky – I don't know whether they can be described better as inaccessible mountains covered with snow or as central intelligences of the universe. They are the keys to the Incarnated Word: Saint John the Evangelist and Saint Thomas Aquinas, enraptured faith on the one hand and subtle reasoning on the other' (Alessandro Francini Bruni, 'Joyce Stripped Naked in the Piazza', *Portraits of the Artist in Exile: Recollections of James Joyce by Europeans*, (ed.) Willard Potts [Seattle: University of Washington Press, 1979], p. 37).

32 See Vicki Mahaffey's chapter on the *Wake* in *States of Desire* (New York: Oxford, University Press, 1998), pp. 142–209.

33 Declan Kiberd, *Inventing Ireland* (Cambridge: Harvard University Press, 1995), p. 332.

34 As such, nation in the *Wake* exceeds the Viconian cycles of civilisation development that present the most obvious model of historical change and societal development in the text. Although the model of civilisation development in Vico's *Scienza Nuova* is more commonly understood as a theory of history, rather than of nation, it can be seen to participate in the rational humanist tradition of the Enlightenment that Benedict Anderson sees as underlying the modern concept of the nation state: 'The century of the Enlightenment, of rationalist secularism, brought with it its own modern darkness. . . . [Few] things were (are) suited to this end better than the idea of nation. If nation states are widely considered to be "new" and "historical", the nation states to which they give political expression always loom out of an immemorial past and . . . glide into a limitless future. What I am proposing is that Nationalism has to be understood, by aligning it not with self-consciously held political ideologies, but with large cultural systems that preceded it, out of which – as well as against which – it came into being' (cited in *Nation and Narration 1*).

35 James Joyce, 'Ireland, Island of Saints and Sages', *The Critical Writings of James Joyce*, ed. Ellsworth Mason and Richard Ellmann, (New York: The Viking Press, 1959), p. 166. Hereafter cited in text.

36 This technique also registers Joyce's ambivalence about nation and nationalism, and more specifically about Irish independence. See Louis Gillet's remembrances of this ambivalence in 'The Living Joyce', pp. 184–5.

37 Homi K. Bhabha sees the discourse of nation as inherently ambivalent – the 'Janus-faced discourse of nation' ('Introduction', *Nation and Narration*, ed. Homi K. Bhabha [New York: Routledge, 1990], p. 3).

38 Homi K. Bhabha notes the fundamentally romantic and metaphorical tradition from which the idea of nation emerges: 'nations, like narratives, lose their origins in the myths of time and only fully realise their horizons in the mind's

eye. Such an image of the nation – or narration – might seem impossibly romantic and excessively metaphorical, but it is from these traditions of political thought and literary language that the nation emerges as a powerful historical idea in the west' (p. 1).

THE TREE WEDDING AND THE (ECO)POLITICS OF IRISH FORESTRY IN 'CYCLOPS' (YI-PENG LAI)

1 The Mesolithic people who arrived in Ireland between eight and ten thousand years ago used to clear the forests 'by felling, by deliberate fire and by grazing stock'. See EoinNeeson, 'Woodland in History and Culture', in John Wilson Foster (ed.), *Nature in Ireland: A Scientific and Cultural History* (Dublin: Lilliput Press, 1997), p. 134.
2 Joyce referred to it as 'this disease-ridden swamp' whose failed reforestation the English government was to blame. See James Joyce, *Occasional, Critical, and Political Writing* (Oxford: Oxford University Press, 2000), p. 144.
3 'The Land Act of 1881 enabled land to be transferred from landlord to tenant, complete with standing timber. Both new owners and vendors found it convenient to sell plantations for additional cash – [. . .] the landlords selling for additional profit before the sale of land, new owners selling after purchase to recoup some of their outlay. With the passing of the Land Act of 1903 transfers took place on a greater scale than ever and much timber was sold [. . .]' (Neeson 1997, p. 150).
4 Afforestation involves planting seeds or saplings to make a forest on land which has not recently been forested, or which has never been a forest, such as bogland.
5 Eoin Neeson, *A History of Irish Forestry* (Dublin: Lilliput Press, 1991), p. 5.
6 U 12.1266–95.
7 Robert Pogue Harrison, *Forests: the Shadow of Civilization* (Chicago: University of Chicago Press, 1992), p. x.
8 Ibid., p. 150.
9 A.C. Forbes, 'Tree Planting in Ireland during Four Centuries' in *Proceedings of the Royal Irish Academy. Section C: Archaeology, Celtic Studies, History, Linguistics, Literature* 41 (1932–1934), p. 168.
10 Eileen McCracken, *The Irish Woods Since Tudor Times: Distribution and Exploitation* (Newton Abbott: David & Charles, 1971), p. 15.
11 Neeson, 1997, p. 140.
12 Ibid., p. 67.
13 *U*, 12.1258–61.
14 Great Britain, Department of Agriculture and Technical Instructions for Ireland, Report of the Departmental Committee on Irish Forestry (Dublin: HMSO, 1908), *House of Commons Parliamentary Papers* (HCPP), Web. 31 Oct. 2010, v.
15 Ibid., p. 35.
16 *U*, 12.1258–61
17 *U*, 12.1267–9
18 *U*, 12.1269–78
19 *U*, 12.1259–60
20 Neeson, *A History of Irish Forestry*, p. 132.
21 Fritz Senn, 'Ovidian Roots of Gigantism in Joyce's "Ulysses"' in *Journal of Modern Literature* 14.4 (Spring 1989), p. 567n.

22 *U*, 12.1265, 1296.
23 Brigitte L. Sanquist, 'The Tree Wedding in "Cyclops" and the Ramifications of Cata-logic', *James Joyce Quarterly* 33.2 (Winter 1996), p. 201.
24 *U*, 12.1265.
25 *U*, 12.1296.
26 Bernard Benstock, 'Vico . . . Joyce. Triv . . . Quad,' *Vico and Joyce*, ed. Donald Phillip Verene (Buffalo: SUNY Press, 1987), p. 66.
27 Ellmann, Richard, *James Joyce*, 2nd edition (Oxford: Oxford University Pdress, 1982) p. 564.
28 Fisch Max Harold and Thomas Goddard Bergin, 'Introduction' to *The Autobiography of Giambattista Vico*, trans. by Max Harold Fisch and Thomas Goddard Bergin (Ithaca: Cornell University Press, 1944), p. 97.
29 JJ p. 693.
30 A. Walton Litz, 'Vico and Joyce,' *Giambattista Vico: an International Symposium*, ed. by Giorgio Tagliacozzo and Hayden V. White (Baltimore: the Johns Hopkins Press, 1969), p. 249.
31 Stuart Gilbert, *James Joyce's 'Ulysses': A Study* (London: Penguin, 1963), p. 338.
32 Samuel Beckett, 'Dante . . . Bruno. Vico . . . Joyce,' *Our Exagmination Round His Factification for Incamination of Work in Progress* (New York: New Directions, 1962), p. 4.
33 Gilbert, *James Joyce's 'Ulysses'*, p. 46.
34 Beckett, 'Dante . . . Bruno. Vico . . . Joyce', p. 5.
35 Joseph Mali, 'Mythology and Counter-history: the New Critical Art of Vico and Joyce,' *Vico and Joyce*, ed. by Donald Phillip Verene (Buffalo: SUNY Press, 1987), p. 40.
36 Giambattista Vico, *The New Science of Giambattista Vico: unabridged translation of the third edition* (1744) with the addition of 'Practice of the New Science,' trans. Thomas Goddard Bergin and Max Harold Fisch (Ithaca: Cornell University Press, 1984), p. 564.
37 Vico, *New Science*, p. 237.
38 Ibid., p. 405.
39 Rosa Maria Bosinelli, '"I use his cycles as a trellis": Joyce's Treatment of Vico in Finnegans Wake', *Vico and Joyce*, ed. Donald Phillip Verene (Buffalo: SUNY Press, 1987), p. 125.
40 *U*, 12.1265, 1296.
41 *U*, 12.1237–8.
42 Sandquist, 'The Tree Wedding in "Cyclops" and the Ramification of Cata-logic', p. 201.
43 Vico, *New Science*, p. 599.
44 Thomas C. Hofheinz, *Joyce and the Invention of Irish History: Finnegans Wake in Context* (Cambridge: Cambridge University Press, 1995), pp. 150–55.
45 Ibid., p. 141.
46 Ibid., p. 141.
47 JJ 340.
48 Vico, *New Science*, p. 553.
49 Ibid., p. 559.
50 Ibid., p. 557.
51 Ibid., p. 556.
52 Ibid., p. 563.
53 Ibid., p. 563.

54 Ibid., p. 564.
55 *FW* 452.21–22.
56 Litz, 'Vico and Joyce,' p. 254.
57 Vico, *New Science*, p. 564.
58 *U*, 12.3.
59 See Anthony D. Buckley, '"On the club": Friendly Societies in Ireland' (*Irish Economic and Social History* 14 (1987), 39–58), Neil Jarman, *Material Conflicts: Parades and Visual Displays in Northern Ireland* (Oxford: Berge, 1997), and John F. Campbell's unpublished M. Litt Thesis 'Friendly Society in Ireland 1850–1960: with particular reference to Ancient Order of Hibernians and the Irish National Foresters' (TCD, Oct 1998), for detailed discussions of the nationalistic sentiment and performativity of the INF parades, banners, and the society's rituals.
60 *U*, 1.638.
61 *U*, 12.69–70.
62 Vico, *New Science*, p. 531.
63 Ibid., p. 531.
64 Ibid., p. 531.
65 Ibid., p. 531.
66 *U*, 10.177–8.
67 *U*, 16.1887–8.
68 Robert Spoo, *James Joyce and the Language of History: Dedalus' Nightmare* (Oxford: Oxford University Press, 1994), p. 84.
69 *Letters* II, p. 148.
70 Spoo, *James Joyce and the Language of History*, p. 84.
71 Senn, '"Trivia Ulysseana" IV', p. 167.
72 Sandquist, 'The Tree Wedding in "Cyclops" and the Ramification of Catalogic,' p. 198.
73 However, what happens in the catalogue is not, as Sandquist argues a few lines earlier, the continuation of maiden-tree transformation that starts as early as from the beginning of 'Cyclops,' where 'lovely maidens sit in proximity to the roots of the lovely trees singing the most lovely songs . . .' (*U*, 12.78–80). Whereas these maidens are indeed illustrated in the mock-bardic language of a classical epic, they show no sign of slightest transformation. The human-tree metamorphoses does take place yet, in my view, in 'Cyclops' it takes place in the tree catalogue only.
74 Sandquist, 'The Tree Wedding in "Cyclops" and the Ramification of Catalogic,' p. 199.
75 Ibid., p. 199.
76 Interestingly, Miss Daphne Bays (bay being part of the laurel family) appears among the tree wedding guests in the list in 'Cyclops' (*U*, 12.1270).
77 Vico, *New Science*, p. 531.
78 Gibson, *Joyce's Revenge*, p. 115.
79 See Fergus Kelly, 'The Old Irish Tree List,' pp. 108–24.
80 Neeson, *A History of Irish Forestry*, p. 29.
81 James Joyce, *Ulysses*, Hans Walter Gabler (ed.), (New York: Vintage, 1986), p. 704.
82 Michael Groden, '"Cyclops" in Progress: 1919', *James Joyce Quarterly* 12 (Fall 1974/Winter1975), p. 133.
83 Vico, *New Science*, p. 260.
84 Hofheinz, *Joyce and the Invention of Irish History*, p. 146.
85 *U*, 12.1288.

86 *U*, 12.1258.
87 Gibson, *Joyce's Revenge*, p. 96n.
88 Ibid., p. 96.
89 Sandquist, 'The Tree Wedding in "Cyclops" and the Ramification of Catalogic,' p. 203.
90 Nolan, *James Joyce and Nationalism*, p. 112.
91 Vico, *New Science*, p. 405.
92 *FW*, 3.1.
93 Bosinelli, '"I use his cycles as a trellis": Joyce's Treatment of Vico in Finnegans Wake,' p. 125.
94 Arthur Symons, *The Symbolist Movement in Literature*, ed. by Richard Ellmann (Kessinger Publishing, 2004), p.5.

NEGATIVE ECOCRITICAL VISIONS IN 'WANDERING ROCK' (NORRIS)

1 Steven Morrison, 'Introduction' in Andrew Gibson and Steven Morrison (eds.), *European Joyce Studies 12: Joyce's 'Wandering Rocks'* (Amsterdam: Rodopi, 2002), pp. 1–16 (1).
2 Michael J. McDowell, 'The Bakhtinian Road to Ecological Insight', in Cheryll Glotfelty and Harold Fromm (eds.), *The Ecocriticsm Reader: Landmarks in Literary Ecology* (Athens: University of Georgia Press, 1996), pp. 371–391 (372).
3 Neil Evernden, 'Beyond Ecology: Self, Place, and the Pathetic Fallacy', in Cheryll Glotfelty and Harold Fromm (eds.), *The Ecocriticism Reader: Landmarks in Literary Ecology* (Athens: University of Georgia Press, 1996), pp. 92–104 (103).
4 See Karla Armbruster and Kathleen R. Wallace (eds.), *Beyond Nature Writing: Expanding the Boundaries of Ecocriticism* (Charlottesville: University of Virginia Press, 2001).
5 Timothy Morton, *Ecology Without Nature: Rethinking Environmental Aesthetics* (Cambridge, MA: Harvard University Press, 2007), p. 169.
6 Richard Brown, 'Time, Space, and the City in 'Wandering Rocks' in Andrew Gibson and Steve Morrison (eds.), *European Joyce Studies 12: Joyce's 'Wandering Rocks'* (Amsterdam: Rodopi, 2002), pp. 57–72 (62).
7 Tim Wenzell, *Emerald Green: An Ecocritical Study of Irish Literature* (Newcastle upon Tyne: Cambridge Scholars Publishing, 2009), p. 1.
8 Ibid., p. 2.
9 Brown, 'Time', p. 58.
10 James Joyce, *Ulysses,* Hans Walter Gabler (ed.), (New York: Vintage, 1986), p. 186; 8.1146–47
11 See 'PS *General Slocum'*, Accessed 10 April 2013, http://en.wikipedia.org/wiki/PS_General_Slocum.
12 Joyce, *Ulysses*, 10.90.
13 Ibid., 8.1146.
14 Ibid., 10.725.
15 Ibid., 10.728.
16 Ibid., 10.731.
17 Ibid., 6.776.
18 Ibid., 6.771.
19 Wenzell, *Emerald Green*, p. 39.
20 Joyce, *Ulysses*, 8.28.

21 Ibid., 8.41.
22 Ibid., 10.662.
23 Ibid., 10.273.
24 Ibid., 10.283.
25 Ibid., 2.338. Joyce may have intended Deasy's concern to gloss one of the terrible ironies of the 'Great Famine', namely that Ireland continued to export food during the entire period. 'Christine Kinealy writes that Irish exports of calves, livestock (except pigs), bacon and ham actually increased during the famine'. See 'Great Famine (Ireland)', accessed 11 April 2013, https://en.wikipedia.org/wiki/Great_Famine_(Ireland).
26 Joyce, *Ulysses*, p. 10.1121.
27 Ibid., 10.706.
28 Ibid., 10.875.
29 Here are the salient lines from the poem's opening:

'The em'rald of Europe, it sparkled and shone,
In the ring of the world the most precious stone.
In her sun, in her soil, in her station thrice blest,
With her back towards Britain, her face to the West,
Erin stands proudly insular, on her steep shore,
And strikes her high harp 'mid the ocean's deep roar'.

See William Drennan, 'When Erin First Met Rose', in Charles A. Read (ed.), *The Cabinet of Irish Literature, Volume 2*, Library Ireland, accessed 10 April 2013, http://www.libraryireland.com/CIL/DrennanErin.php.
30 Joyce, *Ulysses*, 10.805.
31 Ibid., 10.807.
32 Ibid., 10.498.
33 Ibid., 10.101.
34 Ibid., 10.103.
35 Ibid., 10.161.
36 Anne Fogarty, 'States of Memory: Reading History in "Wandering Rocks"', in Ellen Carol Jones and Morris Beja (eds.), *Twenty-first Joyce* (Gainesville: University of Florida Press, 2004), pp. 56–81 (68).
37 Ibid., p. 69.
38 Lawrence Buell, *The Environmental Imagination: Thoreau, Nature Writing, and the Formation of American Culture* (Cambridge, MA: Harvard University Press, 1995), p. 33.
39 Ibid., p. 31.
40 Fogarty, 'States of Memory', p. 69.
41 Joyce, *Ulysses*, 10.184.
42 Morton, *Ecology Without Nature*, p. 2.

JOYCE BEYOND THE PALE (KERSHNER)

1 James Joyce, *Dubliners*, Robert Scholes and Richard Ellmann (eds.), (New York: Viking Press, 1967), p. 46.
2 Michael Bennett and David Teague, 'Introduction', in Michael Bennett and David Teague (eds.), *The Nature of Cities: Ecocriticism and Urban Environments* (Tucson: University of Arizona, 1999), pp. 3–14 (4).
3 While the term 'nature' has become highly debated within ecocriticism, I have retained its usage here simply to signal how the non-urban environment or

surround accrues meaning in Yeats' poetry (and in the work of other Revivalists), and also to show how Joyce redresses this employment of 'nature' in his own work. Throughout this paper I use the term 'nature' to designate a socially constructed zone, rather than an unproblematic given.

4 Tim Wenzell, *Emerald Green: An Ecocritical Study of Irish Literature* (Newcastle upon Tyne: Cambridge Scholars, 2009), p. 1.

5 Catherine Maignant, 'Rural Ireland in the Nineteenth Century and the Advent of the Modern World', in Jacqueline Genet, *Rural Ireland, Real Ireland?* (Oxford: Oxford University Press, 1996), pp. 21–30 (29).

6 Eóin, Flannery, 'Colonialism, Tourism and the Irish Landscape', in Christine Cusick (ed.), *Out of the Earth: Ecocritical Readings of Irish Texts* (Cork: Cork University Press, 2010), pp. 85–107 (87).

7 For more on the relationship between the East and West in Irish literary production, see Joseph Lennon, *Irish Orientalism: A Literary and Intellectual History* (Syracuse: Syracuse University Press, 2004).

8 Wenzell, *Emerald Green*, p. 62.

9 Oona Frawley, *Irish Pastoral: Nostalgia and Twentieth-Century Irish Literature* (Dublin: Irish Academic Press, 2005), p. 54.

10 William Butler Yeats, 'The Song of Wandering Aengus', *The Collected Poems of W.B. Yeats* (New York: Macmillan, 1961), p. 58.

11 James Joyce, *A Portrait of the Artists as a Young Man: Text, Criticism, and Notes*, Chester G. Anderson (ed.), (New York: Viking Press, 1968), p. 251.

12 Declan Kiberd, *Inventing Ireland: The Literature of the Modern Nation* (Cambridge: Harvard University Press, 1995), p. 337.

13 Joyce, *Dubliners*, p. 38.

14 Ibid., p. 107.

15 Ibid., p. 115.

16 Ibid., p. 117.

17 Ibid., p. 117

18 Ibid., p. 189.

19 Ibid., p. 192.

20 Ibid., p. 202.

21 Ibid., p. 223.

22 Ibid., p. 223

23 Ibid., p. 224.

24 Flannery, 'Colonialism, Tourism and the Irish Landscape', p. 87

25 Joyce, *Dubliners*, p. 223.

26 Andrew Ross, 'The Social Claim on Urban Ecology', in Michael Bennett and David W. Teague (eds.), *The Nature of Cities: Ecocriticism and Urban Environments* (Tucson: University of Arizona Press, 1999), pp. 15–32 (22).

27 Joyce, *Portrait*, p. 251.

28 Ibid., p. 167.

29 Ibid., p. 252.

30 For more O'Brien's use of animals in literature, see Maureen O'Connor, '"Becoming Animal" in the Novels of Edna O'Brien', in Christine Cusick (ed.), *Out of the Earth: Ecocritical Readings of Irish Texts* (Cork: Cork University Press, 2010), pp. 151–177.

31 Joyce, *Portrait*, p. 252.

32 Cheryll Glotfelty, 'Introduction: Literary Studies in an Age of Environmental Crisis', in Cheryll Glotfelty and Harold Fromm (eds.), *The Ecocriticism*

Reader: Landmarks in Literary Ecology (Athens: University of Georgia Press, 1996), pp. xv–xxxvii (xix).

33 Greg Garrard, *Ecocriticism* (New York: Routledge, 2004), p. 5.

34 James Joyce, *Ulysses,* Hans Walter Gabler (ed.), (New York: Vintage, 1986), 18.1558–62. Episodes and lines will be cited from this edition.

35 Ibid., 18.1602.

36 Ibid., 3.27–28.

37 Ibid., 3.477–79

38 Ibid., 13.1–5

39 Ibid., 13.1258, 1265

40 Greta Gaard, 'New Directions for Ecofeminism: Toward a More Feminist Ecocriticism', *Interdisciplinary Studies in Literature and Environment* 17.4 (Autumn 2010), pp. 643–665 (653).

41 Brandon R. Kershner, *Joyce, Bakhtin and Popular Literature: Chronicles of Disorder* (Chapel Hill: University of North Carolina Press, 1989), p. 147.

42 Joyce, *Ulysses,* 18.1575.

'AQUACITIES OF THOUGHT AND LANGUAGE' (WINSTON)

1 Charles Fishman, *The Big Thirst: The Secret Life and Turbulent Future of Water* (New York: Simon and Schuster, 2011), p. 3.

2 Alex Prud'homme, *The Ripple Effect: The Fate of Freshwater in the Twenty-First Century* (New York: Scribner, 2011), p. 5.

3 See Fishman, *The Big Thirst*, and Prud'homme, *The Ripple Effect*, above, as well as Steven Solomon, *Water: The Epic Struggle for Wealth, Power, and Civilization* (New York: HarperCollins, 2010).

4 In August 2011, a keyword search of the MLA International Bibliography using the phrase 'blue ecology' resulted in only one (coincidental) hit: a study of American history and ecology in the Kim Stanley Robinson novel *Blue Mars.*

5 At the 2009 ASLE conference in Victoria, British Columbia, the panel 'Blue Ecology: Ecocriticism and the Place of Maritime Literature' included four presentations about oceanic environments and marine resources in canonical fiction, non-fiction and poetry, including Daniel Brayton's paper 'Peter Mathiessen's *Far Tortuga*: Marine Ecology as Human Ecology' and my own '"Somewhere people interfering with the course of nature": Epic Ecology in Derek Walcott's *Omeros*'. Anissa J. Wardi's forthcoming book *Water and African American Memory: An Ecocritical Perspective* (University Press of Florida, 2011) promises to move the conversation in important new directions along racial and historical lines.

6 Lawrence Buell, *Writing for an Endangered World* (Cambridge, MA: Belknap, 2001), p. 199.

7 J.R. McNeill, *Something New Under the Sun: An Environmental History of the Twentieth-Century World* (New York: W.W. Norton, 2000), p. 119.

8 Joseph Conrad, *Heart of Darkness* (London: Penguin, 1989), p. 121.

9 Buell, *Writing for an Endangered World*, p. 249.

10 Ibid., p. 265.

11 Ibid., p. 340n67.

12 Scott Slovic, in Scott Slovic, Serenella Iovino and Shin Yamashiro (eds.), *Concentric* 34.1 (March 2008), pp. 3–4.

13 Fishman, *The Big Thirst*, p. 5.

14 Glen A. Love, *Practical Ecocriticism* (Charlottesville, VA: University of Virgina Press, 2003), p. 34.
15 Lawrence Buell, *The Future of Environmental Criticism: Environmental Crisis and Literary Imagination* (Malden, MA: Blackwell, 2005), p. 17.
16 Robert Kern, 'Ecocriticism: What Is It Good For?' *ISLE* 7 (winter 2000), p. 11.
17 Buell, *The Future of Environmental Criticism*, p. 25.
18 Ibid., p. 86.
19 A pioneering work in this vein is Michael Bennett and David Teague (eds.), *The Nature of Cities: Ecocriticism and Urban Environments* (Tucson: University of Arizona Press, 1999).
20 Karla Armbruster and Kathleen R. Wallace, *Beyond Nature Writing* (Charlottesville, VA: University of Virginia Press, 2001), p. 4.
21 See Robert Adams Day, 'Joyce's AquaCities', in Morris Beja and David Norris, *Joyce in the Hibernian Metropolis* (Columbus: Ohio State University Press, 1996), pp. 3–20, and Ariela Freedman 'Did it Flow?: Bridging Aesthetics and History in Joyce's *Ulysses*', *Modernism/Modernity* 13.1 (2006), pp. 107–22.
22 Michael Rubenstein, *Public Works: Infrastructure, Irish Modernism, and the Postcolonial* (Notre Dame, IN: University of Notre Dame Press, 2010), p. 52.
23 Ibid., p. 58.
24 James Joyce, *Dubliners*, ed. Terence Brown (New York: Penguin, 1992), p. 225.
25 Ibid., pp. 180, 223.
26 James Joyce, *A Portrait of the Artist as a Young Man*, ed. R.B. Kershner (Boston: Bedford/St Martin's, 1993), p. 19.
27 Ibid., pp. 31–33, 62.
28 James Joyce, *Finnegans Wake* (New York: Penguin, 1976), p. 3.
29 Ibid., pp. 3, 23, 44, 90, 113, 257, 314, 332, 414, 424.
30 Ibid., pp. 216, 619–628.
31 James Joyce, *Ulysses*, ed. Hans Walter Gabler (New York: Vintage, 1986), pp. 4–5.
32 Ibid., p. 5.
33 Ibid., p. 41.
34 Ibid., pp. 49, 50.
35 Ibid., pp. 70, 71.
36 Ibid., pp. 345.
37 Ibid., p. 347.
38 Ibid., p. 550, 553.
39 Ibid., p. 548.
40 Fishman, *The Big Thirst*, p. 12.
41 Michael Corcoran, *Our Good Health: A History of Water and Drainage* (Dublin City Council, 2005), p. 50
42 Ibid., p. 54
43 Ibid., p. 48
44 Joyce, *Ulysses*, p. 78.
45 Ibid., p. 123.
46 Yvonne Whelan, 'Monuments, Power, and Contested Space – The Iconography of O'Connell Street (Sackville Street) before Independence (1922)', *Irish Geography*, Volume 34(1), 2001, p. 28.
47 Corcoran, *Our Good Health*, p. 48.
48 Corcoran, *Our Good Health*, p. 59.

49 Fishman, *The Big Thirst*, p. 7.
50 Ibid., p. 9.
51 Joyce, *Ulysses*, p. 549.
52 Ibid., p. 549.
53 Freedman, 'Did it Flow?', p. 110.
54 J.R. McNeill, *Something New Under the Sun*, p. 128.
55 Joyce, *Ulysses*, p. 549.
56 Ibid., p. 549.
57 Ibid.
58 Ibid., p. 548.
59 Corcoran, *Our Good Health*, p. 63.
60 Today, based on projected annual water demand for the Dublin area of 200,000 megalitres, the Irish Government concludes the average Dubliner uses just over 80 gallons per day. Department of the Environment, Heritage and Local Government, 'Economic Analysis of Water Use in Ireland', p. 54, accessed 1 Nov. 2011, http://www.wfdireland.ie/docs/35. By comparison, the average American uses 100 gallons per day. Fishman, *The Big Thirst*, p. 7.
61 Gerald Fitzgerald, 'Correspondence: The Dublin Corporation v. The Guardians South Dublin Union', *Irish Daily Independent*, 10 June 1904, p. 6.
62 'Water Prosecution', *Irish Daily Independent*, 9 June 1904, p. 2.
63 Ibid., p. 2.
64 Fitzgerald, 'Correspondence', p. 6.
65 Ignatius Rice, 'Correspondence. Dublin Corporation v. South Dublin Union', *Irish Daily Independent*, 10 June 1904, p. 6.
66 Ibid., p. 6.
67 Ibid.
68 Joyce, *Ulysses*, p. 548.
69 Prud'homme, *The Ripple Effect*, pp. 265–66.
70 Corcoran, *Our Good Health*, p. 65.
71 Joyce, *Ulysses*, p. 549.
72 Ibid., p. 550.
73 Ibid., p. 550
74 Ibid.
75 Solomon, *Water*, p. 3.
76 Joyce, *Ulysses*, p. 552.
77 'Advertisement for Epps's Cocoa', *Freeman's Journal*, 16 June 1904, p. 2. My italics.
78 David Rothenberg, 'Introduction', in David Rothenberg and Marta Ulvaeus (eds.), *Writing on Water* (Cambridge: MIT Press, 2001), p. xiii.
79 Joyce, *Ulysses*, p. 577.
80 Paul Robbins, *Political Ecology: An Introduction* (Malden, MA: Blackwell, 2004), p. 5.
81 Fishman, *The Big Thirst*, p. 6.
82 Ibid., p. 5.
83 Joyce, *Ulysses*, p. 135.

'CLACKING ALONG THE CONCRETE PAVEMENT' (CUSICK)

1 Neil Evernden, 'Beyond Ecology: Self, Place and the Pathetic Fallacy', in Cheryll Glotfelty and Harold Fromm (eds.), *The Ecocriticism Reader: Landmarks in Literary Ecology* (Athens: University of Georgia P), p. 103.

2 Lawrence Buell, *The Future of Environmental Criticism: Environmental Crisis and Literary Imagination* (Oxford: Blackwell Publishing, 2005), p. 88.
3 James Joyce, *Dubliners* (New York: Penguin Books 1993), p. 22.
4 Glen A. Love, *Practical Ecocriticism: Literature, Biology and the Environment.* (Charlottesville: University of Virginia P, 2003), p. 16.
5 Murray Bookchin, *The Philosophy of Social Ecology: Essays on Dialectical Naturalism* (Montreal: Black Rose Books, 1995), p. 35.
6 Michael Bengal, 'Introduction', in Michael Bengal (ed.), *James Joyce and the City: The Significance of Place* (Syracuse: Syracuse University Press, 2002), p. xv.
7 John Wilson Foster, 'The Culture of Nature', in John Wilson Foster (ed.), *Nature in Ireland: A Scientific and Cultural History* (Dublin: The Lilliput Press, 1997), p. 610.
8 James Joyce, *Dubliners* (New York: Penguin Books, 1993), p. 24
9 Joseph Brady, 'Dublin at the Beginning of the Twentieth Century', in Oona Frawley, *A New and Complex Sensation: Essays on Joyce's Dubliners* (Dublin: The Lilliput Press, 2004), p. 10.
10 Joyce, *Dubliners,* p. 29.
11 Ibid., p. 29
12 Ibid.
13 Ibid., p. 254.
14 Martha Fodaski Black, 'Joyce on Location: Place Names in Joyce's Fiction', in Michael Bengal (ed.), *Joyce and the City: The Significance of Place* (Syracuse: Syracuse UP 2002), p. 19.
15 In this reading it is useful to consider Spurgeon Thompson's survey of recent postcolonial readings of *Dubliners* in which he highlights Seamus Deane's re-envisioning of Joyce's construction of modernity: 'Deane argues, in opposition to conventional readings of *Dubliners* where it is the backwardness of the Irish condition that paralyses the subject that it is, rather, modernity that does so – a modernity coextensive with the kind of colonialism manifested in Ireland'. See 'Recovering *Dubliners* for Postcolonial Theory', in Oona Frawley (ed.), *A New and Complex Sensation: Essays on Joyce's Dubliners* (Dublin: Lilliput Press, 2004), p. 190. While Eveline's paralysis is undoubtedly connected to the constraints of her domestic space, the positioning of her in the liminal space of evening, resting against the transparent glass boundary, suggests a more complex conception of her stagnation.
16 Joyce, *Dubliners,* p. 29.
17 Ibid., p. 29
18 Ibid., p. 30.
19 Ibid., p. 31. Terence Brown refers to the phrase 'down somewhere in the country' as a 'common Dublin mode of reference to the rest of Ireland which bespeaks the city's essential indifference to life outside the capital', ibid., p. 254. For Eveline, however, this phrase seems to bespeak alienation more than indifference. She is so contained not only within the cityscape but also within the walls of the family home that rural Ireland might as well be another country altogether.
20 Ibid., p. 31.
21 Catherine Whitley, 'Gender and Interiority', in Michael Bengal (ed.), *Joyce and the City: The Significance of Place* (Syracuse: Syracuse UP, 2002), p. 38.
22 Ibid., p. 37.

23 Serenella Iovino, 'Ecocriticism and a Non-Anthropocentric Humanism: Reflections on Local Natures and Global Responsibilities', in Laurenz Volkmann, Nancy Grimm, Ines Detmers and Katrin Thomson (eds.), *Local Natures, Global Responsibilities: Ecocritical Perspectives on the New English Literatures* (Amsterdam: Rodopi, 2010), pp. 36–37.
24 Desmond Harding, 'The Dead: Joyce's Epitaph for Dublin', in Michael Bengal (ed.), *Joyce in the City: The Significance of Place* (Syracuse: Syracuse UP 2004), p. 124.
25 Joyce, *Dubliners*, p. 32.
26 Ibid., p. 33.
27 Whitley, p. 40.
28 An ecofeminist reading is especially useful here as it invites us to further explore the parallel hierarchies that perpetuate the oppression of nonhuman nature, women and the economically disadvantaged.
29 Garry Leonard, 'Holding on to the Here and the Now: Juxtaposition and Identity in Modernity and in Joyce', in Michael Patrick Gillespie (ed.), *James Joyce and the Fabrication of an Irish Identity* (Amsterdam: Rodopi, 2001), p. 45.
30 Joyce, *Dubliners*, p. 66.
31 David Pierce and Dan Harper observe of Joyce: 'his imagination was . . . intensely visual – never more so than in his use of maps and in his reconstruction of the streets of Dublin. Indeed, *Dubliners* is not unlike a commentary, an *ekphrasis* on a visual representation – in this case a map of his native city'. See the chapter 'Dubliners, Topography and Social Class' in *James Joyce's Ireland* (New Haven: Yale UP, 1995), p. 83. Little Chandler's position as spectator of the city pathways enacts this imaginative impulse in which Joyce constructs character in relation to the map beneath his window.
32 Joyce, *Dubliners*, p. 66.
33 Ibid., p. 66.
34 Ibid.
35 Ibid.
36 Ibid.
37 Ibid., p. 67.
38 Ibid.
39 Ibid.
40 Ibid., p. 270; p. 67.
41 Ibid., p. 68
42 Martha Fodaski Black makes an important connection between the topography of Chandler's walking route and architectural markers of imperialism: '[Chandler's] walk from Capel Street north of the Liffey over the Grattan Bridge – named for the Anglo-Irish statesman – reinforces the fact that Anglo-Irish influences often dominate Dubliners. . . In Joyce's fiction the Liffey is often the dividing line between chic Georgian (hence Anglo-Irish) Dublin south of the river and lower-middle-class life north of it. Clearly Chandler aspires to identify with the Anglo-Irish set south of the Liffey'. See pp. 20–21. As in 'Eveline', the intersections of class and colonial consequence should not be neglected, and the Dubliner's aspiration to be that which has conquered him reminds us of Joyce's disillusionment with a Nationalism that replicates the very system that it fights.
43 Joyce, *Dubliners*, p. 68.
44 Ibid., p. 68
45 Ibid.

46 Ibid., pp. 68–69.
47 Leonard, 'Holding on to the Here and the Now', p. 45.
48 Ibid., p. 69.
49 Ibid., pp. 68–69.
50 Ibid., p. 69.
51 Desmond Harding, *Writing the City: Urban Visions and Literary Modernisms* (New York: Routledge, 2003), p. 33.
52 Whitley, 'Gender and Interiority', p. 35.
53 Michael Bennett, 'From Wide Open Spaces to Metropolitan Places The Urban Challenge to Ecocriticism', *Interdisciplinary Studies in Literature and Environment* 8.1 (Winter 2001), p. 33.
54 Heyward Ehrlich, 'James Joyce's Four Gated City of Modernisms', in Michael Bengal (ed.), *Joyce and the City: The Significance of Place* (Syracuse: Syracuse UP 2002), p. 16.

Joyce the Travel Writer (Gladwin)

1 Michel de Certeau, *The Practice of Everyday Life*, trans. Steven Randall (Berkeley: University of California Press, 1988), p. 115.
2 Kevin Barry, 'Introduction', in Kevin Barry (ed.), *James Joyce: Occasional, Critical, and Political Writing* (Oxford: Oxford University Press, 2000), p. x.
3 Ibid., pp. x–xxii.
4 Ibid., p. xiii.
5 A. Nicholas Fargnoli and Michael Patrick Gillespie (eds.), *James Joyce A to Z: the Essential Reference to the Life and Work* (Oxford: Oxford University Press, 1995), p. 40.
6 Richard Ellmann and Ellsworth Mason (eds.), *The Critical Writings of James Joyce* (Ithaca: Cornell University Press, 1959), p. 188.
7 Lawrence Buell, *The Future of Environmental Criticism: Environmental Crisis and Literary Imagination* (Malden, MA: Blackwell Publishing, 2005), p. 63.
8 Ibid.
9 Much has been written on the concept of space and place within critical geography, but it has yet to be extensively examined in an ecocritical context. My intent here is not to introduce these as new concepts but to offer a way of looking at Joyce's travel pieces from another angle, particularly one that will reveal an embedded environmental consciousness.
10 Buell, *The Future of Environmental Criticism*, p. 63.
11 Ibid.
12 Eóin Flannery, 'Ireland of the Welcomes: Colonialism, Tourism, and the Irish Landscape', in Christine Cusick (ed.), *Out of the Earth: Ecocritical Readings of Irish Texts* (Cork: University of Cork Press, 2010), p. 87.
13 Arthur Young, *Tour in Ireland (1776–1779)* 2 vols., ed. Arthur Wollaston Hutton (London: George Bell & Sons, 1892).
14 C.J. Woods, 'Irish Travel writings as Source Material', *Irish Historical Studies*, 28.110 (Nov. 2002), pp. 173–175.
15 Ibid., 173.
16 Tim Robinson could be considered one of Ireland's best contemporary examples of this mixed genre. See *Stones of Aran: Pilgrimage* (New York: NY Review of Books, 1986) or his Connemara Trilogy: *Connemara: Listening to the Wind* (London: Penguin, 2006), *Connemara: the Last Pool of Darkness*

(London: Penguin, 2008), and *Connemara: A Little Gaelic Kingdom* (London: Penguin, 2011).

17 Cheryll Glotfelty, 'Introduction: Literary Studies in an Age of Environmental Crisis', in Cheryll Glotfelty and Harold Fromm (eds.), *Ecocriticism Reader: Landmarks in Literary Ecology* (Athens, Georgia: University of Georgia Press, 1996), p. xix.

18 Greg Garrard, *Ecocriticism* (London: Routledge, 2012), p. 5.

19 Buell, *The Future of Environmental Criticism*, p. viii.

20 Gerry Smyth, *Space and the Irish Cultural Imagination* (Basingstoke: Palgrave Macmillan, 2001), p. 11.

21 Michael Cohen, 'Blues in the Green: Ecocriticism Under Critique', *Environmental History*, 9, 1 (Oxford: Oxford University Press, 2004), p. 23.

22 Michael Cronin, 'Fellow Travellers: Contemporary Travel writing and Ireland', in Barbara O'Connor and Michael Cronin (eds.), *Tourism in Ireland: A Critical Analysis* (Cork: Cork University Press, 1993), p. 54.

23 Buell, *The Future of Environmental Criticism*, p. 68.

24 Ibid., p. 67.

25 Robert David Sack, *Homo Geographicus: A Framework for Action, Awareness, and Moral Concern* (Baltimore: Johns Hopkins University Press, 1997), p. 125.

26 Simon Schama, *Landscape and Memory* (New York: Vintage Books, 1995), pp. 9–10.

27 Buell, *The Future of Environmental Criticism*, p. 66.

28 Mitchell Thomashow, 'Toward a Cosmopolitan Bioregionalism', in Michael Vincent McGinnis (ed), *Bioregionalism* (London: Routledge, 1999), p. 121.

29 Buell, *The Future of Environmental Criticism*, p. 84.

30 Ibid., p. 83.

31 Ibid.

32 James Joyce, 'The Mirage of the Fisherman of Aran: England's Safety Valve in Case of War', in Richard Ellmann and Ellsworth Mason (eds.), *The Critical Writings of James Joyce* (Ithaca: Cornell University Press, 1959), p. 234.

33 James Joyce, 'The City of the Tribes: Italian Echoes in an Irish Port', in Richard Ellmann and Ellsworth Mason (eds.), *The Critical Writings of James Joyce* (Ithaca: Cornell, 1959), p. 230.

34 Joyce, 'The Mirage of the Fisherman of Aran', p. 235.

35 James Joyce, 'The City of the Tribes', p. 233.

36 Barry, 'Introduction', pp. x and xv.

37 As I indicate at times throughout this essay, Joyce's version of history is debatable in 'The City of the Tribes' and 'The Mirage of the Fisherman of Aran'. His adulterated history is assembled from, as Barry points out, 'the reference shelves of a library', dates that 'derive from Arthur Griffith's editorials', accounts that come from his wife Nora (a Galway native), and in sections on Galway that have been taken directly from James Hardiman's history of Galway. See Barry's 'Introduction', p. xxi.

38 Catherine Nash, '"Embodying the Nation": The West of Ireland Landscape and Irish Identity', in Barbara O'Connor and Michael Cronin (eds.), *Tourism in Ireland: A Critical Analysis* (Cork: Cork University Press, 1993), p. 87.

39 Joyce, 'The City of the Tribes', p. 230.

40 Bulson, *Novels, Maps, Modernity*, p. 70.

41 Smyth, *Space and the Irish Cultural Imagination*, p. 26.

42 Pascale Casanova, *The World Republic of Letters* (Cambridge: Harvard University Press, 2004), p. 316.

43 Ellmann and Ellsworth, *The Critical Writings of James Joyce*, p. 187.
44 Compared to his other articles such as 'Fenianism: The Last Fenian', 'Home Rule Come of Age', 'The Home Rule Comet, and 'Ireland at the Bar', 'The City of the Tribes' and 'The Mirage of the Fisherman of Aran' might initially appear to be less of a polemic on Irish politics. During the period Joyce wrote the Triestine articles from 1907–1912, he had also been reading two significant nationalist publications, Arthur Griffith's *United Irishman* and later *Sinn Féin*. Therefore, it is clear that all of the pieces in *Il Piccolo* were influenced by Joyce's interest in Irish politics at the time. See Barry's 'Introduction', p. x–xxii.
45 Joyce, 'The City of the Tribes', p. 229.
46 Edward Said, *Culture and Imperialism* (New York: Vintage, 1994), p. 225.
47 Graham Huggan and Helen Tiffin, *Postcolonial Ecocriticism: Literature, Animals, Environment* (London: Routledge, 2010), p. 6.
48 Eric Bulson, *Novels, Maps, Modernity: The Spatial Imagination, 1850–2000* (New York: Routledge, 2007), p. 70.
49 Joyce, 'The City of the Tribes', p. 229.
50 Joyce, 'The Mirage of the Fisherman of Aran', p. 234.
51 Joyce, 'The City of the Tribes', p. 229.
52 Ibid.
53 Nash, '"Embodying the Nation"', p. 89.
54 David Harvey, *The Condition of Postmodernity: An Enquiry into the Origins of Cultural Change* (Oxford: Blackwell, 1989), p. 264.
55 Said, *Culture and Imperialism*, p. 225.
56 Brian Graham, 'Ireland and Irishness: Place, Culture, and Identity', in Brian Graham (ed.), *In Search of Ireland: A Cultural Geography* (London: Routledge, 1997), p. 5.
57 These fourteen aristocratic families were located in Connacht, which is an Irish-speaking region in the West of Ireland. They predominantly dominated politics and commercial life in Galway between the thirteenth and nineteenth centuries respectively. Despite this long period of political and economic control, their power would increase and decrease throughout British colonial rule. See James Hardiman, *The History of the Town and County of Galway* (Dublin: W. Folds and Sons, 1820).
58 Smyth, *Space and the Irish Cultural Imagination*, p. 25.
59 Barbara Bender, 'Introduction' in Barbara Bender and Margot Winer (eds.), *Contested Landscapes: Movement, Exile and Place* (Oxford: Berg, 2001), p. 4.
60 Said, *Culture and Imperialism*, p. 225.
61 James Joyce, 'The Mirage of the Fisherman of Aran', p. 235.
62 Flannery, 'Ireland of the Welcomes', p. 91.
63 Barry, 'Introduction', p. xxxii. Original emphasis.
64 Schama, *Landscape and Memory*, p. 10.
65 Joyce, 'The Mirage of the Fisherman of Aran', p. 237.
66 Ibid.
67 Ibid., p. 236
68 Christine Cusick, 'Mindful Paths: An Interview with Tim Robinson' in Christine Cusick (ed.), *Out of the Earth: Ecocritical Readings of Irish Texts* (Cork: Cork University Press), p. 208.
69 Joyce, 'The City of the Tribes', 231.
70 John Wilson Foster, 'The Culture of Nature', in John Wilson Foster (ed.),

Nature in Ireland: A Scientific and Cultural History (Montreal: McGill-Queens University Press, 1997), p. 597.
71 Joyce, 'The Mirage of the Fisherman of Aran', p. 237.
72 Smyth, *Space and the Irish Cultural Imagination*, p. 11.
73 Graham, 'Ireland and Irishness', p. 2.
74 Schama, *Memory and Landscape*, p. 14.

'CAN EXCREMENT BE ART . . , IF NOT, WHY NOT?' (O'BRIEN)

1 James Joyce, *A Portrait of the Artist as a Young Man*, ed. Seamus Deane (Harmondsworth: Penguin, 2000), p. 229.
2 Umberto Eco, *On Beauty* (London: Secker & Warburg, 2004), p. 41.
3 Ibid., p. 50.
4 Val Plumwood, *Feminism and the Mastery of Nature* (London: Routledge, 1993), p. 115.
5 Greg Garrard, *Ecocriticism* (London: Routledge, 2004), p. 25.
6 Martin Heidegger, *Being and Time*, trans. J. Stambaugh (Albany: State University of New York Press, 1996), p. 183.
7 Maurice Merleau-Ponty, *Phenomenology of Perception* (London: Routledge & Kegan Paul, 1962), p. 159.
8 Karsten Harries, *Art Matters: A Critical Commentary on Heidegger's 'The Origin of the Work of Art', Contributions to Phenomenology* (Dordrecht: Springer, 2009), p. 117.
9 Greg Garrard, 'Heidegger, Heaney and the Problem of Dwelling', in Richard Kerridge and Neil Sammells (eds.), *Writing the Environment: Ecocriticism and Literature* (London: Zed Books, 1998), pp. 167–181.
10 Bill Devall and George Sessions, *Deep Ecology: Living as if Nature Mattered* (Layton, UT: Gibbs Smith, 1985), p. 98.
11 Michael Zimmerman, *Heidegger's Confrontation with Modernity* (Indianapolis: Indiana University Press, 1990), pp. 242–243.
12 Jacques Derrida, *The Animal that Therefore I Am*, trans. D. Wills, ed. M.-L. Mallet (Ashland: Fordham University Press, 2008), p. 72.
13 Derrida, *The Animal that Therefore I Am*, p. 72.
14 Derek Attridge and Daniel Ferrer (eds.), *Post-Sructuralist Joyce: Essays from the French* (Cambridge: Cambridge University Press, 1984), p. 149.
15 Jacques Derrida and Derek Attridge, *Acts of Literature* (London: Routledge, 1992), p. 293.
16 Theodor W. Adorno and Max Horkheimer, *Dialectic of Enlightenment* (Verso Classics. London: Blackwell Verso, 1997), p. 149.
17 Adorno and Horkheimer, *Dialectic of Enlightenment*, p. 23.
18 Miguel de Beistegui, *The New Heidegger* (London Continuum, 2005), p. 127.
19 James Joyce, *Finnegans Wake* [1939] (London: Penguin, 1999), p. 304, l.31.
20 Joyce, *Finnegans* Wake, p. 301, ll.20–25.
21 Merleau-Ponty, *Phenomenology of Perception*, p. xvii.
22 Ibid., p. xvii.
23 Ibid., p. 272.
24 Ibid., p. 274.
25 Ibid., p. 175.
26 Joyce, *A Portrait of the Artist as a Young Man*, p. 232.
27 Martin Heidegger, *What is Called Thinking?*, trans. J.G. Gray (New York: Harper Collins, 2004), p. 14.

28 Martin Heidegger, *Poetry, Language, Thought*, trans. A. Hofstadter (New York: Harper & Row, 1971), p. 211.
29 Jacques Derrida, *Margins of Philosophy*, trans. A. Bass (Brighton: Harvester Press, 1982), p. 239.
30 Harries, *Art Matters*, p. 116.
31 Derrida, *The Animal that Therefore I Am*, p. 73.
32 Heidegger, *Poetry, Language, Thought*, p. xi.
33 Joyce, *A Portrait of the Artist as a Young Man*, p. 4.
34 Ibid., p. 11.
35 Ibid., pp. 12–13.
36 Ibid., p. 19.
37 Ibid., p. 22.
38 Derrida, *The Animal that Therefore I Am*, p. 72.
39 Heidegger, *Poetry, Language, Thought*, p. 147.
40 Martin Heidegger, *Early Greek Thinking*, trans. D. F. Krell and F. A. Capuzzi (New York: Harper and Row, 1975), p. v108.
41 Heidegger, *Poetry, Language, Thought*, p. v44.
42 Julian Young, *Heidegger's Philosophy of Art* (Cambridge: Cambridge University Press, 2001), p. 152.
43 Joyce, *A Portrait of the Artist as a Young Man*, p. 87.
44 Heidegger, *What is Called Thinking?*, p. 16.
45 Joyce, *A Portrait of the Artist as a Young Man*, p. 35.
46 Ibid., p. 35.
47 Ibid., p. 155.
48 Ibid., p. 107.
49 Ibid.
50 Ibid., p. 265.
51 Heidegger, *Poetry, Language, Thought*, p. 6.
52 Heidegger, *What is Called Thinking?*, p. 24.
53 Joyce, *A Portrait of the Artist as a Young Man*, pp. 13–14.
54 Colin MacCabe, *James Joyce and the Revolution of the Word* (London: Macmillan, 1978), p. 4.
55 Jacques Derrida, *Of Grammatology*, ed. G. C. Spivak (Baltimore: Johns Hopkins University Press, 1976), p. lxxiii.
56 Jacques Derrida, *Limited Inc. ABC*, trans. A. B. a. S. Weber (Baltimore: Johns Hopkins University Press, 1977), p. 232.
57 Jacques Derrida, 'Biodegradables Seven Diary Fragments', *Critical Inquiry* 15 (4 Summer 1989): pp. 812–873, p. 841.
58 Jacques Lacan, *Écrits: The First Complete Edition in English*, trans. Bruce Fink (London: W. W. Norton, 2006), p. 76.
59 Joyce, *A Portrait of the Artist as a Young Man*, p. 3.
60 Ibid., p. 3
61 Ibid.
62 Giorgio Agamben, *Infancy and History: The Destruction of Experience* (London: Verso, 1993), p. 47
63 Leland De la Durantaye, *Giorgio Agamben: A Critical Introduction* (Stanford: Stanford University Press, 2009), p. 91.
64 Alison Ross (ed.), spec. issue of *The Agamben Effect*, *South Atlantic Quarterly* 1.107 (2008), pp. 1–220, p.171.
65 Joyce, *A Portrait of the Artist as a Young Man*, p. 220.

66 Ibid., p. 240.
67 Jacques Derrida, *On the Name*, trans. T. Dutoit, *Meridian: Crossing Aesthetics* (Stanford: Stanford University Press, 1995), p. 89.
68 Joyce, *A Portrait of the Artist as a Young Man*, p. 153.
69 Agamben, *Infancy and History*, p. 48.

ENVIRONMENT AND EMBODIMENT IN JOYCE'S 'THE DEAD' (BRAZEAU)

1 Sandra Tropp, '"The Esthetic Instinct in Action': Charles Darwin and Mental Science in *A Portrait of the Artist as a Young Man*', *James Joyce Quarterly* (45.2, 2008), p. 226.
2 Ibid., p. 226.
3 Gerry Smyth, *Space and the Irish Cultural Imagination* (London: Palgrave, 2001), p. 8.
4 Laurence Buell, *The Future of Environmental Criticism* (Oxford, Blackwell, 2005). For Buell, the first wave of ecocriticism was nearly wholly concerned with nature writing, or what Morton, in *Ecology without Nature* refers to as ecomimesis. However, Cheryll Glotfelty's foundational essay 'Introduction: Literary Studies in an Age of Environmental Crisis' does, in fact, address the relationship between culture and nature in a way that clearly marks the connection between them as an early concern of ecocriticism. See Cheryll Glotfelty, 'Introduction: Literary Studies in an Age of Environmental Crisis' in Cheryll Glotfelty and Harold Fromm (eds), *Ecocriticism Reader: Landmarks in Literary Ecology* (Athens, Georgia: University of Georgia Press, 1996), p. xix.
5 See in particular Buell's *Writing for an Endangered World* (Cambridge: Harvard UP, 2001), p. 6.
6 Dana Philips, *The Truth of Ecology* (New York: Oxford UP, 2003), especially pp. 39–41.
7 Greg Garrard, *Ecocriticism* (New York: Taylor and Francis, 2004), p. 10.
8 In a series of lectures at the University of Alberta, Clare Colbrook meticulously traced out the human need to anthropomorphise nature and the attendant theoretical consequences of doing this.
9 Andy Fisher, *Radical Ecopsychology: Psychology in the Service of Life* (Albany: State University of NY Press, 2002), pp. 4–5.
10 Ibid., p. 6.
11 To name one obvious way, Fisher's chapter 'Making Sense of Suffering in a Technological World' (pp. 155–193) could be used productively to read aspects of *Ulysses.*
12 See Isacc Balbus, *Mourning and Modernity: Essays in the Psychoanalysis of Contemporary Society* (New York: Other Press, 2005), especially chapters 9 and 10.
13 Stephen Kaplan, 'The Challenge of Environmental Psychology: A Proposal for a NewFunctionalism', *American Psychologist* 27.2 (1972), p. 140. Kaplan tends to use the masculine pronoun to refer to the general case, and I have retained his usage when citing his work.
14 Stephen Kaplan, 'Environmental Preference in a Knowledge-Seeking, Knowledge-Using Organism' in Jerome H. Barkow, Leda Cosmides and John Tooby (eds) *The Adapted Mind: Evolutionary Psychology and the Generation of Culture* (Oxford: Oxford UP, 1992), p. 590.
15 James Joyce, 'The Dead', *Dubliners* (1914; New York: Penguin, 1992) p. 176.
16 Mary Daly, 'Late Nineteenth and Early Twentieth Century Dublin" in David

Harkness and Mary O'Dowd (eds), *The Town in Ireland* (Belfast: Appletree Press, 1981), p. 222.

17 Ibid., p. 222.
18 Joyce, 'The Dead', p. 192.
19 Ibid., pp. 207–208.
20 Ibid., p. 176.
21 Ibid., p. 209.
22 Ibid., pp. 210–211.
23 Easterlin, 262.
24 Nancy Easterlin, 'Cognitive Ecocriticism: Human Wayfinding, Sociality, and Literary Interpretation', in Lisa Zunshne (ed.), *Introduction to Cognitive Cultural Studies* (Baltimore: Johns Hopkins UP, 2010), p. 263.
25 Ibid., p. 263.
26 Ibid, p. 263.
27 I am grateful to Bonnie Kime Scott and Cheryl Herr for suggesting this way to read Joyce's characterisation of Gretta.
28 In fact, the only significant diversion in 'The Dead' from the autobiographical account of Nora and Michael (Sonny) Bodkin's past is provided in the fact that, at the time of his death, Bodkin was a student at the Royal University. His depiction in 'The Dead' is very much aimed at highlighting the dichotomous relationship between the quiet power of Michael Furey and Garbriel's sometimes overly talkative nature. See Richard Ellmann, *James Joyce* (Oxford: Oxford UP, 1982 [2nd ed.]), p. 158, for material on Michael 'Sonny' Bodkin.
29 Joyce, 'The Dead', p. 214.
30 However, the story makes this point with some subtlety. Because Gretta and Gabriel are walking with D'Arcy and Miss O'Callaghan, they are also being polite by not conversing with each other here. Gretta may well be talking to D'Arcy about the song that has prompted her recollections of the past, and is, of course, thinking of Michael Furey throughout the conclusion of the story.
31 Easterlin, p. 261.
32 Ibid., pp. 260–261.
33 Frederic Jameson, *The Modernist Papers* (London: Verso, 2008), p. 140.
34 Joyce, 'The Dead', p. 217.
35 Ibid., p. 217.
36 Ibid., p. 218.
37 Ibid., p. 218.
38 Ibid., p. 219
39 Ibid., p. 220.
40 Ibid., pp. 221–222.
41 Ibid., p. 224.
42 Raymond Williams, *The Long Revolution* (1961; Peterborough: Broadview, 2001), p. 18.

'SUNFLAWERED' HUMANITY IN *FINNEGANS WAKE* (FAIRHALL)

1 Among others, Katherine Mullin, *James Joyce, Sexuality and Social Purity* (Cambridge: Cambridge University Press, 2003); Richard Brown ed., *Joyce, 'Penelope,' and the Body, European Joyce Studies*, 17 (Amsterdam: Rodopi, 2006); Maud Ellmann, *The Nets of Modernism* (Cambridge: Cambridge University Press, 2010), and Vike Martina Plock, *Joyce, Medicine, and*

Modernity (Gainesville: University of Florida Press, 2010) have done important work on Joyce and the body.

2 Cheryll Glotfelty formulated an influential early definition of ecocriticism – 'the study of the relationship between literature and the physical environment' – which seemingly leaves no room for the human body as nature ('Introduction: Literary Studies in an Age of Environmental Crisis,' in Cheryll Glotfelty and Harold Fromm, eds., *The Ecocriticism Reader* (Athens, GA: University of Georgia Press, 1996), p. xviii.

3 Kate Soper, *What is Nature?* (Oxford: Blackwell, 1995), p. 21.

4 In *Merleau-Ponty's Philosophy of Nature* (Evanston, IL: Northwestern University Press, 2009), Ted Toadvine discusses the conjoined schismatic animality and non-animality of the human condition (see 'Animality,' pp. 76-96).

5 As Stacy Alaimo observes, trans-corporeality recognises 'the interconnections, interchanges, and transits between human bodies and nonhuman natures . . . Imagining human corporeality as trans-corporeality, in which the human is always intermeshed with the more-than-human world, underlines [how] the human is ultimately inseparable from "the environment"' (*Bodily Natures: Science, Environment, and the Material Self* [Bloomington: Indiana University Press, 2010], p. 2). For the purposes of this essay I conjoin trans-corporeality more closely with phenomenology, in particular its focus on ecocentric intercorporeality, than Alaimo does. Phillip G. Payne and Brian Wattchow define 'ecocentric intercorporeality' as the idea that through our bodies we make meaning 'in, about and for the various environments and places in which those bodies interact and relate to nature' ('Phenomenological Deconstruction, Slow Pedagogy, and the Corporeal Turn in Wild Environmental/Outdoor Education', *Canadian Journal of Environmental Education*, 14 [2009], p. 2).

6 Cf. Maurice Merleau-Ponty on 'the sensible in the twofold sense of what one senses and what senses' in *The Visible and the Invisible*, ed. Claude Lefort, trans. Alphonso Lingis (Evanston, IL: Northwestern University Press, 1968), p. 259.

7 'Ineluctable modality of the visible . . . thought through my eyes': James Joyce, *Ulysses*, ed. Hans Walter Gabler et al. (New York and London: Garland, 1984; New York: Penguin, 1986), ch. 3, l. 1–2. Subsequent page citations will appear parenthetically in the text.

8 William R. Jordan III, *The Sunflower Forest* (Berkeley: University of California Press, 2003), p. 46.

9 Ibid., pp. 46–47.

10 Soper continues the passage quoted above: '"Nature" is in this sense both that which we are not *and* that which we are within' (p. 21).

11 Toadvine explicates Merleau-Ponty on the difference between the human and the natural: 'Perception is the discovery of a sense that is not of my making, the response to a demand placed on my body from the outside' (p. 59). Guilty desire (for the apple) is the consequence – not the cause – of Adam and Eve's fall into humanness and alienation from nature, including their own newly perceived physical nature.

12 Jordan, p. 165.

13 Quoted in Jordan, p. 165.

14 James Joyce, *Finnegans Wake* (New York: Viking, 1939), p. 5, l. 14–16. Subsequent page citations will appear parenthetically in the text.

15 Ibid., 3:16–19.

16 Ibid., 3.19, 23.

17 Margot Norris points out the special 'uncertainty and indeterminability of HCE's identity' in *The Decentered Universe of Finnegans Wake* (Baltimore: Johns Hopkins University Press, 1974), p. 59.
18 *Finnegans Wake*, with its centres of consciousness replacing relatively stable, recognizable human actors, lacks the immediacy we enjoy in *Ulysses* of individual characters' thoughts and actions. This immediacy overshadows that novel's exploration of human limitations and mortality; whereas the *Wake*, in spite of its esthetic and intellectual embarrassment of riches, not to mention its funniness, celebrates life through a glass darkly.
19 *Finnegans Wake*, p. 252.36.
20 Ibid., p. 443.1.
21 Ibid., p. 445.16
22 Ibid., p. 548.28.
23 Ibid., p. 556.7, also cf. p. 446.7.
24 John Bishop, *Joyce's Book of the Dark: Finnegans Wake* (Madison: University of Wisconsin Press, 1986), p. 240.
25 *Finnegans Wake* p. 110.30.
26 Ibid., p. 252.28, 29. Dirk Van Hulle explores a set of references to Darwin's *Origin of Species* echoing both the Book of Genesis and the genesis of *Finnegans Wake*. 'Reveiling the Ouragan of Spaces in Less than a Schoppinhour,' paper presented at the 'Genitricksling Joyce' conference, Antwerp, 1997, accessed 21 August 2013, antwerpjamesjoycecenter.com/ ondt.html.
27 James Atherton finds in *Finnegans Wake* the Viconian axioms that 'Every civilisation has its own Jove' and 'Every Jove commits again, to commence his cycle, the same original sin upon which creation depends. It [follows] from this that creation is the original sin' (*The Books at the Wake* [London: Faber and Faber, 1959], p. 32). It is one step further to recognise another axiom: that the creation of human beings – whether by a divinity or by evolution – brings a unique, self-conscious imperfection into the world.
28 *Finnegans Wake*, p. 132.32.
29 Bishop, Joyce's Book of the Dark, pp. 176–77.
30 *Finnegans Wake*, p. 3.1–3
31 Ibid., p. 364.
32 James Joyce, *Letters of James Joyce*, Vol. III, ed. Richard Ellmann (New York: Viking, 1966), p. 312.
33 Briefly, Bergson posits that the time of physics (nature's time) is a quantitative phenomenon that we mistakenly use to define our lives in lieu of the qualitative time of human experience – *durée* – flowing from a constantly re-created past coterminous with the present. Moments when we access our sense of *durée* are transcendent insofar as they lift us from immediate time, even though they include our awareness of ourselves as limited mortal creatures. Outstanding examples of *durée* in *Ulysses* are Bloom's and Molly's memory-reenactments of their tryst on Howth; an outstanding example in the *Wake* is ALP's closing soliloquy, with its memory of meeting her future husband: 'Where you meet I. The day. Remember! Why there that moment and us two only?' (*FW* 626.7–9). See Henri Bergson, *Time and Free Will*, trans. F.L. Pogson (New York: Humanities Press, 1971), pp. 100, 104–06.
34 *Finnegans Wake*, p. 269. fn.3.
35 John Gordon, *Finnegans Wake: A Plot Summary* (Syracuse, NY: Syracuse University Press, 1986), p. 81.

36 *Finnegans Wake*, p. 94.33.
37 Ibid., p. 77.
38 Ibid., p. 459.28.
39 *Ulysses*, p.13.867–68.
40 Ellmann, *Joyce*, p. 398.
41 *Finnegans Wake*, pp. 337.32–355.33.
42 William Sayers, 'The Russian General, Gargantua, and Joyce Writing of "his wit's waste" in *Finnegans Wake*,' *Joyce Studies Annual* (2008): pp. 146–62.
43 Ibid., p. 154.
44 *Finnegans Wake*, p. 353.15–21.
45 'Igorladns' obviously suggests more than just Ireland. The Russian general's self-debasement, in Buckley's eyes, seems to be a more universal insult – a debasing of Russian lads and Russian land, and in fact a letting down of the side for civilised humanity.
46 *Finnegans Wake*, p. 350.11.
47 Ibid., p. 18.26–28.
48 Marcel Mauss, *A General Theory of Magic*, trans. Robert Brain (London & Boston: Routledge & Kegan Paul, 1972), p. 119.
49 Ibid., p. 132.
50 *Finnegans Wake*, p.13.15.
51 Ibid., p. 198.8, 203.31 and p. 84.30–1.
52 I rely here on Bishop's rich discussion of intrauterine regression and the sensory world of the fetus (pp. 354–55, 458).
53 *Finnegans Wake*, p. 563.10.
54 Ibid., p. 198.7.
55 *Ulysses*, p. 3.461–62.
56 *Finnegans Wake*, p. 365.27–28, 32.
57 Ibid., p. 366.12–15.
58 Ibid., pp. 366.17, 23, 30.
59 Ibid., p. 144.2–3.
60 Cf. Thoreau on Walden Pond as 'a perfect forest mirror' that 'betrays the spirit that is in the air'. This spirit, he makes clear a couple of pages earlier, unites nature with human nature: 'A lake . . . is earth's eye; looking into which the beholder measures the depth of his own nature' in Henry David Thoreau, *Walden* (New York: Time, Inc., 1962), pp. 186, 184).
61 *Finnegans Wake*, p. 526.28–32.
62 Ibid., p. 526.34–35.
63 Gordon, *Finnegans Wake: A Plot Summary*, p. 80.
64 *Finnegans Wake*, pp. 504.24, 33.
65 Ibid., p. 505.7–13.
66 Ibid., p. 501.11.
67 Ibid., p. 599.25–26, 34–35.
68 Ibid., p. 628.2.
69 Ibid., p. 404.1.
70 Ibid., p. 297.26–27, 29–30.
71 Bishop, *Joyce's Book of the Dark*, p. 381.
72 *Ulysses*, 3.3.
73 Tyler Volk, *Metapatterns* (New York: Columbia University Press, 1996), p. 234.
74 *Finnegans Wake*, p. 599.29–31.
75 Ibid., p. 215.4.

76 Ibid., pp. 627.11, 23–24; 628.6.
77 Norris remarks: '[T]he inexorable progress from cradle to grave, from innocence to experience, is terrifying for the individual caught up in the cyclical machinery. The *Wake* is also about that fear, about the resistance of Wakean figures to change and decline, about their reluctance to recognize their guilt and mortality, and about their escape into the defenses, disguises, illusions, and myths available to them in the dream' (p. 97). The thing I'd add to Norris's summation is the existential shame that these figures feel as a result of their failures to surmount bodily limitation in particular.
78 *Finnegans Wake*, p. 336.16–17.
79 Ibid., p. 215.23.
80 Christopher Moriarty, *Exploring Dublin* (Dublin: Wolfhound, 1997), pp. 39–40.
81 Joseph Campbell, *The Masks of God* (New York: Viking, 1969), p. 181.
82 Stephen describes nature as 'an omnivorous being' (*U* 14.1286) that consumes everyone.
83 Edward Abbey, *Desert Solitaire* (New York: Ballantine, 1968), p. 45.
84 *Finnegans Wake*, p. 118.21–22.
85 Ibid., p. 29.20.
86 Quoted in Mark Lilla, 'The Hidden Lesson of Montaigne,' *The New York Review of Books*, Vol. LVII, No. 5 (March 24, 2011), p. 21.

INELUCTABLE MODALITY OF THE VISIBLE(LEONARD)

1 James Joyce, *Ulysses: The Corrected Text* (New York: Random House, 1986), p. 42.
2 Ibid., p. 45.
3 James Joyce, *Letters I*. Edited by Richard Ellmann (New York: Viking 1966), p. 55.
4 James Joyce, *Letters I*, p. 52.
5 James Joyce, *Stephen Hero* (New York: New Directions, 1963), pp. 210–211.
6 James Joyce, *Dubliners*, (New York: Penguin, 1976), p. 14.
7 Ibid., p. 9.
8 Ibid., p. 220.
9 Ibid., p. 223.
10 Ibid., p. 35.
11 James Joyce, *A Portrait of the Artist as a Young Man* (New York: St Martin's Press, 1993), p. 192.
12 Ibid., p. 218.
13 Kate Soper, *What is Nature?* (Oxford, England: Blackwell Publishers Ltd, 1995), p.151.
14 James Joyce, *Dubliners* (New York: Penguin), p. 9.
15 James Joyce, *Ulysses*, p. 31.
16 Ibid., p. 40.
17 Ibid., p. 40.
18 Garry Leonard, '"Without Contraries There is No Progression"': Cinematic Montage and the Relationship of Illustration to Text in William Blake's *The [First] Book of Urizen*, *University of Toronto Quarterly* 80.4, 2011, pp. 918–934.
19 Mitchell J. Morse. 'Proteus' in *James Joyce's Ulysses. Critical Essays*, (eds.), Clive Hart and David Hayman (Berkeley: University of California Press, 1974) pp. 29–49. Ernesto Livorni, '"Ineluctable modality of the visible": Diaphane in the "Proteus' Episode" in: *JJQ* 36.2, 1999, pp. 127–169. See Morse and

Livorni for two detailed discussions of Stephen's philosophical hop-scotching. I am emphasising the impulse behind Stephen's restless philosophising rather than discussing the various allusions in and of themselves.

20 Garry Leonard, *Advertising and Commodity Culture in Joyce* (Florida: Florida University Press, 1998). For a thorough discussion of Stephen's aesthetic theory as a defence against feelings, physical sensation and other bodily phenomena, see my commentary in *Advertising and Commodity Culture in Joyce*, pp. 216–236.

21 My reading of Cartesian dualism and the split of Nature is discussed at length by Soper in *What is Nature?*: '[F]or Nature to be conceived as Object, as it is in philosophy from the time of Descartes onwards, it must already be opposed to the mental – as that which differs from the Subject in not possessing mind, spirit or soul . . . replaced an animistic with a mechanistic view of nature . . . for Descartes, the essential being of humanity lies in thinking, and mind can in principle, if not in practice, exist independently of body, Descartes in effect places humanity outside the order of nature, and can only account for its existence in terms of its separate creation by the deity.' What I am bringing to the discussion is the role visuality plays in this split, and how that helps historicise what is seen as 'nature'.

22 Joyce, *Ulysses*, 15.

23 Charlene Spretnak, *The Resurgence of the Real: Body, Nature and Place in a Hypermodern World* (New York: Routledge, 1999), p. 2. Charlene Spretnak traces the effect this has had on nature, place and body: 'In the modern world view, a salvational sense of progress places economic expansion and technological innovation at the center of importance . . . Modern life promised freedom from the vagaries of the body, the limits of nature, and the provincial ties to place. The body came to be seen as a biological machine, the natural world as a mere externality in modern economies, and the sense of place as a primitive precursor to cosmopolitan sophistication.'

24 Garry Leonard, 'He's Got Bette Davis Eyes: James Joyce and Melodrama', *Joyce Studies Annual* (Fordham University Press, 2008): 'For Joyce, in other words, what is visible is irrelevant, or, it is only relevant in the sense that it reveals the field of possibilities that constitutes its own status as "visible" thus revealing the strategies of delimitation that have grown habitual for the subject who "sees". The question is never what is there to see, but why, and how what is seen achieves its constitution as visible, relative to the strategies of delimitation the viewer employs, and how these strategies, in turn, can be seen to be not at all inevitable or natural, but rather the product of years of training all roughly bunched under the heading of "learning how to pay attention"'.

25 *Toronto Star*, 14 December 2011, p. 1.

26 Garry Leonard, '"The Famished Roar of Automobiles": Modernity, the Internal Combustion Engine, and Modernism' in *Disciplining Modernism*, edited by Pamela Caughie (New York: Palgrave Macmillan Press, 2009): p. 231. 'These myths, to suggest four, include: the myth of progress; the myth of efficiency; the myth of satisfaction and the myth of perfectibility. All of these myths are legacies of Enlightenment philosophy, but what is contemporary about them is how much they have been personalised and politicised, written into social policy as well as self-help books. In other words, the myth of modern subjectivity – the myth of our own coherence – depends on upholding these other myths. What this means is that modernity itself, like modern sub-

jectivity, is an irresolvable contradiction: a drive towards something unreachable that must never be understood as such if we are to continue to understand ourselves. In other words, a productive tension: a mechanism. Not man as machine, but man as tension, contradiction, cycles of engagement, explosion, resolution, renewed engagement, explosion – the rhythm of the internal combustion engine'.

27 Garry Leonard, 'Technically Human: Kubrick's Monolith in *2001: A Space Odyssey* and Heidegger's Propriative Event', *Film Criticism* 36, no. 1 (2011): 'The idea of discovering, inventing and progressing as the essence of what makes us human runs strongly through 2001, most brilliantly compressed into the 'jump shot' where the bone thrown by the ape "becomes", four million years later, a space shuttle station. But Kubrick critiques this trope through the film's most famous and mystifying feature: the monolith. A shot by shot analysis of the bone-to-hammer sequence illustrates how Kubrick visualises this "discovery" as a Heideggerean uncovering, leading to the emergence of an attitude – primarily exultant and triumphant – simultaneous with the emergence of a technological mode of consciousness. Because the monolith's unexplained appearance precedes this moment, Kubrick cannot simply be representing"the dawn of man". Instead he depicts the emergence of one mode of knowing among many possible modes'.

28 Jay Martin, 'Scopic Regimes of Modernity', in *Vision and Visuality*, edited by Hal Foster (New York: The New Press, 1988), p. 17.

29 Ibid., p. 21.

30 Joyce, *Ulysses*, p. 28.

31 Garry Leonard, *Reading Dubliners Again: A Lacanian Perspective* (New York: Syracuse University Press, 1988), p. 4.

32 Joyce, *Dubliners*, p. 35.

33 Joyce, *Portrait*, pp. 93–94.

34 Joyce, *Portrait*, p. 94.

35 Joyce, *Portrait*, p. 96.

36 Joyce, *Portrait*, p. 151.

37 Joyce, *Portrait*, p. 152.

38 Joyce, *Portrait*, p. 179.

39 Joyce, *Ulysses*, p. 32.

40 Joyce, *Ulysses*, p. 34.

41 Pico della Mirandola,. *On the Dignity of Man*, trans. Charles Glenn Wallis (Indianappolis, Indiana: Bobbs-Merrill, 1998).

42 Louise Westling, 'Letter', *PMLA* 114.5 (Oct. 1999), pp. 1103–4.

43 Joyce, *Portrait*, p. 32.

44 Joyce, *Portrait*, pp. 124–25.

45 Joyce, *Portrait*, 19.

46 Joyce, *Portrait*, p. 65.

47 Joyce, *Portrait*, pp. 134–35.

48 Joyce, *Portrait*, p. 135.

49 Joyce, *Portrait*, p. 135.

50 Joyce, *Portrait*, p. 186.

51 Joyce, *Ulysses*, p. 31.

52 Joyce, *Ulysses*, p. 41.

53 Joyce, *Ulysses*, p. 40.

54 Joyce, *Ulysses*, p. 40.

55 Joyce, *Ulysses*, 18.
56 Joyce, *Portrait*, p. 107.
57 Joyce, *Portrait*, p. 108.
58 Joyce, *Ulysses*, p. 40.
59 Joyce, *Ulysses*, p. 40. For a discussion of this particular passage as an example of Stephen's suppression of everything wombanly, see Cheryl Herr, 'Old Wives' Tales as Portals of discovery in "Proteus"' in *Ulysses – En-Gendered Perspectives*, editors Kimberly J. Devlin and Marilyn Reizbaum (University of South Carolina Press, 1999), pp. 20–30.
60 Joyce, *Ulysses*, p. 40.
61 Joyce, *Portrait*, p. 160.
62 Joyce, *Ulysses*, pp. 41–42.
63 Joyce, *Portrait*, p. 84.
64 Joyce, *Portrait*, p. 84.
65 Joyce, *Ulysses*, p. 45.
66 Joyce, *Ulysses*, p. 577.
67 Lawrence Buell, *The Environmental Imagination: Thoreau, Nature Writing, and the Formation of American Culture* (Boston: Harvard University Press, 1995), pp. 7–8.
68 William Blake, 'A Grain of Sand' in *Planet Earth: Poems Selected and New*, edited by P.K. Page (Toronto: The Porcupine's Quill, 2002), p. 34.

Bibliography

Aalen, F.H.A., Kevin Whelan and Matthew Stout (eds), *Atlas of the Irish Rural Landscape* 2nd ed. (Cork: Cork University Press, 2011)

Abbey, Edward, *Desert Solitaire* (New York: Ballantine Books, 1968)

Adams Day, Robert, 'Joyce's AquaCities' in Morris Beja and David Norris (eds), *Joyce in the Hibernian Metropolis* (Columbus: Ohio State University Press, 1996), pp. 3–20

Adorno, Theodor W. and Max Horkheimer, *Dialectic of Enlightenment*, Verso Classics (London: Blackwell Verso, 1997)

Agamben, Giorgio, *Infancy and History: The Destruction of Experience* (London: Verso, 1993)

Alaimo, Stacy, *Bodily Natures: Science, Environment and the Material Self* (Bloomington: Indiana University Press, 2010)

Anspaugh, Kelly, 'Death on the Missisliffi: *Huckleberry Finn* and *Finnegans Wake*', *Colby Quarterly* 28 (September 1992), pp. 144–54

Armbruster, Karla and Kathleen R. Wallace (eds), *Beyond Nature Writing: Expanding the Boundaries of Ecocriticism* (Charlottesville: University of Virginia Press, 2001)

Atherton, James S., *The Books at the Wake: A Study of Literary Allusions in James Joyce's Finnegans Wake* (Carbondale: Southern Illinois University Press, 2009)

Attridge, Derek, 'Reading Joyce', in Derek Attridge (ed.), *The Cambridge Companion to James Joyce* (Cambridge: Cambridge University Press, 1990), pp. 1–30

—, 'Unpacking the Portmanteau or Who's Afraid of *Finnegans Wake*?' in Jonathan Culler (ed.), *On Puns: The Foundation of Letters* (New York: Blackwell, 1988), pp. 140–55

Attridge, Derek and Daniel Ferrer (eds), *Post-Sructuralist Joyce: Essays from the French* (Cambridge: Cambridge University Press, 1984)

Balbus, Isaac, *Mourning and Modernity: Essays in the Psychoanalysis of Contemporary Society* (New York: Other Press, 2005)

Ballard, J.G., *The Drowned World* [1962] (London: Millennium, 2000)

—, 'Which Way to Inner Space?' [1962] in David Seed (ed.), *A Companion to Science Fiction* (Malden MA and Oxford: Blackwell, 2008)

Barry, Kevin, 'Introduction' in Kevin Barry (ed.), *James Joyce: Occasional, Critical, and Political Writing* (Oxford: Oxford University Press, 2000), pp. ix–xxxv

Bateson, Gregory, *Steps to an Ecology of Mind* (Chicago: The University of Chicago Press, 2000)

Beckett, Samuel, 'Dante . . . Bruno. Vico . . . Joyce' in *Our Exagmination Round His Factification for Incamination of Work in Progress* (New York: New Directions, 1962)

—, *Murphy* (New York: Grove Press, 1957)

Beistegui, Miguel de, *The New Heidegger* (London: Continuum, 2005)

Bender, Barbara, 'Introduction' in Barbara Bender and Margot Winer (eds), *Contested Landscapes: Movement, Exile and Place* (Oxford: Berg, 2001), pp. 1–18

Bengal, Michael, *James Joyce and the City: The Significance of Place* (Syracuse: Syracuse University Press, 2002)

Bennett, Michael, 'From Wide Open Spaces to Metropolitan Places The Urban Challenge to Ecocriticism', *Interdisciplinary Studies in Literature and Environment* 8.1 (Winter 2001), pp. 31–52

Bennett, Michael and David Teague, 'Introduction' in Michael Bennett and David Teague (eds), *The Nature of Cities: Ecocriticism and Urban Environments* (Tucson: University of Arizona, 1999), pp. 3–14

Benstock, Bernard, 'Vico . . . Joyce. Triv . . . Quad' in Donald Phillip Verene (ed.), *Vico and Joyce* (Buffalo: SUNY Press, 1987), pp. 59–67

Bergson, Henri, *Time and Free Will*, trans. F.L. Pogson (New York: Humanities Press, 1971)

Bhabha, Homi K. (ed.), *Nation and Narration* (New York: Routledge, 1990)

Birkerts, Sven, 'Only God Can Make a Tree: The Joys and Sorrows of Ecocriticism', *The Boston Book Review* 3.1 (Nov./Dec. 1996)

Bishop, John, *Joyce's Book of the Dark: Finnegans Wake* (Madison: The University of Wisconsin Press, 1986)

Black, Martha Fodaski, 'Joyce on Location: Place Names in Joyce's Fiction' in Michael Bengal (eds), *James Joyce and the City: The Significance of Place* (Syracuse: Syracuse University Press, 2002), pp. 18–24

Blake, William, 'A Grain of Sand' in P.K. Page (ed.), *Planet Earth: Poems Selected and New* (Toronto: The Porcupine's Quill, 2002), p. 35

Boland, Eavan, *Domestic Violence: Poems* (New York: W.W. Norton, 2007)

—, 'Eavan Boland at the Symposium', *James Joyce Newestlatter* (November 1992), pp. 8–9

—, 'James Joyce: the Mystery of Influence' in Karen Lawrence (ed.), *Transcultural Joyce* (Cambridge: Cambridge University Press, 1998), pp. 11–20

—, *New Collected Poems* (New York: W.W. Norton, 2008)

—, 'The Woman, the Place, the Poet', *Georgia Review* 4.44 (Spring/Summer 1990), pp. 97–109

Bookchin, Murray, *The Philosophy of Social Ecology: Essays on Dialectical Naturalism* (Montreal: Black Rose Books, 1995)

Borg, Ruben, 'Neologizing in *Finnegans Wake*: Beyond a Typology of the Wakean Portmanteau', *Poetics Today* 28.1 (2007), pp. 143–64

Bosinelli, Rosa Maria, '"I use his cycles as a trellis": Joyce's Treatment of Vico in *Finnegans Wake*' in Donald Phillip Verene (ed.), *Vico and Joyce* (Buffalo: SUNY Press, 1987), pp. 123–31

Boyle, Mark, 'Cleaning Up After the Celtic Tiger: Scalar "fixes" in the Political Ecology of Tiger Economies' *Transactions of the Institute of British Geographers* 27: 2 (2002), pp. 172–94

Brady, Joseph, 'Dublin at the Beginning of the Twentieth Century', in Oona Frawley (ed.), *A New and Complex Sensation: Essays on Joyce's Dubliners* (Dublin: The Lilliput Press, 2004), pp. 10–32

Brown, Richard (ed.), *Joyce, 'Penelope' and the Body, European Joyce Studies* 17 (Amsterdam: Rodopi Press, 2006)

—-, 'Time, Space, and the City in "Wandering Rocks"' in Andrew Gibson and Steve Morrison (eds), *European Joyce Studies 12: Joyce's 'Wandering Rocks'* (Amsterdam: Rodopi, 2002), pp. 57–72

Bruni, Alessandro Francini, 'Joyce Stripped Naked in the Piazza' in Willard Potts (ed.), *Portraits of the Artist in Exile: Recollections of James Joyce by Europeans* (Seattle: University of Washington Press, 1979), pp. 7–39

Buckley, Anthony D., '"On the club": Friendly Societies in Ireland', *Irish Economic and Social History* 14 (1987), pp. 39–58

Buell, Lawrence, *The Environmental Imagination: Thoreau, Nature Writing, and the Formation of American Culture* (Boston: Harvard University Press, 1995)

—-, *The Future of Environmental Criticism: Environmental Crisis and Literary Imagination* (Malden, MA: Blackwell Publishing, 2005)

—-, *Writing for an Endangered World: Literature, Culture, and Environment in the United States and Beyond* (Cambridge, MA: Belknap, 2001)

Bulson, Eric, *Novels, Maps, Modernity: The Spatial Imagination, 1850–2000* (New York: Routledge, 2007)

Campbell, John Francis, *Friendly Societies in Ireland 1850–1960: with particular reference to Ancient Order of Hibernians and the Irish National Foresters*, Unpublished M. Litt. Thesis (Trinity College Dublin, October 1998)

Campbell, Joseph, *The Masks of God: Primitive Mythology* [1959] (New York: Viking Press, 1969)

Campbell, Joseph and Henry Morton Robinson, *A Skeleton Key to* Finnegans Wake*: Unlocking James Joyce's Masterwork* (Novato, CA: New World Library, 2005)

Casanova, Pascale, *The World Republic of Letters* (Cambridge: Harvard University Press, 2004)

Cheng, Vincent, 'White Horse, Darkhorse: Joyce's Allhorse of Another Color', *Joyce Studies Annual* 2 (1991), pp. 101–28

Cohen, Michael, 'Blues in the Green: Ecocriticism Under Critique', *Environmental History*, 9.1 (Oxford: Oxford University Press, 2004), pp. 9–36

Connolly, James, *James Connolly: Selected Writings*, ed. Peter Beresford Ellis (London: Pluto Press, 1997)

Clarke, Suzanne, *Sentimental Modernism: Women Writers and the Revolution of the Word* (Bloomington: Indiana University Press, 1991)

Clark, Timothy, *The Cambridge Introduction to Literature and the Environment* (Cambridge: Cambridge University Press, 2011)

—-, 'Some Climate Change Ironies: Deconstruction, Environmental Politics and the Closure of Ecocriticism', *The Oxford Literary Review* 32.1 (2010), pp. 131–49

Conrad, Joseph, *Heart of Darkness* (London: Penguin, 1989)

Corcoran, Michael, *Our Good Health: A History of Dublin's Water and Drainage* (Dublin: Dublin City Council, 2005)

Cronin, Michael, 'Fellow Travellers: Contemporary Travel Writing and Ireland' in Barbara O'Connor and Michael Cronin (eds), *Tourism in Ireland: A Critical Analysis* (Cork: Cork University Press, 1993), pp. 51–67

Crosby, Alfred, *Ecological Imperialism: The Biological Expansion of Europe, 900–1900* (Cambridge: Cambridge University Press, 1986)

Cusick, Christine, 'Mindful Paths: An Interview with Tim Robinson' in Christine Cusick (ed.), *Out of the Earth: Ecocritical Readings of Irish Texts* (Cork: Cork University Press), pp. 205–11

—, (ed.), *Out of Earth: Ecocritical Readings of Irish Texts* (Cork: Cork University Press, 2010)

Daly, Mary, 'Late Nineteenth and Early Twentieth Century Dublin' in David Harkness and Mary O'Dowd (eds), *The Town in Ireland* (Belfast: Appletree Press, 1981), pp. 221–52

Darwin, Charles, *On the Origin of Species* (New York: Penguin, 1968)

Deane, Seamus, 'Joyce the Irishman' in Derek Attridge (ed.), *The Cambridge Companion to James Joyce* (Cambridge: Cambridge University Press, 1997), pp. 31–53

de Certeau, Michel, *The Practice of Everyday Life*, trans. Steven Randall (Berkeley: University of California Press, 1988)

De la Durantaye, Leland, *Giorgio Agamben: A Critical Introduction* (Stanford: Stanford University Press, 2009)

DeKoven, Marianne, 'Guest Column: Why Animals Now', *PMLA* 124.2 (2009), pp. 361–69

Deleuze, Gilles and Félix Guattari, *Anti-Oedipus: Capitalism and Schizophrenia*, trans. Robert Hurley, Mark Seem and Helen R. Lane (London: The Athlone Press 1990)

—, *A Thousand Plateaus: Capitalism and Schizophrenia*, trans. Brian Massumi (London: The Athlone Press 1992)

Derrida, Jacques, *The Animal That Therefore I Am*, ed. Marie-Louise Mallet, trans. David Wills (New York: Fordham University Press, 2008)

—, 'Biodegradables Seven Diary Fragments', *Critical Inquiry* 15 (Summer 1989), pp. 812–73

—, *Limited Inc. ABC*, trans. Samuel Weber (Baltimore: Johns Hopkins University Press, 1977)

—, *Margins of Philosophy*, trans. A. Bass (Brighton: Harvester Press, 1982)

—, *Of Grammatology*, ed. Gayatri Spivak (Baltimore: Johns Hopkins University Press, 1976)

—, *On the Name*, trans. T. Dutoit, *Meridian: Crossing Aesthetics* (Stanford: Stanford University Press, 1995)

Derrida, Jacques and Derek Attridge, *Acts of Literature* (London: Routledge, 1992)

Devall, Bill and George Sessions, *Deep Ecology: Living as if Nature Mattered* (Layton, UT: Gibbs Smith, 1985)

Drennan, William, 'When Erin First Met Rose' in Charles A. Read (ed.), *The Cabinet of Irish Literature, Volume 2*, Library Ireland, accessed 10 April 2013, http://www.libraryireland.com/CIL/DrennanErin.php

Duffy, Patrick J., *Exploring the History and Heritage of Irish Landscapes* (Dublin: Four Courts Press, 2007)

Eagleton, Terry, *The Ideology of the Aesthetic* (Oxford: Basil Blackwell, 1990)

Easterlin, Nancy, 'Cognitive Ecocriticism: Human Wayfinding, Sociality, and Literary Interpretation' in Lisa Zunshine (ed.), *Introduction to Cognitive Cultural Studies* (Baltimore: Johns Hopkins UP, 2010), pp. 257–74

Eco, Umberto, *The Limits of Interpretation* (Bloomington: Indiana University Press, 1990)

—, *On Beauty* (London: Secker & Warburg, 2000)

Eglinton, John, *New Statesman*, 12 July 1913

Ehrlich, Heyward, 'James Joyce's Four Gated City of Modernisms' in Michael Bengal (ed.), *Joyce and the City: The Significance of Place* (Syracuse: Syracuse University Press 2002), pp. 3–17

Ellmann, Maud, *The Nets of Modernism* (Cambridge: Cambridge University Press, 2010)

Ellmann, Richard, *James Joyce*. 2nd ed. (Oxford: Oxford UP, 1982)

Ellmann, Richard and Ellsworth Mason (eds), *The Critical Writings of James Joyce* (Ithaca: Cornell University Press, 1989)

Evernden, Neil, 'Beyond Ecology: Self, Place, and the Pathetic Fallacy' in Cheryll Glotfelty and Harold Fromm (eds), *The Ecocriticism Reader: Landmarks in Literary Ecology* (Athens: University of Georgia Press, 1996), pp. 92–104

Fairhall, James, 'Ecocriticism, Joyce, and the Politics of Trees in the "Cyclops" Episode of *Ulysses*', *Irish Studies Review* 20.4 (November 2012), pp. 367–87

Fargnoli, A. Nicholas and Michael Patrick Gillespie (eds), *James Joyce A to Z: the Essential Reference to the Life and Work* (Oxford: Oxford University Press, 1995)

Fisch, Max Harold and Thomas Goddard Bergin, 'Introduction' in Max Harold Fisch and Thomas Goddard Bergin (eds and trans.), *The Autobiography of Giambattista Vico* (Ithaca: Cornell University Press, 1944), pp. 1–108

Fisher, Andy, *Radical Ecopsychology: Psychology in the Service of Life* (Albany: State University of NY Press, 2002)

Fishman, Charles, *The Big Thirst: The Secret Life and Turbulent Future of Water* (New York: Simon and Schuster, 2011)

Fitzgerald, Gerald, 'Correspondence: The Dublin Corporation v. The Guardians South Dublin Union', *Irish Daily Independent,* 10 June 1904, p. 6

Flannery, Eóin, 'Ireland of the Welcomes: Colonialism, Tourism, and the Irish Landscape' in Christine Cusick (ed.), *Out of the Earth: Ecocritical Readings of Irish Texts* (Cork: University of Cork Press, 2010), pp. 85–107

Fogarty, Anne, 'States of Memory: Reading History in "Wandering Rocks"' in Ellen Carol Jones and Morris Beja (eds), *Twenty-first Joyce* (Gainesville: University of Florida Press, 2004), pp. 56–81

Forbes, A.C., 'Tree Planting in Ireland during Four Centuries', Proceedings of the Royal Irish Academy, Section C: *Archaeology, Celtic Studies, History, Linguistics, Literature* 41 (1932–1934), pp. 168–99

Foster, John Wilson, 'The Culture of Nature' in John Wilson Foster (ed.), *Nature in Ireland: A Scientific and Cultural History* (Montreal: McGill-Queens University Press, 1997), pp. 597–635

—, 'Preface' in John Wilson Foster (ed.) *Nature in Ireland: A Scientific and Cultural History* (Montreal: McGill-Queens University Press, 1997), pp. ix-xii

Frawley, Oona, *Irish Pastoral: Nostalgia and Twentieth-Century Irish Literature* (Dublin: Irish Academic Press, 2005)

Freedman, Ariela, 'Did it Flow? Bridging Aesthetics and History in Joyce's Ulysses', *Modernism/Modernity* 13.1 (2006), pp. 107–22

Gaard, Greta, 'New Directions for Ecofeminism: Toward a More Feminist

Ecocriticism', *Interdisciplinary Studies in Literature and Environment* 17.4 (Autumn 2010), pp. 643–65

—- 'Toward a Queer Ecofeminism' in Rachel Stein (ed.), *New Perspectives on Environmental Justice* (New Brunswick: Rutgers University Press, 2004), pp. 21–44

Garrard, Greg, *Ecocriticism* (New York: Routledge, 2004)

—, 'Heidegger, Heaney and the Problem of Dwelling' in Richard Kerridge and Neil Sammells (eds), *Writing the Environment: Ecocriticism and Literature* (London: Zed Books, 1998), pp. 167–81

Gibson, Andrew, *Joyce's Revenge: History, Politics, and Aesthetics in Ulysses* (Oxford: Oxford University Press, 2005)

Gibson, George Cinclair, *Wake Rites: The Ancient Irish Rituals of* Finnegans Wake (Gainesville, FL: University Press of Florida, 2005)

Gifford, Don, with Robert J. Seidman, *Ulysses Annotated: Notes for James Joyce's Ulysses*, 2nd ed. (Berkeley: University of California Press, 1974)

Gilbert, Stuart, *James Joyce's 'Ulysses': a study* (London: Penguin, 1963)

Gillet, Louis, 'The Living Joyce' in Willard Potts (ed.), *Portraits of the Artist in Exile* (Seattle: University of Washington Press, 1979), pp. 170–204

Glotfelty, Cheryll, 'Introduction: Literary Studies in an Age of Environmental Crisis' in Cheryll Glotfelty and Harold Fromm (eds), *Ecocriticism Reader: Landmarks in Literary Ecology* (Athens, Georgia: University of Georgia Press, 1996), pp. xv–xxxvii

Gogarty, Oliver St John, 'James Joyce: A Portrait of the Artist', in E.H. Mikhail (ed.), *James Joyce: Interviews and Recollections* (New York: St Martins, 1990), pp. 21–32

Gordon, John, *Finnegans Wake: A Plot Summary* (Syracuse, NY: Syracuse University Press, 1986)

Graham, Brian (ed.), *In Search of Ireland: A Cultural Geography* (London: Routledge, 1997)

—, 'Ireland and Irishness: Place, Culture, and Identity' in Brian Graham (ed.), *In Search of Ireland: A Cultural Geography* (London: Routledge, 1997), pp. 1–15

Great Britain, Department of Agriculture and Technical Instructions for Ireland, *Report of the Departmental Committee on Irish Forestry, House of Commons Parliamentary Papers (HCPP)* (Dublin: HMSO, 1908), accessed 31 October 2010

'Great Famine (Ireland)', accessed 10 April 2013, https://en.wikipedia.org/wiki/Great_Famine_(Ireland)

Groden, Michael, '"Cyclops" in Progress: 1919', *James Joyce Quarterly* 12 (Fall 1974/Winter 1975), pp. 123–68

Haraway, Donna, *When Species Meet* (Minneapolis: University of Minnesota Press, 2008)

Hardiman, James, *The History of the Town and County of the Town of Galway* (Dublin: W. Folds and Sons, 1820)

Harding, Desmond, 'The Dead: Joyce's Epitaph for Dublin' in Michael Bengal (ed.), *Joyce in the City: The Significance of Place* (Syracuse: Syracuse University Press, 2004), pp. 123–48

—, *Writing the City: Urban Visions and Literary Modernisms* (New York: Routledge, 2003)

Harries, Karsten, *Art Matters: A Critical Commentary on Heidegger's 'The*

Origin of the Work of Art', Contributions to Phenomenology (Dordrecht: Springer, 2009)

Harrison, Robert Pogue, 'The Forest of Literature' in Laurence B. Coupe (ed.), *The Green Studies Reader: From Romanticism to Ecocriticism* (London and New York: Routledge, 2000), pp. 212–18

—, *Forests: the Shadow of Civilization* (Chicago: University of Chicago Press, 1992)

Harvey, David, *The Condition of Postmodernity: An Enquiry into the Origins of Cultural Change* (Oxford: Blackwell, 1989)

Heidegger, Martin, *Being and Time*, trans. J. Stambaugh (Albany: State University of New York Press, 1996)

—, *Early Greek Thinking*, trans. D.F. Krell and F.A. Capuzzi (New York: Harper and Row, 1975)

—, *Poetry, Language, Thought*, trans. A. Hofstadter (New York: Harper & Row, 1971)

—, *What is Called Thinking?* trans. J.G. Gray (New York: Harper Collins, 2004)

Heise, Ursula K., *Sense of Place and Sense of Planet: the Environmental Imagination of the Global* (Oxford: Oxford University Press, 2008)

Herr, Cheryl, 'Art and Life, Nature and Culture, *Ulysses*' in Robert D. Newman and Weldon Thornton (eds), *Joyce's Ulysses: The Larger Perspective* (Newark: University of Delaware Press, 1987), pp. 19–38

—, 'Old Wives' Tales as Portals of Discovery in "Proteus"' in Kimberly J. Devlin and Marilyn Reizbaum (eds), *Ulysses: En-Gendered Perspectives* (Charleston: University of South Carolina Press, 1999), pp. 20–30

Herring, Phillip F. (ed.), *Joyce's Notes and Early Drafts for Ulysses: Selections from the Buffalo Collection* (Charlottesville: University of Virginia Press, 1977)

Hoffmeister, Adolph, 'Portrait of Joyce' in Willard Potts (ed.), *Portraits of the Artist in Exile: Recollections of James Joyce by Europeans* (Seattle: University of Washington Press, 1979), pp. 127–36

Hofheinz, Thomas C., *Joyce and the Invention of Irish History: Finnegans Wake in Context* (Cambridge: Cambridge University Press, 1995)

Huggan, Graham and Helen Tiffin, *Postcolonial Ecocriticism: Literature, Animals, Environment* (London: Routledge, 2010)

Iovino, Serenella, 'Ecocriticism and a Non-Anthropocentric Humanism: Reflections on Local Natures and Global Responsibilities' in Laurenz Volkmann, Nancy Grimm, Ines Detmers and Katrin Thomson (eds), *Local Natures, Global Responsibilities: Ecocritical Perspectives on the New English Literatures* (Amsterdam: Rodopi, 2010), pp. 29–51

'Ireland in the Early Twentieth Century', National Archives of Ireland, accessed 1 September 2011, http://www.census.nationalarchives.ie/exhibition/dublin/main.html

Jameson, Frederic, *The Modernist Papers* (London: Verso, 2008)

Jarman, Neil, *Material Conflicts: Parades and Visual Displays in Northern Ireland* (Oxford: Berge, 1997)

Jay, Martin, 'Scopic Regimes of Modernity' in Hal Foster (ed.), *Vision and Visuality* (New York: The New Press, 1988), pp. 3–23

Jordan III, William R., *The Sunflower Forest: Ecological Restoration and the New Communion with Nature* (Berkeley: University of California Press, 2003)

Joyce, James, 'The City of the Tribes: Italian Echoes in an Irish Port' in Richard

Ellmann and Ellsworth Mason (eds), *James Joyce: the Critical Writings* (Ithaca: Cornell University Press, 1959), pp. 229–33
—, 'The Dead', *Dubliners* [1914] (New York: Penguin, 1992)
—, *Dubliners* (New York: Penguin Books, 1993)
—, *Dubliners*, ed. Terence Brown (New York: Penguin, 1992)
—, *Dubliners: Text Criticism, and Notes*, eds Robert Scholes and A Walton Litz (New York: Viking, 1969)
—, *Finnegans Wake* (London: Penguin, 1999)
—, *Finnegans Wake* (New York: Penguin, 1976)
—, *Finnegans Wake* (New York: Viking, 1939)
—, 'Ireland, Island of Saints and Sages' in Ellsworth Mason and Richard Ellmann (eds), *The Critical Writings of James Joyce* (New York: The Viking Press, 1959), pp. 153–74
—, *The Letters of James Joyce*, ed. Stuart Gilbert (New York: Viking, 1957)
—, *Letters I, II* and *III*, ed. Richard Ellmann (New York: Viking, 1966)
—, 'The Mirage of the Fisherman of Aran: England's Safety Valve in Case of War' in Richard Ellmann and Ellsworth Mason (eds), *James Joyce: the Critical Writings* (Ithaca: Cornell University Press, 1959), pp. 234–37
—, *A Portrait of the Artist as a Young Man*, ed. Seamus Deane (Harmondsworth: Penguin, 2000)
—, *A Portrait of the Artist as a Young Man* (New York: St Martin's Press, 1993)
—. *A Portrait of the Artist as a Young Man*, ed. R.B. Kershner (Boston: Bedford/St Martin's, 1993)
—, *A Portrait of the Artist as a Young Man* (St Albans: Triad/Panther Books, 1977)
—, *A Portrait of the Artists as a Young Man: Text, Criticism, and Notes*, ed. Chester G. Anderson (New York: Viking Press, 1968)
—, *A Portrait of the Artist as a Young Man* [1916] (New York: Viking, 1964)
—, *Selected Letters of James Joyce*, ed. Richard Ellmann (New York: Viking, 1975)
—, *Stephen Hero* (New York: New Directions, 1963)
—. *Ulysses*, ed. Hans Walter Gabler (New York: Vintage, 1986)
Kaplan, Stephen, 'The Challenge of Environmental Psychology: A Proposal for a New Functionalism', *American Psychologist* 27.2 (1972), pp. 140–43
—, 'Environmental Preference in a Knowledge-Seeking, Knowledge-Using Organism' in Jerome H. Barkow, Leda Cosmides and John Tooby (eds), *The Adapted Mind: Evolutionary Psychology and the Generation of Culture* (Oxford: Oxford University Press, 1992), pp. 581–98
Kelly, Fergus, 'The Old Irish Tree List', *Celtica* 11 (1976), pp. 107–24
Kelly, Michelle McSwiggan, 'Oceanic Longing: an Ecocritical Approach to Joyce' in Franca Ruggieri, John McCourt and Enrico Terrinoni (eds), *Joyce in Progress: Proceedings of the 2008 James Joyce Graduate Conference in Rome* (Newcastle: Cambridge Scholars Publishing, 2009), pp. 135–47
Kern, Robert, 'Ecocriticism: What Is It Good For'? *ISLE* 7 (Winter 2000), pp. 9–32
Kerridge, Richard, 'Introduction' in Richard Kerridge and Neil Sammells (eds), *Writing the Environment: Ecocriticism and Literature* (London and New York: Zed Books, 1998), pp. 1–9
Kershner, Brandon R., *Joyce, Bakhtin and Popular Literature: Chronicles of Disorder* (Chapel Hill: University of North Carolina Press, 1989)
Kiberd, Declan, *Inventing Ireland* (Cambridge: Harvard University Press, 1995)

Lacan, Jacques, *Écrits: The First Complete Edition in English*, trans. Bruce Fink (London: W.W. Norton, 2006)

Ladrón, Marisol Morales, 'James Joyce's Early Writings and Ecocritical Theory: A New Turn?' in Universidad de Deusto, *New Perspective on James Joyce* (La Rioja: Dialnet, 2010), pp. 197–210

Latham, Sean, 'Twenty-first-century Critical Contexts' in John McCourt (ed.), *James Joyce in Context* (Cambridge: Cambridge University Press, 2009)

Lawrence, D.H., *The Complete Poems*, eds Vivian de Sola Pinto and F. Warren Roberts (London: Penguin, 1993)

Lennon, Joseph, *Irish Orientalism: A Literary and Intellectual History* (Syracuse: Syracuse University Press, 2004)

Leonard, Garry, *Advertising and Commodity Culture in Joyce* (Florida: Florida University Press, 1988)

—, 'He's Got Bette Davis Eyes: James Joyce and Melodrama', *Joyce Studies Annual* (New York: Fordham University Press, 2008)

—, 'Holding on to the Here and the Now: Juxtaposition and Identity in Modernity and in Joyce', in Michael Patrick Gillespie (ed.), *James Joyce and the Fabrication of an Irish Identity* (Amsterdam: Rodopi, 2001), pp. 39–51

—, '"The Famished Roar of Automobiles": Modernity, the Internal Combustion Engine, and Modernism', in Pamela Caughie (ed.), *Disciplining Modernism* (New York: Palgrave Macmillan Press, 2009), pp. 221–41

—, 'Technically Human: Kubrick's Monolith in *2001: A Space Odyssey* and Heidegger's Propriative Event', *Film Criticism* 36.1 (Fall 2011), pp. 44–67

—, *Reading Dubliners Again: A Lacanian Perspective* (New York: Syracuse University Press, 1988)

—, '"Without Contraries There is No Progression": Cinematic Montage and the Relationship of Illustration to Text in William Blake's *The [First] Book of Urizen*', *University of Toronto Quarterly* 80.4 (2011), pp. 918–34

Leonard, Liam, *The Environmental Movement in Ireland* (New York: Springer, 2008)

Lilla, Mark, 'The Hidden Lesson of Montaigne', *The New York Review of Books*, Vol. LVII, No. 5 (24 March 2011), p. 21

Litz, Walton A., *The Art of James Joyce: Method and Design in Ulysses and Finnegans Wake* (Oxford: Oxford University Press, 1964)

Livorni, Ernesto, '"Ineluctable modality of the visible": Diaphane in the "Proteus" Episode', *James Joyce Quarterly* 36.2 (1999), pp. 127–69

Lorentz, Pare, *FDR's Moviemaker: Memoirs and Scripts by Pare Lorentz* (Las Vegas and London: University of Nevada Press, 1992)

Love, Glen A., *Practical Ecocriticism: Literature, Biology and the Environment* (Charlottesville: University of Virginia Press, 2003)

MacCabe, Colin, *James Joyce and the Revolution of the Word* (London: Macmillan, 1978)

Mahaffey, Vicki, *States of Desire* (New York: Oxford, University Press, 1998)

Maignant, Catherine, 'Rural Ireland in the Nineteenth Century and the Advent of the Modern World' in Jacqueline Genet (ed.), *Rural Ireland, Real Ireland?* (Oxford: University of Oxford Press, 1996), pp. 21–30

Mali, Joseph, 'Mythology and Counter-history: the New Critical Art of Vico and Joyce' in Donald Phillip Verene (ed.), *Vico and Joyce* (Buffalo: SUNY Press, 1987), pp. 32–47

Manes, Christopher, 'Nature and Silence' in Cheryll Glotfelty and Harold Fromm (eds), *The Ecocriticism Reader: Landmarks in Literary Ecology* (Athens: University of Georgia Press, 1996), pp. 15–29

Mariani, Paul, *Gerard Manley Hopkins: A Life* (New York: Viking, 2008)

Marvin, John, '*Finnegans Wake* III.3 and the Third Millennium: The Ghost of Modernisms Yet to Come', *Hypermedia Joyce Studies* 6.1 (Jul. 2005), un-paginated, accessed 2 October 2011, *http://www.geocities.com/hypermedia_joyce/marvin.html*

Marx, Karl, *Capital* (Oxford: Oxford University Press, 1999)

Mauss, Marcel, *A General Theory of Magic* [1950], trans. Robert Brain (London & Boston: Routledge & Kegan Paul, 1972)

McCarthy, Patrick A., 'Making Herself Tidal: Chapter I.8' in Luca Crispi and Sam Slote (eds), *How Joyce Wrote Finnegans Wake: A Chapter-by-Chapter Genetic Guide* (Madison: University of Wisconsin Press, 2007)

McCracken, Eileen, *The Irish Woods Since Tudor Times: Distribution and Exploitation*(Newton, Abbott: David & Charles, 1971)

McDowell, Michael J., 'The Bakhtinian Road to Ecological Insight' in Cheryll Glotfelty and Harold Fromm (eds), *The Ecocriticsm Reader: Landmarks in Literary Ecology* (Athens: University of Georgia Press, 1996), pp. 371–91

McHugh, Roland, *Annotations to* Finnegans Wake (Baltimore: The Johns Hopkins University Press, 1991)

McNeill, J.R., *Something New Under the Sun: An Environmental History of the Twentieth-Century World* (New York: W.W. Norton, 2000)

Merleau-Ponty, Maurice, *Phenomenology of Perception* (London: Routledge & Kegan Paul, 1962)

—. *The Visible and the Invisible*, ed. Claude Lefort, trans. Alphonos Lingis (Evanston: Northwestern University Press, 1968)

Mink, Louis O., *A Finnegans Wake Gazetteer* (Bloomington and London: Indiana University Press, 1978)

Mirandolla, Pico della, *On the Dignity of Man*, trans. Charles Glenn Wallis (Indianapolis, Indiana: Bobbs-Merrill, 1998)

Moriarty, Christopher, *Exploring Dublin: Wildlife, Parks, Waterways* (Dublin: Wolfhound Press, 1997)

Morrison, Steven, 'Introduction' in Andrew Gibson and Steven Morrison (eds), *European Joyce Studies 12: Joyce's 'Wandering Rocks'* (Amsterdam: Rodopi, 2002), pp. 1–16

Morse, J. Mitchell, 'Proteus' in Clive Hart and David Hayman (eds), *James Joyce's Ulysses: Critical Essays* (Berkeley: University of California Press, 1974), pp. 29–49

Morton, Timothy, 'Ecology as Text, Text as Ecology', *Oxford Literary Review*, 32 (2010), pp. 1–17

—, *Ecology Without Nature: Rethinking Environmental Aesthetics* (Cambridge: Harvard University Press, 2007)

Nash, Catherine, '"Embodying the Nation": The West of Ireland Landscape and Irish Identity' in Barbara O'Connor and Michael Cronin (eds), *Tourism in Ireland: A Critical Analysis* (Cork: Cork University Press, 1993), pp. 86–112

Neeson, Eoin, *A History of Irish Forestry* (Dublin: Lilliput Press, 1991)

—, 'Woodland in History and Culture' in John Wilson Foster (ed.), *Nature in*

Ireland: A Scientific and Cultural History (Dublin: Lilliput Press, 1997), pp. 133–56

Nolan, Emer, *James Joyce and Nationalism* (London: Routledge, 1995)

Norris, Margot, *Beasts of the Modern Imagination: Darwin, Nietzsche, Kafka, Ernst and Lawrence* (Baltimore, MD: Johns Hopkins University Press, 1985)

—, *The Decentered Universe of* Finnegans Wake: *A Structuralist Analysis* (Baltimore: Johns Hopkins University Press, 1974)

O'Brien, Joseph V., *Dear, Dirty Dublin: A City in Distress, 1899–1916* (Berkeley, CA: University of California Press, 1982)

O'Connor, Barbara and Michael Cronin (eds), *Tourism in Ireland: A Critical Analysis* (Cork: Cork University Press, 1993)

O'Connor, Maureen, '"Becoming Animal" in the Novels of Edna O'Brien' in Christine Cusick (ed.), *Out of the Earth: Ecocritical Readings of Irish Texts* (Cork: Cork University Press, 2010), pp. 151–77

'Papers by Command', *Royal Commission on Sewage Disposal*, vol. 31, 113 (Great Britain: Parliament, House of Commons, Royal Commission on Sewage Disposal, 1903)

Peck, George, 'The Night Soil Men', *George Peck's Memories of Stafford Street*, Accessed 1 September 2010,http://www.localhistory.scit.wlv.ac.uk/articles/GeorgePeck2/NightSoilMen.htm

Phillips, Dana, *The Truth of Ecology: Nature, Culture, and Literature in America* (New York: Oxford University Press, 2003)

Pierce, David and Dan Harper, *James Joyce's Ireland* (New Haven: Yale UP, 1995)

Plumwood, Val, *Environmental Culture: The Ecological Crisis of Reason* (London: Routledge, 2002)

—, *Feminism and the Mastery of Nature* (London: Routledge, 1993)

Powys, John Cowper, *Wolf Solent* [1964] (London: Penguin, 2000)

Preston, Carrie J., *Modernism's Mythic Pose: Gender, Genre, Solo Performance* (New York: Oxford University Press, 2011)

Prud'homme, Alex, *The Ripple Effect: The Fate of Freshwater in the Twenty-First Century* (New York: Scribner, 2011)

Prunty, Jacinta, *Dublin Slums 1800–1925: A Study in Urban Geography* (Dublin: Irish Academic Press, 1998)

Rathjen, Friedhelm, 'Horses versus Cattle in *Ulysses*', *Joyce Studies Annual* 12 (2001), pp. 172–75.

Rice, Ignatius, 'Correspondence: Dublin Corporation v. South Dublin Union', *Irish Daily Independent*, 10 June 1904, p. 6

Ritvo, Harriet, *The Animal Estate: The English and Other Creatures in the Victorian Age* (Cambridge: Harvard University Press, 1987)

Robbins, Paul, *Political Ecology: An Introduction* (Malden, MA: Blackwell, 2004)

Robinson, Tim, *Connemara: A Little Gaelic Kingdom* (London: Penguin, 2011)

—, *Connemara: The Last Pool of Darkness* (London: Penguin, 2008)

—, *Connemara: Listening to the Wind* (London: Penguin, 2006)

—, *Stones of Aran: Pilgrimage* (New York: NY Review of Books, 1986)

Rohman, Carrie, *Stalking the Subject: Modernism and the Animal* (New York: Columbia University Press, 2009)

Ross, Alison (ed.), spec. issue of *The Agamben Effect*, *South Atlantic Quarterly* 1.107 (2008), pp. 1–220

Ross, Andrew, 'The Social Claim on Urban Ecology' in Michael Bennett and David W. Teague (eds), *The Nature of Cities: Ecocriticism and Urban Environments* (Tucson: University of Arizona Press, 1999), pp. 15–32

Rothenberg, David, 'Introduction', in David Rothenberg and Marta Ulvaeus (eds), *Writing on Water* (Cambridge: MIT Press, 2001), pp. ix–xv

Rowntree, B. Seebohm, *Poverty: A Study of Town Life* (London: Macmillan, 1902)

Rubenstein, Michael, *Public Works: Infrastructure, Irish Modernism, and The Postcolonial* (Notre Dame: University of Notre Dame Press, 2011)

Rueckert, William, 'Literature and Ecology' in Cheryl Glotfelty and Harold Fromm (eds), *The Ecocriticism Reader: Landmarks in Literary Ecology* (Athens, GA: University of Georgia Press, 1996), pp. 121–23

Saá, Margarita Estévez, 'Could We Speak About an Eco-Feminist Joyce?' in Universidad de Deusto, *New Perspective on James Joyce* (La Rioja: Dialnet, 2010), pp. 211–24

Sack, Robert David, *Homo Geographicus: A Framework for Action, Awareness, and Moral Concern* (Baltimore: Johns Hopkins University Press, 1997)

Said, Edward, *Culture and Imperialism* (New York: Vintage Books, 1994)

Sandilands, Catriona, *The Good-Natured Feminist: Ecofeminism and the Quest for Democracy* (Minneapolis: University of Minnesota Press, 1999)

Sandquist, Brigitte L., 'The Tree Wedding in "Cyclops" and the Ramifications of Cata-logic', *James Joyce Quarterly* 33.2 (Winter 1996), pp. 195–209

Sayers, William, 'The Russian General, Gargantua, and Writing of "Wit's Waste"', *Joyce Studies Annual* (2008), pp. 146–62

Scott, Bonnie Kime, *James Joyce* (Briton, Sussex: The Harvester Press, 1987)

Senn, Fritz, 'Ovidian Roots of Gigantism in Joyce's "Ulysses"', *Journal of Modern Literature* 14.4 (Spring 1989), pp. 561–77

—, 'A Reading Exercise in *Finnegans Wake*' in Patrick A. McCarthy (ed.), *Critical Essays on James Joyce's* Finnegans Wake (New York: G.K. Hall & Co., 1992), pp. 48–58

—, '"Trivia Ulysseana" IV', *James Joyce Quarterly* 19.2 (Winter 1982), pp. 151–78

Schama, Simon, *Landscape and Memory* (New York: Vintage Books, 1995)

Slovic, Scott, 'Introduction Part I: The Rain in Reno' in Scott Slovic, Serenella Iovino and Shin Yamashiro (eds), *Concentric* 34.1 (March 2008), pp. 3–19

Smyth, Gerry, 'Shite and Sheep: An Ecocritical Perspective on Two Recent Irish Novels' in special issue of *Contemporary Irish Fiction*, *Irish University Review* 30: 1 (2000), pp. 163–78

—, *Space and the Irish Cultural Imagination* (New York: Palgrave, 2001)

Solomon, Steve, *Water: The Epic Struggle for Wealth, Power, and Civilization* (New York: HarperCollins, 2010)

Soper, Kate, *What is Nature? Culture, Politics and the Non-Human* (Oxford: Blackwell, 1995)

Spoo, Robert, *James Joyce and the Language of History: Dedalus's Nightmare* (Oxford: Oxford University Press, 1994)

Spretnak, Charlene, *The Resurgence of the Real: Body, Nature and Place in a Hypermodern World* (New York: Routledge, 1999)

Symons, Arthur, *The Symbolist Movement in Literature*, ed. Richard Ellmann (Kessinger Publishing, 2004)

Tindall, William York, *A Reader's Guide to* Finnegans Wake (Syracuse: Syracuse University Press, 1996)

Toadvine, Ted, *Merleau-Ponty's Philosophy of Nature* (Evanston, IL: Northwestern University Press, 2009)

Thomashow, Mitchell, 'Toward a Cosmopolitan Bioregionalism' in Michael Vincent McGinnis (eds), *Bioregionalism* (London: Routledge, 1999), pp. 121–32

Thompson, Spurgeon, 'The Politics of Photography: Travel Writing and the Irish Countryside, 1900–14', in Lawrence McBride (ed.), *Images, Icons and the Irish Nationalist Imagination* (Dublin: Four Courts Press, 1999), pp. 113–29

—, 'Recovering *Dubliners* for Postcolonial Theory' in Oona Frawley (ed.), *A New and Complex Sensation: Essays on Joyce's Dubliners* (Dublin: Lilliput Press, 2004), pp. 186–96

Thoreau, Henry David, *Walden* (New York: Time, Inc., 1962)

Tropp, Sandra, '"The Esthetic Instinct in Action": Charles Darwin and Mental Science in *A Portrait of the Artist as a Young Man*', *James Joyce Quarterly* 45.2 (2008), pp. 221–44

Tymoczko, Maria, *The Irish Ulysses* (Berkeley: University of California Press, 1994)

Vico, Giambattista, *The New Science of Giambattista Vico: unabridged translation of the third edition (1744) with the addition of 'Practic of the New Science'*, trans. Thomas Goddard Bergin and Max Harold Fisch (Ithaca: Cornell University Press, 1984)

Volk, Tyler, *Metapatterns* (New York: Columbia University Press, 1996)

Wall, Eamonn, *Writing the Irish West: Ecologies and Traditions* (South Bend, IN: University of Notre Dame Press, 2011)

Wardi, Anissa J, *Water and African American Memory: An Ecocritical Perspective* (University Press of Florida, 2011)

Wells, H.G., 'James Joyce', *New Republic*, 10 March 1917, pp. 158–60

Wenzell, Tim, *Emerald Green: An Ecocritical Study of Irish Literature* (Newcastle: Cambridge Scholars, 2009)

Westling, Louise, 'Letter', *PMLA* 114.5 (1999), pp. 1103–04

Whelan, Yvonne, 'Monuments, Power, and Contested Space – The Iconography of O'Connell Street (Sackville Street) before Independence (1922)', *Irish Geography* 34.1 (2001), pp. 11–33

White, Norman, *Hopkins: A Literary Biography* (Oxford: Oxford Univ. Press, 1995)

White, W.L., 'Pare Lorentz', *Scribner's Magazine*, Vol. 105, No. 1 (January 1939), p. 11

Whitley, Catherine, 'Gender and Interiority' in Michael Bengal (ed.) *Joyce and the City: The Significance of Place* (Syracuse: Syracuse University Press, 2002), pp. 35–50

Wiener, Norbert, *Cybernetics: Control and Communication in the Animal and the Machine* (New York: MIT Press, 1961)

Williams, Chris, *Ecology and Socialism* (Chicago: Haymarket Books, 2010)

Williams, Raymond, *The Country and the City* (Oxford: Oxford University Press, 1973)

—, *The Long Revolution* [1961] (Peterborough: Broadview, 2001)

Wolfe, Cary, *Animal Rites: American Culture, the Discourse of Species, and Posthumanist Theory* (Chicago: University of Chicago Press, 2003)

Woods, C.J. 'Irish Travel writings as Source Material', *Irish Historical Studies*, 28.110 (Nov. 2002), pp. 171–183

Wright, Lawrence, *Clean and Decent: The Fascinating History of the Bathroom and the Water-Closet* (London: Penguin, 1960)

Wright, Laura, *'Wilderness into Civilized Shapes': Reading the Postcolonial Environment* (Athens, GA: University of Georgia Press, 2010)

Yeats, William Butler, *The Collected Poems of W.B. Yeats* (New York: Macmillan, 1961)

Young, Arthur, *Tour in Ireland (1776–1779)* 2 Vols., ed. Arthur Wollaston Hutton (London: George Bell & Sons, 1892)

Young, Julian, *Heidegger's Philosophy of Art* (Cambridge: Cambridge University Press, 2001)

Zimmerman, Michael, *Heidegger's Confrontation with Modernity* (Indianapolis: Indiana University Press, 1990)

Žižek, Slavoj, *Looking Awry: An Introduction to Jacques Lacan through Popular Culture* (Cambridge MA: MIT Press, 1991)

—. 'Žižek: the Lecture', University of Leeds, 18 March 2008

Index